Abortion
The Supreme Court Decisions

Abortion

The Supreme Court Decisions

Edited,
with an Introduction,
by
Ian Shapiro

Hackett Publishing Company, Inc.
Indianapolis/Cambridge

00 99 98 97 96 95   1 2 3 4 5 6 7

For further information, please address

Hackett Publishing Company, Inc.
P.O. Box 44937
Indianapolis, Indiana 46244-0937

Design by Dan Kirklin

Production Coordination: Elizabeth Shaw Editorial & Publishing Services

Library of Congress Cataloging-in-Publication Data

Abortion: the Supreme Court decisions/edited,
    with introduction, by Ian Shapiro.
        p.   cm.
    Includes bibliographical references and index.
    ISBN 0-87220-274-7 (cloth).   ISBN 0-87220-273-9 (pbk.)
    1. Abortion—Law and legislation—United States—Cases.
I. Shapiro, Ian. II. United States Supreme Court.
KF3771.A7A26   1995
344.73'04192—dc20
[347.3044192]   94-44150
                                                           CIP

The paper used in this publication meets the minimum requirements of American National Standard for Information Sciences—Permanence of Paper for Printed Library Materials, ANSI Z39.48-1984.

Preface

Editor's Introduction

PREFACE

The United States Supreme Court is the American constitutional court of last resort. It has the final say in interpreting the constitution, and—curiously in a modern democracy—its members are not elected: They are appointed with life tenure that can be revoked only in exceptional circumstances. The Court's appropriate place in the American political order has been the subject of much debate, and this will likely continue to be so for as long as the republic endures. Critics see the Court as an anachronistic throwback to predemocratic times and are skeptical that it does much to guard human liberties.[1] For defenders, by contrast, the Court protects democracy from itself in a variety of indispensable ways. It insulates us from the expedient passions of the moment that govern electoral politics; it guards individual rights against the excesses of majority tyranny; and it is a cornerstone of the separation of constitutional powers that is the lifeblood of modern republican government.[2]

The Court captivates insiders and fascinates outsiders. Whereas other American public officials are generally held in low public esteem, Supreme Court Justices are often greatly revered. There is, indeed, no more distinguished achievement for a lawyer than to be named to the nation's highest judicial bench. The quality of debate on the Court also sets it apart from

1. Perhaps the most persistent critic of both the justification for and the effectiveness of judicial review is Robert Dahl. See *A Preface to Democratic Theory* (Chicago: University of Chicago Press, 1956), pp. 105–12, "Decision-making in a democracy: The Supreme Court as national policy maker," *Journal of Public Law,* vol. 6 (1958), pp. 279–95, and *Democracy and Its Critics* (New Haven: Yale University Press, 1989), pp. 188–92. See also Michael Walzer, "Philosophy and Democracy," *Political Theory,* Vol. 9, No. 3 (August, 1981).

2. For a sampling of different views of the Court's appropriate role, see Alexander M. Bickel, *The Least Dangerous Branch* (New Haven: Yale University Press, 1962), John Hart Ely, *Democracy and Distrust: A Theory of Judicial Review* (Cambridge, Mass.: Harvard University Press, 1980), Michael Perry, *The Constitution, The Courts, and Human Rights* (New Haven: Yale University Press, 1982), Rogers M. Smith, *Liberalism and American Constitutional Law* (Cambridge, Mass.: Harvard University Press, 1985), and Ronald Dworkin, *Law's Empire* (Cambridge, Mass.: Harvard University Press, 1986), Bruce Ackerman, *We the People: Foundations* (Cambridge, Mass.: Harvard University Press, 1991), and Robert A. Burt, *The Constitution in Conflict* (Cambridge, Mass.: Harvard University Press, 1992).

other American public institutions. In stark contrast to the cliché-ridden sound bites of electoral politics, argument on the Court—while often no less divisive or ideologically charged than political debate—is generally carried on at an exceedingly high intellectual level. Most Justices are persons of considerable intellectual ability and training. They probe one another's arguments with great acuity, and their deliberations exhibit a degree of thoroughness and rigor seldom found elsewhere in American public life.

The Supreme Court is a complex institution, and its operations and decisions can sometimes be opaque to outsiders. The Court's powers are set out in Article III of the United States Constitution. Apart from a small class of limited exceptions, it is a court of appellate, rather than original, jurisdiction. This means that the Supreme Court may only review decisions of lower courts. In addition, the "cases" or "controversies" clause of Article III limits the Court to deciding the issue before it as this has come up from the courts below. Unlike appellate courts elsewhere in the world, the American Supreme Court is not supposed to venture beyond these confines or to issue advisory opinions about the validity of laws and statutes before they are tested by particular litigants who are engaged in actual disputes. Although the Supreme Court differs from lower courts in that it can reverse itself and alter its precedents, it does this rarely. The doctrine of *stare decisis* (discussed in the introduction) creates a presumption of continuity in the law that further limits what the Court may do in a given case. Justices are often accused—and often accuse one another—of exceeding the scope of their proper authority, but in theory at least, this authority is comparatively limited.

Although the Court's decisions are governed by strict majority rule, the five members needed for a majority when the Court is at full complement may reach the same result by different reasoning, or they may agree with one another in part only. In such cases, Justices may issue plurality or concurring opinions in order to explain their differences and the reasons for them, rather than sign a single majority opinion.[3] Justices who disagree with a decision may write dissenting opinions. These have a number of purposes. They may be simple expressions of outrage or anger; they may be designed to limit the majority holding as much as possible; they may be intended as

---

3. A plurality opinion is an opinion that commands the largest number of votes on the winning side when there is no majority opinion. The author of a concurrence "in the result" accepts the conclusion in the majority or plurality opinion but reaches it by different reasoning. However, a concurring opinion might not actually reject the reasoning in the majority or plurality opinion; its author may merely want to express arguments or reservations that he or she thinks have not been adequately dealt with in the other opinions.

signals to future litigants about how best to present an issue; and, perhaps most important, they sometimes provide conceptual resources for future majorities on the Court who might see an issue differently.[4] If the Court's decision is arrived at by an argument over the merits of a particular case, it is thus always somewhat more than merely that: It is an argument that extends backward and forward in time, engaging the present generation of Justices with their predecessors and successors. Nowhere is this more clearly evident than in the evolution of the constitutional law of abortion.

The present volume contains all the United States Supreme Court cases on abortion from the handing down of *Roe* v. *Wade* on January 22, 1973 through *Planned Parenthood of Pennsylvania* v. *Casey*, decided on June 29, 1992. It also contains *Griswold* v. *Connecticut* (1965) and *Eisenstadt* v. *Baird* (1972), the decisions which provided the often commented-upon jurisprudential foundations for Justice Blackmun's majority opinion in *Roe*. The cases deal with the nature of a woman's right to abortion; with the evolving justifications of and limits to that right over some two decades; with informed consent and waiting periods; with definitions of fetal viability; with the rights of physicians, husbands, parents, and the state in the making of abortion decisions; with abortion funding; and with a host of related issues. The only cases that have been excluded are those arising out of conflicts surrounding demonstrations outside abortion clinics. Despite the attention they often receive in the media when the topic of abortion comes up, they turn on freedom of speech matters rooted in the First Amendment; they actually have nothing to do with the constitutional law of abortion.

I have ended with *Casey* because it is the last major abortion decision as the present volume goes to press, and, given the membership of the Court and the entrenched majority support for the changes *Casey* has codified, it seems likely that the main contours of the constitutional law of abortion are now set for some time to come. To be sure, prediction is a dangerous business as far as Supreme Court behavior is concerned. Chief Justice Rehnquist and Justices Scalia and Thomas remain ferociously opposed to the result in *Casey*, and it is not altogether inconceivable that two more Justices could be appointed who share their view of the matter. But the pro-*Casey* majority coalition—recently reinforced by President Clinton's appointments—is younger and likely, therefore, to continue to uphold its basic ruling. This is not to say that abortion litigation is at an end. On the contrary, as I note in the introduction, *Casey* will encourage litigation of certain kinds; this is

4. Concurrences and dissents can be complete or partial. That is, their authors may reject the majority or plurality opinion completely, or only aspects of it. Partial dissents and concurrences can be a source of considerable confusion as to what the Court has actually held. See the *Webster* decision in this volume.

already going on in the lower federal courts. But this litigation will not be about the fundamental nature of the constitutional right to abortion, which now seems to be embedded in the fabric of American constitutional law for the medium term at least.

The cases have been edited for use in undergraduate and graduate courses in a variety of disciplines. I have included many dissenting opinions as well as majority and plurality ones, in order to convey something of the flavor of argument on the Court and the manner in which constitutional doctrine evolves out of that argument over time. The principal cases—*Griswold, Roe, Webster* v. *Reproductive Health Services,* and *Casey*—have been less heavily edited than the others. They are also the focus of my discussion in the introduction. I have tried there to set these cases in political, historical, and philosophical context, and to give the reader a sense of what the main issues in the constitutional law of abortion are likely to be in the future. The footnotes to the introduction refer the reader to literatures in philosophy, law, and the social sciences that deal with the subject of abortion; they should be a useful starting point for further study.

For scholarly purposes, the original footnote references in the cases have been preserved; the editing has thus caused occasional discontinuities in the numbering of footnotes. The deletion of material from the original is indicated by ellipses (. . .).

Sara Taylor and Marian Swanzy-Parker have both been excellent research assistants on this project; their help is gratefully acknowledged.

Abortion
The Supreme Court Decisions

For all their contradictory impulses—indeed, perhaps partly because of them—it seems that people also expect to resolve the abortion debate. They argue in books, legislatures, and the media. They take issue with one another's reasoning and adduce statistics that they regard as decisive for one or another aspect of the issue. Even as they sense, perhaps, that the abortion debate is beyond resolution, at some level many people cannot accept this. There *must* be a reasonable resolution of the debate, they seem to think; the question is how to arrive at it.

For over two decades the United States Supreme Court has been engaged in a struggle over the abortion question. The 1973 decision in *Roe* v. *Wade*, supported by a majority of seven to two on the Court, seemed at the time to be a decisive resolution of the controversy. However, those who expected this decision to settle the matter by removing the abortion question from the realm of charged political debate were quickly disappointed; if anything *Roe* seemed to intensify and further polarize the public abortion debate. Nor has there been stability in the Supreme Court's view of the abortion question in the years since *Roe* was handed down. Although the right recognized in that decision was reaffirmed by a bare majority on the Court in *Planned Parenthood* v. *Casey*[4] in June 1992, both the content of the right in question and the jurisprudential basis on which it rests have evolved substantially in a number of the Court's decisions in the intervening two decades. Indeed, as will become plain below, the reasoning on which the original *Roe* decision rested has largely been abandoned by the Court.

Part of the evolution in the Court's understanding of the right to abortion reflects changes in its personnel. In 1973 Justices Rehnquist and White were the only dissenters from the majority opinion authored by Justice Blackmun. By 1993 Rehnquist was Chief Justice, and most of the original *Roe* majority had departed. Justices Burger, Douglas, Brennan, Stewart, Marshall, and Powell had all retired (as had the other dissenter from *Roe*, Justice White), and been replaced by Justices Stevens, Scalia, O'Connor, Kennedy, Souter, Thomas, and Ginsburg.[5] All the replacements other than Ginsburg (appointed by President Clinton in 1993) were Republican appointees who were in varying degrees uncomfortable with the reasoning, the outcome, or both in *Roe*. Indeed, even Ginsburg was known to be uncomfortable with aspects of the reasoning (see below).

The evolution of the right to abortion since *Roe* has also been driven by things other than the changing faces on the bench, however. It is possible to

---

4. 112 S.Ct 2791 (1992).

5. In the spring of 1994 Justice Blackmun announced that he would retire at the end of the 1993–94 term, and President Clinton nominated Judge Stephen Breyer, a known supporter of the constitutional right to abortion, to replace him.

discern in that evolution attempts by various members of the Court to reconcile the apparently irreconcilable, to find a middle ground that could satisfy at least some of the contending parties who have sought to influence the Court's handling of the abortion issue. Several Justices have struggled mightily in this regard. How successful they have been will be taken up below. Before getting to that, I begin with a sketch of the right's historical evolution and an examination of the jurisprudential issues that are at stake in the abortion controversy.

HISTORY OF THE CONSTITUTIONAL RIGHT TO ABORTION

There is a significant respect in which the Supreme Court debate about constitutional protection for the right to abortion is detached from the public abortion debate. The slogans and posters at demonstrations outside abortion clinics, at rallies for and against *Roe*, and in much of the discussion in the media might reasonably lead one to assume that the central question at issue is whether or not a fetus is a person. Kristin Luker is surely correct when she says of the public abortion debate that it is fundamentally "a debate about personhood."[6] In fact no Justice on the Supreme Court has ever been committed to the view that the constitution should regard a fetus as a person, and if the Court were ever to embrace such a view the implications would be more radical than even the most ardent opponents of *Roe* appear to realize.[7] If the Court were to decide that a fetus is a legal person within the

---

6. Kristin Luker, *Abortion and the Politics of Motherhood* (Los Angeles: University of California Press, 1984), p. 5.

7. Judith Jarvis Thompson has famously argued that the common perception that whether or not one is in favor of abortion depends on whether or not one thinks a fetus is a person is false. She argues that if a woman awoke one day to discover that a brilliant but sick violinist had been attached by tubes to her kidneys and that the attachment must be maintained for nine months if the violinist was not to die, the woman would have no moral obligation to maintain the attachment against her will. "A defense of abortion," *Philosophy and Public Affairs*, Vol. 1, No. 1 (Fall 1971), pp. 47–66. Ronald Dworkin points out that Thompson's argument, although influential among philosophers, is not legally dispositive because "abortion normally requires a physical attack on a fetus, not just a failure to aid it, and, in any case, parents are invariably made an exception to the general doctrine [that one ordinarily has no affirmative legal duty to save a stranger] because they have a legal duty to care for their children." *Life's Dominion: An Argument about Abortion, Euthanasia, and Individual Freedom* (New York: Knopf, 1993), p. 111. For a more elaborate discussion of the legal implications of Thompson's argument, see Donald Regan, "Rewriting *Roe* v. *Wade*," *Michigan Law Review*, Vol. 77, No. 7 (1979), pp. 1569–1646.

meaning of the Fourteenth Amendment to the U.S. Constitution, this might well bring with it an obligation to *proscribe* abortion as a matter of federal constitutional law, at least a large class of circumstances. Jurists and legal commentators who argue that the decision in *Roe* is unconstitutional and that it should be repealed are not partisans of that view.[8] Rather, they are advocates of restoring the status quo ante that existed before *Roe*'s passage, when the law of abortion was regulated differently in different states— sometimes by state legislatures and sometimes as a matter of state constitutional law. This status quo ante was quite varied, ranging from liberal states like New York, which had permitted abortion, to states like Texas, which had blanket prohibitions, to various intermediate regulatory regimes.[9] Opposition to *Roe* from such Justices as Rehnquist, White, Scalia, and Thomas is not, therefore, necessarily tantamount to opposition to abortion rights as such. Rather, it is opposition to federalizing and constitutionalizing the abortion-rights question.

That government should regulate or limit women's access to abortion in order to protect the fetus is a relatively recent idea in American law and politics. Historically its emergence seems to have been linked to the increase in abortions sought by white, Protestant, married middle- and upper-class women (as opposed to poor women of other races) in the mid-to-late nineteenth century, and the threat to the existing social order that these developments implied.[10] Prior to this, abortion had been regulated, but the argument for regulation was that it protected the health of the mother. Abortion was a dangerous procedure that often led to infection and death. However, as Justice Blackmun noted in his majority opinion in *Roe*, by 1973 medical developments were such that statistically a woman was at greater medical risk if she carried the child to term than if she had an early abortion.[11]

This altered reality set the context for the Court's analysis of the right to abortion in *Roe*, in which a Texas statute that had made it a crime to "pro-

---

8. See, for example, Justice Rehnquist's dissent in *Roe*, in which he concedes that he has "little doubt" that statutes proscribing abortion in all circumstances would not survive constitutional scrutiny. 410 U.S. 113, at p. 173 (1973).

9. It should be noted that prior to *Roe* no American state had ever regarded the fetus as a legal person. As Dworkin points out, even states with the most stringent anti-abortion laws did not punish abortion as severely as murder, which they ought to have done had they thought a fetus a constitutional person, nor did they try to prevent women from procuring abortion in jurisdictions where it was legal. Dworkin, "The great abortion case," p. 50.

10. See James Mohr, *Abortion in America: The Origins and Evolution of National Policy* (Oxford: Oxford University Press, 1978), especially chapters 3 and 4.

11. 410 U.S. 113 (1973), at p. 149.

cure an abortion" unless the life of the mother was threatened by continuing the pregnancy, was held unconstitutional. For reasons that will be taken up later, such statutes were held to violate the Due Process Clause of the Fourteenth Amendment.[12] First let us get clear on the holding. Blackmun's majority opinion deals with abortion differently during the three trimesters of a normal pregnancy:

(a) For the stage prior to approximately the end of the first trimester, the abortion decision and its effectuation must be left to the medical judgment of the pregnant woman's attending physician.

(b) For the stage subsequent to approximately the end of the first trimester, the State, in promoting its interest in the health of the mother, may, if it chooses, regulate the abortion procedure in ways that are reasonably related to maternal health.

(c) For the stage subsequent to viability, the State in promoting its interest in the potentiality of human life may, if it chooses, regulate, and even proscribe, abortion except where it is necessary, in appropriate medical judgment, for the preservation of the life or health of the mother.[13]

This trimester-based test greatly limited the power of states to regulate abortion. Before the end of the first trimester, abortion could no longer be regulated at all; prior to the point of viability it could only be regulated in the interests of the health of the mother; and even after viability if a state chose to regulate or proscribe abortion acting on its interest "in the potentiality of human life," this could be trumped if the attending physician made an "appropriate" judgment that this was necessary for the "life or health" of the mother.

In *Roe* the Court acknowledged that the state has an interest in potential human life, but circumscribed that right and effectively subordinated it to the woman's right to an abortion, even (if with qualification) after the point of viability. In the years following *Roe*, various modifications to the constitutional right that it created were added by the evolving majority on the Court. In a number of respects the right recognized in *Roe* was secured and expanded. In *Doe* v. *Boulton*,[14] also decided in 1973, the Court struck down restrictions on places that could be used to perform abortions, giving rise to

12. The Due Process Clause states: "No State shall . . . deprive any person of life, liberty, or property, without due process of law."

13. 410 U.S. 113 (1973), at pp. 164–65.

14. 410 U.S. 179 (1973).

the modern abortion clinic. Three years later, in *Planned Parenthood* v. *Danforth*,[15] the Court denied states the authority to give husbands veto power over their wives' decisions to abort pregnancies, and also held that parents of unwed minor girls could not be given an absolute veto power over abortions. In 1979, in *Colautti* v. *Franklin*,[16] the Court affirmed its intention to give physicians broad discretion to determine when a fetus can live outside the womb. The Justices said that although a state may seek to protect a viable fetus, the determination of viability must be left to doctors. In 1983 the Court placed additional limits on the types of regulations that states may place on abortion. In a trio of decisions, *City of Akron* v. *Akron Center for Reproductive Health*,[17] *Planned Parenthood of Kansas City* v. *Ashcroft*,[18] and *Simopoulos* v. *Virginia*[19] by a six-to-three vote a majority on the Court denied states and local communities the power to require that women more than three months pregnant have their abortions in a hospital and struck down regulations that, among other things, imposed a twenty-four-hour waiting period between the signing of an abortion consent form and the medical procedure. Three years later (this time by a five-to-four vote that reflected the conservative drift on the Court that was by then well under way), a bare majority struck down Pennsylvania regulations that had required doctors to inform women seeking abortions about potential risks and about available benefits for prenatal care and childbirth.[20] In 1987 the Justices split four to four in *Hartigan* v. *Zbaraz*,[21] thereby letting stand a lower decision invalidating an Illinois law that might have restricted access to abortions for some teenagers.

Despite the elaboration and deepening of the woman's constitutional right to an abortion brought about by these decisions, the Court had also begun to limit the right to abortion in various ways long before the *Roe* majority began to erode. One important area of constraint concerned abortion funding. In 1977 the Court ruled, in *Maher* v. *Roe*,[22] that states have no constitutional obligation to pay for "nontherapeutic" abortions, and three years

15. 428 U.S. 476 (1976).

16. 439 U.S. 379 (1979).

17. 462 U.S. 416 (1983).

18. 462 U.S. 476 (1983).

19. 462 U.S. 506 (1983).

20. *Thornburgh* v. *American College of Obstetricians and Gynecologists.* 476 U.S. 747 (1986).

21. 484 U.S. 171 (1987).

22. 432 U.S. 464 (1977).

later a five-to-four majority held, in *Harris* v. *McRae*,[23] that, even for medically necessary abortions sought by women on welfare, neither states nor the federal government is under any constitutional obligation to provide public funding. In 1979, in the first of what was to turn out to be a string of decisions regulating the rights of dependent minors to abortion, an eight-to-one majority on the Court held, in *Bellotti* v. *Baird*,[24] that states may be able to require a pregnant, unmarried minor to obtain parental consent to an abortion so long as the state provides a "bypass" procedure, such as allowing the minor to seek a judge's permission instead. In 1981 a six-to-three majority held, in *H. L.* v. *Matheson*,[25] that states may require physicians approached by some girls who are still dependent on their parents and too "immature" to decide such matters for themselves to try to inform parents before performing abortions. Two 1990 decisions, *Hodgson* v. *Minnesota*[26] and *Ohio* v. *Akron Center for Reproductive Health*,[27] further elaborated the law of parental notification. In the Ohio case, a six-to-three majority upheld the state law requiring notification of at least one parent so long as it provided a judicial bypass, although in the Minnesota case a five-to-four majority made it clear that statutes requiring both parents to be informed before a minor can have an abortion would not survive in the future.

By the time of the 1990 decisions, much of the reasoning underlying *Roe* had been compromised by the watershed decision in *Webster* v. *Reproductive Health Services*,[28] handed down by a multiply divided Court eleven months earlier. With that decision, majority support for *Roe* on the Court seemed finally to have evaporated, as Justice Blackmun acknowledged in a bitter dissent. In its controlling opinion, the *Webster* Court upheld a Missouri statute requiring that, before a physician performs an abortion on a woman whom he has reason to believe is twenty or more weeks pregnant, he shall first determine whether the unborn child is viable. More important than this comparatively minor new restriction of a woman's right to an abortion was that the plurality launched a frontal assault on *Roe*'s trimester-based framework of analysis that had been law for the preceding decade and a half.

Justice Blackmun's throwaway remark in *Roe* that the state has an interest in "the potentiality of human life" had come back to haunt him. In Chief Justice Rehnquist's hands it became a stake that he seemed poised to drive

23. 448 U.S. 297 (1980).

24. 428 U.S. 132 (1979).

25. 430 U.S. 398 (1981).

26. 497 U.S. 417 (1990).

27. 497 U.S. 502 (1990).

28. 492 U.S. 490 (1989).

into *Roe*'s heart. In an opinion signed also by Justices Kennedy and White, Rehnquist flatly rejected *Roe*'s "rigid" framework as "hardly consistent with the notion of a Constitution cast in general terms, as ours is, and usually speaking in general principles." Rehnquist went on to say that the plurality did "not see why the State's interest in protecting potential human life should come into existence only at the point of viability, and that there should therefore be a rigid line allowing state regulation after viability but prohibiting it before viability."[29]

Justice O'Connor had announced her opposition to *Roe*'s trimester framework as early as 1985,[30] and Justice Scalia's only objection to the plurality opinion in *Webster* was that it should have gone further and done explicitly what he insisted it did implicitly, namely overrule *Roe*. This appeared to mean that there were now five votes in favor of overruling *Roe*, even if the five Justices in question were not yet all prepared to reach that matter on the grounds that the Missouri statute in question did not in fact try to regulate abortions prior to viability. The principle had been conceded, even if what Scalia dismissed as the Court's "newly contracted abstemiousness" meant that "the mansion of constitutionalized abortion-law, constructed overnight in *Roe* v. *Wade*, must be disassembled doorjamb by doorjamb."[31] No more impressed than Scalia by what he saw as the plurality's "feigned restraint," Justice Blackmun, writing in dissent (also for Brennan and Marshall), declared that it "implicitly invites every state legislature to enact more and more restrictive abortion regulations in order to provoke more and more test cases, in the hope that sometime down the line the Court will return the law of procreative freedom to the severe limitations that generally prevailed in this country before January 22, 1973." "Thus, 'not with a bang, but a whimper,'" Blackmun concluded, "the plurality discards a landmark case of the last generation, and casts into darkness the hopes and visions of every woman in this country who had come to believe that the Constitution guaranteed her the right to exercise some control over her unique ability to bear children."[32]

That some of Blackmun's own formulations in *Roe* could be used to undermine its result in *Webster* is characteristic of the haphazard way in which constitutional interpretation often evolves over time. Perhaps this very fact should have alerted Blackmun to the possibility that all was not lost from his

---

29. 492 U.S. 490 (1989), at pp. 518–19.

30. See her dissenting opinion in *Thornburgh* v. *American College of Obstetricians and Gynecologists* 476 U.S. 747 (1985), at p. 828.

31. 492 U.S. 490, at p. 537.

32. *Ibid.*, at pp. 538, 557.

point of view. Although *Roe*'s trimester framework had been jettisoned and a majority on the Court had embraced the idea that states may assert an interest in protecting "potential" human life even before the point at which a fetus is viable, this did not necessarily mean that the constitutional protection of a woman's right to an abortion would soon follow the trimester framework into the annals of constitutional history. Everything would now turn on what the nature of states' interest in potential life would turn out to be. Until that was determined, just what the impact of *Webster* would be on a woman's constitutionally protected right to an abortion could not be known. This would remain unclear for almost three years.

In retrospect we can say that there were clues dating back to the 1970s. In *Maher* v. *Roe* the Court had declared that the right recognized in *Roe* "protects the woman from unduly burdensome interference with her freedom to decide whether to terminate her pregnancy."[33] This notion that state interference with a woman's right to an abortion must not be "unduly burdensome" had first appeared in 1976 in *Bellotti* v. *Baird*, in which the Court had held that states may not "impose undue burdens upon a minor capable of giving informed consent."[34] Since that time, various members of the Court, including several majorities, had held that no state may "unduly burden the right to seek an abortion,"[35] that the constitutional right affirmed in *Roe* "protects the woman from unduly burdensome interference with her freedom to decide whether to terminate her pregnancy,"[36] that informed consent requirements for first trimester abortions will be upheld if they do not "unduly burden the right to seek an abortion,"[37] and that the state interest in protecting human life "does not, at least until approximately the third trimester, become sufficiently compelling to justify unduly burdensome state interference. . . ."[38] In 1982 Justice O'Connor made it clear in her dissent in *City of Akron* v. *Akron Center for Reproductive Health* that, for her at least, the issue of abortion revolved around finding restrictions that do not "infringe substantially" or impose "unduly burdensome" interference on the woman's right to an abortion,[39] a view that she reasserted in *Hodgson* v. *Minnesota* in the course of arguing that only when a state regulation imposes an "undue burden" on a woman's ability to make the abortion decision does

33. *Maher* v. *Roe*, 432 U.S. 464, at pp. 473–74 (1977).

34. 428 U.S. 132, 147 (1976).

35. *Bellotti* v. *Baird* 443 U.S. 622, at p. 640 (1979).

36. *Maher* v. *Roe*, 432 U.S. 464, at pp. 473–74 (1977).

37. *Bellotti* v. *Baird*, 428 U.S. 132, 147 (1976).

38. *Beal* v. *Doe*, 432 U.S. 438, at p. 446 (1977).

39. 462 U.S. 416, at pp. 461–62 (1982).

the power of the State reach into the heart of the liberty protected by the Due Process Clause.[40]

In view of these formulations, it should perhaps not come as a surprise that Justices O'Connor and Kennedy—who had declined Justice Scalia's invitation to overrule *Roe* in *Webster*—would be part of a centrist bloc on the Court (the other member being Justice Souter) committed to reformulating the constitutional right to abortion by reference to an "undue burden" standard rooted in the Due Process Clause of the Fourteenth Amendment. This was the step taken in *Planned Parenthood* v. *Casey*, handed down in June 1992, in which a once more multiply divided Court reaffirmed *Roe*'s basic holding while detaching it from Blackmun's now-defunct trimester-based framework of analysis, and tethering it instead to the notion of undue burden.[41] The *Casey* decision left many matters unresolved; indeed it created new areas of uncertainty in the constitutional law of abortion as is discussed below. But two fundamental matters about which *Webster* had generated considerable confusion were now clarified. The first was that "the essential holding of *Roe* v. *Wade* should be retained and once again reaffirmed."[42] This meant not only that the Constitution guarantees women a right to abortion that no legislature has the power to destroy, but also that Court decided not to divorce itself from Blackmun's original reasoning that had located the constitutional protection in question in a right to privacy thought to be entailed by the Due Process Clause. This was a notable development, because Blackmun's reasoning had been much criticized in the academic literature (see below), and several of the newer appointees to the Court—not to mention Chief Justice Rehnquist—were on record as being unimpressed by it. This was perhaps the principal reason that *Webster* was thought by so many to be the beginning of the end of *Roe*, prompting the introduction of legislation intended to reverse *Webster* in Congress and turning abortion into a lightning-rod political issue in the run-up to the 1992 presidential election. In the event, declaring that "[l]iberty finds no refuge in a jurisprudence of doubt,"[43] the plurality invoked the doctrine of *stare decisis*. This doctrine rests on the notion that "no judicial system could do society's work if it eyed each issue afresh in every case that raised it," and that consequently once a decision has become part of the law on which people have come to rely, it should not lightly be overturned. *Stare decisis* is not an "inexorable com-

---

40. 497 U.S. 417, at pp. 458–59 (1990).

41. 112 S.Ct. 2791 (1992).

42. *Ibid.*, p. 2796.

43. *Ibid.*, p. 2803.

mand" to uphold every precedent, and it might reasonably be ignored if a rule has "proved to be intolerable simply in defying practical workability," if it is "subject to a kind of reliance that would lend a special hardship to the consequences of overruling and add inequity to the cost of repudiation," or if "facts have so changed or come to be seen so differently, as to have robbed the old rule of significant application or justification."[44] But the plurality held that none of these considerations applied in the case of *Roe*, so that it should be upheld, even though "[w]e do not need to say whether each of us, had we been Members of the Court when the valuation of the State interest [in protecting potential life] came before it . . . would have concluded, as the *Roe* Court did, that its weight is insufficient to justify a ban on abortions prior to viability even when it is subject to certain exceptions."[45] By appeal to this reasoning, the plurality in *Casey* held that a woman does have a constitutionally protected right to an abortion until the point of viability, and that after that point states have the power to "restrict abortions," provided the law contains "exceptions for pregnancies that endanger women's life or health."[46]

The second matter resolved by the *Casey* decision was that the state's interest in protecting potential life would be seen as subordinate to the woman's constitutionally protected right to an abortion. The plurality's discussion of this issue did not amount to a definitive account of the status of the state's interest, but it set some limits on what states may do. Following the point of viability, threats to the woman's life or health may trump legitimate abortion restrictions rooted in the state's interest in protecting potential life. Depending on how broadly "health" is defined (in particular whether it includes psychological well-being), and bearing in mind that it will generally be a physician of the patient's choosing who decides whether the woman's health is threatened, this might turn out to be a substantial constraint on the state's power even after the point of viability.

The *Casey* decision amounted to a rejection of *Roe*'s underlying logic not only because the trimester-based analysis was explicitly abandoned but also because the state's interest in potential life was held unequivocally to begin before the point at which the fetus is viable. The state's interest is conceived of strengthening as the fetus develops, justifying graduated increases in interference by the state with the constitutionally protected rights of pregnant women over the course of their pregnancies. Before the point of viability,

44. *Ibid.*, pp. 2808–9.
45. *Ibid.*, p. 2817.
46. *Ibid.*, p. 2791.

the Court's "undue burden" test rules out "[u]nnecessary health regulations that have the purpose or effect of presenting a substantial obstacle to a woman seeking an abortion. . . ."[47] But this does not mean that the state is powerless to try to influence a woman's decision to abort in the early stages of pregnancy. "What is at stake," the *Casey* plurality insisted, "is the woman's right to make the ultimate decision, not a right to be insulated from all others in doing so."[48] From the onset of a pregnancy states "may enact rules and regulations designed to encourage [a woman] to know that there are philosophic and social arguments of great weight that can be brought to bear in favor of continuing the pregnancy."[49] So long as neither the purpose nor effect of the regulations in question is to place an "undue burden" on women by imposing "substantial obstacles" on their choice in favor of abortion, states may try to get women to reflect on that choice and encourage them to consider alternatives.[50]

Just what would count as an undue burden in particular cases was by no means clear and was bound to invite further litigation, as the dissenters in *Casey* were quick to point out. In *Casey* itself, the Court held that a Pennsylvania statute placed an undue burden on women insofar as it required a married woman seeking an abortion to sign a statement that she had notified her husband, but that a variety of the Pennsylvania statute's other provisions could survive the test. These included regulations designed to ensure that the woman was giving informed consent to the procedure by requiring that she receive certain information at least twenty-four hours before undergoing the abortion procedure, that for a minor to undergo an abortion there must be informed consent from at least one parent at least twenty-four hours before the procedure (with provisions for a judicial bypass procedure), and that abortion clinics could be obliged to comply with a variety of reporting requirements. The spousal-notification requirement was thought to differ from the others in that although most women would tell their husbands voluntarily what their intentions were, women who are victims of physical and psychological spousal abuse "may have very good reasons for not wishing to inform their husbands of their decision to obtain an abortion."[51] If the Court was clear that this tipped the scale of "undue burden" while the twenty-four-hour waiting period did not, the reasoning behind the distinction was less than entirely lucid. In particular, the Court seemed to have run

47. *Ibid.*, p. 2821.
48. *Ibid.*
49. *Ibid.*, p. 2818.
50. *Ibid.*
51. *Ibid.* p. 2828.

together the quite different considerations of trying to ensure that the woman make a well-thought-out decision (in the sense of not being one that *she* would subsequently come to regret) and the state's right to further *its* interest in potential life by regulating the woman's abortion choice. For this and other reasons *Casey* raised as many questions as it settled, as subsequent litigation soon began to reveal.[52]

ABORTION JURISPRUDENCE

Much of the heat generated by the abortion controversy stems from its symbolic role in American politics; arguments over "life" versus "choice" serve as proxies for conflicts over the role of women in American society, the controversial status of "traditional" and "family" values, and the place of religion in American politics.[53] However, part of the heat has been internally generated, by the manner in which *Roe* was decided and the privacy argument on which it rested. This stemmed partly from the sweeping nature of the holding in *Roe* and partly from the fact that the right of privacy on which Justice Blackmun based his argument is not explicitly mentioned in the Constitution.

Arguments about privacy and reproductive freedom are rooted in the Supreme Court's 1965 decision in *Griswold* v. *Connecticut*.[54] *Griswold* was the culmination of a fifty-year battle to organize formal opposition to birth-control statutes.[55] By a seven-to-two majority, the Court struck down an 1879 statute that had made it illegal "to use any drug or article to prevent conception," holding that a zone of privacy encompasses the marital relationship that outweighs any legitimate state interest in preventing sexual immorality.[56] This decision provided part of the logical foundation for Justice Blackmun's reasoning in *Roe*, in which he maintained that the zone of privacy encompasses decisions about abortion as well as about contraception. But *Griswold* applied to married couples only; by itself this could not generate the right to *individual* privacy on which *Roe* rests. The bridging argument was supplied in *Eisenstadt* v. *Baird* in 1972, when Justice Brennan,

---

52. See *Fargo Women's Health Organization* v. *Schafer* 113 S.Ct. 1668 (1993) and *Planned Parenthood* v. *Casey II* 114 S.Ct. 909 (1994).

53. An excellent treatment of this subject is Luker, *Abortion and the Politics of Motherhood*, especially chapters 3–7.

54. 381 U.S. 479 (1965).

55. For an account of this history, see David J. Garrow, *The Right to Privacy and the Making of* Roe v. Wade (New York: Lisa Drew Books, 1993).

56. 381 U.S. 479–84 (1965).

writing for the majority, observed of the contraception cases that if "the right of privacy means anything, it is the right of the *individual*, married or single, to be free from unwarranted governmental intrusions into matters so fundamentally affecting a person as the decision whether to bear or beget a child."[57]

The *Griswold* result has often been criticized as a poor piece of constitutional jurisprudence, and Blackmun's extension of it to *Roe* has never been secure. The principal charge its defenders have had to deal with is that *Griswold* is alleged to be an example of "judicial legislation," that in deciding it the Court set itself up as a kind of superlegislature. There are two possible responses to this line of criticism for those who support the outcome in *Roe*. One is to insist that what the Court did in *Griswold* is not unusual. Every clause of the Bill of Rights has to be interpreted in light of background philosophical assumptions.[58] Moreover, this line of response goes, few critics of *Griswold* would want to live with the full implications of abandoning the notion that there is a constitutionally protected right to privacy. Indeed, critics of *Roe*, such as President Reagan's solicitor general Charles Fried, usually deny that *Griswold* should be overruled.[59] As Ronald Dworkin—the most articulate defender of *Griswold* and its extension to *Roe*—has noted, it is difficult to discern a principled basis for this view. Once *Griswold* is accepted, it seems inevitably to lead to *Roe*, partly because the technologies of contraception and abortion overlap (and may do so increasingly over time)[60] and partly because it is difficult to articulate compelling grounds for distinguishing the two cases from one another. The Court's reasoning in *Griswold* was that decisions affecting marriage and childbirth are of such an intimate and personal character that people must in principle be free to make the decisions for themselves. As Dworkin notes, decisions regarding abortion are at least as private as those concerning contraception; indeed, in one respect they are more so because the abortion decision "involves a woman's control not just of her sexual relations but of changes within her own body, and the Supreme Court has recognized in various

---

57. *Eisenstadt* v. *Baird* 405 U.S. 453 (1972), emphasis in original.

58. See Ronald Dworkin, *Taking Rights Seriously* (Cambridge, Mass.: Harvard University Press, 1977), pp. 14–80.

59. As he maintained in oral argument before the Court in *Webster* in 1990. The exception here is Robert Bork, who argued in his confirmation hearings for the Supreme Court that both *Roe* and *Griswold* should be overruled. This view has the merit of internal consistency, but it was so far out of the mainstream of even conservative jurisprudential opinion that it led many conservative Democrats and Republicans in the Senate to oppose his nomination.

60. Some intrauterine devices and many popular birth-control pills, if they fail to prevent fertilization, destroy fertilized ova.

ways the importance of physical integrity."[61] Accordingly, Dworkin defends both *Griswold* and *Roe,* as well as the Supreme Court's refashioning of the *Roe* doctrine in *Casey* by reference to an "undue burden" standard that places gradually more stringent burdens on the women seeking an abortion as pregnancy advances, designed to get her to reflect on the seriousness of her proposed abortion and to further the state's interest in protecting potential human life.[62]

To defend *Roe* on the grounds that it cannot be distinguished from *Griswold* in a principled way is to appeal to what is at bottom an ad hominem argument, as conservatives like Robert Bork are quick to point out, since it begs the question of whether *Griswold* was correctly decided. On the left, the *Griswold* doctrine has also been rejected by radical feminists. *Griswold's* privacy doctrine is seen by them as male ideology that contributes to the subjugation of women.[63] Indeed, in other contexts—such as in arguing for the passage of marital-rape statutes—feminists have been concerned to weaken the common-law presumption that the marital relationship shields "intimate" behavior from the criminal law.[64] Partly for these reasons, an alternate line of response to the perceived weakness of *Griswold* and *Roe* has been put forward by defenders of the right to abortion, one which jettisons the privacy argument altogether and relies instead on the constitutional commitment to equal protection of the laws, explicit in the Fourteenth Amendment and implied in the Due Process Clause of the Fifth Amendment.

The equality argument turns on the claim that restrictions on abortion discriminate against women by placing constraints on their freedom that

61. Dworkin, *Life's Dominion,* p. 107.

62. Though Dworkin would apply the standard more permissively than does the Court. For instance, his view is that the Court should have struck down the mandatory waiting periods that were upheld in *Casey.* Dworkin, *Life's Dominion,* pp. 172–74.

63. See Catherine MacKinnon, *Feminism Unmodified: Discourses on Life and Law* (Cambridge, Mass.: Harvard University Press, 1987), pp. 93–102, and Robin West, "Jurisprudence and gender," *University of Chicago Law Review,* Vol. 55, No. 1 (1988), pp. 67–70.

64. On the changing law of marital rape in the U.S., see Michael Freeman, "If you can't rape your wife, who[m] can you rape? The marital rape exception reexamined," *Family Law Quarterly,* Vol. 15, No. 1 (Spring 1981), pp. 1–29, Deborah Rhode, *Justice and Gender* (Cambridge, Mass.: Harvard University Press, 1989), pp. 249–51, Rene I. Augustine, "Marriage: The safe haven for rapists," *The Journal of Family Law,* Vol. 29, No. 3 (1990–91), pp. 559–90, and Sandra Ryder and Sheryl Kuzmenka, "Legal rape: The marital exception," *John Marshall Law Review,* Vol. 24, pp. 393–421. On the English evolution of the exception, see P. M. Bromley and N. V. Lowe, *Family Law,* 7th ed. (Butterworths, 1987), pp. 109–12.

men do not have to bear. This was the view defended by then–Appellate Court Federal Judge Ruth Bader Ginsberg in her 1993 Madison Lecture at New York University, which prompted some sharp questioning in her confirmation hearings for the Supreme Court, because it revealed her discomfort with *Roe*'s privacy doctrine.[65] On Ginsburg's account, abortion regulations affect "a woman's autonomous charge of her full life's course—her ability to stand in relation to man, society, and the state as an independent, self-sustaining citizen."[66] In Ginsburg's view the *Roe* court should have "homed in more precisely on the woman's equality dimension of the issue," enabling it to argue that "disadvantageous treatment of a woman because of her pregnancy and reproductive choice is a paradigm case of discrimination on the basis of sex."[67] It is true that equal-protection arguments have been of declining effectiveness in the Burger and Rehnquist Courts, but Ginsburg points out that, in the very term *Roe* was decided, the Supreme Court had a case on its calendar that could have served as a bridge, "linking reproductive choice to disadvantageous treatment of women on the basis of their sex."[68] Accordingly, she saw the decision to opt for the *Griswold* line of reasoning in *Roe* as a missed opportunity to place the right to abortion on a firmer conceptual and constitutional footing.[69]

Whatever the jurisprudential basis for the right to abortion, it is arguable that it was the manner in which *Roe* was decided—as much as the content of the decision—that was to render its legitimacy suspect. After all, in *Roe* the Court did a good deal more than strike down a Texas abortion statute. The majority opinion laid out a detailed test to determine the conditions under which any abortion statute could be expected to pass muster; in effect, Justice Blackmun authored a federal abortion statute of his own. Ginsburg

65. Ruth Bader Ginsburg, "Speaking in a judicial voice," Madison Lecture, New York University Law School, March 9, 1993, *mimeo*. For the hearings, see "Nomination of Ruth Bader Ginsburg to Be an Associate Justice of the United States Supreme Court: Report together with Additional Views," Exec Report. 103-6 - 93 - 1 United States Senate, pp. 17–19.

66. "Nomination of Ruth Bader Ginsburg . . . ," p. 17.

67. Ginsburg, Madison Lecture, pp. 24, 28. For a more elaborate defense of the equality-based view, see Sylvia A. Law, "Rethinking sex and the Constitution," *University of Pennsylvania Law Review*, Vol. 132, No. 2 (1983–84), pp.1002–13.

68. Ginsburg, Madison Lecture, p. 24. The case, *Struck* v. *Secretary of Defense*, 409 U.S. 947 (1973), was remanded for consideration of mootness.

69. It is of course possible that Blackmun canvassed this possibility and could not find support for it among his brethren on the Court, though—given his failure even to mention it—it seems more likely that, like Ronald Dworkin, Blackmun simply thought *Griswold* compelling.

makes a powerful case that decisions of this kind tend to undermine the Court's legitimacy. Although she thinks that it is sometimes necessary for the Court to step "ahead" of the political process to achieve reforms that the Constitution requires, if it gets too far ahead it can produce a backlash and provoke charges that it is overreaching its appropriate place in a democratic constitutional order.[70] This line of reasoning about the Court's role has been more fully developed by Robert Burt.[71] He contrasts the Court's handling of the abortion question with its approach in the school-desegregation cases of the 1950s. In *Brown* v. *Board of Education* the Justices declared the doctrine of "separate but equal" to be an unconstitutional violation of the Equal Protection Clause,[72] but they did not describe schooling conditions that would be acceptable. Rather, they turned the problem back to Southern state legislatures, requiring them to fashion acceptable remedies themselves.[73] These remedies came before the Court as a result of subsequent litigation, were evaluated when they did, and were often found to be wanting.[74] But the Court avoided designing the remedy itself and thus also avoided the charge that it was usurping the legislative function. In *Roe*, by contrast, as Ginsburg puts it, the Court "invited no dialogue with legislators. Instead, it seemed entirely to remove the ball from the legislators' court" by wiping out virtually every form of abortion regulation then in existence.[75]

On the Ginsburg-Burt view, the sweeping holding in *Roe* diminished the Court's democratic legitimacy at the same time that it ended various schemes to liberalize abortion laws that were under way in different states. Between 1967 and 1973 statutes had been passed in nineteen states liberalizing the permissible grounds for abortion. Many feminists had been dissatisfied with the pace and extent of this reform, and they mounted the campaign that resulted in *Roe*. Burt concedes that in 1973 it was "not clear whether the recently enacted state laws signified the beginning of a national trend toward abolishing all abortion restrictions or even whether in the so-called liberalized states, the new enactments would significantly increase access to abortion for anyone." Nonetheless, he insists that "the abortion issue was openly, avidly, controverted in a substantial number of public forums, and unlike the regimen extant as recently as 1967, it was no longer clear who

70. Ginsburg, Madison Lecture, pp. 30–38.

71. Robert A. Burt, *The Constitution in Conflict* (Harvard University Press, 1992), pp. 344–52.

72. *Brown* v. *Board of Education I* 347 U.S. 483 (1954).

73. *Brown* v. *Board of Education II* 349 U.S. 294 (1955).

74. Burt, *Constitution in Conflict*, pp. 271–310.

75. Ginsburg, Madison Lecture, p. 32.

was winning the battle."[76] Following the *Brown* model, the Court might have struck down the Texas abortion statute in *Roe* (whether by appeal to Blackmun's privacy argument or to the equality argument favored by Ginsburg, Burt, and others) and remanded the matter for further action at the state level, thereby setting limits on what legislatures might do in the matter of regulating abortion without involving the Court directly in designing that regulation. On the Ginsburg-Burt view, this would have left space for democratic resolution of the conflict that would have ensured the survival of the right to abortion while at the same time preserving the legitimacy of the Court's role in a democratic constitutional order.[77]

FUTURE OF THE CONSTITUTIONAL RIGHT TO ABORTION

It is ironic, perhaps, that although *Casey* was decided before Ruth Ginsburg's elevation to the Supreme Court, that decision brought the Court's stance into line with the Ginsburg-Burt view of the manner in which the Court should approach the abortion question. By affirming the existence of a woman's fundamental constitutional right to an abortion, recognizing the legitimacy of the state's interest in potential life, and insisting that states may not pursue the vindication of that interest in a manner that is unduly burdensome to women, the Court set some basic parameters within which legislatures must now fashion regulations that govern abortion. The *Casey* dissenters are right to point out that there will be a degree of unpredictability and confusion as different regulatory regimes are enacted in different states and tested through the courts.[78] Particularly given the developmental dimension to the test—which permits increasingly burdensome

---

76. Burt, *Constitution in Conflict*, p. 348.

77. *Ibid.*, pp. 349–52.

78. In his partly dissenting opinion, Rehnquist—joined by White and Scalia—said of the controlling opinion in *Casey:* "The end result of the joint opinion's paens for praise of legitimacy is the enunciation of a brand new standard for evaluating state regulation of a woman's right to abortion—the undue burden standard. . . . *Roe* v. *Wade* adopted a 'fundamental right' standard under which state regulations could survive only if they met the requirement of 'strict scrutiny.' While we disagree with that standard, it at least had a recognized basis in constitutional law at the time *Roe* was decided. The same cannot be said for the 'undue burden' standard, which is created largely out of whole cloth by the authors of the joint opinion. It is a standard which even today does not command the support of a majority of this Court. And it will not, we believe, result in the sort of 'simple implementation,' easily applied, which the joint opinion anticipates." 112 S.Ct. 2791, at p. 2866 (1992).

regulation as pregnancy advances—this is inevitable. On views of adjudication that encourage efficiency and clarity above all else, this will appear to be a reprehensible invitation to further litigation.[79] On the Ginsburg-Burt view, however, the fact that *Casey* invites litigation may be a cost worth paying. It places the burden of coming up with modes of regulating abortion that are not unduly burdensome on democratically elected legislatures and forces them to do this in the knowledge that the statutes they enact will be tested through the courts and thrown out if they are found wanting. This gives legislators incentives to devise regimes of regulation that minimize the burdens placed on women when they seek to vindicate states' legitimate interests in protecting potential life. It also assigns the federal courts a defensible role in a constitutional democracy. "Without taking giant strides and thereby risking a backlash too forceful to contain, the Court, through constitutional adjudication, can reinforce or signal a green light for social change."[80]

By adopting the Ginsburg-Burt approach to the manner in which abortion regulations are approached, the Court has arguably begun to belie MacIntyre's claim—mentioned at the outset of this introduction—that the different sides in the abortion controversy operate from conceptually incommensurable premises between which it is impossible either rationally to adjudicate or to find common ground. On the contrary, as the debate has moved away from metaphysical imponderables—about when life begins and whether a fetus is a person—and toward consideration of what constitutes an undue burden on a woman's constitutionally protected rights, it has become plain that there is a good deal of room for rational argument about the legal right to abortion. That abortion *can* be a politically polarizing issue does not mean that the debate *has* to be polarized, and it is certainly an advantage of the *Casey* approach that it pushes the debate away from issues that cannot be resolved in a pluralist culture and toward areas where compromise and accommodation are possible.

Questions of approach aside, the substance of the "undue burden" standard offers possibilities for limiting abortion regulations that may be more robust than critics of *Casey* have realized. Certainly it seems to be a plausible interpretive strategy to claim in the wake of *Casey*, as Dworkin does,

---

79. See Rehnquist's remarks immediately following those quoted in the preceding footnote. For a more general defense of efficiency in appellate federal adjudication, see Richard Posner, *The Federal Courts: Crisis and Reform* (Cambridge, Mass.: Harvard University Press, 1985), pp. 169–315. For criticism of Posner's view, see my "Richard Posner's Praxis," *Ohio State Law Review*, Vol. 48, No. 4 (1987), pp. 1009–26.

80. Ginsburg, Madison Lecture, p. 36.

that any regulation of abortion decisions should be deemed unnecessarily coercive and therefore "undue" if the same "improvement in responsibility of decisions about abortion could have been achieved in some different way with less coercive consequences."[81] This line of reasoning suggests that, if plaintiffs can show that less restrictive regulations can achieve states' stated goals in regulating abortion, existing regulations will have to be struck down. Knowing this, legislatures contemplating the passage of abortion statutes will have incentives not to adopt unnecessarily stringent regulations.

Yet perhaps the most important and least noticed feature of the "undue burden" standard around which the constitutional law of abortion has come to revolve since *Casey* is that it has the potential to reinvigorate the egalitarian considerations that Blackmun sidestepped when he looked to *Griswold*'s privacy doctrine as a basis for his decision in *Roe*. The reason is that it will likely prove exceedingly difficult to hammer out a jurisprudence of due and undue burdens without reference to egalitarian considerations. A hint of this can be found in the *Casey* opinions. The dissenters in that case point out that it is difficult to discern a principled basis for the Court's holding, on the one hand, that spousal notification requirements impose undue burdens on women because some women may face abusive husbands, while holding, on the other, that parental consent requirements do not, even though, presumably, some pregnant teenagers will face abusive parents.[82] Dworkin extends this critique, pointing out that it is no less difficult to find a principled basis for the Court's rejection of the claim that a twenty-four-hour waiting period fails the undue burden test, even though it is conceded by the Court to place a heavier burden on poorer women. If a restraint that does not make abortion practically impossible for anyone nonetheless "makes it sufficiently more expensive or difficult that it will deter some women from having an abortion that they, on reflection, want" it should fail the undue burden test, on his view.[83] Dworkin's logic is hard to resist, once the Court has embraced the idea that a regulation that may impose severe costs on *some* women fails to pass constitutional muster for that reason. Although this argument is not explicitly egalitarian, it is implicitly so because it suggests that, in order to survive, abortion regulations must not impose burdens on poor women merely in virtue of their poverty.

Dworkin's reasoning is rooted in the reality that it is difficult—perhaps impossible—to make sense of the idea of "dueness" without reference to the concept of equality. This is perhaps nowhere better illustrated than in

81. Dworkin, *Life's Dominion*, p. 173.

82. 120 L.Ed.2d 674, at 774–97 (1992).

83. Dworkin, *Life's Dominion*, p. 173.

the evolution of the concept of Due Process in American criminal procedure, and it may be illuminating to conclude by mentioning some possible parallels between that history and the future of the undue burden standard in the constitutional law of abortion. The famous 1963 case *Gideon v. Wainright* centered on the question whether states must supply indigent criminal defendants in capital cases with legal counsel paid for by the government.[84] The Court held that they must, partly on the grounds that wealthy defendants typically are in a position to hire counsel.[85] In the decades following *Gideon,* the notion that the poor should not have to bear burdens in pursuit of their constitutionally protected rights that the rich do not have to bear became embedded in the notion of criminal Due Process. As a result, substantial protections were built into the law of criminal procedure in the 1960s and 1970s, relating to the right to counsel for appeals as well as trials, for noncapital offenses if a defendant is to be imprisoned if found guilty, and related areas.[86] It is true that egalitarian readings of the Due Process Clause in criminal procedure have been cut back by the Burger and Rehnquist Courts,[87] so that it is by no means necessary that robustly egalitarian interpretations of the idea of "dueness" will always prevail in this area or any other. Nonetheless, egalitarian considerations have not been entirely abandoned by the Court in this area, and at times even the conservative Courts of the 1980s have expanded upon them—as in the 1985 holding that an indigent defendant who offers an insanity plea should be allowed his own court-appointed psychiatrist at the government's expense.[88] Once again the idea of "dueness" in the Due Process Clause was unpacked by reference to the concept of equality.

It does not take great leaps of imagination to discern the creative possibilities for analogous reasoning as the federal courts begin to unpack the meaning of "undue burden" in the constitutional law of abortion. The notion that a burden is less than due if it imposes substantial costs on some women has a foothold in the language of the controlling opinion in *Casey,* as we have seen, though, as with the case of due process in criminal procedure, the

84. For an excellent account, see Anthony Lewis, *Gideon's Trumpet* (New York: Vintage, 1966).

85. 372 U.S. 335 (1963).

86. For examples, see *Douglas* v. *California* 372 U.S. 353 (1963) and *Argesinger* v. *Hamlin* 407 U.S. 25 (1972).

87. See *Scott* v. *Illinois* 440 U.S. 367 (1979), *Ross* v. *Moffitt* 417 U.S. 600 (1974), *United States* v. *Cronic* 466 U.S. 648 (1984), and *Strickland* v. *Washington* 466 U.S. 668 (1984).

88. *Ake* v. *Oklahoma* 470 U.S. 68 (1985).

implications of this are contradictory in the Court's opinions and have yet to be fully worked out. One obvious area that might be explored concerns abortion funding. Just as Clarence Earl Gideon's constitutional right to counsel was held to require the government to appoint counsel at its own expense for indigent defendants in certain circumstances, so one can imagine analogous arguments being explored in the abortion context. What the parallel class of circumstances would turn out to be is difficult to discern in advance, but the case of rape—where the pregnant woman has no responsibility at all for her pregnancy—is an obvious place to start. From the standpoint of radical feminists this might seem like a small potential gain, given what has been lost since *Webster* and *Casey,* but since the Court has never looked favorably on plaintiffs seeking abortion funding in the past, a potential gain in this area should not be seen as insignificant from their point of view.

The egalitarian possibilities are not exhausted by playing out the implications of the notion that regulations that impose substantial burdens on some women should fail the "undue burden" test. *Casey* identifies two sources of the state's interest in regulating abortion: to ensure that the woman has given her informed consent to the abortion procedure, and vindicating its interest in protecting potential life. The first of these interests is individual-regarding, in the sense that the state may encourage the woman contemplating an abortion to reflect on the seriousness of her proposed course of action and to consider alternatives to it, so long as this does not unnecessarily burden her decision. The state's interest here is in the quality of the woman's decision: that it should be authentic and informed. As I have indicated, egalitarian considerations implicitly affect the evaluation of regulations designed to achieve this goal, because the same regulations that will not be burdensome to wealthy women may impose substantial costs on poor women. A different—and potentially stronger—type of egalitarian consideration arises, however, once we reflect on the state regulation of abortion in order to further its interest in protecting potential human life. This opens up the possibility of reviving the equal protection considerations that Ginsburg, MacKinnon, West, and others think were lost when Blackmun decided to base *Roe* on Griswold's privacy doctrine. Why, it can and will be asked, should states be permitted to vindicate *this* interest in any way that imposes the costs of so doing disproportionately on some women or, indeed, on women rather than men? The possibilities offered by this line of thinking are difficult to discern in the abstract. Clearly the Court in the mid-1990s is unreceptive to the feminist view that virtually all regulation of abortion discriminates against women and should be rejected for that reason.[89] But the possibility of an equal protection argument lurks in the logic of *Casey,* if

89. See footnote 63 above.

not in its language, and it seems at least possible that this logic might generate substantial constraints on abortion regulations in the future.

It seems safe to conclude that *Casey*'s "undue burden" standard offers possibilities that future generations of creative litigators on both sides of the abortion controversy will likely explore with profit. It would be no small historical irony if the *Casey* decision, which has been criticized by many defenders of constitutionally protected abortion rights for women as substantially weakening *Roe*, turned out to be a vehicle by which the right to abortion actually was actually strengthened in certain respects. But as the tumultuous history of the Supreme Court's abortion decisions since 1973 has revealed, it would not be the first such irony. Nor, most likely, would it be the last.

GRISWOLD ET AL. *v.* CONNECTICUT.

APPEAL FROM THE SUPREME COURT OF ERRORS OF CONNECTICUT.

No. 496. Argued March 29–30, 1965.—Decided June 7, 1965.

DOUGLAS, J. delivered the opinion of the Court. GOLDBERG, J., and BRENNAN, J., filed concurring opinions. BLACK, J., and STEWART, J., filed dissenting opinions.

MR. JUSTICE DOUGLAS delivered the opinion of the Court.

Appellant Griswold is Executive Director of the Planned Parenthood League of Connecticut. Appellant Buxton is a licensed physician and a professor at the Yale Medical School who served as Medical Director for the League at its Center in New Haven—a center open and operating from November 1 to November 10, 1961, when appellants were arrested.

They gave information, instruction, and medical advice to *married persons* as to the means of preventing conception. They examined the wife and prescribed the best contraceptive device or material for her use. Fees were usually charged, although some couples were serviced free.

The statutes whose constitutionality is involved in this appeal are §§ 53–32 and 54–196 of the General Statutes of Connecticut (1958 rev.). The former provides:

"Any person who uses any drug, medicinal article or instrument for the purpose of preventing conception shall be fined not less than fifty dollars or imprisoned not less than sixty days nor more than one year or be both fined and imprisoned."

Section 54–196 provides:

"Any person who assists, abets, counsels, causes, hires or commands another to commit any offense may be prosecuted and punished as if he were the principal offender."

The appellants were found guilty as accessories and fined $100 each, against the claim that the accessory statute as so applied violated the Fourteenth Amendment. The Appellate Division of the Circuit Court affirmed. The Supreme Court of Errors affirmed that judgment. 151 Conn. 544, 200 A. 2d 479. We noted probable jurisdiction. 379 U. S. 926.

We think that appellants have standing to raise the constitutional rights of the married people with whom they had a professional relationship. *Tileston* v. *Ullman*, 318 U. S. 44, is different, for there the plaintiff seeking to represent others asked for a declaratory judgment. In that situation we thought that the requirements of standing should be strict, lest the standards of "case or controversy" in Article III of the Constitution become blurred. Here those doubts are removed by reason of a criminal conviction for serving married couples in violation of an aiding-and-abetting statute. Certainly the accessory should have standing to assert that the offense which he is charged with assisting is not, or cannot constitutionally be, a crime.

This case is more akin to *Truax* v. *Raich*, 239 U. S. 33, where an employee was permitted to assert the rights of his employer; to *Pierce* v. *Society of Sisters*, 268 U. S. 510, where the owners of private schools were entitled to assert the rights of potential pupils and their parents; and to *Barrows* v. *Jackson*, 346 U. S. 249, where a white defendant, party to a racially restrictive covenant, who was being sued for damages by the covenantors because she had conveyed her property to Negroes, was allowed to raise the issue that enforcement of the covenant violated the rights of prospective Negro purchasers to equal protection, although no Negro was a party to the suit. And see *Meyer* v. *Nebraska*, 262 U. S. 390; *Adler* v. *Board of Education*, 342 U. S. 485; *NAACP* v. *Alabama*, 357 U. S. 449; *NAACP* v. *Button*, 371 U. S. 415. The rights of husband and wife, pressed here, are likely to be diluted or adversely affected unless those rights are considered in a suit involving those who have this kind of confidential relation to them.

Coming to the merits, we are met with a wide range of questions that implicate the Due Process Clause of the Fourteenth Amendment. Overtones of some arguments suggest that *Lochner* v. *New York*, 198 U. S. 45, should be our guide. But we decline that invitation. . . . We do not sit as a superlegislature to determine the wisdom, need, and propriety of laws that touch economic problems, business affairs, or social conditions. This law, however, operates directly on an intimate relation of husband and wife and their physician's role in one aspect of that relation.

The association of people is not mentioned in the Constitution nor in the Bill of Rights. The right to educate a child in a school of the parents' choice—whether public or private or parochial—is also not mentioned. Nor is the right to study any particular subject or any foreign language. Yet the First Amendment has been construed to include certain of those rights.

By *Pierce* v. *Society of Sisters, supra*, the right to educate one's children as one chooses is made applicable to the States by the force of the First and Fourteenth Amendments. By *Meyer* v. *Nebraska, supra*, the same dignity is given the right to study the German language in a private school. In other words, the State may not, consistently with the spirit of the First Amendment, contract the spectrum of available knowledge. The right of freedom of speech and press includes not only the right to utter or to print, but the right to distribute, the right to receive, the right to read (*Martin* v. *Struthers,* 319 U. S. 141, 143) and freedom of inquiry, freedom of thought, and freedom to teach (see *Wieman* v. *Updegraff,* 344 U. S. 183, 195)—indeed the freedom of the entire university community. *Sweezy* v. *New Hampshire,* 354 U. S. 234, 249–250, 261–263; *Barenblatt* v. *United States,* 360 U. S. 109, 112; *Baggett* v. *Bullitt,* 377 U. S. 360, 369. Without those peripheral rights the specific rights would be less secure. And so we reaffirm the principle of the *Pierce* and the *Meyer* cases.

In *NAACP* v. *Alabama,* 357 U. S. 449, 462, we protected the "freedom to associate and privacy in one's associations," noting that freedom of association was a peripheral First Amendment right. Disclosure of membership lists of a constitutionally valid association, we held, was invalid "as entailing the likelihood of a substantial restraint upon the exercise by petitioner's members of their right to freedom of association." *Ibid.* In other words, the First Amendment has a penumbra where privacy is protected from governmental intrusion. In like context, we have protected forms of "association" that are not political in the customary sense but pertain to the social, legal, and economic benefit of the members. *NAACP* v. *Button,* 371 U. S. 415, 430–431. In *Schware* v. *Board of Bar Examiners,* 353 U. S. 232, we held it not permissible to bar a lawyer from practice, because he had once been a member of the Communist Party. The man's "association with that Party" was not shown to be "anything more than a political faith in a political party" (*id.,* at 244) and was not action of a kind proving bad moral character. *Id.,* at 245–246.

Those cases involved more than the "right of assembly"—a right that extends to all irrespective of their race or ideology. *De Jonge* v. *Oregon,* 299 U. S. 353. The right of "association," like the right of belief (*Board of Education* v. *Barnette,* 319 U. S. 624), is more than the right to attend a meeting; it includes the right to express one's attitudes or philosophies by membership in a group or by affiliation with it or by other lawful means. Association in that context is a form of expression of opinion; and while it is not expressly included in the First Amendment its existence is necessary in making the express guarantees fully meaningful.

The foregoing cases suggest that specific guarantees in the Bill of Rights have penumbras, formed by emanations from those guarantees that help give them life and substance. See *Poe* v. *Ullman,* 367 U. S. 497, 516–522 (dissenting opinion). Various guarantees create zones of privacy. The right of association contained in the penumbra of the First Amendment is one, as we have seen. The Third Amendment in its prohibition against the quartering of soldiers "in any house" in time of peace without the consent of the owner is another facet of that privacy. The Fourth Amendment explicitly affirms the "right of the people to be secure in their persons, houses, papers, and effects, against unreasonable searches and seizures." The Fifth Amendment in its Self-Incrimination Clause enables the citizen to create a zone of privacy which government may not force him to surrender to his detriment. The Ninth Amendment provides: "The enumeration in the Constitution, of certain rights, shall not be construed to deny or disparage others retained by the people."

The Fourth and Fifth Amendments were described in *Boyd* v. *United States*, 116 U. S. 616, 630, as protection against all governmental invasions "of the sanctity of a man's home and the privacies of life."* We recently referred in *Mapp* v. *Ohio*, 367 U. S. 643, 656, to the Fourth Amendment as creating a "right to privacy, no less important than any other right carefully and particularly reserved to the people." See Beaney, The Constitutional Right to Privacy, 1962 Sup. Ct. Rev. 212; Griswold, The Right to be Let Alone, 55 Nw. U. L. Rev. 216 (1960).

We have had many controversies over these penumbral rights of "privacy and repose." See, *e.g.*, *Breard* v. *Alexandria*, 341 U. S. 622, 626, 644; *Public Utilities Comm'n* v. *Pollak*, 343 U. S. 451; *Monroe* v. *Pape*, 365 U. S. 167; *Lanza* v. *New York*, 370 U. S. 139; *Frank* v. *Maryland*, 359 U. S. 360; *Skinner* v. *Oklahoma*, 316 U. S. 535, 541. These cases bear witness that the right of privacy which presses for recognition here is a legitimate one.

The present case, then, concerns a relationship lying within the zone of privacy created by several fundamental constitutional guarantees. And it concerns a law which, in forbidding the *use* of contraceptives rather than regulating their manufacture or sale, seeks to achieve its goals by means having a maximum destructive impact upon that relationship. Such a law cannot stand in light of the familiar principle, so often applied by this Court, that a "governmental purpose to control or prevent activities constitutionally subject to state regulation may not be achieved by means which sweep unnecessarily broadly and thereby invade the area of protected free-

---

*The Court said in full about this right of privacy:

"The principles laid down in this opinion [by Lord Camden in *Entick* v. *Carrington*, 19 How. St. Tr. 1029] affect the very essence of constitutional liberty and security. They reach farther than the concrete form of the case then before the court, with its adventitious circumstances; they apply to all invasions on the part of the government and its employes of the sanctity of a man's home and the privacies of life. It is not the breaking of his doors, and the rummaging of his drawers, that constitutes the essence of the offence; but it is the invasion of his indefeasible right of personal security, personal liberty and private property, where that right has never been forfeited by his conviction of some public offence—it is the invasion of this sacred right which underlies and constitutes the essence of Lord Camden's judgment. Breaking into a house and opening boxes and drawers are circumstances of aggravation; but any forcible and compulsory extortion of a man's own testimony or of his private papers to be used as evidence to convict him of crime or to forfeit his goods, is within the condemnation of that judgment. In this regard the Fourth and Fifth Amendments run almost into each other." 116 U. S., at 630.

doms." *NAACP* v. *Alabama*, 377 U. S. 288, 307. Would we allow the police to search the sacred precincts of marital bedrooms for telltale signs of the use of contraceptives? The very idea is repulsive to the notions of privacy surrounding the marriage relationship.

We deal with a right of privacy older than the Bill of Rights—older than our political parties, older than our school system. Marriage is a coming together for better or worse, hopefully enduring, and intimate to the degree of being sacred. It is an association that promotes a way of life, not causes; a harmony in living, not political faiths; a bilateral loyalty, not commercial or social projects. Yet it is an association for as noble a purpose as any involved in our prior decisions.

Reversed.

MR. JUSTICE GOLDBERG, whom THE CHIEF JUSTICE and MR. JUSTICE BRENNAN join, concurring.

I agree with the Court that Connecticut's birth-control law unconstitutionally intrudes upon the right of marital privacy, and I join in its opinion and judgment. Although I have not accepted the view that "due process" as used in the Fourteenth Amendment incorporates all of the first eight Amendments (see my concurring opinion in *Pointer* v. *Texas*, 380 U. S. 400, 410, and the dissenting opinion of MR. JUSTICE BRENNAN in *Cohen* v. *Hurley*, 366 U. S. 117, 154), I do agree that the concept of liberty protects those personal rights that are fundamental, and is not confined to the specific terms of the Bill of Rights. My conclusion that the concept of liberty is not so restricted and that it embraces the right of marital privacy though that right is not mentioned explicitly in the Constitution[1] is supported both

---

1. My Brother STEWART dissents on the ground that he "can find no . . . general right of privacy in the Bill of Rights, in any other part of the Constitution, or in any case ever before decided by this Court." *Post*, at 530. He would require a more explicit guarantee than the one which the Court derives from several constitutional amendments. This Court, however, has never held that the Bill of Rights or the Fourteenth Amendment protects only those rights that the Constitution specifically mentions by name. See, *e. g.*, *Bolling* v. *Sharpe*, 347 U. S. 497; *Aptheker* v. *Secretary of State*, 378 U. S. 500; *Kent* v. *Dulles*, 357 U. S. 116; *Carrington* v. *Rash*, 380 U. S. 89, 96; *Schware* v. *Board of Bar Examiners*, 353 U. S. 232; *NAACP* v. *Alabama*, 360 U. S. 240; *Pierce* v. *Society of Sisters*, 268 U. S. 510; *Meyer* v. *Nebraska*, 262 U. S. 390. To the contrary, this Court, for example, in *Bolling* v. *Sharpe, supra*, while recognizing that the Fifth Amendment does not contain the "explicit safeguard" of an equal protection clause, *id.*, at 499, nevertheless derived an equal protection principle from that Amendment's Due Process Clause. And in *Schware* v. *Board of Bar Examiners, supra*, the Court held that the Fourteenth Amendment protects from arbitrary state action the right to pursue an occupation, such as the practice of law.

by numerous decisions of this Court, referred to in the Court's opinion, and by the language and history of the Ninth Amendment. In reaching the conclusion that the right of marital privacy is protected, as being within the protected penumbra of specific guarantees of the Bill of Rights, the Court refers to the Ninth Amendment, *ante*, at 484. I add these words to emphasize the relevance of that Amendment to the Court's holding.

The Court stated many years ago that the Due Process Clause protects those liberties that are "so rooted in the traditions and conscience of our people as to be ranked as fundamental." *Snyder* v. *Massachusetts,* 291 U. S. 97, 105. In *Gitlow* v. *New York,* 268 U. S. 652, 666, the Court said:

> "For present purposes we may and do assume that freedom of speech and of the press—which are protected by the First Amendment from abridgment by Congress—are among the *fundamental* personal rights and 'liberties' protected by the due process clause of the Fourteenth Amendment from impairment by the States." (Emphasis added.)

And, in *Meyer* v. *Nebraska,* 262 U. S. 390, 399, the Court, referring to the Fourteenth Amendment, stated:

> "While this Court has not attempted to define with exactness the liberty thus guaranteed, the term has received much consideration and some of the included things have been definitely stated. Without doubt, it denotes not merely freedom from bodily restraint but also [for example,] the right . . . to marry, establish a home and bring up children. . . ."

This Court, in a series of decisions, has held that the Fourteenth Amendment absorbs and applies to the States those specifics of the first eight amendments which express fundamental personal rights.[2] The language and history of the Ninth Amendment reveal that the Framers of the Constitution believed that there are additional fundamental rights, protected from governmental infringement, which exist alongside those fundamental rights specifically mentioned in the first eight constitutional amendments.

The Ninth Amendment reads, "The enumeration in the Constitution, of certain rights, shall not be construed to deny or disparage others retained by the people." The Amendment is almost entirely the work of James Madison. It was introduced in Congress by him and passed the House and

---

2. See, *e. g., Chicago, B. & Q. R. Co.* v. *Chicago,* 166 U. S. 226; *Gitlow* v. *New York, supra; Cantwell* v. *Connecticut,* 310 U. S. 296; *Wolf* v. *Colorado,* 338 U. S. 25; *Robinson* v. *California,* 370 U. S. 660; *Gideon* v. *Wainwright,* 372 U. S. 335; *Malloy* v. *Hogan,* 378 U. S. 1; *Pointer* v. *Texas, supra; Griffin* v. *California,* 380 U. S. 609.

Senate with little or no debate and virtually no change in language. It was proffered to quiet expressed fears that a bill of specifically enumerated rights[3] could not be sufficiently broad to cover all essential rights and that the specific mention of certain rights would be interpreted as a denial that others were protected.[4]

In presenting the proposed Amendment, Madison said:

"It has been objected also against a bill of rights, that, by enumerating particular exceptions to the grant of power, it would disparage those rights which were not placed in that enumeration; and it might follow by implication, that those rights which were not singled out, were intended to be assigned into the hands of the General Government, and were consequently insecure. This is one of the most plausible arguments I have ever heard urged against the admission of a bill of rights into this system; but, I conceive, that it may be guarded against. I have attempted it, as gentlemen may see by turning to the last clause of the fourth resolution [the Ninth Amendment]." I Annals of Congress 439 (Gales and Seaton ed. 1834).

Mr. Justice Story wrote of this argument against a bill of rights and the meaning of the Ninth Amendment:

3. Madison himself had previously pointed out the dangers of inaccuracy resulting from the fact that "no language is so copious as to supply words and phrases for every complex idea." The Federalist, No. 37 (Cooke ed. 1961), at 236.

4. Alexander Hamilton was opposed to a bill of rights on the ground that it was unnecessary because the Federal Government was a government of delegated powers and it was not granted the power to intrude upon fundamental personal rights. The Federalist, No. 84 (Cooke ed. 1961), at 578–579. He also argued,

"I go further, and affirm that bills of rights, in the sense and in the extent in which they are contended for, are not only unnecessary in the proposed constitution, but would even be dangerous. They would contain various exceptions to powers which are not granted; and on this very account, would afford a colourable pretext to claim more than were granted. For why declare that things shall not be done which there is no power to do? Why for instance, should it be said, that the liberty of the press shall not be restrained, when no power is given by which restrictions may be imposed? I will not contend that such a provision would confer a regulating power; but it is evident that it would furnish, to men disposed to usurp, a plausible pretence for claiming that power." *Id.*, at 579.

The Ninth Amendment and the Tenth Amendment, which provides, "The powers not delegated to the United States by the Constitution, nor prohibited by it to the States, are reserved to the States respectively, or to the people," were apparently also designed in part to meet the above-quoted argument of Hamilton.

"In regard to . . . [a] suggestion, that the affirmance of certain rights might disparage others, or might lead to argumentative implications in favor of other powers, it might be sufficient to say that such a course of reasoning could never be sustained upon any solid basis. . . . But a conclusive answer is, that such an attempt may be interdicted (as it has been) by a positive declaration in such a bill of rights that the enumeration of certain rights shall not be construed to deny or disparage others retained by the people." II Story, Commentaries on the Constitution of the United States 626–627 (5th ed. 1891).

He further stated, referring to the Ninth Amendment:

"This clause was manifestly introduced to prevent any perverse or ingenious misapplication of the well-known maxim, that an affirmation in particular cases implies a negation in all others; and, *e converso*, that a negation in particular cases implies an affirmation in all others." *Id.*, at 651.

These statements of Madison and Story make clear that the Framers did not intend that the first eight amendments be construed to exhaust the basic and fundamental rights which the Constitution guaranteed to the people.[5]

While this Court has had little occasion to interpret the Ninth Amendment,[6] "[i]t cannot be presumed that any clause in the constitution is intended to be without effect." *Marbury* v. *Madison*, 1 Cranch 137, 174. In

---

5. The Tenth Amendment similarly made clear that the States and the people retained all those powers not expressly delegated to the Federal Government.

6. This Amendment has been referred to as "The Forgotten Ninth Amendment," in a book with that title by Bennett B. Patterson (1955). Other commentary on the Ninth Amendment includes Redlich, Are There "Certain Rights . . . Retained by the People"? 37 N. Y. U. L. Rev. 787 (1962), and Kelsey, The Ninth Amendment of the Federal Constitution, 11 Ind. L. J. 309 (1936). As far as I am aware, until today this Court has referred to the Ninth Amendment only in *United Public Workers* v. *Mitchell*, 330 U. S. 75, 94–95; *Tennessee Electric Power Co.* v. *TVA*, 306 U. S. 118, 143–144; and *Ashwander* v. *TVA*, 297 U. S. 288, 330–331. See also *Calder* v. *Bull*, 3 Dall. 386, 388; *Loan Assn.* v. *Topeka*, 20 Wall. 655, 662–663.

In *United Public Workers* v. *Mitchell, supra*, at 94–95, the Court stated: "We accept appellants' contention that the nature of political rights reserved to the people by the Ninth and Tenth Amendments [is] involved. The right claimed as inviolate may be stated as the right of a citizen to act as a party official or worker to further his own political views. Thus we have a measure of interference by the Hatch Act and the Rules with what otherwise would be the freedom of the civil servant under the First, Ninth and Tenth Amendments. And, if we look upon due process as a guarantee of freedom in those fields, there is a corresponding impairment of that right under the Fifth Amendment."

interpreting the Constitution, "real effect should be given to all the words it uses." *Myers* v. *United States,* 272 U. S. 52, 151. The Ninth Amendment to the Constitution may be regarded by some as a recent discovery and may be forgotten by others, but since 1791 it has been a basic part of the Constitution which we are sworn to uphold. To hold that a right so basic and fundamental and so deep-rooted in our society as the right of privacy in marriage may be infringed because that right is not guaranteed in so many words by the first eight amendments to the Constitution is to ignore the Ninth Amendment and to give it no effect whatsoever. Moreover, a judicial construction that this fundamental right is not protected by the Constitution because it is not mentioned in explicit terms by one of the first eight amendments or elsewhere in the Constitution would violate the Ninth Amendment, which specifically states that "[t]he enumeration in the Constitution, of certain rights, shall not be *construed* to deny or disparage others retained by the people." (Emphasis added.) . . .

MR. JUSTICE HARLAN, concurring in the judgment.

I fully agree with the judgment of reversal, but find myself unable to join the Court's opinion. The reason is that it seems to me to evince an approach to this case very much like that taken by my Brothers BLACK and STEWART in dissent, namely: the Due Process Clause of the Fourteenth Amendment does not touch this Connecticut statute unless the enactment is found to violate some right assured by the letter or penumbra of the Bill of Rights.

In other words, what I find implicit in the Court's opinion is that the "incorporation" doctrine may be used to *restrict* the reach of Fourteenth Amendment Due Process. For me this is just as unacceptable constitutional doctrine as is the use of the "incorporation" approach to *impose* upon the States all the requirements of the Bill of Rights as found in the provisions of the first eight amendments and in the decisions of this Court interpreting them. See, *e. g.,* my concurring opinions in *Pointer* v. *Texas,* 380 U. S. 400, 408, and *Griffin* v. *California,* 380 U. S. 609, 615, and my dissenting opinion in *Poe* v. *Ullman,* 367 U. S. 497, 522, at pp. 539–545.

In my view, the proper constitutional inquiry in this case is whether this Connecticut statute infringes the Due Process Clause of the Fourteenth Amendment because the enactment violates basic values "implicit in the concept of ordered liberty," *Palko* v. *Connecticut,* 302 U. S. 319, 325. For reasons stated at length in my dissenting opinion in *Poe* v. *Ullman, supra,* I believe that it does. While the relevant inquiry may be aided by resort to one or more of the provisions of the Bill of Rights, it is not dependent on them or any of their radiations. The Due Process Clause of the Fourteenth Amendment stands, in my opinion, on its own bottom.

A further observation seems in order respecting the justification of my

Brothers BLACK and STEWART for their "incorporation" approach to this case. Their approach does not rest on historical reasons, which are of course wholly lacking (see Fairman, Does the Fourteenth Amendment Incorporate the Bill of Rights? The Original Understanding, 2 Stan. L. Rev. 5 (1949)), but on the thesis that by limiting the content of the Due Process Clause of the Fourteenth Amendment to the protection of rights which can be found elsewhere in the Constitution, in this instance in the Bill of Rights, judges will thus be confined to "interpretation" of specific constitutional provisions, and will thereby be restrained from introducing their own notions of constitutional right and wrong into the "vague contours of the Due Process Clause." *Rochin* v. *California*, 342 U. S. 165, 170.

While I could not more heartily agree that judicial "self restraint" is an indispensable ingredient of sound constitutional adjudication, I do submit that the formula suggested for achieving it is more hollow than real. "Specific" provisions of the Constitution, no less than "due process," lend themselves as readily to "personal" interpretations by judges whose constitutional outlook is simply to keep the Constitution in supposed "tune with the times" (*post,* p. 522). Need one go further than to recall last Term's reapportionment cases, *Wesberry* v. *Sanders,* 376 U. S. 1, and *Reynolds* v. *Sims,* 377 U. S. 533, where a majority of the Court "interpreted" "by the People" (Art. I, § 2) and "equal protection" (Amdt. 14) to command "one person, one vote," an interpretation that was made in the face of irrefutable and still unanswered history to the contrary? See my dissenting opinions in those cases, 376 U. S., at 20; 377 U. S., at 589.

Judicial self-restraint will not, I suggest, be brought about in the "due process" area by the historically unfounded incorporation formula long advanced by my Brother BLACK, and now in part espoused by my Brother STEWART. It will be achieved in this area, as in other constitutional areas, only by continual insistence upon respect for the teachings of history, solid recognition of the basic values that underlie our society, and wise appreciation of the great roles that the doctrines of federalism and separation of powers have played in establishing and preserving American freedoms. See *Adamson* v. *California,* 332 U. S. 46, 59 (Mr. Justice Frankfurter, concurring). Adherence to these principles will not, of course, obviate all constitutional differences of opinion among judges, nor should it. Their continued recognition will, however, go farther toward keeping most judges from roaming at large in the constitutional field than will the interpolation into the Constitution of an artificial and largely illusory restriction on the content of the Due Process Clause.*

---

*Indeed, my Brother BLACK, in arguing his thesis, is forced to lay aside a host of cases in which the Court has recognized fundamental rights in the Fourteenth Amendment without specific reliance upon the Bill of Rights.

MR. JUSTICE WHITE, concurring in the judgment.

In my view this Connecticut law as applied to married couples deprives them of "liberty" without due process of law, as that concept is used in the Fourteenth Amendment. I therefore concur in the judgment of the Court reversing these convictions under Connecticut's aiding and abetting statute.

It would be unduly repetitious, and belaboring the obvious, to expound on the impact of this statute on the liberty guaranteed by the Fourteenth Amendment against arbitrary or capricious denials or on the nature of this liberty. Suffice it to say that this is not the first time this Court has had occasion to articulate that the liberty entitled to protection under the Fourteenth Amendment includes the right "to marry, establish a home and bring up children," *Meyer* v. *Nebraska*, 262 U. S. 390, 399, and "the liberty . . . to direct the upbringing and education of children," *Pierce* v. *Society of Sisters*, 268 U. S. 510, 534–535, and that these are among "the basic civil rights of man." *Skinner* v. *Oklahoma*, 316 U. S. 535, 541. These decisions affirm that there is a "realm of family life which the state cannot enter" without substantial justification. *Prince* v. *Massachusetts*, 321 U. S. 158, 166. Surely the right invoked in this case, to be free of regulation of the intimacies of the marriage relationship, "come[s] to this Court with a momentum for respect lacking when appeal is made to liberties which derive merely from shifting economic arrangements." *Kovacs* v. *Cooper*, 336 U. S. 77, 95 (opinion of Frankfurter, J.).

The Connecticut anti-contraceptive statute deals rather substantially with this relationship. For it forbids all married persons the right to use birth-control devices, regardless of whether their use is dictated by considerations of family planning, *Trubek* v. *Ullman*, 147 Conn. 633, 165 A. 2d 158, health, or indeed even of life itself. *Buxton* v. *Ullman*, 147 Conn. 48, 156 A. 2d 508. The anti-use statute, together with the general aiding and abetting statute, prohibits doctors from affording advice to married persons on proper and effective methods of birth control. *Tileston* v. *Ullman*, 129 Conn. 84, 26 A. 2d 582. And the clear effect of these statutes, as enforced, is to deny disadvantaged citizens of Connecticut, those without either adequate knowledge or resources to obtain private counseling, access to medical assistance and up-to-date information in respect to proper methods of birth control. *State* v. *Nelson*, 126 Conn. 412, 11 A. 2d 856; *State* v. *Griswold*, 151 Conn. 544, 200 A. 2d 479. In my view, a statute with these effects bears a substantial burden of justification when attacked under the Fourteenth Amendment. *Yick Wo* v. *Hopkins*, 118 U. S. 365; *Skinner* v. *Oklahoma*, 316 U. S. 535; *Schware* v. *Board of Bar Examiners*, 353 U. S. 232; *McLaughlin* v. *Florida*, 379 U. S. 184, 192.

An examination of the justification offered, however, cannot be avoided by saying that the Connecticut anti-use statute invades a protected area of privacy and association or that it demeans the marriage relationship. The nature of the right invaded is pertinent, to be sure, for statutes regulating sensitive areas of liberty do, under the cases of this Court, require "strict scrutiny," *Skinner* v. *Oklahoma*, 316 U. S. 535, 541, and "must be viewed in the light of less drastic means for achieving the same basic purpose." *Shelton* v. *Tucker*, 364 U. S. 479, 488. "Where there is a significant encroachment upon personal liberty, the State may prevail only upon showing a subordinating interest which is compelling." *Bates* v. *Little Rock*, 361 U. S. 516, 524. See also *McLaughlin* v. *Florida*, 379 U. S. 184. But such statutes, if reasonably necessary for the effectuation of a legitimate and substantial state interest, and not arbitrary or capricious in application, are not invalid under the Due Process Clause. *Zemel* v. *Rusk*, 381 U. S. 1. . . .

MR. JUSTICE BLACK, with whom MR. JUSTICE STEWART joins, dissenting.

I agree with my Brother STEWART'S dissenting opinion. And like him I do not to any extent whatever base my view that this Connecticut law is constitutional on a belief that the law is wise or that its policy is a good one. In order that there may be no room at all to doubt why I vote as I do, I feel constrained to add that the law is every bit as offensive to me as it is to my Brethren of the majority and my Brothers HARLAN, WHITE and GOLDBERG who, reciting reasons why it is offensive to them, hold it unconstitutional. There is no single one of the graphic and eloquent strictures and criticisms fired at the policy of this Connecticut law either by the Court's opinion or by those of my concurring Brethren to which I cannot subscribe—except their conclusion that the evil qualities they see in the law make it unconstitutional.

Had the doctor defendant here, or even the nondoctor defendant, been convicted for doing nothing more than expressing opinions to persons coming to the clinic that certain contraceptive devices, medicines or practices would do them good and would be desirable, or for telling people how devices could be used, I can think of no reasons at this time why their expressions of views would not be protected by the First and Fourteenth Amendments, which guarantee freedom of speech. Cf. *Brotherhood of Railroad Trainmen* v. *Virginia ex rel. Virginia State Bar*, 377 U. S. 1; *NAACP* v. *Button*, 371 U. S. 415. But speech is one thing; conduct and physical activities are quite another. See, *e.g., Cox* v. *Louisiana*, 379 U. S. 536, 554–555; *Cox* v. *Louisiana*, 379 U. S. 559, 563–564; *id* 575–584 (concurring opinion); *Giboney* v. *Empire Storage & Ice Co.*, 336 U. S. 490; cf. *Reynolds* v. *United States*, 98 U. S. 145, 163–164. The two defendants here were active participants in an organization which gave physical examinations to women, advised them what kind of contraceptive devices or medicines would most likely be satisfactory for them, and then supplied the devices themselves, all for a graduated scale of fees, based on the family income. Thus these defendants admittedly engaged with others in a planned course of conduct to help people violate the Connecticut law. Merely because some speech was used in carrying on that conduct—just as in ordinary life some speech accompanies most kinds of conduct—we are not in my view justified in holding that the First Amendment forbids the State to punish their conduct. Strongly as I desire to protect all First Amendment freedoms, I am unable to stretch the Amendment so as to afford protection to the conduct of these defendants in violating the Connecticut law. What would be the constitutional fate of the law if hereafter applied to punish nothing but speech is, as I have said, quite another matter.

The Court talks about a constitutional "right of privacy" as though there is some constitutional provision or provisions forbidding any law ever to be passed which might abridge the "privacy" of individuals. But there is not. There are, of course, guarantees in certain specific constitutional provisions which are designed in part to protect privacy at certain times and places with respect to certain activities. Such, for example, is the Fourth Amendment's guarantee against "unreasonable searches and seizures." But I think it belittles that Amendment to talk about it as though it protects nothing but "privacy." To treat it that way is to give it a niggardly interpretation, not the kind of liberal reading I think any Bill of Rights provision should be given. The average man would very likely not have his feelings soothed any more by having his property seized openly than by having it seized privately and by stealth. He simply wants his property left alone. And a person can be just as much, if not more, irritated, annoyed and injured by an unceremonious public arrest by a policeman as he is by a seizure in the privacy of his office or home.

One of the most effective ways of diluting or expanding a constitutionally guaranteed right is to substitute for the crucial word or words of a constitutional guarantee another word or words, more or less flexible and more or less restricted in meaning. This fact is well illustrated by the use of the term "right of privacy" as a comprehensive substitute for the Fourth Amendment's guarantee against "unreasonable searches and seizures." "Privacy" is a broad, abstract and ambiguous concept which can easily be shrunken in meaning but which can also, on the other hand, easily be interpreted as a constitutional ban against many things other than searches and seizures. I have expressed the view many times that First Amendment freedoms, for example, have suffered from a failure of the courts to stick to the simple language of the First Amendment in construing it, instead of invoking multitudes of words substituted for those the Framers used. See, *e.g., New York*

Times Co. v. *Sullivan,* 376 U. S. 254, 293 (concurring opinion); cases collected in *City of El Paso* v. *Simmons,* 379 U. S. 497, 517, n. 1 (dissenting opinion); Black, The Bill of Rights, 35 N. Y. U. L. Rev. 865. For these reasons I get nowhere in this case by talk about a constitutional "right of privacy" as an emanation from one or more constitutional provisions.[1] I like my privacy as well as the next one, but I am nevertheless compelled to admit that government has a right to invade it unless prohibited by some specific constitutional provision. For these reasons I cannot agree with the Court's judgment and the reasons it gives for holding this Connecticut law unconstitutional. . . .

MR. JUSTICE STEWART, whom MR. JUSTICE BLACK joins, dissenting.

Since 1879 Connecticut has had on its books a law which forbids the use of contraceptives by anyone. I think this is an uncommonly silly law. As a practical matter, the law is obviously unenforceable, except in the oblique context of the present case. As a philosophical matter, I believe the use of contraceptives in the relationship of marriage should be left to personal and private choice, based upon each individual's moral, ethical, and religious beliefs. As a matter of social policy, I think professional counsel about methods of birth control should be available to all, so that each individual's choice can be meaningfully made. But we are not asked in this case to say whether we think this law is unwise, or even asinine. We are asked to hold that it violates the United States Constitution. And that I cannot do.

1. The phrase "right to privacy" appears first to have gained currency from an article written by Messrs. Warren and (later Mr. Justice) Brandeis in 1890 which urged that States should give some form of tort relief to persons whose private affairs were exploited by others. The Right to Privacy, 4 Harv. L. Rev. 193. Largely as a result of this article, some States have passed statutes creating such a cause of action, and in others state courts have done the same thing by exercising their powers as courts of common law. See generally 41 Am. Jur. 926–927. Thus the Supreme Court of Georgia, in granting a cause of action for damages to a man whose picture had been used in a newspaper advertisement without his consent, said that "A right of privacy in matters purely private is . . . derived from natural law" and that "The conclusion reached by us seems to be . . . thoroughly in accord with natural justice, with the principles of the law of every civilized nation, and especially with the elastic principles of the common law. . . . " *Pavesich* v. *New England Life Ins. Co.,* 122 Ga. 190, 194, 218, 50 S. E. 68, 70, 80. Observing that "the right of privacy . . . presses for recognition here," today this Court, which I did not understand to have power to sit as a court of common law, now appears to be exalting a phrase which Warren and Brandeis used in discussing grounds for tort relief, to the level of a constitutional rule which prevents state legislatures from passing any law deemed by this Court to interfere with "privacy."

In the course of its opinion the Court refers to no less than six Amendments to the Constitution: the First, the Third, the Fourth, the Fifth, the Ninth, and the Fourteenth. But the Court does not say which of these Amendments, if any, it thinks is infringed by this Connecticut law.

We *are* told that the Due Process Clause of the Fourteenth Amendment is not, as such, the "guide" in this case. With that much I agree. There is no claim that this law, duly enacted by the Connecticut Legislature, is unconstitutionally vague. There is no claim that the appellants were denied any of the elements of procedural due process at their trial, so as to make their convictions constitutionally invalid. And, as the Court says, the day has long passed since the Due Process Clause was regarded as a proper instrument for determining "the wisdom, need, and propriety" of state laws. Compare *Lochner* v. *New York*, 198 U. S. 45, with *Ferguson* v. *Skrupa*, 372 U. S. 726. My Brothers HARLAN and WHITE to the contrary, "[w]e have returned to the original constitutional proposition that courts do not substitute their social and economic beliefs for the judgment of legislative bodies, who are elected to pass laws." *Ferguson* v. *Skrupa, supra,* at 730.

As to the First, Third, Fourth, and Fifth Amendments, I can find nothing in any of them to invalidate this Connecticut law, even assuming that all those Amendments are fully applicable against the States.[1] It has not even been argued that this is a law "respecting an establishment of religion, or prohibiting the free exercise thereof."[2] And surely, unless the solemn process of constitutional adjudication is to descend to the level of a play on words, there is not involved here any abridgment of "the freedom of speech, or of the press; or the right of the people peaceably to assemble, and to petition the Government for a redress of grievances."[3] No soldier has been

1. The Amendments in question were, as everyone knows, originally adopted as limitations upon the power of the newly created Federal Government, not as limitations upon the powers of the individual States. But the Court has held that many of the provisions of the first eight amendments are fully embraced by the Fourteenth Amendment as limitations upon state action, and some members of the Court have held the view that the adoption of the Fourteenth Amendment made every provision of the first eight amendments fully applicable against the States. See *Adamson* v. *California*, 332 U. S. 46, 68 (dissenting opinion of MR. JUSTICE BLACK).

2. U. S. Constitution, Amendment I. To be sure, the injunction contained in the Connecticut statute coincides with the doctrine of certain religious faiths. But if that were enough to invalidate a law under the provisions of the First Amendment relating to religion, then most criminal laws would be invalidated. See, *e.g.,* the Ten Commandments. The Bible, Exodus 20:2–17 (King James).

3. U. S. Constitution, Amendment I. If all the appellants had done was to advise people that they thought the use of contraceptives was desirable, or even to counsel their use, the appellants would, of course, have a substantial First Amendment

quartered in any house.[4] There has been no search, and no seizure.[5] Nobody has been compelled to be a witness against himself.[6]

The Court also quotes the Ninth Amendment, and my Brother GOLD-BERG's concurring opinion relies heavily upon it. But to say that the Ninth Amendment has anything to do with this case is to turn somersaults with history. The Ninth Amendment, like its companion the Tenth, which this Court held "states but a truism that all is retained which has not been surrendered," *United States* v. *Darby,* 312 U. S. 100, 124, was framed by James Madison and adopted by the States simply to make clear that the adoption of the Bill of Rights did not alter the plan that the *Federal* Government was to be a government of express and limited powers, and that all rights and powers not delegated to it were retained by the people and the individual States. Until today no member of this Court has ever suggested that the Ninth Amendment meant anything else, and the idea that a federal court could ever use the Ninth Amendment to annul a law passed by the elected representatives of the people of the State of Connecticut would have caused James Madison no little wonder.

What provision of the Constitution, then, does make this state law invalid? The Court says it is the right of privacy "created by several fundamental constitutional guarantees." With all deference, I can find no such general right of privacy in the Bill of Rights, in any other part of the Constitution, or in any case ever before decided by this Court.[7]

At the oral argument in this case we were told that the Connecticut law

---

claim. But their activities went far beyond mere advocacy. They prescribed specific contraceptive devices and furnished patients with the prescribed contraceptive materials.

4. U. S. Constitution, Amendment III.

5. U. S. Constitution, Amendment IV.

6. U. S. Constitution, Amendment V.

7. Cases like *Shelton* v. *Tucker,* 364 U. S. 479 and *Bates* v. *Little Rock,* 361 U. S. 516, relied upon in the concurring opinions today, dealt with true First Amendment rights of association and are wholly inapposite here. See also, *e.g., NAACP* v. *Alabama,* 357 U. S. 449; *Edwards* v. *South Carolina,* 372 U. S. 229. Our decision in *McLaughlin* v. *Florida,* 379 U. S. 184, is equally far afield. That case held invalid under the Equal Protection Clause, a state criminal law which discriminated against Negroes.

The Court does not say how far the new constitutional right of privacy announced today extends. See, *e.g.,* Mueller, Legal Regulation of Sexual Conduct, at 127; Ploscowe, Sex and the Law, at 189. I suppose, however, that even after today a State can constitutionally still punish at least some offenses which are not committed in public.

does not "conform to current community standards." But it is not the function of this Court to decide cases on the basis of community standards. We are here to decide cases "agreeably to the Constitution and laws of the United States." It is the essence of judicial duty to subordinate our own personal views, our own ideas of what legislation is wise and what is not. If, as I should surely hope, the law before us does not reflect the standards of the people of Connecticut, the people of Connecticut can freely exercise their true Ninth and Tenth Amendment rights to persuade their elected representatives to repeal it. That is the constitutional way to take this law off the books.[8]

8. See *Reynolds* v. *Sims,* 377 U. S. 533, 562. The Connecticut House of Representatives recently passed a bill (House Bill No. 2462) repealing the birth control law. The State Senate has apparently not yet acted on the measure, and today is relieved of that responsibility by the Court. New Haven Journal-Courier, Wed., May 19, 1965, p. 1, col. 4, and p. 13, col. 7.

EISENSTADT, SHERIFF *v.* BAIRD

APPEAL FROM THE UNITED STATES COURT OF APPEALS
FOR THE FIRST CIRCUIT

No. 70–17. Argued November 17–18, 1971—Decided March 22, 1972

BRENNAN, J., delivered the opinion of the Court, in which DOUGLAS, STEWART, and MARSHALL, JJ., joined. DOUGLAS, J., filed a concurring opinion. WHITE, J., filed an opinion concurring in the result, in which BLACKMUN, J., joined. BURGER, C. J., filed a dissenting opinion. POWELL and REHNQUIST, JJ., took no part in the consideration or decision of the case.

MR. JUSTICE BRENNAN delivered the opinion of the Court.

Appellee William Baird was convicted at a bench trial in the Massachusetts Superior Court under Massachusetts General Laws Ann., c. 272, § 21, first, for exhibiting contraceptive articles in the course of delivering a lecture on contraception to a group of students at Boston University and, second, for giving a young woman a package of Emko vaginal foam at the close of his address. . . . The Massachusetts Supreme Judicial Court unanimously set aside the conviction for exhibiting contraceptives on the ground that it violated Baird's First Amendment rights, but by a four-to-three vote sustained the conviction for giving away the foam. *Commonwealth* v. *Baird*, 355 Mass. 746, 247 N. E. 2d 574 (1969). Baird subsequently filed a petition for a federal writ of habeas corpus, which the District Court dismissed. 310 F. Supp. 951 (1970). On appeal, however, the Court of Appeals for the First Circuit vacated the dismissal and remanded the action with directions to grant the writ discharging Baird. 429 F. 2d 1398 (1970). This appeal by the Sheriff of Suffolk County, Massachusetts, followed, and we noted probable jurisdiction. 401 U. S. 934 (1971). We affirm.

Massachusetts General Laws Ann., c. 272, § 21, under which Baird was convicted, provides a maximum five-year term of imprisonment for "whoever . . . gives away . . . any drug, medicine, instrument or article whatever for the prevention of conception," except as authorized in § 21A. Under § 21A, "[a] registered physician may administer to or prescribe for any married person drugs or articles intended for the prevention of pregnancy or conception. [And a] registered pharmacist actually engaged in the business of pharmacy may furnish such drugs or articles to any married person presenting a prescription from a registered physician." . . . As interpreted by the State Supreme Judicial Court, these provisions make it a felony for anyone, other than a registered physician or pharmacist acting in accordance with the terms of § 21A, to dispense any article with the intention that it be used for the prevention of conception. The statutory scheme distinguishes among three distinct classes of distributees—*first*, married persons may obtain contraceptives to prevent pregnancy, but only from doctors or druggists on prescription; *second*, single persons may not obtain contraceptives from anyone to prevent pregnancy; and, *third*, married or single persons may obtain contraceptives from anyone to prevent, not pregnancy, but the spread of disease. This construction of state law is, of course, binding on us. *E. g.,* *Groppi* v. *Wisconsin,* 400 U. S. 505, 507 (1971). . . .

The basic principles governing application of the Equal Protection Clause of the Fourteenth Amendment are familiar. As THE CHIEF JUSTICE only recently explained in *Reed* v. *Reed,* 404 U. S. 71, 75–76 (1971):

"In applying that clause, this Court has consistently recognized that the Fourteenth Amendment does not deny to States the power to treat different classes of persons in different ways. *Barbier* v. *Connolly,* 113 U. S. 27 (1885); *Lindsley* v. *Natural Carbonic Gas Co.,* 220 U. S. 61 (1911); *Railway Express Agency* v. *New York,* 336 U. S. 106 (1949); *McDonald* v. *Board of Election Commissioners,* 394 U. S. 802 (1969). The Equal Protection Clause of that amendment does, however, deny to States the power to legislate that different treatment be accorded to persons placed by a statute into different classes on the basis of criteria wholly unrelated to the objective of that statute. A classification 'must be reasonable, not arbitrary, and must rest upon some ground of difference having a fair and substantial relation to the object of the legislation, so that all persons similarly circumstanced shall be treated alike.' *Royster Guano Co.* v. *Virginia,* 253 U. S. 412, 415 (1920)."

The question for our determination in this case is whether there is some ground of difference that rationally explains the different treatment accorded married and unmarried persons under Massachusetts General Laws Ann., c. 272, §§ 21 and 21A.[7] For the reasons that follow, we conclude that no such ground exists.

7. Of course, if we were to conclude that the Massachusetts statute impinges upon fundamental freedoms under *Griswold,* the statutory classification would have to be not merely *rationally related* to a valid public purpose but *necessary* to the achievement of a *compelling* state interest. *E. g.,* *Shapiro* v. *Thompson,* 394 U. S. 618 (1969); *Loving* v. *Virginia,* 388 U. S. 1 (1967). But just as in *Reed* v. *Reed,* 404 U. S. 71 (1971), we do not have to address the statute's validity under that test because the law fails to satisfy even the more lenient equal protection standard.

First. Section 21 stems from Mass. Stat. 1879, c. 159, § 1, which prohibited, without exception, distribution of articles intended to be used as contraceptives. In *Commonwealth* v. *Allison,* 227 Mass. 57, 62, 116 N. E. 265, 266 (1917), the Massachusetts Supreme Judicial Court explained that the law's "plain purpose is to protect purity, to preserve chastity, to encourage continence and self restraint, to defend the sanctity of the home, and thus to engender in the State and nation a virile and virtuous race of men and women." Although the State clearly abandoned that purpose with the enactment of § 21A, at least insofar as the illicit sexual activities of married persons are concerned, see n. 3, *supra,* the court reiterated in *Sturgis* v. *Attorney General, supra,* that the object of the legislation is to discourage premarital sexual intercourse. Conceding that the State could, consistently with the Equal Protection Clause, regard the problems of extramarital and premarital sexual relations as "[e]vils . . . of different dimensions and proportions, requiring different remedies," *Williamson* v. *Lee Optical Co.,* 348 U. S. 483, 489 (1955), we cannot agree that the deterrence of premarital sex may reasonably be regarded as the purpose of the Massachusetts law.

It would be plainly unreasonable to assume that Massachusetts has prescribed pregnancy and the birth of an unwanted child as punishment for fornication, which is a misdemeanor under Massachusetts General Laws Ann., c. 272, § 18. Aside from the scheme of values that assumption would attribute to the State, it is abundantly clear that the effect of the ban on distribution of contraceptives to unmarried persons has at best a marginal relation to the proffered objective. What Mr. Justice Goldberg said in *Griswold* v. *Connecticut, supra,* at 498 (concurring opinion), concerning the effect of Connecticut's prohibition on the use of contraceptives in discouraging extramarital sexual relations, is equally applicable here. "The rationality of this justification is dubious, particularly in light of the admitted widespread availability to all persons in the State of Connecticut, unmarried as well as married, of birth-control devices for the prevention of disease, as distinguished from the prevention of conception." See also *id.,* at 505–507 (WHITE, J., concurring in judgment). Like Connecticut's laws, §§ 21 and 21A do not at all regulate the distribution of contraceptives when they are to be used to prevent, not pregnancy, but the spread of disease. *Commonwealth* v. *Corbett,* 307 Mass. 7, 29 N. E. 2d 151 (1940), cited with approval in *Commonwealth* v. *Baird,* 355 Mass., at 754, 247 N. E. 2d, at 579. Nor, in making contraceptives available to married persons without regard to their intended use, does Massachusetts attempt to deter married persons from engaging in illicit sexual relations with unmarried persons. Even on the assumption that the fear of pregnancy operates as a deterrent to fornication, the Massachusetts statute is thus so riddled with exceptions that deterrence of premarital sex cannot reasonably be regarded as its aim. . . .

If under *Griswold* the distribution of contraceptives to married persons cannot be prohibited, a ban on distribution to unmarried persons would be equally impermissible. It is true that in *Griswold* the right of privacy in question inhered in the marital relationship. Yet the marital couple is not an independent entity with a mind and heart of its own, but an association of two individuals each with a separate intellectual and emotional makeup. If the right of privacy means anything, it is the right of the *individual,* married or single, to be free from unwarranted governmental intrusion into matters so fundamentally affecting a person as the decision whether to bear or beget a child. See *Stanley* v. *Georgia,* 394 U. S. 557 (1969). . . . See also *Skinner* v. *Oklahoma,* 316 U. S. 535 (1942); *Jacobson* v. *Massachusetts,* 197 U. S. 11, 29 (1905).

On the other hand, if *Griswold* is no bar to a prohibition on the distribution of contraceptives, the State could not, consistently with the Equal Protection Clause, outlaw distribution to unmarried but not to married persons. In each case the evil, as perceived by the State, would be identical, and the underinclusion would be invidious. . . .

ROE ET AL. *v.* WADE, DISTRICT ATTORNEY OF DALLAS COUNTY

APPEAL FROM THE UNITED STATES DISTRICT COURT FOR THE
NORTHERN DISTRICT OF TEXAS

No. 70–18. Argued December 13, 1971—Reargued October 11,
1972—Decided January 22, 1973

BLACKMUN, J., delivered the opinion of the Court, in which BURGER, C. J., and DOUGLAS, BRENNAN, STEWART, MARSHALL, and POWELL, JJ., joined. BURGER, C. J., DOUGLAS, J., and STEWART, J., filed concurring opinions. WHITE, J., filed a dissenting opinion, in which REHNQUIST, J., joined. REHNQUIST, J., filed a dissenting opinion.

MR. JUSTICE BLACKMUN delivered the opinion of the Court.

This Texas federal appeal and its Georgia companion, *Doe* v. *Bolton*, present constitutional challenges to state criminal abortion legislation. The Texas statutes under attack here are typical of those that have been in effect in many States for approximately a century. The Georgia statutes, in contrast, have a modern cast and are a legislative product that, to an extent at least, obviously reflects the influences of recent attitudinal change, of advancing medical knowledge and techniques, and of new thinking about an old issue.

We forthwith acknowledge our awareness of the sensitive and emotional nature of the abortion controversy, of the vigorous opposing views, even among physicians, and of the deep and seemingly absolute convictions that the subject inspires. One's philosophy, one's experiences, one's exposure to the raw edges of human existence, one's religious training, one's attitudes toward life and family and their values, and the moral standards one establishes and seeks to observe, are all likely to influence and to color one's thinking and conclusions about abortion.

In addition, population growth, pollution, poverty, and racial overtones tend to complicate and not to simplify the problem.

Our task, of course, is to resolve the issue by constitutional measurement, free of emotion and of predilection. We seek earnestly to do this, and, because we do, we have inquired into, and in this opinion place some emphasis upon, medical and medical-legal history and what that history reveals about man's attitudes toward the abortion procedure over the centuries. We bear in mind, too, Mr. Justice Holmes' admonition in his now vindicated dissent in *Lochner* v. *New York*, 198 U. S. 45, 76 (1905):

"[The Constitution] is made for people of fundamentally differing views, and the accident of our finding certain opinions natural and familiar or novel and even shocking ought not to conclude our judgment upon the question whether statutes embodying them conflict with the Constitution of the United States."

I

The Texas statutes that concern us here are Arts. 1191–1194 and 1196 of the State's Penal Code.[1] These make it a crime to "procure an abortion," as therein defined, or to attempt one, except with respect to "an abortion pro-

---

1. "Article 1191. Abortion
    "If any person shall designedly administer to a pregnant woman or knowingly procure to be administered with her consent any drug or medicine, or shall use towards her any violence or means whatever externally or internally applied, and thereby procure an abortion, he shall be confined in the penitentiary not less than two nor more than five years; if it be done without her consent, the punishment shall be doubled. By 'abortion' is meant that the life of the fetus or embryo shall be destroyed in the woman's womb or that a premature birth thereof be caused.
    "Art. 1192. Furnishing the means
    "Whoever furnishes the means for procuring an abortion knowing the purpose intended is guilty as an accomplice.
    "Art. 1193. Attempt at abortion
    "If the means used shall fail to produce an abortion, the offender is nevertheless guilty of an attempt to produce abortion, provided it be shown that such means were calculated to produce that result, and shall be fined not less than one hundred nor more than one thousand dollars.
    "Art. 1194. Murder in producing abortion
    "If the death of the mother is occasioned by an abortion so produced or by an attempt to effect the same it is murder."
    "Art. 1196. By medical advice
    "Nothing in this chapter applies to an abortion procured or attempted by medical advice for the purpose of saving the life of the mother."
    The foregoing Articles, together with Art. 1195, compose Chapter 9 of Title 15 of the Penal Code. Article 1195, not attacked here, reads:
    "Art. 1195. Destroying unborn child
    "Whoever shall during parturition of the mother destroy the vitality or life in a child in a state of being born and before actual birth, which child would otherwise have been born alive, shall be confined in the penitentiary for life or for not less than five years."

cured or attempted by medical advice for the purpose of saving the life of the mother." Similar statutes are in existence in a majority of the States. . . .

Texas first enacted a criminal abortion statute in 1854. Texas Laws 1854, c. 49, § 1, set forth in 3 H. Gammel, Laws of Texas 1502 (1898). This was soon modified into language that has remained substantially unchanged to the present time. See Texas Penal Code of 1857, c. 7, Arts. 531–536; G. Paschal, Laws of Texas, Arts. 2192–2197 (1866); Texas Rev. Stat., c. 8, Arts. 536–541 (1879); Texas Rev. Crim. Stat., Arts. 1071–1076 (1911). The final article in each of these compilations provided the same exception, as does the present Article 1196, for an abortion by "medical advice for the purpose of saving the life of the mother." . . .

II

Jane Roe,[4] a single woman who was residing in Dallas County, Texas, instituted this federal action in March 1970 against the District Attorney of the county. She sought a declaratory judgment that the Texas criminal abortion statutes were unconstitutional on their face, and an injunction restraining the defendant from enforcing the statutes.

Roe alleged that she was unmarried and pregnant; that she wished to terminate her pregnancy by an abortion "performed by a competent, licensed physician, under safe, clinical conditions"; that she was unable to get a "legal" abortion in Texas because her life did not appear to be threatened by the continuation of her pregnancy; and that she could not afford to travel to another jurisdiction in order to secure a legal abortion under safe conditions. She claimed that the Texas statutes were unconstitutionally vague and that they abridged her right of personal privacy, protected by the First, Fourth, Fifth, Ninth, and Fourteenth Amendments. By an amendment to her complaint Roe purported to sue "on behalf of herself and all other women" similarly situated. . . . and the licensed practicing physician, all joining in the attack on the Texas criminal abortion statutes. . . .

V

The principal thrust of appellant's attack on the Texas statutes is that they improperly invade a right, said to be possessed by the pregnant woman, to choose to terminate her pregnancy. Appellant would discover this right in the concept of personal "liberty" embodied in the Fourteenth Amendment's Due Process Clause; or in personal, marital, familial, and sexual privacy said to be protected by the Bill of Rights or its penumbras, see *Gris-*

---

4. The name is a pseudonym.

wold v. *Connecticut,* 381 U. S. 479 (1965); *Eisenstadt* v. *Baird,* 405 U. S. 438 (1972); *id.,* at 460 (WHITE, J., concurring in result); or among those rights reserved to the people by the Ninth Amendment, *Griswold* v. *Connecticut,* 381 U. S., at 486 (Goldberg, J., concurring). Before addressing this claim, we feel it desirable briefly to survey, in several aspects, the history of abortion, for such insight as that history may afford us, and then to examine the state purposes and interests behind the criminal abortion laws.

#

VI

It perhaps is not generally appreciated that the restrictive criminal abortion laws in effect in a majority of States today are of relatively recent vintage. Those laws, generally proscribing abortion or its attempt at any time during pregnancy except when necessary to preserve the pregnant woman's life, are not of ancient or even of common-law origin. Instead, they derive from statutory changes effected, for the most part, in the latter half of the 19th century.

    1. *Ancient attitudes.* These are not capable of precise determination. We are told that at the time of the Persian Empire abortifacients were known and that criminal abortions were severely punished.[8] We are also told, however, that abortion was practiced in Greek times as well as in the Roman Era,[9] and that "it was resorted to without scruple."[10] The Ephesian, Soranos, often described as the greatest of the ancient gynecologists, appears to have been generally opposed to Rome's prevailing free-abortion practices. He found it necessary to think first of the life of the mother, and he resorted to abortion when, upon this standard, he felt the procedure advisable.[11] Greek and Roman law afforded little protection to the unborn. If abortion was prosecuted in some places, it seems to have been based on a

8. A. Castiglioni, A History of Medicine 84 (2d ed. 1947), E. Krumbhaar, translator and editor (hereinafter Castiglioni).

9. J. Ricci, The Genealogy of Gynaecology 52, 84, 113, 149 (2d ed. 1950) (hereinafter Ricci); L. Lader, Abortion 75–77 (1966) (hereinafter Lader); K. Niswander, Medical Abortion Practices in the United States, in Abortion and the Law 37, 38–40 (D. Smith ed. 1967); G. Williams, The Sanctity of Life and the Criminal Law 148 (1957) (hereinafter Williams); J. Noonan, An Almost Absolute Value in History, in The Morality of Abortion 1, 3–7 (J. Noonan ed. 1970) (hereinafter Noonan); Quay, Justifiable Abortion—Medical and Legal Foundations (pt. 2), 49 Geo. L. J. 395, 406–422 (1961) (hereinafter Quay).

10. L. Edelstein, The Hippocratic Oath 10 (1943) (hereinafter Edelstein). But see Castiglioni 227.

11. Edelstein 12; Ricci 113–114, 118–119; Noonan 5.

concept of a violation of the father's right to his offspring. Ancient religion did not bar abortion.[12]

2. *The Hippocratic Oath*. What then of the famous Oath that has stood so long as the ethical guide of the medical profession and that bears the name of the great Greek (460(?)–377(?) B. C.), who has been described as the Father of Medicine, the "wisest and the greatest practitioner of his art," and the "most important and most complete medical personality of antiquity," who dominated the medical schools of his time, and who typified the sum of the medical knowledge of the past?[13] The Oath varies somewhat according to the particular translation, but in any translation the content is clear: "I will give no deadly medicine to anyone if asked, nor suggest any such counsel; and in like manner I will not give to a woman a pessary to produce abortion,"[14] or "I will neither give a deadly drug to anyone if asked for it, nor will I make a suggestion to this effect. Similarly, I will not give to a woman an abortive remedy."[15]

Although the Oath is not mentioned in any of the principal briefs in this case or in *Doe* v. *Bolton*, . . . it represents the apex of the development of strict ethical concepts in medicine, and its influence endures to this day. Why did not the authority of Hippocrates dissuade abortion practice in his time and that of Rome? The late Dr. Edelstein provides us with a theory:[16] The Oath was not uncontested even in Hippocrates' day; only the Pythagorean school of philosophers frowned upon the related act of suicide. Most Greek thinkers, on the other hand, commended abortion, at least prior to viability. See Plato, Republic, V, 461; Aristotle, Politics, VII, 1335b 25. For the Pythagoreans, however, it was a matter of dogma. For them the embryo was animate from the moment of conception, and abortion meant destruction of a living being. The abortion clause of the Oath, therefore, "echoes Pythagorean doctrines," and "[i]n no other stratum of Greek opinion were such views held or proposed in the same spirit of uncompromising austerity."[17]

Dr. Edelstein then concludes that the Oath originated in a group representing only a small segment of Greek opinion and that it certainly was not accepted by all ancient physicians. He points out that medical writings down to Galen (A. D. 130–200) "give evidence of the violation of almost every

12. Edelstein 13–14.
13. Castiglioni 148.
14. *Id.*, at 154.
15. Edelstein 3.
16. *Id.*, at 12, 15–18.
17. *Id.*, at 18; Lader 76.

one of its injunctions."[18] But with the end of antiquity a decided change took place. Resistance against suicide and against abortion became common. The Oath came to be popular. The emerging teachings of Christianity were in agreement with the Pythagorean ethic. The Oath "became the nucleus of all medical ethics" and "was applauded as the embodiment of truth." Thus, suggests Dr. Edelstein, it is "a Pythagorean manifesto and not the expression of an absolute standard of medical conduct."[19]

This, it seems to us, is a satisfactory and acceptable explanation of the Hippocratic Oath's apparent rigidity. It enables us to understand, in historical context, a long-accepted and revered statement of medical ethics.

3. *The common law.* It is undisputed that at common law, abortion performed *before* "quickening"—the first recognizable movement of the fetus *in utero*, appearing usually from the 16th to the 18th week of pregnancy[20]— was not an indictable offense.[21] The absence of a common-law crime for pre-quickening abortion appears to have developed from a confluence of earlier philosophical, theological, and civil and canon law concepts of when life begins. These disciplines variously approached the question in terms of the point at which the embryo or fetus became "formed" or recognizably human, or in terms of when a "person" came into being, that is, infused with a "soul" or "animated." A loose consensus evolved in early English law that these events occurred at some point between conception and live birth.[22] This was "mediate animation." Although Christian theology and the canon law came to fix the point of animation at 40 days for a male and

18. Edelstein 63.

19. *Id.,* at 64.

20. Dorland's Illustrated Medical Dictionary 1261 (24th ed. 1965).

21. E. Coke, Institutes III *50; 1 W. Hawkins, Pleas of the Crown, c. 31, § 16 (4th ed. 1762); 1 W. Blackstone, Commentaries *129–130; M. Hale, Pleas of the Crown 433 (1st Amer. ed. 1847). For discussions of the role of the quickening concept in English common law, see Lader 78; Noonan 223–226; Means, The Law of New York Concerning Abortion and the Status of the Foetus, 1664–1968: A Case of Cessation of Constitutionality (pt. 1), 14 N. Y. L. F. 411, 418–428 (1968) (hereinafter Means I); Stern, Abortion: Reform and the Law, 59 J. Crim. L. C. & P. S. 84 (1968) (hereinafter Stern); Quay 430–432; Williams 152.

22. Early philosophers believed that the embryo or fetus did not become formed and begin to live until at least 40 days after conception for a male, and 80 to 90 days for a female. See, for example, Aristotle, Hist. Anim. 7.3.583b; Gen. Anim. 2.3.736, 2.5.741; Hippocrates, Lib. de Nat. Puer., No. 10. Aristotle's thinking derived from his three-stage theory of life: vegetable, animal, rational. The vegetable stage was reached at conception, the animal at "animation," and the rational soon after live birth. This theory, together with the 40/80 day view, came to be accepted by early Christian thinkers.

80 days for a female, a view that persisted until the 19th century, there was otherwise little agreement about the precise time of formation or animation. There was agreement, however, that prior to this point the fetus was to be regarded as part of the mother, and its destruction, therefore, was not homicide. Due to continued uncertainty about the precise time when animation occurred, to the lack of any empirical basis for the 40–80-day view, and perhaps to Aquinas' definition of movement as one of the two first principles of life, Bracton focused upon quickening as the critical point. The significance of quickening was echoed by later common-law scholars and found its way into the received common law in this country.

Whether abortion of a *quick* fetus was a felony at common law, or even a lesser crime, is still disputed. Bracton, writing early in the 13th century, thought it homicide.[23] But the later and predominant view, following the great common-law scholars, has been that it was, at most, a lesser offense. In a frequently cited passage, Coke took the position that abortion of a woman "quick with childe" is "a great misprision, and no murder."[24] Blackstone followed, saying that while abortion after quickening had once been consid-

---

The theological debate was reflected in the writings of St. Augustine, who made a distinction between *embryo inanimatus,* not yet endowed with a soul, and *embryo animatus.* He may have drawn upon Exodus 21:22. At one point, however, he expressed the view that human powers cannot determine the point during fetal development at which the critical change occurs. See Augustine, De Origine Animae 4.4 (Pub. Law 44.527). See also W. Reany, The Creation of the Human Soul, c. 2 and 83–86 (1932); Huser, The Crime of Abortion in Canon Law 15 (Catholic Univ. of America, Canon Law Studies No. 162, Washington, D. C., 1942).

Galen, in three treatises related to embryology, accepted the thinking of Aristotle and his followers. Quay 426–427. Later, Augustine on abortion was incorporated by Gratian into the Decretum, published about 1140. Decretum Magistri Gratiani 2.32.2.7 to 2.32.2.10, in 1 Corpus Juris Canonici 1122, 1123 (A. Friedburg, 2d ed. 1879). This Decretal and the Decretals that followed were recognized as the definitive body of canon law until the new Code of 1917.

For discussions of the canon-law treatment, see Means I, pp. 411–412; Noonan 20–26; Quay 426–430; see also J. Noonan, Contraception: A History of Its Treatment by the Catholic Theologians and Canonists 18–29 (1965).

23. Bracton took the position that abortion by blow or poison was homicide "if the foetus be already formed and animated, and particularly if it be animated." 2 H. Bracton, De Legibus et Consuetudinibus Angliae 279 (T. Twiss ed. 1879), or, as a later translation puts it, "if the foetus is already formed or quickened, especially if it is quickened," 2 H. Bracton, On the Laws and Customs of England 341 (S. Thorne ed. 1968). See Quay 431; see also 2 Fleta 60–61 (Book 1, c. 23) (Selden Society ed. 1955).

24. E. Coke, Institutes III *50.

ered manslaughter (though not murder), "modern law" took a less severe view.[25] A recent review of the common-law precedents argues, however, that those precedents contradict Coke and that even post-quickening abortion was never established as a common-law crime.[26] This is of some importance because while most American courts ruled, in holding or dictum, that abortion of an unquickened fetus was not criminal under their received common law,[27] others followed Coke in stating that abortion of a quick fetus was a "misprision," a term they translated to mean "misdemeanor."[28] That their reliance on Coke on this aspect of the law was uncritical and, apparently in all the reported cases, dictum (due probably to the paucity of common-law prosecutions for post-quickening abortion), makes it now appear doubtful that abortion was ever firmly established as a common-law crime even with respect to the destruction of a quick fetus.

4. *The English statutory law.* England's first criminal abortion statute, Lord Ellenborough's Act, 43 Geo. 3, c. 58, came in 1803. It made abortion

25. 1 W. Blackstone, Commentaries *129–130.

26. Means, The Phoenix of Abortional Freedom: Is a Penumbral or Ninth-Amendment Right About to Arise from the Nineteenth-Century Legislative Ashes of a Fourteenth-Century Common-Law Liberty?, 17 N. Y. L. F. 335 (1971) (hereinafter Means II). The author examines the two principal precedents cited marginally by Coke, both contrary to his dictum, and traces the treatment of these and other cases by earlier commentators. He concludes that Coke, who himself participated as an advocate in an abortion case in 1601, may have intentionally misstated the law. The author even suggests a reason: Coke's strong feelings against abortion, coupled with his determination to assert common-law (secular) jurisdiction to assess penalties for an offense that traditionally had been an exclusively ecclesiastical or canon-law crime. See also Lader 78–79, who notes that some scholars doubt that the common law ever was applied to abortion; that the English ecclesiastical courts seem to have lost interest in the problem after 1527; and that the preamble to the English legislation of 1803, 43 Geo. 3, c. 58, § 1, referred to in the text, *infra*, at 136, states that "no adequate means have been hitherto provided for the prevention and punishment of such offenses."

27. *Commonwealth* v. *Bangs*, 9 Mass. 387, 388 (1812); *Commonwealth* v. *Parker*, 50 Mass. (9 Metc.) 263, 265–266 (1845); *State* v. *Cooper*, 22 N. J. L. 52, 58 (1849); *Abrams* v. *Foshee*, 3 Iowa 274, 278–280 (1856); *Smith* v. *Gaffard*, 31 Ala. 45, 51 (1857); *Mitchell* v. *Commonwealth*, 78 Ky. 204, 210 (1879); *Eggart* v. *State*, 40 Fla. 527, 532, 25 So. 144, 145 (1898); *State* v. *Alcorn*, 7 Idaho 599, 606, 64 P. 1014, 1016 (1901); *Edwards* v. *State*, 79 Neb. 251, 252, 112 N. W. 611, 612 (1907); *Gray* v. *State*, 77 Tex. Cr. R. 221, 224, 178 S. W. 337, 338 (1915); *Miller* v. *Bennett*, 190 Va. 162, 169, 56 S. E. 2d 217, 221 (1949). Contra, *Mills* v. *Commonwealth*, 13 Pa. 631, 633 (1850); *State* v. *Slagle*, 83 N. C. 630, 632 (1880).

28. See *Smith* v. *State*, 33 Me. 48, 55 (1851); *Evans* v. *People*, 49 N. Y. 86, 88 (1872); *Lamb* v. *State*, 67 Md. 524, 533, 10 A. 208 (1887).

of a quick fetus, § 1, a capital crime, but in § 2 it provided lesser penalties for the felony of abortion before quickening, and thus preserved the "quickening" distinction. This contrast was continued in the general revision of 1828, 9 Geo. 4, c. 31, § 13. It disappeared, however, together with the death penalty, in 1837, 7 Will. 4 & 1 Vict., c. 85, § 6, and did not reappear in the Offenses Against the Person Act of 1861, 24 & 25 Vict., c. 100, § 59, that formed the core of English anti-abortion law until the liberalizing reforms of 1967. In 1929, the Infant Life (Preservation) Act, 19 & 20 Geo. 5, c. 34, came into being. Its emphasis was upon the destruction of "the life of a child capable of being born alive." It made a willful act performed with the necessary intent a felony. It contained a proviso that one was not to be found guilty of the offense "unless it is proved that the act which caused the death of the child was not done in good faith for the purpose only of preserving the life of the mother."

A seemingly notable development in the English law was the case of *Rex* v. *Bourne*, [1939] 1 K. B. 687. This case apparently answered in the affirmative the question whether an abortion necessary to preserve the life of the pregnant woman was excepted from the criminal penalties of the 1861 Act. In his instructions to the jury, Judge Macnaghten referred to the 1929 Act, and observed that the Act related to "the case where a child is killed by a wilful act at the time when it is being delivered in the ordinary course of nature." *Id.,* at 691. He concluded that the 1861 Act's use of the word "unlawfully," imported the same meaning expressed by the specific proviso in the 1929 Act, even though there was no mention of preserving the mother's life in the 1861 Act. He then construed the phrase "preserving the life of the mother" broadly, that is, "in a reasonable sense," to include a serious and permanent threat to the mother's *health,* and instructed the jury to acquit Dr. Bourne if it found he had acted in a good-faith belief that the abortion was necessary for this purpose. *Id.,* at 693–694. The jury did acquit.

Recently, Parliament enacted a new abortion law. This is the Abortion Act of 1967, 15 & 16 Eliz. 2, c. 87. The Act permits a licensed physician to perform an abortion where two other licensed physicians agree (a) "that the continuance of the pregnancy would involve risk to the life of the pregnant woman, or of injury to the physical or mental health of the pregnant woman or any existing children of her family, greater than if the pregnancy were terminated," or (b) "that there is a substantial risk that if the child were born it would suffer from such physical or mental abnormalities as to be seriously handicapped." The Act also provides that, in making this determination, "account may be taken of the pregnant woman's actual or reasonably foreseeable environment." It also permits a physician, without the concurrence of others, to terminate a pregnancy where he is of the good-faith opinion that the abortion "is immediately necessary to save the life or to prevent grave permanent injury to the physical or mental health of the pregnant woman."

5. *The American law.* In this country, the law in effect in all but a few States until mid-19th century was the pre-existing English common law. Connecticut, the first State to enact abortion legislation, adopted in 1821 that part of Lord Ellenborough's Act that related to a woman "quick with child."[29] The death penalty was not imposed. Abortion before quickening was made a crime in that State only in 1860.[30] In 1828, New York enacted legislation[31] that, in two respects, was to serve as a model for early anti-abortion statutes. First, while barring destruction of an unquickened fetus as well as a quick fetus, it made the former only a misdemeanor, but the latter second-degree manslaughter. Second, it incorporated a concept of therapeutic abortion by providing that an abortion was excused if it "shall have been necessary to preserve the life of such mother, or shall have been advised by two physicians to be necessary for such purpose." By 1840, when Texas had received the common law,[32] only eight American States had statutes dealing with abortion.[33] It was not until after the War Between the States that legislation began generally to replace the common law. Most of these initial statutes dealt severely with abortion after quickening but were lenient with it before quickening. Most punished attempts equally with completed abortions. While many statutes included the exception for an abortion thought by one or more physicians to be necessary to save the mother's life, that provision soon disappeared and the typical law required that the procedure actually be necessary for that purpose.

Gradually, in the middle and late 19th century the quickening distinction disappeared from the statutory law of most States and the degree of the offense and the penalties were increased. By the end of the 1950's, a large majority of the jurisdictions banned abortion, however and whenever performed, unless done to save or preserve the life of the mother.[34] The

29. Conn. Stat., Tit. 20, § 14 (1821).

30. Conn. Pub. Acts, c. 71, § 1 (1860).

31. N. Y. Rev. Stat., pt. 4, c. 1, Tit. 2, Art. 1, § 9, p. 661, and Tit. 6, § 21, p. 694 (1829).

32. Act of Jan. 20, 1840, § 1, set forth in 2 H. Gammel, Laws of Texas 177–178 (1898); see *Grigsby* v. *Reib,* 105 Tex. 597, 600, 153 S. W. 1124, 1125 (1913).

33. The early statutes are discussed in Quay 435–438. See also Lader 85–88; Stern 85–86; and Means II 375–376.

34. Criminal abortion statutes in effect in the States as of 1961, together with historical statutory development and important judicial interpretations of the state statutes, are cited and quoted in Quay 447–520. See Comment, A Survey of the Present Statutory and Case Law on Abortion: The Contradictions and the Problems, 1972 U. Ill. L. F. 177, 179, classifying the abortion statutes and listing 25 States as permitting abortion only if necessary to save or preserve the mother's life.

exceptions, Alabama and the District of Columbia, permitted abortion to preserve the mother's health.[35] Three States permitted abortions that were not "unlawfully" performed or that were not "without lawful justification," leaving interpretation of those standards to the courts.[36] In the past several years, however, a trend toward liberalization of abortion statutes has resulted in adoption, by about one-third of the States, of less stringent laws, most of them patterned after the ALI Model Penal Code, § 230.3,[37] set forth as Appendix B to the opinion in *Doe* v. *Bolton.*

It is thus apparent that at common law, at the time of the adoption of our Constitution, and throughout the major portion of the 19th century, abortion was viewed with less disfavor than under most American statutes currently in effect. Phrasing it another way, a woman enjoyed a substantially broader right to terminate a pregnancy than she does in most States today. At least with respect to the early stage of pregnancy, and very possibly without such a limitation, the opportunity to make this choice was present in this country well into the 19th century. Even later, the law continued for some time to treat less punitively an abortion procured in early pregnancy. . . .

VII

Three reasons have been advanced to explain historically the enactment of criminal abortion laws in the 19th century and to justify their continued existence.

35. Ala. Code, Tit. 14, § 9 (1958); D. C. Code Ann. § 22–201 (1967).

36. Mass. Gen. Laws Ann., c. 272, § 19 (1970); N. J. Stat. Ann. § 2A:87–1 (1969); Pa. Stat. Ann., Tit. 18, §§ 4718, 4719 (1963).

37. Fourteen States have adopted some form of the ALI statute. See Ark. Stat. Ann. §§ 41–303 to 41–310 (Supp. 1971); Calif. Health & Safety Code §§ 25950–25955.5 (Supp. 1972); Colo. Rev. Stat. Ann. §§ 40–2–50 to 40–2–53 (Cum. Supp. 1967); Del. Code Ann., Tit. 24, §§ 1790–1793 (Supp. 1972); Florida Law of Apr. 13, 1972, c. 72–196, 1972 Fla. Sess. Law Serv., pp. 380–382; Ga. Code §§ 26–1201 to 26–1203 (1972); Kan. Stat. Ann § 21–3407 (Supp. 1971); Md. Ann. Code, Art. 43, §§ 137–139 (1971); Miss. Code Ann. § 2223 (Supp. 1972); N. M. Stat. Ann. §§ 40A–5–1 to 40A–5–3 (1972); N. C. Gen. Stat. § 14–45.1 (Supp. 1971); Ore. Rev. Stat. §§ 435.405 to 435.495 (1971); S C. Code Ann. §§ 16–82 to 16–89 (1962 and Supp. 1971); Va. Code Ann. §§ 18.1–62 to 18.1–62.3 (Supp. 1972). Mr. Justice Clark described some of these States as having "led the way." Religion, Morality, and Abortion: A Constitutional Appraisal, 2 Loyola U. (L. A.) L. Rev. 1, 11 (1969).

By the end of 1970, four other States had repealed criminal penalties for abortions performed in early pregnancy by a licensed physician, subject to stated procedural and health requirements. Alaska Stat. § 11.15.060 (1970); Haw. Rev. Stat. § 453–16 (Supp. 1971); N. Y. Penal Code § 125.05, subd. 3 (Supp. 1972–1973); Wash. Rev. Code §§ 9.02.060 to 9.02.080 (Supp. 1972). The precise status of criminal abortion laws in some States is made unclear by recent decisions in state and federal courts striking down existing state laws, in whole or in part.

It has been argued occasionally that these laws were the product of a Victorian social concern to discourage illicit sexual conduct. Texas, however, does not advance this justification in the present case, and it appears that no court or commentator has taken the argument seriously.[42] The appellants and *amici* contend, moreover, that this is not a proper state purpose at all and suggest that, if it were, the Texas statutes are overbroad in protecting it since the law fails to distinguish between married and unwed mothers.

A second reason is concerned with abortion as a medical procedure. When most criminal abortion laws were first enacted, the procedure was a hazardous one for the woman.[43] This was particularly true prior to the development of antisepsis. Antiseptic techniques, of course, were based on discoveries by Lister, Pasteur, and others first announced in 1867, but were not generally accepted and employed until about the turn of the century. Abortion mortality was high. Even after 1900, and perhaps until as late as the development of antibiotics in the 1940's, standard modern techniques such as dilation and curettage were not nearly so safe as they are today. Thus, it has been argued that a State's real concern in enacting a criminal abortion law was to protect the pregnant woman, that is, to restrain her from submitting to a procedure that placed her life in serious jeopardy.

Modern medical techniques have altered this situation. Appellants and various *amici* refer to medical data indicating that abortion in early pregnancy, that is, prior to the end of the first trimester, although not without its risk, is now relatively safe. Mortality rates for women undergoing early abortions, where the procedure is legal, appear to be as low as or lower than the rates for normal childbirth.[44] Consequently, any interest of the State in protecting the woman from an inherently hazardous procedure, except when it would be equally dangerous for her to forgo it, has largely disappeared. Of course, important state interests in the areas of health and medical standards do remain. The State has a legitimate interest in seeing to it that abortion,

42. See, for example, *YWCA* v. *Kugler*, 342 F. Supp. 1048, 1074 (N. J. 1972); *Abele* v. *Markle*, 342 F. Supp. 800, 805–806 (Conn. 1972) (Newman, J., concurring in result), appeal docketed, No. 72–56; *Walsingham* v. *State*, 250 So. 2d 857, 863 (Ervin, J., concurring) (Fla. 1971); *State* v. *Gedicke*, 43 N. J. L. 86, 90 (1881); Means II 381–382.

43. See C. Haagensen & W. Lloyd, A Hundred Years of Medicine 19 (1943).

44. Potts, Postconceptive Control of Fertility, 8 Int'l J. of G. & O. 957, 967 (1970) (England and Wales); Abortion Mortality, 20 Morbidity and Mortality 208, 209 (June 12, 1971) (U. S. Dept. of HEW, Public Health Service) (New York City); Tietze, United States: Therapeutic Abortions, 1963–1968, 59 Studies in Family Planning 5, 7 (1970); Tietze, Mortality with Contraception and Induced Abortion, 45 Studies in Family Planning 6 (1969) (Japan, Czechoslovakia, Hungary); Tietze & Lehfeldt, Legal Abortion in Eastern Europe, 175 J. A. M. A. 1149, 1152 (April 1961). Other sources are discussed in Lader 17–23.

like any other medical procedure, is performed under circumstances that in-sure maximum safety for the patient. This interest obviously extends at least to the performing physician and his staff, to the facilities involved, to the availability of after-care, and to adequate provision for any complication or emergency that might arise. The prevalence of high mortality rates at illegal "abortion mills" strengthens, rather than weakens, the State's interest in regulating the conditions under which abortions are performed. Moreover, the risk to the woman increases as her pregnancy continues. Thus, the State retains a definite interest in protecting the woman's own health and safety when an abortion is proposed at a late stage of pregnancy.

The third reason is the State's interest—some phrase it in terms of duty—in protecting prenatal life. Some of the argument for this justifica-tion rests on the theory that a new human life is present from the moment of conception.[45] The State's interest and general obligation to protect life then extends, it is argued, to prenatal life. Only when the life of the pregnant mother herself is at stake, balanced against the life she carries within her, should the interest of the embryo or fetus not prevail. Logically, of course, a legitimate state interest in this area need not stand or fall on acceptance of the belief that life begins at conception or at some other point prior to live birth. In assessing the State's interest, recognition may be given to the less rigid claim that as long as at least *potential* life is involved, the State may assert interests beyond the protection of the pregnant woman alone.

Parties challenging state abortion laws have sharply disputed in some courts the contention that a purpose of these laws, when enacted, was to protect prenatal life.[46] Pointing to the absence of legislative history to sup-port the contention, they claim that most state laws were designed solely to protect the woman. Because medical advances have lessened this concern, at least with respect to abortions in early pregnancy, they argue that with re-spect to such abortions the laws can no longer be justified by any state inter-est. There is some scholarly support for this view of original purpose.[47] The few state courts called upon to interpret their laws in the late 19th and early 20th centuries did focus on the State's interest in protecting the woman's health rather than in preserving the embryo and fetus.[48] Proponents of this

45. See Brief of *Amicus* National Right to Life Committee; R. Drinan, The Invio-lability of the Right to Be Born, in Abortion and the Law 107 (D. Smith ed. 1967); Louisell, Abortion, The Practice of Medicine and the Due Process of Law, 16 U. C. L. A. L. Rev. 233 (1969); Noonan 1.

46. See, *e. g., Abele* v. *Markle,* 342 F. Supp. 800 (Conn. 1972), appeal docketed, No. 72–56.

47. See discussions in Means I and Means II.

48. See, *e. g., State* v. *Murphy,* 27 N. J. L. 112, 114 (1858).

view point out that in many States, including Texas,[49] by statute or judicial interpretation, the pregnant woman herself could not be prosecuted for self-abortion or for cooperating in an abortion performed upon her by another.[50] They claim that adoption of the "quickening" distinction through received common law and state statutes tacitly recognizes the greater health hazards inherent in late abortion and impliedly repudiates the theory that life begins at conception.

It is with these interests, and the weight to be attached to them, that this case is concerned.

VIII

The Constitution does not explicitly mention any right of privacy. In a line of decisions, however, going back perhaps as far as *Union Pacific R. Co.* v. *Botsford*, 141 U. S. 250, 251 (1891), the Court has recognized that a right of personal privacy, or a guarantee of certain areas or zones of privacy, does exist under the Constitution. In varying contexts, the Court or individual Justices have, indeed, found at least the roots of that right in the First Amendment, *Stanley* v. *Georgia*, 394 U. S. 557, 564 (1969); in the Fourth and Fifth Amendments, *Terry* v. *Ohio*, 392 U. S. 1, 8–9 (1968), *Katz* v. *United States*, 389 U. S. 347, 350 (1967), *Boyd* v. *United States*, 116 U. S. 616 (1886), see *Olmstead* v. *United States*, 277 U. S. 438, 478 (1928) (Brandeis, J., dissenting); in the penumbras of the Bill of Rights, *Griswold* v. *Connecticut*, 381 U. S., at 484–485; in the Ninth Amendment, *id.*, at 486 (Goldberg, J., concurring); or in the concept of liberty guaranteed by the first section of the Fourteenth Amendment, see *Meyer* v. *Nebraska*, 262 U. S. 390, 399 (1923). These decisions make it clear that only personal rights that can be deemed "fundamental" or "implicit in the concept of ordered liberty," *Palko* v. *Connecticut*, 302 U. S. 319, 325 (1937), are included in this guarantee of personal privacy. They also make it clear that the right has some extension to activities relating to marriage, *Loving* v. *Virginia*, 388 U. S. 1, 12

49. *Watson* v. *State*, 9 Tex. App. 237, 244–245 (1880); *Moore* v. *State*, 37 Tex. Cr. R. 552, 561, 40 S. W. 287, 290 (1897); *Shaw* v. *State*, 73 Tex. Cr. R. 337, 339, 165 S. W. 930, 931 (1914); *Fondren* v. *State*, 74 Tex. Cr. R. 552, 557, 169 S. W. 411, 414 (1914); *Gray* v. *State*, 77 Tex. Cr. R. 221, 229, 178 S. W. 337, 341 (1915). There is no immunity in Texas for the father who is not married to the mother. *Hammett* v. *State*, 84 Tex. Cr. R. 635, 209 S. W. 661 (1919); *Thompson* v. *State* (Ct. Crim. App. Tex. 1971), appeal docketed, No. 71–1200.

50. See *Smith* v. *State*, 33 Me., at 55; *In re Vince*, 2 N. J. 443, 450, 67 A. 2d 141, 144 (1949). A short discussion of the modern law on this issue is contained in the Comment to the ALI's Model Penal Code § 207.11, at 158 and nn. 35–37 (Tent. Draft No. 9, 1959).

(1967); procreation, *Skinner* v. *Oklahoma,* 316 U. S. 535, 541–542 (1942); contraception, *Eisenstadt* v. *Baird,* 405 U. S., at 453–454; *id.,* at 460, 463–465 (WHITE, J., concurring in result); family relationships, *Prince* v. *Massachusetts,* 321 U. S. 158, 166 (1944); and child rearing and education, *Pierce* v. *Society of Sisters,* 268 U. S. 510, 535 (1925), *Meyer* v. *Nebraska, supra.*

This right of privacy, whether it be founded in the Fourteenth Amendment's concept of personal liberty and restrictions upon state action, as we feel it is, or, as the District Court determined, in the Ninth Amendment's reservation of rights to the people, is broad enough to encompass a woman's decision whether or not to terminate her pregnancy. The detriment that the State would impose upon the pregnant woman by denying this choice altogether is apparent. Specific and direct harm medically diagnosable even in early pregnancy may be involved. Maternity, or additional offspring, may force upon the woman a distressful life and future. Psychological harm may be imminent. Mental and physical health may be taxed by child care. There is also the distress, for all concerned, associated with the unwanted child, and there is the problem of bringing a child into a family already unable, psychologically and otherwise, to care for it. In other cases, as in this one, the additional difficulties and continuing stigma of unwed motherhood may be involved. All these are factors the woman and her responsible physician necessarily will consider in consultation.

On the basis of elements such as these, appellant and some *amici* argue that the woman's right is absolute and that she is entitled to terminate her pregnancy at whatever time, in whatever way, and for whatever reason she alone chooses. With this we do not agree. Appellant's arguments that Texas either has no valid interest at all in regulating the abortion decision, or no interest strong enough to support any limitation upon the woman's sole determination, are unpersuasive. The Court's decisions recognizing a right of privacy also acknowledge that some state regulation in areas protected by that right is appropriate. As noted above, a State may properly assert important interests in safeguarding health, in maintaining medical standards, and in protecting potential life. At some point in pregnancy, these respective interests become sufficiently compelling to sustain regulation of the factors that govern the abortion decision. The privacy right involved, therefore, cannot be said to be absolute. In fact, it is not clear to us that the claim asserted by some *amici* that one has an unlimited right to do with one's body as one pleases bears a close relationship to the right of privacy previously articulated in the Court's decisions. The Court has refused to recognize an unlimited right of this kind in the past. *Jacobson* v. *Massachusetts,* 197 U. S. 11 (1905) (vaccination); *Buck* v. *Bell,* 274 U. S. 200 (1927) (sterilization).

We, therefore, conclude that the right of personal privacy includes the abortion decision, but that this right is not unqualified and must be considered against important state interests in regulation.

We note that those federal and state courts that have recently considered abortion law challenges have reached the same conclusion. A majority, in addition to the District Court in the present case, have held state laws unconstitutional, at least in part, because of vagueness or because of overbreadth and abridgment of rights. *Abele* v. *Markle,* 342 F. Supp. 800 (Conn. 1972), appeal docketed, No. 72–56; *Abele* v. *Markle,* 351 F. Supp. 224 (Conn. 1972), appeal docketed, No. 72–730; *Doe* v. *Bolton,* 319 F. Supp. 1048 (ND Ga. 1970), appeal decided today, *post,* p. 179; *Doe* v. *Scott,* 321 F. Supp. 1385 (ND Ill. 1971), appeal docketed, No. 70–105; *Poe* v. *Menghini,* 339 F. Supp. 986 (Kan. 1972); *YWCA* v. *Kugler,* 342 F. Supp. 1048 (NJ 1972); *Babbitz* v. *McCann,* 310 F. Supp. 293 (ED Wis. 1970), appeal dismissed, 400 U. S. 1 (1970); *People* v. *Belous,* 71 Cal. 2d 954, 458 P. 2d 194 (1969), cert. denied, 397 U. S. 915 (1970); *State* v. *Barquet,* 262 So. 2d 431 (Fla. 1972).

Others have sustained state statutes. *Crossen* v. *Attorney General,* 344 F. Supp. 587 (ED Ky. 1972), appeal docketed, No. 72–256; *Rosen* v. *Louisiana State Board of Medical Examiners,* 318 F. Supp. 1217 (ED La. 1970), appeal docketed, No. 70–42; *Corkey* v. *Edwards,* 322 F. Supp. 1248 (WDNC 1971), appeal docketed, No. 71–92; *Steinberg* v. *Brown,* 321 F. Supp. 741 (ND Ohio 1970); *Doe* v. *Rampton* (Utah 1971), appeal docketed, No. 71–5666; *Cheaney* v. *State,* Ind., 285 N. E. 2d 265 (1972); *Spears* v. *State,* 257 So. 2d 876 (Miss. 1972); *State* v. *Munson,* 86 S. D. 663, 201 N. W. 2d 123 (1972), appeal docketed, No. 72–631.

Although the results are divided, most of these courts have agreed that the right of privacy, however based, is broad enough to cover the abortion decision; that the right, nonetheless, is not absolute and is subject to some limitations; and that at some point the state interests as to protection of health, medical standards, and prenatal life, become dominant. We agree with this approach.

Where certain "fundamental rights" are involved, the Court has held that regulation limiting these rights may be justified only by a "compelling state interest," *Kramer* v. *Union Free School District,* 395 U. S. 621, 627 (1969); *Shapiro* v. *Thompson,* 394 U. S. 618, 634 (1969); *Sherbert* v. *Verner,* 374 U. S. 398, 406 (1963), and that legislative enactments must be narrowly drawn to express only the legitimate state interests at stake. *Griswold* v. *Connecticut,* 381 U. S., at 485; *Aptheker* v. *Secretary of State,* 378 U. S. 500, 508 (1964); *Cantwell* v. *Connecticut,* 310 U. S. 296, 307–308 (1940); see *Eisenstadt* v. *Baird,* 405 U. S., at 460, 463–464 (WHITE, J., concurring in result).

In the recent abortion cases, cited above, courts have recognized these principles. Those striking down state laws have generally scrutinized the State's interests in protecting health and potential life, and have concluded that neither interest justified broad limitations on the reasons for which a physician and his pregnant patient might decide that she should have an abortion in the early stages of pregnancy. Courts sustaining state laws have held that the State's determinations to protect health or prenatal life are dominant and constitutionally justifiable.

IX

The District Court held that the appellee failed to meet his burden of demonstrating that the Texas statute's infringement upon Roe's rights was necessary to support a compelling state interest, and that, although the appellee presented "several compelling justifications for state presence in the area of abortions," the statutes outstripped these justifications and swept "far beyond any areas of compelling state interest." 314 F. Supp., at 1222–1223. Appellant and appellee both contest that holding. Appellant, as has been indicated, claims an absolute right that bars any state imposition of criminal penalties in the area. Appellee argues that the State's determination to recognize and protect prenatal life from and after conception constitutes a compelling state interest. As noted above, we do not agree fully with either formulation.

A. The appellee and certain *amici* argue that the fetus is a "person" within the language and meaning of the Fourteenth Amendment. In support of this, they outline at length and in detail the well-known facts of fetal development. If this suggestion of personhood is established, the appellant's case, of course, collapses, for the fetus' right to life would then be guaranteed specifically by the Amendment. The appellant conceded as much on reargument.[51] On the other hand, the appellee conceded on reargument[52] that no case could be cited that holds that a fetus is a person within the meaning of the Fourteenth Amendment.

The Constitution does not define "person" in so many words. Section 1 of the Fourteenth Amendment contains three references to "person." The first, in defining "citizens," speaks of "persons born or naturalized in the United States." The word also appears both in the Due Process Clause and in the Equal Protection Clause. "Person" is used in other places in the Constitution: in the listing of qualifications for Representatives and Senators, Art. I, § 2, cl. 2, and § 3, cl. 3; in the Apportionment Clause, Art. I, § 2, cl. 3;[53] in the Migration and Importation provision, Art. I, § 9, cl. 1; in the Emolument Clause, Art. I, § 9, cl. 8; in the Electors provisions, Art. II, § 1, cl. 2, and the superseded cl. 3; in the provision outlining qualifications for the office of President, Art. II, § 1, cl. 5; in the Extradition provisions,

---

51. Tr. of Oral Rearg. 20–21.

52. Tr. of Oral Rearg. 24.

53. We are not aware that in the taking of any census under this clause, a fetus has ever been counted.

Art. IV, § 2, cl. 2, and the superseded Fugitive Slave Clause 3; and in the Fifth, Twelfth, and Twenty-second Amendments, as well as in §§ 2 and 3 of the Fourteenth Amendment. But in nearly all these instances, the use of the word is such that it has application only postnatally. None indicates, with any assurance, that it has any possible prenatal application.[54]

All this, together with our observation, *supra*, that throughout the major portion of the 19th century prevailing legal abortion practices were far freer than they are today, persuades us that the word "person," as used in the Fourteenth Amendment, does not include the unborn.[55] This is in accord with the results reached in those few cases where the issue has been squarely presented. *McGarvey* v. *Magee-Womens Hospital*, 340 F. Supp. 751 (WD Pa. 1972); *Byrn* v. *New York City Health & Hospitals Corp.*, 31 N. Y. 2d 194, 286 N. E. 2d 887 (1972), appeal docketed, No. 72–434; *Abele* v. *Markle*, 351 F. Supp. 224 (Conn. 1972), appeal docketed, No. 72–730. Cf. *Cheaney* v. *State*, Ind., 285 N. E. 2d, at 270; *Montana* v. *Rogers*, 278 F. 2d 68, 72 (CA7 1960), aff'd *sub nom. Montana* v. *Kennedy*, 366 U. S. 308 (1961); *Keeler* v. *Superior Court*, 2 Cal. 3d 619, 470 P. 2d 617 (1970); *State* v. *Dickinson*, 28 Ohio St. 2d 65, 275 N. E. 2d 599 (1971). Indeed, our decision in *United States* v. *Vuitch*, 402 U. S. 62 (1971), inferentially is to the same effect, for we there would not have indulged in statutory interpretation favorable to abortion in specified circumstances if the necessary consequence was the termination of life entitled to Fourteenth Amendment protection.

54. When Texas urges that a fetus is entitled to Fourteenth Amendment protection as a person, it faces a dilemma. Neither in Texas nor in any other State are all abortions prohibited. Despite broad proscription, an exception always exists. The exception contained in Art. 1196, for an abortion procured or attempted by medical advice for the purpose of saving the life of the mother, is typical. But if the fetus is a person who is not to be deprived of life without due process of law, and if the mother's condition is the sole determinant, does not the Texas exception appear to be out of line with the Amendment's command?

There are other inconsistencies between Fourteenth Amendment status and the typical abortion statute. It has already been pointed out, n. 49, *supra*, that in Texas the woman is not a principal or an accomplice with respect to an abortion upon her. If the fetus is a person, why is the woman not a principal or an accomplice? Further, the penalty for criminal abortion specified by Art. 1195 is significantly less than the maximum penalty for murder prescribed by Art. 1257 of the Texas Penal Code. If the fetus is a person, may the penalties be different?

55. Cf. the Wisconsin abortion statute, defining "unborn child" to mean "a human being from the time of conception until it is born alive," Wis. Stat. § 940.04 (6)(1969), and the new Connecticut statute, Pub. Act No. 1 (May 1972 special session), declaring it to be the public policy of the State and the legislative intent "to protect and preserve human life from the moment of conception."

This conclusion, however, does not of itself fully answer the contentions raised by Texas, and we pass on to other considerations.

B. The pregnant woman cannot be isolated in her privacy. She carries an embryo and, later, a fetus, if one accepts the medical definitions of the developing young in the human uterus. See Dorland's Illustrated Medical Dictionary 478–479, 547 (24th ed. 1965). The situation therefore is inherently different from marital intimacy, or bedroom possession of obscene material, or marriage, or procreation, or education, with which *Eisenstadt* and *Griswold, Stanley, Loving, Skinner,* and *Pierce* and *Meyer* were respectively concerned. As we have intimated above, it is reasonable and appropriate for a State to decide that at some point in time another interest, that of health of the mother or that of potential human life, becomes significantly involved. The woman's privacy is no longer sole and any right of privacy she possesses must be measured accordingly.

Texas urges that, apart from the Fourteenth Amendment, life begins at conception and is present throughout pregnancy, and that, therefore, the State has a compelling interest in protecting that life from and after conception. We need not resolve the difficult question of when life begins. When those trained in the respective disciplines of medicine, philosophy, and theology are unable to arrive at any consensus, the judiciary, at this point in the development of man's knowledge, is not in a position to speculate as to the answer.

It should be sufficient to note briefly the wide divergence of thinking on this most sensitive and difficult question. There has always been strong support for the view that life does not begin until live birth. This was the belief of the Stoics.[56] It appears to be the predominant, though not the unanimous, attitude of the Jewish faith.[57] It may be taken to represent also the position of a large segment of the Protestant community, insofar as that can be ascertained; organized groups that have taken a formal position on the abortion issue have generally regarded abortion as a matter for the conscience of the individual and her family.[58] As we have noted, the common law found greater significance in quickening. Physicians and their scientific colleagues have regarded that event with less interest and have tended to focus either upon conception, upon live birth, or upon the interim point at which the fetus becomes "viable," that is, potentially able to live outside the mother's

56. Edelstein 16.

57. Lader 97–99; D. Feldman, Birth Control in Jewish Law 251–294 (1968). For a stricter view, see I. Jakobovits, Jewish Views on Abortion, in Abortion and the Law 124 (D. Smith ed. 1967).

58. Amicus Brief for the American Ethical Union et al. For the position of the National Council of Churches and of other denominations, see Lader 99–101.

womb, albeit with artificial aid.[59] Viability is usually placed at about seven months (28 weeks) but may occur earlier, even at 24 weeks.[60] The Aristotelian theory of "mediate animation," that held sway throughout the Middle Ages and the Renaissance in Europe, continued to be official Roman Catholic dogma until the 19th century, despite opposition to this "ensoulment" theory from those in the Church who would recognize the existence of life from the moment of conception.[61] The latter is now, of course, the official belief of the Catholic Church. As one brief *amicus* discloses, this is a view strongly held by many non-Catholics as well, and by many physicians. Substantial problems for precise definition of this view are posed, however, by new embryological data that purport to indicate that conception is a "process" over time, rather than an event, and by new medical techniques such as menstrual extraction, the "morning-after" pill, implantation of embryos, artificial insemination, and even artificial wombs.[62]

In areas other than criminal abortion, the law has been reluctant to endorse any theory that life, as we recognize it, begins before live birth or to accord legal rights to the unborn except in narrowly defined situations and except when the rights are contingent upon live birth. For example, the traditional rule of tort law denied recovery for prenatal injuries even though the child was born alive.[63] That rule has been changed in almost every jurisdiction. In most States, recovery is said to be permitted only if the fetus was viable, or at least quick, when the injuries were sustained, though few courts have squarely so held.[64] In a recent development, generally opposed by the commentators, some States permit the parents of a stillborn child to main-

---

59. L. Hellman & J. Pritchard, Williams Obstetrics 493 (14th ed. 1971); Dorland's Illustrated Medical Dictionary 1689 (24th ed. 1965).

60. Hellman & Pritchard, *supra,* n. 59, at 493.

61. For discussions of the development of the Roman Catholic position, see D. Callahan, Abortion: Law, Choice, and Morality 409–447 (1970); Noonan 1.

62. See Brodie, The New Biology and the Prenatal Child, 9 J. Family L. 391, 397 (1970); Gorney, The New Biology and the Future of Man, 15 U. C. L. A. L. Rev. 273 (1968); Note, Criminal Law—Abortion—The "Morning-After Pill" and Other Pre-Implantation Birth-Control Methods and the Law, 46 Ore. L. Rev. 211 (1967); G. Taylor, The Biological Time Bomb 32 (1968); A. Rosenfeld, The Second Genesis 138–139 (1969); Smith, Through a Test Tube Darkly: Artificial Insemination and the Law, 67 Mich. L. Rev. 127 (1968); Note, Artificial Insemination and the Law, 1968 U. Ill. L. F. 203.

63. W. Prosser, The Law of Torts 335–338 (4th ed. 1971); 2 F. Harper & F. James, The Law of Torts 1028–1031 (1956); Note, 63 Harv. L. Rev. 173 (1949).

64. See cases cited in Prosser, *supra,* n. 63, at 336–338; Annotation, Action for Death of Unborn Child, 15 A. L. R. 3d 992 (1967).

tain an action for wrongful death because of prenatal injuries.[65] Such an action, however, would appear to be one to vindicate the parents' interest and is thus consistent with the view that the fetus, at most, represents only the potentiality of life. Similarly, unborn children have been recognized as acquiring the rights or interests by way of inheritance or other devolution of property, and have been represented by guardians *ad litem*.[66] Perfection of the interests involved, again, has generally been contingent upon live birth. In short, the unborn have never been recognized in the law as persons in the whole sense.

X

In view of all this, we do not agree that, by adopting one theory of life, Texas may override the rights of the pregnant woman that are at stake. We repeat, however, that the State does have an important and legitimate interest in preserving and protecting the health of the pregnant woman, whether she be a resident of the State or a nonresident who seeks medical consultation and treatment there, and that it has still *another* important and legitimate interest in protecting the potentiality of human life. These interests are separate and distinct. Each grows in substantiality as the woman approaches term and, at a point during pregnancy, each becomes "compelling."

With respect to the State's important and legitimate interest in the health of the mother, the "compelling" point, in the light of present medical knowledge, is at approximately the end of the first trimester. This is so because of the now-established medical fact, referred to above at 149, that until the end of the first trimester mortality in abortion may be less than mortality in normal childbirth. It follows that, from and after this point, a State may regulate the abortion procedure to the extent that the regulation reasonably relates to the preservation and protection of maternal health. Examples of permissible state regulation in this area are requirements as to the qualifications of the person who is to perform the abortion; as to the licensure of that person; as to the facility in which the procedure is to be performed, that is, whether it must be a hospital or may be a clinic or some other place of less-than-hospital status; as to the licensing of the facility; and the like.

65. Prosser, *supra*, n. 63, at 338; Note, The Law and the Unborn Child: The Legal and Logical Inconsistencies, 46 Notre Dame Law. 349, 354–360 (1971).

66. Louisell, Abortion, The Practice of Medicine and the Due Process of Law, 16 U. C. L. A. L. Rev. 233, 235–238 (1969); Note, 56 Iowa L. Rev. 994, 999–1000 (1971); Note, The Law and the Unborn Child, 46 Notre Dame Law. 349, 351–354 (1971).

This means, on the other hand, that, for the period of pregnancy prior to this "compelling" point, the attending physician, in consultation with his patient, is free to determine, without regulation by the State, that, in his medical judgment, the patient's pregnancy should be terminated. If that decision is reached, the judgment may be effectuated by an abortion free of interference by the State.

With respect to the State's important and legitimate interest in potential life, the "compelling" point is at viability. This is so because the fetus then presumably has the capability of meaningful life outside the mother's womb. State regulation protective of fetal life after viability thus has both logical and biological justifications. If the State is interested in protecting fetal life after viability, it may go so far as to proscribe abortion during that period, except when it is necessary to preserve the life or health of the mother.

Measured against these standards, Art. 1196 of the Texas Penal Code, in restricting legal abortions to those "procured or attempted by medical advice for the purpose of saving the life of the mother," sweeps too broadly. The statute makes no distinction between abortions performed early in pregnancy and those performed later, and it limits to a single reason, "saving" the mother's life, the legal justification for the procedure. The statute, therefore, cannot survive the constitutional attack made upon it here.

This conclusion makes it unnecessary for us to consider the additional challenge to the Texas statute asserted on grounds of vagueness. See *United States* v. *Vuitch,* 402 U. S., at 67–72.

XI

To summarize and to repeat:

1. A state criminal abortion statute of the current Texas type, that excepts from criminality only a *life-saving* procedure on behalf of the mother, without regard to pregnancy stage and without recognition of the other interests involved, is violative of the Due Process Clause of the Fourteenth Amendment.

(a) For the stage prior to approximately the end of the first trimester, the abortion decision and its effectuation must be left to the medical judgment of the pregnant woman's attending physician.

(b) For the stage subsequent to approximately the end of the first trimester, the State, in promoting its interest in the health of the mother, may, if it chooses, regulate the abortion procedure in ways that are reasonably related to maternal health.

(c) For the stage subsequent to viability, the State in promoting its interest in the potentiality of human life may, if it chooses, regulate, and even proscribe, abortion except where it is necessary, in appropriate medical judgment, for the preservation of the life or health of the mother. . . .

This holding, we feel, is consistent with the relative weights of the respective interests involved, with the lessons and examples of medical and legal history, with the lenity of the common law, and with the demands of the profound problems of the present day. The decision leaves the State free to place increasing restrictions on abortion as the period of pregnancy lengthens, so long as those restrictions are tailored to the recognized state interests. The decision vindicates the right of the physician to administer medical treatment according to his professional judgment up to the points where important state interests provide compelling justifications for intervention. Up to those points, the abortion decision in all its aspects is inherently, and primarily, a medical decision, and basic responsibility for it must rest with the physician. If an individual practitioner abuses the privilege of exercising proper medical judgment, the usual remedies, judicial and intra-professional, are available. . . .

MR. JUSTICE REHNQUIST, dissenting.

The Court's opinion brings to the decision of this troubling question both extensive historical fact and a wealth of legal scholarship. While the opinion thus commands my respect, I find myself nonetheless in fundamental disagreement with those parts of it that invalidate the Texas statute in question, and therefore dissent.

I

The Court's opinion decides that a State may impose virtually no restriction on the performance of abortions during the first trimester of pregnancy. Our previous decisions indicate that a necessary predicate for such an opinion is a plaintiff who was in her first trimester of pregnancy at some time during the pendency of her lawsuit. While a party may vindicate his own constitutional rights, he may not seek vindication for the rights of others. *Moose Lodge* v. *Irvis,* 407 U. S. 163 (1973); *Sierra Club* v. *Morton,* 405 U. S. 727 (1972). The Court's statement of facts in this case makes clear, however, that the record in no way indicates the presence of such a plaintiff. We know only that plaintiff Roe at the time of filing her complaint was a pregnant woman; for aught that appears in this record, she may have been in her *last* trimester of pregnancy as of the date the complaint was filed.

Nothing in the Court's opinion indicates that Texas might not constitutionally apply its proscription of abortion as written to a woman in that stage of pregnancy. Nonetheless, the Court uses her complaint against the Texas statute as a fulcrum for deciding that States may impose virtually no restrictions on medical abortions performed during the *first* trimester of pregnancy. In deciding such a hypothetical lawsuit, the Court departs from the longstanding admonition that it should never "formulate a rule of constitutional law broader than is required by the precise facts to which it is to be applied." *Liverpool, New York & Philadelphia S. S. Co.* v. *Commissioners of Emigration,* 113 U. S. 33, 39 (1885). See also *Ashwander* v. *TVA,* 297 U. S. 288, 345 (1936) (Brandeis, J., concurring).

II

Even if there were a plaintiff in this case capable of litigating the issue which the Court decides, I would reach a conclusion opposite to that reached by the Court. I have difficulty in concluding, as the Court does, that the right of "privacy" is involved in this case. Texas, by the statute here challenged, bars the performance of a medical abortion by a licensed physician on a plaintiff such as Roe. A transaction resulting in an operation such as this is not "private" in the ordinary usage of that word. Nor is the "privacy" that the Court finds here even a distant relative of the freedom from searches and seizures protected by the Fourth Amendment to the Constitution, which the Court has referred to as embodying a right to privacy. *Katz* v. *United States,* 389 U. S. 347 (1967).

If the Court means by the term "privacy" no more than that the claim of a person to be free from unwanted state regulation of consensual transactions may be a form of "liberty" protected by the Fourteenth Amendment, there is no doubt that similar claims have been upheld in our earlier decisions on the basis of that liberty. I agree with the statement of MR. JUSTICE STEWART in his concurring opinion that the "liberty," against deprivation of which without due process the Fourteenth Amendment protects, embraces more than the rights found in the Bill of Rights. But that liberty is not guaranteed absolutely against deprivation, only against deprivation without due process of law. The test traditionally applied in the area of social and economic legislation is whether or not a law such as that challenged has a rational relation to a valid state objective. *Williamson* v. *Lee Optical Co.,* 348 U. S. 483, 491 (1955). The Due Process Clause of the Fourteenth Amendment undoubtedly does place a limit, albeit a broad one, on legislative power to enact laws such as this. If the Texas statute were to prohibit an abortion even where the mother's life is in jeopardy, I have little doubt that such a statute would lack a rational relation to a valid state objective under the test stated in *Williamson, supra.* But the Court's sweeping invalidation of any restrictions on abortion during the first trimester is impossible to justify under that standard, and the conscious weighing of competing factors that the Court's opinion apparently substitutes for the established test is far more appropriate to a legislative judgment than to a judicial one.

The Court eschews the history of the Fourteenth Amendment in its reliance on the "compelling state interest" test. See *Weber* v. *Aetna Casualty & Surety Co.*, 406 U. S. 164, 179 (1972) (dissenting opinion). But the Court adds a new wrinkle to this test by transposing it from the legal considerations associated with the Equal Protection Clause of the Fourteenth Amendment to this case arising under the Due Process Clause of the Fourteenth Amendment. Unless I misapprehend the consequences of this transplanting of the "compelling state interest test," the Court's opinion will accomplish the seemingly impossible feat of leaving this area of the law more confused than it found it.

While the Court's opinion quotes from the dissent of Mr. Justice Holmes in *Lochner* v. *New York*, 198 U. S. 45, 74 (1905), the result it reaches is more closely attuned to the majority opinion of Mr. Justice Peckham in that case. As in *Lochner* and similar cases applying substantive due process standards to economic and social welfare legislation, the adoption of the compelling state interest standard will inevitably require this Court to examine the legislative policies and pass on the wisdom of these policies in the very process of deciding whether a particular state interest put forward may or may not be "compelling." The decision here to break pregnancy into three distinct terms and to outline the permissible restrictions the State may impose in each one, for example, partakes more of judicial legislation than it does of a determination of the intent of the drafters of the Fourteenth Amendment.

The fact that a majority of the States reflecting, after all, the majority sentiment in those States, have had restrictions on abortions for at least a century is a strong indication, it seems to me, that the asserted right to an abortion is not "so rooted in the traditions and conscience of our people as to be ranked as fundamental," *Snyder* v. *Massachusetts*, 291 U. S. 97, 105 (1934). Even today, when society's views on abortion are changing, the very existence of the debate is evidence that the "right" to an abortion is not so universally accepted as the appellant would have us believe. . . .

DOE ET AL. *v.* BOLTON, ATTORNEY GENERAL OF GEORGIA, ET AL.

APPEAL FROM THE UNITED STATES DISTRICT COURT FOR
THE NORTHERN DISTRICT OF GEORGIA

No. 70–40. Argued December 13, 1971—Reargued October 11, 1972—
Decided January 22, 1973

BLACKMUN, J., delivered the opinion of the Court, in which BURGER, C. J., and DOUGLAS, BRENNAN, STEWART, MARSHALL, and POWELL, JJ., joined. BURGER, C. J., and DOUGLAS, J., filed concurring opinions. WHITE, J., filed a dissenting opinion, in which REHNQUIST, J., joined. REHNQUIST, J., filed a dissenting opinion.

MR. JUSTICE BLACKMUN delivered the opinion of the Court.

In this appeal, the criminal abortion statutes recently enacted in Georgia are challenged on constitutional grounds. The statutes are §§ 26–1201 through 26–1203 of the State's Criminal Code, formulated by Georgia Laws, 1968 Session, pp. 1249, 1277–1280. In *Roe* v. *Wade, ante,* p. 113, we today have struck down, as constitutionally defective, the Texas criminal abortion statutes that are representative of provisions long in effect in a majority of our States. The Georgia legislation, however, is different and merits separate consideration. . . .

Section 26–1201, with a referenced exception, makes abortion a crime, and § 26–1203 provides that a person convicted of that crime shall be punished by imprisonment for not less than one nor more than 10 years. Section 26–1202 (a) states the exception and removes from § 1201's definition of criminal abortion, and thus makes noncriminal, an abortion "performed by a physician duly licensed" in Georgia when, "based upon his best clinical judgment . . . an abortion is necessary because:

"(1) A continuation of the pregnancy would endanger the life of the pregnant woman or would seriously and permanently injure her health; or
"(2) The fetus would very likely be born with a grave, permanent, and irremediable mental or physical defect; or
"(3) The pregnancy resulted from forcible or statutory rape."[5]

5. In contrast with the ALI model, the Georgia statute makes no specific reference to pregnancy resulting from incest. We were assured by the State at reargument that this was because the statute's reference to "rape" was intended to include incest. Tr. of Oral Rearg. 32.

71

Section 26–1202 also requires, by numbered subdivisions of its subsection (b), that, for an abortion to be authorized or performed as a noncriminal procedure, additional conditions must be fulfilled. These are (1) and (2) residence of the woman in Georgia; (3) reduction to writing of the performing physician's medical judgment that an abortion is justified for one or more of the reasons specified by § 26–1202 (a), with written concurrence in that judgment by at least two other Georgia-licensed physicians, based upon their separate personal medical examinations of the woman; (4) performance of the abortion in a hospital licensed by the State Board of Health and also accredited by the Joint Commission on Accreditation of Hospitals; (5) advance approval by an abortion committee of not less than three members of the hospital's staff; (6) certifications in a rape situation; and (7), (8), and (9) maintenance and confidentiality of records. There is a provision (subsection (c)) for judicial determination of the legality of a proposed abortion on petition of the judicial circuit law officer or of a close relative, as therein defined, of the unborn child, and for expeditious hearing of that petition. There is also a provision (subsection (e)) giving a hospital the right not to admit an abortion patient and giving any physician and any hospital employee or staff member the right, on moral or religious grounds, not to participate in the procedure.

II

On April 16, 1970, Mary Doe,[6] 23 other individuals (nine described as Georgia-licensed physicians, seven as nurses registered in the State, five as clergymen, and two as social workers), and two nonprofit Georgia corporations that advocate abortion reform instituted this federal action in the Northern District of Georgia against the State's attorney general, the district attorney of Fulton County, and the chief of police of the city of Atlanta. The plaintiffs sought a declaratory judgment that the Georgia abortion statutes were unconstitutional in their entirety. They also sought injunctive relief restraining the defendants and their successors from enforcing the statutes.

Mary Doe alleged:

(1) She was a 22-year-old Georgia citizen, married, and nine weeks pregnant. She had three living children. The two older ones had been placed in a foster home because of Doe's poverty and inability to care for them. The youngest, born July 19, 1969, had been placed for adoption. Her husband had recently abandoned her and she was forced to live with her indigent parents and their eight children. She and her husband, however, had become

6. Appellants by their complaint, App. 7, allege that the name is a pseudonym.

reconciled. He was a construction worker employed only sporadically. She had been a mental patient at the State Hospital. She had been advised that an abortion could be performed on her with less danger to her health than if she gave birth to the child she was carrying. She would be unable to care for or support the new child.

(2) On March 25, 1970, she applied to the Abortion Committee of Grady Memorial Hospital, Atlanta, for a therapeutic abortion under § 26–1202. Her application was denied 16 days later, on April 10, when she was eight weeks pregnant, on the ground that her situation was not one described in § 26–1202 (a).[7]

(3) Because her application was denied, she was forced either to relinquish "her right to decide when and how many children she will bear" or to seek an abortion that was illegal under the Georgia statutes. This invaded her rights of privacy and liberty in matters related to family, marriage, and sex, and deprived her of the right to choose whether to bear children. This was a violation of rights guaranteed her by the First, Fourth, Fifth, Ninth, and Fourteenth Amendments. The statutes also denied her equal protection and procedural due process and, because they were unconstitutionally vague, deterred hospitals and doctors from performing abortions. She sued "on her own behalf and on behalf of all others similarly situated."

The other plaintiffs alleged that the Georgia statutes "chilled and deterred" them from practicing their respective professions and deprived them of rights guaranteed by the First, Fourth, and Fourteenth Amendments. These plaintiffs also purported to sue on their own behalf and on behalf of others similarly situated. . . .

IV

The appellants attack on several grounds those portions of the Georgia abortion statutes that remain after the District Court decision: undue restriction of a right to personal and marital privacy; vagueness; deprivation of substantive and procedural due process; improper restriction to Georgia residents; and denial of equal protection.

A. *Roe* v. *Wade, supra,* sets forth our conclusion that a pregnant woman does not have an absolute constitutional right to an abortion on her demand. What is said there is applicable here and need not be repeated.

B. The appellants go on to argue, however, that the present Georgia statutes must be viewed historically, that is, from the fact that prior to the 1968

---

7. In answers to interrogatories, Doe stated that her application for an abortion was approved at Georgia Baptist Hospital on May 5, 1970, but that she was not approved as a charity patient there and had no money to pay for an abortion. App. 64.

Act an abortion in Georgia was not criminal if performed to "preserve the life" of the mother. It is suggested that the present statute, as well, has this emphasis on the mother's rights, not on those of the fetus. Appellants contend that it is thus clear that Georgia has given little, and certainly not first, consideration to the unborn child. Yet, it is the unborn child's rights that Georgia asserts in justification of the statute. Appellants assert that this justification cannot be advanced at this late date.

Appellants then argue that the statutes do not adequately protect the woman's right. This is so because it would be physically and emotionally damaging to Doe to bring a child into her poor, "fatherless"[10] family, and because advances in medicine and medical techniques have made it safer for a woman to have a medically induced abortion than for her to bear a child. Thus, "a statute that requires a woman to carry an unwanted pregnancy to term infringes not only on a fundamental right of privacy but on the right to life itself." Brief 27.

The appellants recognize that a century ago medical knowledge was not so advanced as it is today, that the techniques of antisepsis were not known, and that any abortion procedure was dangerous for the woman. To restrict the legality of the abortion to the situation where it was deemed necessary, in medical judgment, for the preservation of the woman's life was only a natural conclusion in the exercise of the legislative judgment of that time. A State is not to be reproached, however, for a past judgmental determination made in the light of then-existing medical knowledge. It is perhaps unfair to argue, as the appellants do, that because the early focus was on the preservation of the woman's life, the State's present professed interest in the protection of embryonic and fetal life is to be downgraded. That argument denies the State the right to readjust its views and emphases in the light of the advanced knowledge and techniques of the day. . . .

D. The appellants next argue that the District Court should have declared unconstitutional three procedural demands of the Georgia statute: (1) that the abortion be performed in a hospital accredited by the Joint Commission on Accreditation of Hospitals;[11] (2) that the procedure be approved by the hospital staff abortion committee; and (3) that the performing physician's judgment be confirmed by the independent examinations of the patient by two other licensed physicians. The appellants attack these provisions not only on the ground that they unduly restrict the woman's right of privacy, but also on procedural due process and equal protection grounds. The physician-appellants also argue that, by subjecting a doctor's individual

10. Brief for Appellants 25.

11. We were advised at reargument, Tr. of Oral Rearg. 10, that only 54 of Georgia's 159 counties have a JCAH-accredited hospital.

medical judgment to committee approval and to confirming consultations, the statute impermissibly restricts the physician's right to practice his profession and deprives him of due process.

1. *JCAH accreditation.* The Joint Commission on Accreditation of Hospitals is an organization without governmental sponsorship or overtones. No question whatever is raised concerning the integrity of the organization or the high purpose of the accreditation process. . . . That process, however, has to do with hospital standards generally and has no present particularized concern with abortion as a medical or surgical procedure. . . . In Georgia, there is no restriction on the performance of nonabortion surgery in a hospital not yet accredited by the JCAH so long as other requirements imposed by the State, such as licensing of the hospital and of the operating surgeon, are met. See Georgia Code §§ 88–1901 (a) and 88–1905 (1971) and 84–907 (Supp. 1971). Furthermore, accreditation by the Commission is not granted until a hospital has been in operation at least one year. The Model Penal Code, § 230.3, Appendix B hereto, contains no requirement for JCAH accreditation. And the Uniform Abortion Act (Final Draft, Aug. 1971) . . . approved by the American Bar Association in February 1972, contains no JCAH-accredited hospital specification. . . . Some courts have held that a JCAH-accreditation requirement is an overbroad infringement of fundamental rights because it does not relate to the particular medical problems and dangers of the abortion operation. *E. g., Poe* v. *Menghini,* 339 F. Supp., at 993–994.

We hold that the JCAH-accreditation requirement does not withstand constitutional scrutiny in the present context. It is a requirement that simply is not "based on differences that are reasonably related to the purposes of the Act in which it is found." *Morey* v. *Doud,* 354 U. S. 457, 465 (1957).

This is not to say that Georgia may not or should not, from and after the end of the first trimester, adopt standards for licensing all facilities where abortions may be performed so long as those standards are legitimately related to the objective the State seeks to accomplish. The appellants contend that such a relationship would be lacking even in a lesser requirement that an abortion be performed in a licensed hospital, as opposed to a facility, such as a clinic, that may be required by the State to possess all the staffing and services necessary to perform an abortion safely (including those adequate to handle serious complications or other emergency, or arrangements with a nearby hospital to provide such services). Appellants and various *amici* have presented us with a mass of data purporting to demonstrate that some facilities other than hospitals are entirely adequate to perform abortions if they possess these qualifications. The State, on the other hand, has not presented persuasive data to show that only hospitals meet its acknowledged interest in insuring the quality of the operation and the full protection of the patient.

We feel compelled to agree with appellants that the State must show more than it has in order to prove that only the full resources of a licensed hospital, rather than those of some other appropriately licensed institution, satisfy these health interests. We hold that the hospital requirement of the Georgia law, because it fails to exclude the first trimester of pregnancy, see *Roe* v. *Wade*, is also invalid. In so holding we naturally express no opinion on the medical judgment involved in any particular case, that is, whether the patient's situation is such that an abortion should be performed in a hospital, rather than in some other facility.

2. *Committee approval.* The second aspect of the appellants' procedural attack relates to the hospital abortion committee and to the pregnant woman's asserted lack of access to that committee. Relying primarily on *Goldberg* v. *Kelly*, 397 U. S. 254 (1970), concerning the termination of welfare benefits, and *Wisconsin* v. *Constantineau*, 400 U. S. 433 (1971), concerning the posting of an alcoholic's name, Doe first argues that she was denied due process because she could not make a presentation to the committee. It is not clear from the record, however, whether Doe's own consulting physician was or was not a member of the committee or did or did not present her case, or, indeed, whether she herself was or was not there. We see nothing in the Georgia statute that explicitly denies access to the committee by or on behalf of the woman. If the access point alone were involved, we would not be persuaded to strike down the committee provision on the unsupported assumption that access is not provided.

Appellants attack the discretion the statute leaves to the committee. The most concrete argument they advance is their suggestion that it is still a badge of infamy "in many minds" to bear an illegitimate child, and that the Georgia system enables the committee members' personal views as to extramarital sex relations, and punishment therefor, to govern their decisions. This approach obviously is one founded on suspicion and one that discloses a lack of confidence in the integrity of physicians. To say that physicians will be guided in their hospital committee decisions by their predilections on extramarital sex unduly narrows the issue to pregnancy outside marriage. (Doe's own situation did not involve extramarital sex and its product.) The appellants' suggestion is necessarily somewhat degrading to the conscientious physician, particularly the obstetrician, whose professional activity is concerned with the physical and mental welfare, the woes, the emotions, and the concern of his female patients. He, perhaps more than anyone else, is knowledgeable in this area of patient care, and he is aware of human frailty, so-called "error," and needs. The good physician—despite the presence of rascals in the medical profession, as in all others, we trust that most physicians are "good"—will have sympathy and understanding for the pregnant patient that probably are not exceeded by those who participate in other areas of professional counseling. . . .

Saying all this, however, does not settle the issue of the constitutional propriety of the committee requirement. Viewing the Georgia statute as a whole, we see no constitutionally justifiable pertinence in the structure for the advance approval by the abortion committee. With regard to the protection of potential life, the medical judgment is already completed prior to the committee stage, and review by a committee once removed from diagnosis is basically redundant. We are not cited to any other surgical procedure made subject to committee approval as a matter of state criminal law. The woman's right to receive medical care in accordance with her licensed physician's best judgment and the physician's right to administer it are substantially limited by this statutorily imposed overview. And the hospital itself is otherwise fully protected. Under § 26–1202 (e), the hospital is free not to admit a patient for an abortion. It is even free not to have an abortion committee. Further, a physician or any other employee has the right to refrain, for moral or religious reasons, from participating in the abortion procedure. These provisions obviously are in the statute in order to afford appropriate protection to the individual and to the denominational hospital. Section 26–1202 (e) affords adequate protection to the hospital, and little more is provided by the committee prescribed by § 26–1202 (b)(5).

We conclude that the interposition of the hospital abortion committee is unduly restrictive of the patient's rights and needs that, at this point, have already been medically delineated and substantiated by her personal physician. To ask more serves neither the hospital nor the State.

3. *Two-doctor concurrence.* The third aspect of the appellants' attack centers on the "time and availability of adequate medical facilities and personnel." It is said that the system imposes substantial and irrational roadblocks and "is patently unsuited" to prompt determination of the abortion decision. Time, of course, is critical in abortion. Risks during the first trimester of pregnancy are admittedly lower than during later months. . . .

The statute's emphasis, as has been repetitively noted, is on the attending physician's "best clinical judgment that an abortion is necessary." That should be sufficient. The reasons for the presence of the confirmation step in the statute are perhaps apparent, but they are insufficient to withstand constitutional challenge. Again, no other voluntary medical or surgical procedure for which Georgia requires confirmation by two other physicians has been cited to us. If a physician is licensed by the State, he is recognized by the State as capable of exercising acceptable clinical judgment. If he fails in this, professional censure and deprivation of his license are available remedies. Required acquiescence by co-practitioners has no rational connection with a patient's needs and unduly infringes on the physician's right to practice. . . .

F. The last argument on this phase of the case is one that often is made, namely, that the Georgia system is violative of equal protection because it discriminates against the poor. The appellants do not urge that abortions should be performed by persons other than licensed physicians, so we have no argument that because the wealthy can better afford physicians, the poor should have non-physicians made available to them. The appellants acknowledged that the procedures are "nondiscriminatory in . . . express terms" but they suggest that they have produced invidious discriminations. The District Court rejected this approach out of hand. 319 F. Supp., at 1056. It rests primarily on the accreditation and approval and confirmation requirements, discussed above, and on the assertion that most of Georgia's counties have no accredited hospital. We have set aside the accreditation, approval, and confirmation requirements, however, and with that, the discrimination argument collapses in all significant aspects. . . .

MR. JUSTICE WHITE, with whom MR. JUSTICE REHNQUIST joins, dissenting.*

At the heart of the controversy in these cases are those recurring pregnancies that pose no danger whatsoever to the life or health of the mother but are, nevertheless, unwanted for any one or more of a variety of reasons—convenience, family planning, economics, dislike of children, the embarrassment of illegitimacy, etc. The common claim before us is that for any one of such reasons, or for no reason at all, and without asserting or claiming any threat to life or health, any woman is entitled to an abortion at her request if she is able to find a medical advisor willing to undertake the procedure.

The Court for the most part sustains this position: During the period prior to the time the fetus becomes viable, the Constitution of the United States values the convenience, whim, or caprice of the putative mother more than the life or potential life of the fetus; the Constitution, therefore, guarantees the right to an abortion as against any state law or policy seeking to protect the fetus from an abortion not prompted by more compelling reasons of the mother.

With all due respect, I dissent. I find nothing in the language or history of the Constitution to support the Court's judgment. The Court simply fashions and announces a new constitutional right for pregnant mothers and, with scarcely any reason or authority for its action, invests that right with sufficient substance to override most existing state abortion statutes. The upshot is that the people and the legislatures of the 50 States are constitutionally disentitled to weigh the relative importance of the continued existence and development of the fetus, on the one hand, against a spectrum of

*[This opinion applies also to No. 70–18, *Roe* v. *Wade.*]

possible impacts on the mother, on the other hand. As an exercise of raw judicial power, the Court perhaps has authority to do what it does today; but in my view its judgment is an improvident and extravagant exercise of the power of judicial review that the Constitution extends to this Court.

The Court apparently values the convenience of the pregnant mother more than the continued existence and development of the life or potential life that she carries. Whether or not I might agree with that marshaling of values, I can in no event join the Court's judgment because I find no constitutional warrant for imposing such an order of priorities on the people and legislatures of the States. In a sensitive area such as this, involving as it does issues over which reasonable men may easily and heatedly differ, I cannot accept the Court's exercise of its clear power of choice by interposing a constitutional barrier to state efforts to protect human life and by investing mothers and doctors with the constitutionally protected right to exterminate it. This issue, for the most part, should be left with the people and to the political processes the people have devised to govern their affairs.

It is my view, therefore, that the Texas statute is not constitutionally infirm because it denies abortions to those who seek to serve only their convenience rather than to protect their life or health. Nor is this plaintiff, who claims no threat to her mental or physical health, entitled to assert the possible rights of those women whose pregnancy assertedly implicates their health. This, together with *United States* v. *Vuitch,* 402 U. S. 62 (1971), dictates reversal of the judgment of the District Court.

Likewise, because Georgia may constitutionally forbid abortions to putative mothers who, like the plaintiff in this case, do not fall within the reach of § 26–1202 (a) of its criminal code, I have no occasion, and the District Court had none, to consider the constitutionality of the procedural requirements of the Georgia statute as applied to those pregnancies posing substantial hazards to either life or health. I would reverse the judgment of the District Court in the Georgia case. . . .

PLANNED PARENTHOOD OF CENTRAL MISSOURI ET AL. *v.* DANFORTH, ATTORNEY GENERAL OF MISSOURI, ET AL.

APPEAL FROM THE UNITED STATES DISTRICT COURT FOR THE
EASTERN DISTRICT OF MISSOURI

No. 74–1151. Argued March 23, 1976—Decided July 1, 1976

BLACKMUN, J., delivered the opinion of the Court, in which BRENNAN, STEWART, MARSHALL, and POWELL, JJ., joined, in all but Parts IV–D and IV–E of which STEVENS, J., joined, and in all but Parts IV–C, IV–D, IV–E, and IV–G of which BURGER, C. J., and WHITE and REHNQUIST, JJ., joined. STEWART, J., filed a concurring opinion, in which POWELL, J., joined. WHITE, J., filed an opinion concurring in part and dissenting in part, in which BURGER, C. J., and REHNQUIST, J., joined. STEVENS, J., filed an opinion concurring in part and dissenting in part.

MR. JUSTICE BLACKMUN delivered the opinion of the Court.

This case is a logical and anticipated corollary to *Roe* v. *Wade,* 410 U. S. 113 (1973), and *Doe* v. *Bolton,* 410 U. S. 179 (1973), for it raises issues secondary to those that were then before the Court. Indeed, some of the questions now presented were forecast and reserved in *Roe* and *Doe.* 410 U. S., at 165 n. 67.

I

After the decisions in *Roe* and *Doe,* this Court remanded for reconsideration a pending Missouri federal case in which the State's then-existing abortion legislation, Mo. Rev. Stat. §§ 559.100, 542.380, and 563.300 (1969), was under constitutional challenge. *Rodgers* v. *Danforth,* 410 U. S. 949 (1973). A three-judge federal court for the Western District of Missouri, in an unreported decision, thereafter declared the challenged Missouri statutes unconstitutional and granted injunctive relief. On appeal here, that judgment was summarily affirmed. *Danforth* v. *Rodgers,* 414 U. S. 1035 (1973).

In June 1974, somewhat more than a year after *Roe* and *Doe* had been decided, Missouri's 77th General Assembly, in its Second Regular Session, enacted House Committee Substitute for House Bill No. 1211 (hereinafter

Act). The legislation was approved by the Governor on June 14, 1974, and became effective immediately by reason of an emergency clause contained in § A of the statute. The Act is set forth in full as the Appendix to this opinion. It imposes a structure for the control and regulation of abortions in Missouri during all stages of pregnancy.

II

Three days after the Act became effective, the present litigation was instituted in the United States District Court for the Eastern District of Missouri. The plaintiffs are Planned Parenthood of Central Missouri, a not-for-profit Missouri corporation which maintains a facility in Columbia, Mo., for the performance of abortions; David Hall, M. D.; and Michael Freiman, M. D. Doctor Hall is a resident of Columbia, is licensed as a physician in Missouri, is chairman of the Department and Professor of Obstetrics and Gynecology at the University of Missouri Medical School at Columbia, and supervises abortions at the Planned Parenthood facility. He was described by the three-judge court in the 1973 case as one of four plaintiffs who were "eminent, Missouri-licensed obstetricians and gynecologists." Jurisdictional Statement, App. 47, in *Danforth* v. *Rodgers,* No. 73-426, O. T. 1973. Doctor Freiman is a resident of St. Louis, is licensed as a physician in Missouri, is an instructor of Clinical Obstetrics and Gynecology at Washington University Medical School, and performs abortions at two St. Louis hospitals and at a clinic in that city.

The named defendants are the Attorney General of Missouri and the Circuit Attorney of the city of St. Louis "in his representative capacity" and "as the representative of the class of all similar Prosecuting Attorneys of the various counties of the State of Missouri." Complaint 10. . . .

IV

With the exception specified in n. 2, *infra,* we agree with the District Court that the physician-appellants clearly have standing. This was established in *Doe* v. *Bolton,* 410 U. S., at 188. Like the Georgia statutes challenged in that case, "[t]he physician is the one against whom [the Missouri Act] directly operate[s] in the event he procures an abortion that does not meet the statutory exceptions and conditions. The physician-appellants, therefore, assert a sufficiently direct threat of personal detriment. They should not be required to await and undergo a criminal prosecution as the sole means of seeking relief." . . . *Ibid.*

Our primary task, then, is to consider each of the challenged provisions of the new Missouri abortion statute in the particular light of the opinions and decisions in *Roe* and in *Doe*. To this we now turn, with the assistance of helpful briefs from both sides and from some of the *amici*.

A

The definition of viability. Section 2 (2) of the Act defines "viability" as "that stage of fetal development when the life of the unborn child may be continued indefinitely outside the womb by natural or artificial life-supportive systems." Appellants claim that this definition violates and conflicts with the discussion of viability in our opinion in *Roe*. 410 U. S., at 160, 163. In particular, appellants object to the failure of the definition to contain any reference to a gestational time period, to its failure to incorporate and reflect the three stages of pregnancy, to the presence of the word "indefinitely," and to the extra burden of regulation imposed. It is suggested that the definition expands the Court's definition of viability, as expressed in *Roe*, and amounts to a legislative determination of what is properly a matter for medical judgment. It is said that the "mere possibility of momentary survival is not the medical standard of viability." Brief for Appellants 67.

In *Roe*, we used the term "viable," properly we thought, to signify the point at which the fetus is "potentially able to live outside the mother's womb, albeit with artificial aid," and presumably capable of "meaningful life outside the mother's womb," 410 U. S., at 160, 163. We noted that this point "is usually placed" at about seven months or 28 weeks, but may occur earlier. *Id.*, at 160.

We agree with the District Court and conclude that the definition of viability in the Act does not conflict with what was said and held in *Roe*. In fact, we believe that § 2 (2), even when read in conjunction with § 5 (proscribing an abortion "not necessary to preserve the life or health of the mother . . . unless the attending physician first certifies with reasonable medical certainty that the fetus is not viable"), the constitutionality of which is not explicitly challenged here, reflects an attempt on the part of the Missouri General Assembly to comply with our observations and discussion in *Roe* relating to viability. Appellant Hall, in his deposition, had no particular difficulty with the statutory definition.[3] As noted above, we recognized in *Roe* that viability was a matter of medical judgment, skill, and technical ability, and we preserved the flexibility of the term. Section 2 (2) does the same. Indeed, one might argue, as the appellees do, that the presence of the statute's words "continued indefinitely" favor, rather than disfavor, the appellants, for, arguably, the point when life can be "continued indefinitely

---

3. "[A]lthough I agree with the definition of 'viability,' I think that it must be understood that viability is a very difficult state to assess." Tr. 369.

outside the womb" may well occur later in pregnancy than the point where the fetus is "potentially able to live outside the mother's womb." *Roe* v. *Wade*, 410 U. S., at 160.

In any event, we agree with the District Court that it is not the proper function of the legislature or the courts to place viability, which essentially is a medical concept, at a specific point in the gestation period. The time when viability is achieved may vary with each pregnancy, and the determination of whether a particular fetus is viable is, and must be, a matter for the judgment of the responsible attending physician. The definition of viability in § 2 (2) merely reflects this fact. The appellees do not contend otherwise, for they insist that the determination of viability rests with the physician in the exercise of his professional judgment. . . .

B

The woman's consent. Under § 3 (2) of the Act, a woman, prior to submitting to an abortion during the first 12 weeks of pregnancy, must certify in writing her consent to the procedure and "that her consent is informed and freely given and is not the result of coercion." Appellants argue that this requirement is violative of *Roe* v. *Wade*, 410 U. S., at 164–165, by imposing an extra layer and burden of regulation on the abortion decision. See *Doe* v. *Bolton*, 410 U. S., at 195–200. Appellants also claim that the provision is overbroad and vague. . . .

. . . It is true that *Doe* and *Roe* clearly establish that the State may not restrict the decision of the patient and her physician regarding abortion during the first stage of pregnancy. Despite the fact that apparently no other Missouri statute, with the exceptions referred to in n. 6, *supra*, requires a patient's prior written consent to a surgical procedure,[7] the imposition by § 3 (2) of such a requirement for termination of pregnancy even during the first stage, in our view, is not in itself an unconstitutional requirement. The decision to abort, indeed, is an important, and often a stressful one, and it is desirable and imperative that it be made with full knowledge of its nature and consequences. The woman is the one primarily concerned, and her awareness of the decision and its significance may be assured, constitutionally, by the State to the extent of requiring her prior written consent. . . .

The spouse's consent. Section 3 (3) requires the prior written consent of the spouse of the woman seeking an abortion during the first 12 weeks of preg-

---

7. There is some testimony in the record to the effect that taking from the patient a prior written consent to surgery is the custom. That may be so in some areas of Missouri, but we definitely refrain from characterizing it extremely as "the universal practice of the medical profession," as the appellees do. Brief for Appellee Danforth 32.

nancy, unless "the abortion is certified by a licensed physician to be necessary in order to preserve the life of the mother."[9]

The appellees defend § 3 (3) on the ground that it was enacted in the light of the General Assembly's "perception of marriage as an institution," Brief for Appellee Danforth 34, and that any major change in family status is a decision to be made jointly by the marriage partners. Reference is made to an abortion's possible effect on the woman's childbearing potential. It is said that marriage always has entailed some legislatively imposed limitations: Reference is made to adultery and bigamy as criminal offenses; to Missouri's general requirement, Mo. Rev. Stat. § 453.030.3 (1969), that for an adoption of a child born in wedlock the consent of both parents is necessary; to similar joint-consent requirements imposed by a number of States with respect to artificial insemination and the legitimacy of children so conceived; to the laws of two States requiring spousal consent for voluntary sterilization; and to the long-established requirement of spousal consent for the effective disposition of an interest in real property. It is argued that "[r]ecognizing that the consent of both parties is generally necessary . . . to begin a family, the legislature has determined that a change in the family structure set in motion by mutual consent should be terminated only by mutual consent," Brief for Appellee Danforth 38, and that what the legislature did was to exercise its inherent policy-making power "for what was believed to be in the best interests of all the people of Missouri." *Id.,* at 40.

The appellants, on the other hand, contend that § 3 (3) obviously is designed to afford the husband the right unilaterally to prevent or veto an abortion, whether or not he is the father of the fetus, and that this not only violates *Roe* and *Doe* but is also in conflict with other decided cases. See, *e. g., Poe* v. *Gerstein,* 517 F. 2d 787, 794–796 (CA5 1975), appeal docketed, No. 75–713; *Wolfe* v. *Schroering,* 388 F. Supp., at 636–637; *Doe* v. *Rampton,* 366 F. Supp. 189, 193 (Utah 1973). They also refer to the situation where the husband's consent cannot be obtained because he cannot be located. And they assert that § 3 (3) is vague and overbroad.

In *Roe* and *Doe* we specifically reserved decision on the question whether a requirement for consent by the father of the fetus, by the spouse, or by the parents, or a parent, of an unmarried minor, may be constitutionally imposed. 410 U. S., at 165 n. 67. We now hold that the State may not constitutionally require the consent of the spouse, as is specified under § 3 (3) of the Missouri Act, as a condition for abortion during the first 12 weeks of pregnancy. We thus agree with the dissenting judge in the present case, and with the courts whose decisions are cited above, that the State cannot "delegate to

9. It is of some interest to note that the condition does not relate, as most statutory conditions in this area do, to the preservation of the life or *health* of the mother.

a spouse a veto power which the state itself is absolutely and totally prohibited from exercising during the first trimester of pregnancy." 392 F.
Supp., at 1375. Clearly, since the State cannot regulate or proscribe abortion
during the first stage, when the physician and his patient make that decision,
the State cannot delegate authority to any particular person, even the
spouse, to prevent abortion during that same period.

We are not unaware of the deep and proper concern and interest that a
devoted and protective husband has in his wife's pregnancy and in the
growth and development of the fetus she is carrying. Neither has this Court
failed to appreciate the importance of the marital relationship in our society.
See, *e. g., Griswold* v. *Connecticut,* 381 U. S. 479, 486 (1965); *Maynard* v.
Hill, 125 U. S. 190, 211 (1888). . . . Moreover, we recognize that the decision whether to undergo or to forgo an abortion may have profound effects
on the future of any marriage, effects that are both physical and mental, and
possibly deleterious. Notwithstanding these factors, we cannot hold that the
State has the constitutional authority to give the spouse unilaterally the ability to prohibit the wife from terminating her pregnancy, when the State itself lacks that right. See *Eisenstadt* v. *Baird,* 405 U. S. 438, 453 (1972).[11]

It seems manifest that, ideally, the decision to terminate a pregnancy
should be one concurred in by both the wife and her husband. No marriage
may be viewed as harmonious or successful if the marriage partners are fundamentally divided on so important and vital an issue. But it is difficult to
believe that the goal of fostering mutuality and trust in a marriage, and of
strengthening the marital relationship and the marriage institution, will be
achieved by giving the husband a veto power exercisable for any reason
whatsoever or for no reason at all. Even if the State had the ability to delegate to the husband a power it itself could not exercise, it is not at all likely
that such action would further, as the District Court majority phrased it, the
"interest of the state in protecting the mutuality of decisions vital to the
marriage relationship." 392 F. Supp., at 1370.

We recognize, of course, that when a woman, with the approval of her
physician but without the approval of her husband, decides to terminate her
pregnancy, it could be said that she is acting unilaterally. The obvious fact is
that when the wife and the husband disagree on this decision, the view of

---

11. As the Court recognized in *Eisenstadt* v. *Baird,* "the marital couple is not an independent entity with a mind and heart of its own, but an association of two individuals each with a separate intellectual and emotional makeup. If the right of privacy
means anything, it is the right of the *individual,* married or single, to be free from
unwarranted governmental intrusion into matters so fundamentally affecting a person as the decision whether to bear or beget a child." 405 U. S., at 453 (emphasis in
original). . . .

only one of the two marriage partners can prevail. Inasmuch as it is the woman who physically bears the child and who is the more directly and immediately affected by the pregnancy, as between the two, the balance weighs in her favor. Cf. *Roe* v. *Wade*, 410 U. S., at 153. . . .

D

Parental Consent. Section 3 (4) requires, with respect to the first 12 weeks of pregnancy, where the woman is unmarried and under the age of 18 years, the written consent of a parent or person *in loco parentis* unless, again, "the abortion is certified by a licensed physician as necessary in order to preserve the life of the mother." . . .

We agree with appellants . . . that the State may not impose a blanket provision, such as § 3 (4), requiring the consent of a parent or person *in loco parentis* as a condition for abortion of an unmarried minor during the first 12 weeks of her pregnancy. Just as with the requirement of consent from the spouse, so here, the State does not have the constitutional authority to give a third party an absolute, and possibly arbitrary, veto over the decision of the physician and his patient to terminate the patient's pregnancy, regardless of the reason for withholding the consent.

Constitutional rights do not mature and come into being magically only when one attains the state-defined age of majority. Minors, as well as adults, are protected by the Constitution and possess constitutional rights. See, *e. g., Breed* v. *Jones,* 421 U. S. 519 (1975); *Goss* v. *Lopez,* 419 U. S. 565 (1975); *Tinker* v. *Des Moines School Dist.,* 393 U. S. 503 (1969); *In re Gault,* 387 U. S. 1 (1967). The Court indeed, however, long has recognized that the State has somewhat broader authority to regulate the activities of children than of adults. *Prince* v. *Massachusetts,* 321 U. S., at 170; *Ginsberg* v. *New York,* 390 U. S. 629 (1968). It remains, then, to examine whether there is any significant state interest in conditioning an abortion on the consent of a parent or person *in loco parentis* that is not present in the case of an adult.

One suggested interest is the safeguarding of the family unit and of parental authority. 392 F. Supp., at 1370. It is difficult, however, to conclude that providing a parent with absolute power to overrule a determination, made by the physician and his minor patient, to terminate the patient's pregnancy will serve to strengthen the family unit. Neither is it likely that such veto power will enhance parental authority or control where the minor and the nonconsenting parent are so fundamentally in conflict and the very existence of the pregnancy already has fractured the family structure. Any independent interest the parent may have in the termination of the minor daughter's pregnancy is no more weighty than the right of privacy of the competent minor mature enough to have become pregnant.

We emphasize that our holding that § 3 (4) is invalid does not suggest that every minor, regardless of age or maturity, may give effective consent for termination of her pregnancy. See *Bellotti* v. *Baird.* The fault with § 3 (4) is that it imposes a special-consent provision, exercisable by a person other than the woman and her physician, as a prerequisite to a minor's termination of her pregnancy and does so without a sufficient justification for the restriction. It violates the strictures of *Roe* and *Doe.*

E

Saline amniocentesis. Section 9 of the statute prohibits the use of saline amniocentesis, as a method or technique of abortion, after the first 12 weeks of pregnancy. It describes the method as one whereby the amniotic fluid is withdrawn and "a saline or other fluid" is inserted into the amniotic sac. The statute imposes this proscription on the ground that the technique "is deleterious to maternal health," and places it in the form of a legislative finding. . . .

We held in *Roe* that after the first stage, "the State, in promoting its interest in the health of the mother, may, if it chooses, regulate the abortion procedure in ways that are reasonably related to maternal health." 410 U. S., at 164. The question with respect to § 9 therefore is whether the flat prohibition of saline amniocentesis is a restriction which "reasonably relates to the preservation and protection of maternal health." . . .

. . . The State, through § 9, would prohibit the use of a method which the record shows is the one most commonly used nationally by physicians after the first trimester and which is safer, with respect to maternal mortality, than even continuation of the pregnancy until normal childbirth. Moreover, as a practical matter, it forces a woman and her physician to terminate her pregnancy by methods more dangerous to her health than the method outlawed.

As so viewed, particularly in the light of the present unavailability—as demonstrated by the record—of the prostaglandin technique, the outright legislative proscription of saline fails as a reasonable regulation for the protection of maternal health. It comes into focus, instead, as an unreasonable or arbitrary regulation designed to inhibit, and having the effect of inhibiting, the vast majority of abortions after the first 12 weeks. As such, it does not withstand constitutional challenge. See *Wolfe* v. *Schroering*, 388 F. Supp., at 637.

MR. JUSTICE WHITE, with whom THE CHIEF JUSTICE and MR. JUSTICE REHNQUIST join, concurring in part and dissenting in part.

In *Roe* v. *Wade*, 410 U. S. 113 (1973), this Court recognized a right to an abortion free from state prohibition. The task of policing this limitation on state police power is and will be a difficult and continuing venture in substantive due process. However, even accepting *Roe* v. *Wade,* there is nothing in the opinion in that case and nothing articulated in the Court's opinion in this case which justifies the invalidation of four provisions of House Committee Substitute for House Bill No. 1211 (hereafter Act) enacted by the Missouri 77th General Assembly in 1974 in response to *Roe* v. *Wade.* Accordingly, I dissent, in part.

I

Roe v. *Wade* holds that until a fetus becomes viable, the interest of the State in the life or potential life it represents is outweighed by the interest of the mother in choosing "whether or not to terminate her pregnancy." 410 U. S., at 153. Section 3 (3) of the Act provides that a married woman may not obtain an abortion without her husband's consent. The Court strikes down this statute in one sentence. It says that "since the State cannot . . . proscribe abortion . . . the State cannot delegate authority to any particular person, even the spouse, to prevent abortion. . . . " *Ante,* at 69. But the State is not—under § 3 (3)—delegating to the husband the power to vindicate the *State*'s interest in the future life of the fetus. It is instead recognizing that the husband has an interest of his own in the life of the fetus which should not be extinguished by the unilateral decision of the wife.[1] It by no means follows, from the fact that the mother's interest in deciding "whether or not to terminate her pregnancy" outweighs the *State*'s interest in the potential life of the fetus, that the husband's interest is also outweighed and may not be protected by the State. A father's interest in having a child—perhaps his only child—may be unmatched by any other interest in his life. See *Stanley* v. *Illinois,* 405 U. S. 645, 651 (1972), and cases there cited. It is truly surprising that the majority finds in the United States Constitution, as it must in order to justify the result it reaches, a rule that the State must assign a greater value to a mother's decision to cut off a potential human life by abortion than to a father's decision to let it mature into a live child. Such a rule cannot be found there, nor can it be found in *Roe* v. *Wade, supra.* These are matters which a State should be able to decide free from the

---

1. There are countless situations in which the State prohibits conduct only when it is objected to by a private person most closely affected by it. Thus a State cannot forbid anyone to enter on private property with the owner's consent, but it may enact and enforce trespass laws against unauthorized entrances. It cannot forbid transfer of property held in tenancy by the entireties but it may require consent by both husband and wife to such a transfer. These situations plainly do not involve delegations of legislative power to private parties; and neither does the requirement in §3 (3) that a woman not deprive her husband of his future child without his consent.

suffocating power of the federal judge, purporting to act in the name of the Constitution.

In describing the nature of a mother's interest in terminating a pregnancy, the Court in *Roe* v. *Wade* mentioned only the post-birth burdens of rearing a child, 410 U. S., at 153, and rejected a rule based on her interest in controlling her own body during pregnancy. *Id.,* at 154. Missouri has a law which prevents a woman from putting a child up for adoption over her husband's objection, Mo. Rev. Stat. § 453.030 (1969). This law represents a judgment by the State that the mother's interest in avoiding the burdens of child rearing do not outweigh or snuff out the father's interest in participating in bringing up his own child. That law is plainly valid, but no more so than § 3 (3) of the Act now before us, resting as it does on precisely the same judgment.

II

Section 3 (4) requires that an unmarried woman under 18 years of age obtain the consent of a parent or a person *in loco parentis* as a condition to an abortion. Once again the Court strikes the provision down in a sentence. It states: "Just as with the requirement of consent from the spouse, so here, the State does not have the constitutional authority to give a third party an absolute, and possibly arbitrary, veto over the decision of the physician and his patient to terminate the patient's pregnancy. . . . " The Court rejects the notions that the *State* has an interest in strengthening the family unit, or that the *parent* has an "independent interest" in the abortion decision, sufficient to justify § 3 (4) and apparently concludes that the provision is therefore unconstitutional. But the purpose of the parental-consent requirement is not merely to vindicate any interest of the parent or of the State. The purpose of the requirement is to vindicate the very right created in *Roe* v. *Wade, supra*—the right of the pregnant woman to decide "whether or *not* to terminate her pregnancy." 410 U. S., at 153 (emphasis added). The abortion decision is unquestionably important and has irrevocable consequences whichever way it is made. Missouri is entitled to protect the minor unmarried woman from making the decision in a way which is not in her own best interests, and it seeks to achieve this goal by requiring parental consultation and consent. This is the traditional way by which States have sought to protect children from their own immature and improvident decisions; . . . and there is absolutely no reason expressed by the majority why the State may not utilize that method here.

III

Section 9 of the Act prohibits abortion by the method known as saline amniocentesis—a method used at the time the Act was passed for 70% of abortions performed after the first trimester. Legislative history reveals that the Missouri Legislature viewed saline amniocentesis as far less safe a method of abortion than the so-called prostaglandin method. The court below took evidence on the question and summarized it as follows:

"The record of trial discloses that use of the saline method exposes a woman to the danger of severe complications, regardless of the skill of the physician or the precaution taken. Saline may cause one or more of the following conditions: Disseminated intravascular coagulation or 'consumptive coagulapathy' (disruption of the blood clotting mechanism [Dr. Warren, Tr. 57–58; Dr. Klaus, Tr. 269–270; Dr. Anderson, Tr. 307; Defts' Exs. H & M]), which may result in severe bleeding and possibly death (Dr. Warren, Tr. 58); hypernatremia (increase in blood sodium level), which may lead to convulsions and death (Dr. Klaus, Tr. 268); and water intoxication (accumulated water in the body tissue which may occur when oxytoxin is used in conjunction with the injection of saline), resulting in damage to the central nervous system or death (Dr. Warren, Tr. 76; Dr. Klaus, Tr. 270–271; Dr. Anderson, Tr. 310; Defts' Ex. L). There is also evidence that saline amniocentesis causes massive tissue destruction to the inside of the uterus (Dr. Anderson, Tr. 308)." 392 F. Supp. 1362, 1372–1373 (1975).

The District Court also cited considerable evidence establishing that the prostaglandin method is safer. In fact, the Chief of Obstetrics at Yale University, Dr. Anderson, suggested that "physicians should be liable for malpractice if they chose saline over prostaglandin after having been given all the facts on both methods." *Id.,* at 1373. The Court nevertheless reverses the decision of the District Court sustaining § 9 against constitutional challenge. It does so apparently because saline amniocentesis was widely used before the Act was passed; because the prostaglandin method was seldom used and was not generally available; and because other abortion techniques more dangerous than saline amniocentesis were not banned. At bottom the majority's holding—as well as the concurrence—rests on its *factual* finding that the prostaglandin method is unavailable to the women of Missouri. It therefore concludes that the ban on the saline method is "an unreasonable or arbitrary regulation designed to inhibit, and having the effect of inhibiting, the vast majority of abortions after the first 12 weeks," *ante,* at 79. This factual finding was not made either by the majority or by the dissenting judge below. Appellants have not argued that the record below supports such a finding. In fact the record below does not support such a finding. There is *no* evidence in the record that women in Missouri will be unable to obtain abortions by the prostaglandin method. What evidence there is in the record on this question supports the contrary conclusion.[3] The record discloses that the prostaglandin method of abortion was the country's second most common method of abortion during the second trimester, Tr. 42, 89–90; that although the prostaglandin method had previously been available only on an experimental basis, it was, at the time of trial available in "small hospitals all over the country," *id.*, at 342; that in another year or so the prostaglandin method would become—even in the absence of legislation on the subject—the most prevalent method. Anderson deposition, at 69. Moreover, one doctor quite sensibly testified that if the saline method were banned, hospitals would quickly switch to the prostaglandin method.

The majority relies on the testimony of one doctor that—as already noted—prostaglandin had been available on an experimental basis only until January 1, 1974; and that its manufacturer, the Upjohn Co., restricted its sales to large medical centers for the following six months, after which sales were to be unrestricted. Tr. 334–335. In what manner this evidence supports the proposition that prostaglandin is unavailable to the women of Missouri escapes me. . . .

The only other basis for its factual finding which the majority offers is a citation to *another* case—*Wolfe* v. *Schroering,* 388 F. Supp. 631, 637 (WD Ky. 1974)—in which a different court concluded that the record in its case showed the prostaglandin method to be unavailable in another State—Kentucky—at another time—two years ago. This case must be decided on its own record. I am not yet prepared to accept the notion that normal rules of law, procedure, and constitutional adjudication suddenly become irrelevant solely because a case touches on the subject of abortion. The majority's finding of fact that women in Missouri will be unable to obtain abortions after the first trimester if the saline method is banned is wholly unjustifiable. . . .

IV

In my opinion, . . . the parental-consent requirement is consistent with the holding in *Roe.* The State's interest in the welfare of its young citizens justifies a variety of protective measures. Because he may not foresee the consequences of his decision, a minor may not make an enforceable bargain. He may not lawfully work or travel where he pleases, or even attend exhibitions of constitutionally protected adult motion pictures. Persons below a certain age may not marry without parental consent. Indeed, such consent is

3. The absence of more evidence on the subject in the record seems to be a result of the fact that the claim that the prostaglandin method is unavailable was not part of plaintiffs' litigating strategy below.

essential even when the young woman is already pregnant. The State's interest in protecting a young person from harm justifies the imposition of restraints on his or her freedom even though comparable restraints on adults would be constitutionally impermissible. Therefore, the holding in *Roe* v. *Wade* that the abortion decision is entitled to constitutional protection merely emphasizes the importance of the decision; it does not lead to the conclusion that the state legislature has no power to enact legislation for the purpose of protecting a young pregnant woman from the consequences of an incorrect decision.

The abortion decision is, of course, more important than the decision to attend or to avoid an adult motion picture, or the decision to work long hours in a factory. It is not necessarily any more important than the decision to run away from home or the decision to marry. But even if it is the most important kind of a decision a young person may ever make, that assumption merely enhances the quality of the State's interest in maximizing the probability that the decision be made correctly and with full understanding of the consequences of either alternative. . . .

SINGLETON, CHIEF, BUREAU OF MEDICAL SERVICES, DEPARTMENT OF HEALTH AND WELFARE OF MISSOURI *v.* WULFF ET AL.

CERTIORARI TO THE UNITED STATES COURT OF APPEALS
FOR THE EIGHTH CIRCUIT

No. 74–1393. Argued March 23, 1976—Decided July 1, 1976

[This litigation concerned the constitutionality of a Missouri statute that denied Medicaid funding for abortions that are not "medically indicated." At issue was not only the constitutionality of the statute, but whether or not physicians had standing to bring suits of this kind. The Court did not decide the substantive question, on the grounds that it had not been properly presented in the courts below, but it did deal with the issue of physicians' standing in abortion litigation.]

BLACKMUN, J., announced the judgment of the Court and delivered an opinion of the Court with respect to Parts I, II-A, and III, in which all Members joined, and in which, as to Part II-B, BRENNAN, WHITE, and MARSHALL, JJ., joined. STEVENS, J., filed an opinion concurring in part, *post,* p 121. POWELL, J., filed an opinion concurring in part and dissenting in part, in which BURGER, C. J., and STEWART and REHNQUIST, JJ., joined, *post,* p. 122.

MR. JUSTICE BLACKMUN delivered the opinion of the Court (Parts I, II–A, and III) together with an opinion (Part II–B), in which MR. JUSTICE BRENNAN, MR. JUSTICE WHITE, and MR. JUSTICE MARSHALL joined.

I

. . . The closeness of the relationship is patent, as it was in *Griswold* and in *Doe.* A woman cannot safely secure an abortion without the aid of a physician, and an impecunious woman cannot easily secure an abortion without the physician's being paid by the State. The woman's exercise of her right to an abortion, whatever its dimension, is therefore necessarily at stake here. Moreover, the constitutionally protected abortion decision is one in which the physician is intimately involved. See *Roe* v. *Wade,* 410 U. S., at 153–156. Aside from the woman herself, therefore, the physician is uniquely qualified

93

to litigate the constitutionality of the State's interference with, or discrimination against, that decision.

As to the woman's assertion of her own rights, there are several obstacles. For one thing, she may be chilled from such assertion by a desire to protect the very privacy of her decision from the publicity of a court suit. A second obstacle is the imminent mootness, at least in the technical sense, of any individual woman's claim. Only a few months, at the most, after the maturing of the decision to undergo an abortion, her right thereto will have been irrevocably lost, assuming, as it seems fair to assume, that unless the impecunious woman can establish Medicaid eligibility she must forgo abortion. It is true that these obstacles are not insurmountable. Suit may be brought under a pseudonym, as so frequently has been done. A woman who is no longer pregnant may nonetheless retain the right to litigate the point because it is "'capable of repetition yet evading review.'" *Roe* v. *Wade*, 410 U. S., at 124–125. And it may be that a class could be assembled, whose fluid membership always included some women with live claims. But if the assertion of the right is to be "representative" to such an extent anyway, there seems little loss in terms of effective advocacy from allowing its assertion by a physician.

For these reasons, we conclude that it generally is appropriate to allow a physician to assert the rights of women patients as against governmental interference with the abortion decision, and we decline to restrict our holding to that effect in *Doe* to its purely criminal context. . . .

MR. JUSTICE POWELL, with whom THE CHIEF JUSTICE, MR. JUSTICE STEWART, and MR. JUSTICE REHNQUIST join, concurring in part and dissenting in part.

The Court holds that the respondents have standing to bring this suit and to assert their own constitutional rights, if any, in an attack on Mo. Rev. Stat. § 208.152 (12) (Supp. 1975). The Court also holds that the Court of Appeals erred in proceeding to the merits of respondents' challenge. I agree with both of these holdings and therefore concur in Parts I, II–A, and III of JUSTICE BLACKMUN's opinion, as well as in the first four sentences of Part II–B.

The Court further holds that after remand to the District Court the respondents may assert, in addition to their own rights, the constitutional rights of their patients who would be eligible for Medicaid assistance in obtaining elective abortions but for the exclusion of such abortions in § 208.152 (12). I dissent from this holding. . . .

. . . The usual—and wise—stance of the federal courts when policing their own exercise of power . . . is one of cautious reserve. See generally *Ashwander* v. *TVA*, 297 U. S. 288, 346–348 (1936) (Brandeis, J., concurring).

This caution has given rise to the general rule that a party may not defend against or attack governmental action on the ground that it infringes the rights of some third party, and to the corollary that any exception must rest on specific factors outweighing the policies behind the rule itself. . . . See *Barrows* v. *Jackson*, 346 U. S. 249, 257 (1953); cf. generally *United States* v. *Richardson*, 418 U. S. 166, 188–197 (1974) (POWELL, J., concurring).

The plurality acknowledges this general rule, but identifies "two factual elements"—thought to be derived from prior cases—that justify the adjudication of the asserted third-party rights: (i) obstacles to the assertion by the third party of her own rights, and (ii) the existence of some "relationship" such as the one between physician and patient. In my view these factors do not justify allowing these physicians to assert their patients' rights.

A

Our prior decisions are enlightening. In *Barrows* v. *Jackson, supra,* a covenantor who breached a racially restrictive covenant by selling to Negroes was permitted to set up the buyers' rights to equal protection in defense against a damages action by the covenantees. See *Shelley* v. *Kraemer,* 334 U. S. 1 (1948). The Court considered the general rule outweighed by "the need to protect [these] fundamental rights" in a situation "in which it would be difficult if not impossible for the persons whose rights are asserted to present their grievance before any court." 346 U. S., at 257. It would indeed have been difficult if not impossible for the rightholders to assert their own rights: the operation of the restrictive covenant and the threat of damages actions for its breach tended to insure they would not come into possession of the land, and there was at the time little chance of a successful suit based on a covenantor's failure to sell to them. In a second case, *NAACP* v. *Alabama,* 357 U. S. 449 (1958), an organization was allowed to resist an order to produce its membership list by asserting the associational rights of its members to anonymity because, as the plurality notes, *ante,* at 116, the members themselves would have had to forgo the rights in order to assert them. And in *Eisenstadt* v. *Baird,* 405 U. S. 438 (1972), the Court considered it necessary to relax the rule and permit a distributor of contraceptives to assert the constitutional rights of the recipients because the statutory scheme operating to deny the contraceptives to the recipients appeared to offer them no means of challenge. *Id.,* at 446.

The plurality purports to derive from these cases the principle that a party may assert another's rights if there is "some genuine obstacle" to the third party's own litigation. But this understates the teaching of those cases: On their facts they indicate that such an assertion is proper, not when there is merely some "obstacle" to the rightholder's own litigation, but when such litigation is in all practicable terms impossible. Thus, in its framing of this principle, the plurality has gone far beyond our major precedents. . . .

B

The plurality places primary reliance on a second element, the existence of a "confidential relationship" between the rightholder and the party seeking to assert her rights.[5] Focusing on the professional relationships present in *Griswold, Doe* and *Planned Parenthood of Missouri* v. *Danforth, ante*, p. 52, the plurality suggests that allowing the physicians in this case to assert their patients' rights flows naturally from those three. Indeed, its conclusion is couched in terms of the general appropriateness of allowing physicians to assert the privacy interests of their patients in attacks on "governmental interference with the abortion decision."

With all respect, I do not read these cases as merging the physician and his patient for constitutional purposes. The principle they support turns not upon the confidential nature of a physician-patient relationship but upon the nature of the State's impact upon that relationship. In each instance the State directly interdicted the normal functioning of the physician-patient relationship by criminalizing certain procedures. In the circumstances of direct interference, I agree that one party to the relationship should be permitted to assert the constitutional rights of the other, for a judicial rule of self-restraint should not preclude an attack on a State's proscription of constitutionally protected activity. See also *Meyer* v. *Nebraska*, 262 U. S. 390 (1923). But Missouri has not directly interfered with the abortion decision—neither the physicians nor their patients are forbidden to engage in the procedure. . . . The only impact of § 208.152 (12) is that, because of the way Missouri chose to structure its Medicaid payments, it causes these doctors financial detriment. This affords them Art. III standing because they aver injury in fact, but it does not justify abandonment of the salutary rule against assertion of third-party rights. . . .

5. The plurality's primary emphasis upon this relationship is in marked contrast to the Court's previous position that the relationship between litigant and rightholder was subordinate in importance to "the impact of the litigation on the third-party interests." *Eisenstadt* v. *Baird*, 405 U. S. 438, 445 (1972). I suspect the plurality's inversion of the previous order results from the weakness of the argument that this litigation is necessary to protect third-party interests. I would keep the emphasis where it has been before, and would consider the closeness of any "relationship" only as a factor imparting confidence that third-party interests will be represented adequately in a case in which allowing their assertion is justified on other grounds. Cf. n. 2, *supra.*

BEAL, SECRETARY, DEPARTMENT OF PUBLIC WELFARE OF PENNSYLVANIA, ET AL. *v.* DOE ET AL.

CERTIORARI TO THE UNITED STATES COURT OF APPEALS
FOR THE THIRD CIRCUIT

No. 75–554. Argued January 11, 1977—Decided June 20, 1977

POWELL, J., delivered the opinion of the Court, in which BURGER, C. J., and STEWART, WHITE, REHNQUIST, and STEVENS, JJ., joined. BRENNAN, J., filed a dissenting opinion, in which MARSHALL and BLACKMUN, JJ., joined. MARSHALL, J., filed a dissenting opinion. BLACKMUN, J., filed a dissenting opinion, in which BRENNAN and MARSHALL, JJ., joined.

MR. JUSTICE POWELL delivered the opinion of the Court.

The issue in this case is whether Title XIX of the Social Security Act, as added, 79 Stat. 343, and amended, 42 U. S. C. § 1396 *et seq.* (1970 ed. and Supp. V), requires States that participate in the Medical Assistance (Medicaid) program to fund the cost of nontherapeutic abortions. . . .

The only question before us is one of statutory construction: whether Title XIX requires Pennsylvania to fund under its Medicaid program the cost of *all* abortions that are permissible under state law. "The starting point in every case involving construction of a statute is the language itself." *Blue Chip Stamps* v. *Manor Drug Stores,* 421 U. S. 723, 756 (1975) (POWELL, J., concurring). Title XIX makes no reference to abortions, or, for that matter, to any other particular medical procedure. Instead, the statute is cast in terms that require participating States to provide financial assistance with respect to five broad categories of medical treatment. See n. 2, *supra.* But nothing in the statute suggests that participating States are required to fund every medical procedure that falls within the delineated categories of medical care. Indeed, the statute expressly provides:

> "A State plan for medical assistance must . . . include reasonable standards . . . for determining eligibility for and the extent of medical assistance under the plan which . . . are consistent with the objectives of this [Title]. . . . " 42 U. S. C. § 1396a (a) (17) (1970 ed., Supp. V).

This language confers broad discretion on the States to adopt standards for determining the extent of medical assistance, requiring only that such standards be "reasonable" and "consistent with the objectives" of the Act. . . .

Pennsylvania's regulation comports fully with Title XIX's broadly stated primary objective to enable each State, as far as practicable, to furnish medical assistance to individuals whose income and resources are insufficient to meet the costs of necessary medical services. See 42 U. S. C. §§ 1396, 1396a (10) (C) (1970 ed., Supp. V). Although serious statutory questions might be presented if a state Medicaid plan excluded necessary medical treatment from its coverage, it is hardly inconsistent with the objectives of the Act for a State to refuse to fund *unnecessary*—though perhaps desirable—medical services. . . .

Our interpretation of the statute is reinforced by two other relevant considerations. First, when Congress passed Title XIX in 1965, nontherapeutic abortions were unlawful in most States. . . . In view of the then-prevailing state law, the contention that Congress intended to require—rather than permit—participating States to fund nontherapeutic abortions requires far more convincing proof than respondents have offered. Second, the Department of Health, Education, and Welfare, the agency charged with the administration of this complicated statute, . . . takes the position that Title XIX allows—but does not mandate—funding for such abortions. "[W]e must be mindful that 'the construction of a statute by those charged with its execution should be followed unless there are compelling indications that it is wrong. . . . '" *New York Dept. of Soc. Services* v. *Dublino,* 413 U. S. 405, 421 (1973), quoting *Red Lion Broadcasting Co.* v. *FCC,* 395 U. S. 367, 381 (1969). Here, such indications are completely absent.

We therefore hold that Pennsylvania's refusal to extend Medicaid coverage to nontherapeutic abortions is not inconsistent with Title XIX. . . . We make clear, however, that the federal statute leaves a State free to provide such coverage if it so desires. . . .

MR. JUSTICE BRENNAN, with whom MR. JUSTICE MARSHALL and MR. JUSTICE BLACKMUN join, dissenting.

The Court holds that the "necessary medical services" which Pennsylvania must fund for individuals eligible for Medicaid do not include services connected with elective abortions. I dissent.

Though the question presented by this case is one of statutory interpretation, a difficult constitutional question would be raised where Title XIX of the Social Security Act, as amended, 42 U. S. C. § 1396 *et seq.* (1970 ed. and Supp. V), is read not to require funding of elective abortions. *Maher* v. *Roe, post,* p. 464; *Doe* v. *Bolton,* 410 U. S. 179 (1973); *Roe* v. *Wade,* 410 U. S. 113 (1973). Since the Court should "first ascertain whether a construction of the statute is fairly possible by which the [constitutional] question may be avoided," *Ashwander* v. *TVA,* 297 U. S. 288, 341, 348 (1936) (Brandeis, J., concurring); see *Westby* v. *Doe*, 420 U. S. 968 (1975), Title XIX, in my view, read fairly in light of the principle of avoidance of unnecessary constitutional decisions, requires agreement with the Court of Appeals that the legislative history of Title XIX and our abortion cases compel the conclusion that elective abortions constitute medically necessary treatment for the condition of pregnancy. I would therefore find that Title XIX requires that Pennsylvania pay the costs of elective abortions for women who are eligible participants in the Medicaid program.

Pregnancy is unquestionably a condition requiring medical services. See *Roe* v. *Norton*, 380 F. Supp. 726, 729 (Conn. 1974); *Klein* v. *Nassau County Medical Center*, 347 F. Supp. 496, 500 (EDNY 1972), vacated for further consideration (in light of *Roe* v. *Wade* and *Doe* v. *Bolton*), 412 U. S. 925 (1973). Treatment for the condition may involve medical procedures for its termination, or medical procedures to bring the pregnancy to term, resulting in a live birth. "[A]bortion and childbirth, when stripped of the sensitive moral arguments surrounding the abortion controversy, are simply two alternative medical methods of dealing with pregnancy. . . . " *Roe* v. *Norton*, 408 F. Supp. 660, 663 n. 3 (Conn. 175). The Medicaid statutes leave the decision as to choice among pregnancy procedures exclusively with the doctor and his patient, and make no provision whatever for intervention by the State in that decision. Section 1396a (a) (19) expressly imposes the obligation upon participating States to incorporate safeguards in their programs that assure medical "care and services will be provided, in a manner consistent with . . . the best interests of the recipients." And, significantly, the Senate Finance Committee Report on the Medicaid bill expressly stated that the "physician is to be the key figure in determining utilization of health services." S. Rep. No. 404, 89th Cong., 1st Sess., 46 (1965). Thus the very heart of the congressional scheme is that the physician and patient should have complete freedom to choose those medical procedures for a given condition which are best suited to the needs of the patient. . . .

If Pennsylvania is not obligated to fund medical services rendered in performing elective abortions because they are not "necessary" within the meaning of 42 U. S. C. § 1396 (1970 ed., Supp. V), it must follow that Pennsylvania also would not violate the statute if it refused to fund medical services for "therapeutic" abortions or live births. For if the availability of therapeutic abortions and live births makes elective abortions "unnecessary," the converse must also be true. This highlights the violence done the congressional mandate by today's decision. If the State must pay the costs of therapeutic abortions and of live birth as constituting medically necessary responses to the condition of pregnancy, it must, under the command of § 1396, also pay the costs of elective abortions; the procedures in each case constitute necessary medical treatment for the condition of pregnancy.

The 1972 family-planning amendment to the Act, 42 U. S. C. § 1396d (a) (4) (c) (1970 ed., Supp. V), buttresses my conclusion that the Court's construction frustrates the objectives of the Medicaid program. Section 1396 (2) states that an explicit purpose of Medicaid is to assist eligible indigent recipients to "attain or retain capability for independence or self-care." The 1972 amendment furthered this objective by assisting those who "desire to control family size in order to enhance their capacity and ability to seek employment and better meet family needs." S. Rep. No. 92–1230, p. 297 (1972). Though far less than an ideal family-planning mechanism, elective abortions are one method for limiting family size and avoiding the financial and emotional problems that are the daily lot of the impoverished. See Special Subcommittee on Human Resources of the Senate Committee on Labor and Public Welfare, 92d Cong., 1st Sess., Report of the Secretary of Health, Education, and Welfare Submitting Five-Year Plan for Family Planning Services and Population Research Programs 319 (Comm. Print 1971).

MR. JUSTICE BLACKMUN, with whom MR. JUSTICE BRENNAN and MR. JUSTICE MARSHALL join, dissenting.*

The Court today, by its decisions in these cases, allows the States, and such municipalities as choose to do so, to accomplish indirectly what the Court in Roe v. Wade, 410 U. S. 113 (1973), and Doe v. Bolton, 410 U. S. 179 (1973)—by a substantial majority and with some emphasis, I had thought—said they could not do directly. The Court concedes the existence of a constitutional right but denies the realization and enjoyment of that right on the ground that existence and realization are separate and distinct. For the individual woman concerned, indigent and financially helpless, as the Court's opinions in the three cases concede her to be, the result is punitive and tragic. Implicit in the Court's holdings is the condescension that she may go elsewhere for her abortion. I find that disingenuous and alarming, almost reminiscent of: "Let them eat cake."

The result the Court reaches is particularly distressing in Poelker v. Doe, where a presumed majority, in electing as mayor one whom the record shows campaigned on the issue of closing public hospitals to nontherapeutic abortions, punitively impresses upon a needy minority its own concepts of the socially desirable, the publicly acceptable, and the morally sound, with a touch of the devil-take-the-hindmost. This is not the kind of thing for which our Constitution stands.

―――――――――
*[This opinion applies also to No. 75–1440, *Maher, Commissioner of Social Services of Connecticut* v. *Roe et al.*, post, p. 464, and No. 75–442, *Poelker, Mayor of St. Louis, et al.* v. *Doe*, post, p. 519.]

The Court's financial argument, of course, is specious. To be sure, welfare funds are limited and welfare must be spread perhaps as best meets the community's concept of its needs. But the cost of a nontherapeutic abortion is far less than the cost of maternity care and delivery, and holds no comparison whatsoever with the welfare costs that will burden the State for the new indigents and their support in the long, long years ahead.

Neither is it an acceptable answer, as the Court well knows, to say that the Congress and the States are free to authorize the use of funds for nontherapeutic abortions. Why should any politician incur the demonstrated wrath and noise of the abortion opponents when mere silence and nonactivity accomplish the results the opponents want?

There is another world "out there," the existence of which the Court, I suspect, either chooses to ignore or fears to recognize. And so the cancer of poverty will continue to grow. This is a sad day for those who regard the Constitution as a force that would serve justice to all evenhandedly and, in so doing, would better the lot of the poorest among us.

MAHER, COMMISSIONER OF SOCIAL SERVICES OF CONNECTICUT v. ROE ET AL.

APPEAL FROM THE UNITED STATES DISTRICT COURT FOR THE
DISTRICT OF CONNECTICUT

No. 75–1140. Argued January 11, 1977—Decided June 20, 1977

POWELL, J., delivered the opinion of the Court, in which BURGER, C. J., and STEWART, WHITE, REHNQUIST, and STEVENS, JJ., joined. BURGER, C. J., filed a concurring statement. BRENNAN, J., filed a dissenting opinion, in which MARSHALL and BLACKMUN, JJ., joined. MARSHALL, J., filed a dissenting opinion. BLACKMUN, J., filed a dissenting opinion, in which BRENNAN and MARSHALL, JJ., joined.

I

A regulation of the Connecticut Welfare Department limits state Medicaid benefits for first trimester abortions[1] to those that are "medically necessary," a term defined to include psychiatric necessity. Connecticut Welfare Department, Public Assistance Program Manual, Vol. 3, c. III, § 275 (1975).[2] Connecticut enforces this limitation through a system of prior authorization from its Department of Social Services. In order to obtain authorization for a first trimester abortion, the hospital or clinic where the

---

1. The procedures governing abortions beyond the first trimester are not challenged here.

2. Section 275 provides in relevant part:

"The Department makes payment for abortion services under the Medical Assistance (Title XIX) Program when the following conditions are met:

"1. In the opinion of the attending physician the abortion is medically necessary. The term 'Medically Necessary' includes psychiatric necessity.

"2. The abortion is to be performed in an accredited hospital or licensed clinic when the patient is in the first trimester of pregnancy. . . .

"3. The written request for the abortion is submitted by the patient, and in the case of a minor, from the parent or guardian.

. . . . .

"4. Prior authorization for the abortion is secured from the Chief of Medical Services, Division of Health Services, Department of Social Services."

See n. 4, *infra*.

abortion is to be performed must submit, among other things, a certificate from the patient's attending physician stating that the abortion is medically necessary.

This attack on the validity of the Connecticut regulation was brought against appellant Maher, the Commissioner of Social Services, by appellees Poe and Roe, two indigent women who were unable to obtain a physician's certificate of medical necessity.[3] In a complaint filed in the United States District Court for the District of Connecticut, they challenged the regulation both as inconsistent with the requirements of Title XIX of the Social Security Act, as added, 79 Stat. 343, as amended, 42 U. S. C. § 1396 *et seq.* (1970 ed. Supp. V), and as violative of their constitutional rights, including the Fourteenth Amendment's guarantees of due process and equal protection. . . .

II

The Constitution imposes no obligation on the States to pay the pregnancy-related medical expenses of indigent women, or indeed to pay any of the medical expenses of indigents. . . . But when a State decides to alleviate some of the hardships of poverty by providing medical care, the manner in which it dispenses benefits is subject to constitutional limitations. Appellees' claim is that Connecticut must accord equal treatment to both abortion and childbirth, and may not evidence a policy preference by funding only the medical expenses incident to childbirth. This challenge to the classifications established by the Connecticut regulation presents a question arising under the Equal Protection Clause of the Fourteenth Amendment. The basic framework of analysis of such a claim is well settled:

"We must decide, first, whether [state legislation] operates to the disadvantage of some suspect class or impinges upon a fundamental right explicitly or implicitly protected by the Constitution, thereby requiring

3. At the time this action was filed, Mary Poe, a 16-year-old high school junior, had already obtained an abortion at a Connecticut hospital. Apparently because of Poe's inability to obtain a certificate of medical necessity, the hospital was denied reimbursement by the Department of Social Services. As a result, Poe was being pressed to pay the hospital bill of $244. Susan Roe, an unwed mother of three children, was unable to obtain an abortion because of her physician's refusal to certify that the procedure was medically necessary. By consent, a temporary restraining order was entered by the District Court enjoining the Connecticut officials from refusing to pay for Roe's abortion. After the remand from the Court of Appeals, the District Court issued temporary restraining orders covering three additional women. *Roe* v. *Norton,* 408 F. Supp. 660, 663 (1975).

strict judicial scrutiny. . . . If not, the [legislative] scheme must still be examined to determine whether it rationally furthers some legitimate, articulated state purpose and therefore does not constitute an invidious discrimination. . . . " *San Antonio School Dist.* v. *Rodriguez,* 411 U. S. 1, 17 (1973).

Accord, *Massachusetts Bd. of Retirement* v. *Murgia,* 427 U. S. 307, 312, 314 (1976). Applying this analysis here, we think the District Court erred in holding that the Connecticut regulation violated the Equal Protection Clause of the Fourteenth Amendment.

A

This case involves no discrimination against a suspect class. An indigent woman desiring an abortion does not come within the limited category of disadvantaged classes so recognized by our cases. Nor does the fact that the impact of the regulation falls upon those who cannot pay lead to a different conclusion. In a sense, every denial of welfare to an indigent creates a wealth classification as compared to nonindigents who are able to pay for the desired goods or services. But this Court has never held that financial need alone identifies a suspect class for purposes of equal protection analysis. See *Rodriguez, supra,* at 29; *Dandridge* v. *Williams,* 397 U. S. 471 (1970).[6] Accordingly, the central question in this case is whether the regulation "impinges upon a fundamental right explicitly or implicitly protected by the Constitution." The District Court read our decisions in *Roe* v. *Wade,* 410 U. S. 113 (1973), and the subsequent cases applying it, as establishing a fundamental right to abortion and therefore concluded that nothing less than a compelling state interest would justify Connecticut's different treatment of abortion and childbirth. We think the District Court misconceived the nature and scope of the fundamental right recognized in *Roe.* . . .

B

These cases recognize a constitutionally protected interest "in making certain kinds of important decisions" free from governmental compulsion.

6. In cases such as *Griffin* v. *Illinois,* 351 U. S. 12 (1956) and *Douglas* v. *California,* 372 U. S. 353 (1963), the Court held that the Equal Protection Clause requires States that allow appellate review of criminal convictions to provide indigent defendants with trial transcripts and appellate counsel. These cases are grounded in the criminal justice system, a governmental monopoly in which participation is compelled. Cf. n. 5, *supra.* Our subsequent decisions have made it clear that the principles underlying *Griffin* and *Douglas* do not extend to legislative classifications generally.

Whalen v. *Roe*, 429 U. S. 589, 599–600, and nn. 24 and 26 (1977). As *Whalen* makes clear, the right in *Roe* v. *Wade* can be understood only by considering both the woman's interest and the nature of the State's interference with it. *Roe* did not declare an unqualified "constitutional right to an abortion," as the District Court seemed to think. Rather, the right protects the woman from unduly burdensome interference with her freedom to decide whether to terminate her pregnancy. It implies no limitation on the authority of a State to make a value judgment favoring childbirth over abortion, and to implement that judgment by the allocation of public funds.

The Connecticut regulation before us is different in kind from the laws invalidated in our previous abortion decisions. The Connecticut regulation places no obstacles—absolute or otherwise—in the pregnant woman's path to an abortion. An indigent woman who desires an abortion suffers no disadvantage as a consequence of Connecticut's decision to fund childbirth; she continues as before to be dependent on private sources for the service she desires. The State may have made childbirth a more attractive alternative, thereby influencing the woman's decision, but it has imposed no restriction on access to abortions that was not already there. The indigency that may make it difficult—and in some cases, perhaps, impossible—for some women to have abortions is neither created nor in any way affected by the Connecticut regulation. We conclude that the Connecticut regulation does not impinge upon the fundamental right recognized in *Roe*. . . .

In conclusion, we emphasize that our decision today does not proscribe government funding of nontherapeutic abortions. It is open to Congress to require provision of Medicaid benefits for such abortions as a condition of state participation in the Medicaid program. Also, under Title XIX as construed in *Beal* v. *Doe*. Connecticut is free—through normal democratic processes—to decide that such benefits should be provided. We hold only that the Constitution does not require a judicially imposed resolution of these difficult issues. . . .

MR. JUSTICE BRENNAN, with whom MR. JUSTICE MARSHALL and MR. JUSTICE BLACKMUN join, dissenting.

The District Court held:

"When Connecticut refuses to fund elective abortions while funding therapeutic abortions and prenatal and postnatal care, it weights the choice of the pregnant mother against choosing to exercise her constitutionally protected right to an elective abortion. . . . Her choice is affected not simply by the absence of payment for the abortion, but by the availability of public funds for childbirth if she chooses not to have the abortion. When the state thus infringes upon a fundamental interest, it must assert a compelling state interest." *Roe* v. *Norton,* 408 F. Supp. 660, 663–664 (1975).

This Court reverses on the ground that "the District Court misconceived the nature and scope of the fundamental right recognized in *Roe* [v. *Wade,* 410 U. S. 113 (1973)]," and therefore that Connecticut was not required to meet the "compelling interest" test to justify its discrimination against elective abortion but only "the less demanding test of rationality that applies in the absence of . . . the impingement of a fundamental right." This holding, the Court insists, "places no obstacles—absolute or otherwise—in the pregnant woman's path to an abortion"; she is still at liberty to finance the abortion from "private sources." True, "the State may [by funding childbirth] have made childbirth a more attractive alternative, thereby influencing the woman's decision, but it has imposed no restriction on access to abortions that was not already there." *Ibid.* True, also, indigency "may make it difficult—and in some cases, perhaps impossible—for some women to have abortions," but that regrettable consequence "is neither created nor in any way affected by the Connecticut regulation." *Ibid.*

But a distressing insensitivity to the plight of impoverished pregnant women is inherent in the Court's analysis. The stark reality for too many, not just "some," indigent pregnant women is that indigency makes access to competent licensed physicians not merely "difficult" but "impossible." As a practical matter, many indigent women will feel they have no choice but to carry their pregnancies to term because the State will pay for the associated medical services, even though they would have chosen to have abortions if the State had also provided funds for that procedure, or indeed if the State had provided funds for neither procedure. This disparity in funding by the State clearly operates to coerce indigent pregnant women to bear children they would not otherwise choose to have, and just as clearly, this coercion can only operate upon the poor, who are uniquely the victims of this form of financial pressure. Mr. Justice Frankfurter's words are apt:

> "To sanction such a ruthless consequence, inevitably resulting from a money hurdle erected by the State, would justify a latter-day Anatole France to add one more item to his ironic comments on the 'majestic equality' of the law. "The law, in its majestic equality, forbids the rich as well as the poor to sleep under bridges, to beg in the streets, and to steal bread'. . . . " *Griffin* v. *Illinois,* 351 U. S. 12, 23 (1956) (concurring opinion).

None can take seriously the Court's assurance that its "conclusion signals no retreat from *Roe* [v. *Wade*] or the cases applying it." . . . That statement must occasion great surprise among the Courts of Appeals and District Courts that, relying upon *Roe* v. *Wade* and *Doe* v. *Bolton,* 410 U. S. 179 (1973), have held that States are constitutionally required to fund elective abortions if they fund pregnancies carried to term. See *Doe* v. *Rose,* 499 F. 2d 1112 (CA10 1974); *Wulff* v. *Singleton,* 508 F. 2d 1211 (CA8 1974), rev'd and remanded on other grounds, 428 U. S. 106 (1976); *Doe* v. *Westby,* 383 F. Supp. 1143 (WDSD 1974), vacated and remanded (in light of *Hagans* v. *Lavine,* 415 U. S. 528 (1974)), 420 U. S. 968, on remand, 402 F. Supp. 140 (1975); *Doe* v. *Wohlgemuth,* 376 F. Supp. 173 (WD Pa. 1974), aff'd on statutory grounds *sub nom. Doe* v. *Beal,* 523 F. 2d 611 (CA3 1975), rev'd and remanded, *ante,* p. 438; *Doe* v. *Rampton,* 366 F. Supp. 189 (Utah 1973); *Klein* v. *Nassau County Medical Center,* 347 F. Supp. 496 (EDNY 1972), vacated and remanded (in light of *Roe* v. *Wade* and *Doe* v. *Bolton,* 412 U. S. 925 (1973)), on remand, 409 F. Supp. 731 (1976). Indeed, it cannot be gainsaid that today's decision seriously erodes the principles that *Roe* and *Doe* announced to guide the determination of what constitutes an unconstitutional infringement of the fundamental right of pregnant women to be free to decide whether to have an abortion.

The Court's premise is that only an equal protection claim is presented here. Claims of interference with enjoyment of fundamental rights have, however, occupied a rather protean position in our constitutional jurisprudence. Whether or not the Court's analysis may reasonably proceed under the Equal Protection Clause, the Court plainly errs in ignoring, as it does, the unanswerable argument of appellees, and the holding of the District Court, that the regulation unconstitutionally impinges upon their claim of privacy derived from the Due Process Clause.

Roe v. *Wade* and cases following it hold that an area of privacy invulnerable to the State's intrusion surrounds the decision of a pregnant woman whether or not to carry her pregnancy to term. The Connecticut scheme clearly impinges upon that area of privacy by bringing financial pressures on indigent women that force them to bear children they would not otherwise have. That is an obvious impairment of the fundamental right established by *Roe* v. *Wade.* Yet the Court concludes that "the Connecticut regulation does not impinge upon [that] fundamental right." . . . This conclusion is based on a perceived distinction, on the one hand, between the imposition of criminal penalties for the procurement of an abortion present in *Roe* v. *Wade* and *Doe* v. *Bolton* and the absolute prohibition present in *Planned Parenthood of Central Missouri* v. *Danforth,* 428 U. S. 52 (1976), and, on the other, the assertedly lesser inhibition imposed by the Connecticut scheme. . . .

The last time our Brother POWELL espoused the concept in an abortion case that "[t]here is a basic difference between direct state interference with a protected activity and state encouragement of an alternative activity consonant with legislative policy," *ante*, at 475, the Court refused to adopt it. *Singleton* v. *Wulff*, 428 U. S. 106, 122 (1976). This was made explicit in Part II of our Brother BLACKMUN's opinion for four of us and is implicit in our Brother STEVENS' essential agreement with the analysis of Part II–B. *Id.*, at 121–122 (concurring in part). Part II–B stated:

"MR. JUSTICE POWELL would so limit *Doe* and the other cases cited, explaining them as cases in which the State 'directly interfered with the abortion decision' and 'directly interdicted the normal functioning of the physician-patient relationship by criminalizing certain procedures,' [428 U. S.,] at 128. There is no support in the language of the cited cases for this distinction. . . . Moreover, a 'direct interference' or 'interdiction' test does not appear to be supported by precedent. . . . For a doctor who cannot afford to work for nothing, and a woman who cannot afford to pay him, the State's refusal to fund an abortion is as effective an 'interdiction' of it as would ever be necessary. Furthermore, since the right . . . is not simply the right to have an abortion, but the right to have abortions nondiscriminatorily funded, the denial of such funding is as complete an 'interdiction' of the exercise of the right as could ever exist." *Id.*, at 118 n. 7.

We have also rejected this approach in other abortion cases. *Doe* v. *Bolton*, the companion to *Roe* v. *Wade*, in addition to striking down the Georgia criminal prohibition against elective abortions, struck down the procedural requirements of certification of hospitals, of approval by a hospital committee, and of concurrence in the abortion decision by two doctors other than the woman's own doctor. None of these requirements operated as an absolute bar to elective abortions in the manner of the criminal prohibitions present in the other aspect of the case or in *Roe*, but this was not sufficient to save them from unconstitutionality. In *Planned Parenthood, supra*, we struck down a requirement for spousal consent to an elective abortion which the Court characterizes today simply as an "absolute obstacle" to a woman's obtaining an abortion. But the obstacle was "absolute" only in the limited sense that a woman who was unable to persuade her spouse to agree to an elective abortion was prevented from obtaining one. Any woman whose husband agreed, or could be persuaded to agree, was free to obtain an abortion, and the State never imposed directly any prohibition of its own. This requirement was qualitatively different from the criminal statutes that the Court today says are comparable, but we nevertheless found it unconstitutional. . . .

Until today, I had not thought the nature of the fundamental right established in *Roe* was open to question, let alone susceptible of the interpretation advanced by the Court. The fact that the Connecticut scheme may not operate as an absolute bar preventing all indigent women from having abortions is not critical. What is critical is that the State has inhibited their fundamental right to make that choice free from state interference. . . .

POELKER, MAYOR OF ST. LOUIS, ET AL. *v.* DOE

CERTIORARI TO THE UNITED STATES COURT OF APPEALS
FOR THE EIGHTH CIRCUIT

No. 75–442. Argued January 11, 1977—Decided June 20, 1977

PER CURIAM.

Respondent Jane Doe, an indigent, sought unsuccessfully to obtain a non-therapeutic abortion at Starkloff Hospital, one of two city-owned public hospitals in St. Louis, Mo. She subsequently brought this class action under 42 U. S. C. § 1983 against the Mayor of St. Louis and the Director of Health and Hospitals, alleging that the refusal by Starkloff Hospital to provide the desired abortion violated her constitutional rights. Although the District Court ruled against Doe following a trial, the Court of Appeals for the Eighth Circuit reversed in an opinion that accepted both her factual and legal arguments. 515 F. 2d 541 (1975). . . .

The Court of Appeals concluded that Doe's inability to obtain an abortion resulted from a combination of a policy directive by the Mayor and a longstanding staffing practice at Starkloff Hospital. The directive, communicated to the Director of Health and Hospitals by the Mayor, prohibited the performance of abortions in the city hospitals except when there was a threat of grave physiological injury or death to the mother. Under the staffing practice, the doctors and medical students at the obstetrics-gynecology clinic at the hospital are drawn from the faculty and students at the St. Louis University School of Medicine, a Jesuit-operated institution opposed to abortion. Relying on our decisions in *Roe* v. *Wade*, 410 U. S. 113 (1973), and *Doe* v. *Bolton*, 410 U. S. 179 (1973), the Court of Appeals held that the city's policy and the hospital's staffing practice denied the "constitutional rights of indigent pregnant women . . . long after those rights had been clearly enunciated" in *Roe* and *Doe*. 515 F. 2d, at 547. The court cast the issue in an equal protection mold, finding that the provision of publicly financed hospital services for childbirth but not for elective abortions constituted invidious discrimination. In support of its equal protection analysis, the court also emphasized the contrast between nonindigent women who can afford to obtain abortions in private hospitals and indigent women who cannot. Particular reliance was placed upon the previous decision in *Wulff* v. *Singleton*, 508 F. 2d 1211 (CA8 1974), reversed on other grounds, 428 U. S. 106 (1976), in which the Court of Appeals had held unconstitutional a state Medicaid statute that provided benefits for women who carried their pregnancies to term but denied them for women who sought elective abortions. The court stated that "[t]here is no practical distinction between that case and this one." 515 F. 2d, at 545.

We agree that the constitutional question presented here is identical in principle with that presented by a State's refusal to provide Medicaid benefits for abortions while providing them for childbirth. This was the issue before us in *Maher* v. *Roe*. For the reasons set forth in our opinion in that case, we find no constitutional violation by the city of St. Louis in electing, as a policy choice, to provide publicly financed hospital services for childbirth without providing corresponding services for nontherapeutic abortions. . . .

MR. JUSTICE BRENNAN, with whom MR. JUSTICE MARSHALL and MR. JUSTICE BLACKMUN join, dissenting.

The Court holds that St. Louis may constitutionally refuse to permit the performance of elective abortions in its city-owned hospitals while providing hospital services to women who carry their pregnancies to term. As stated by the Court of Appeals:

"Stripped of all rhetoric, the city here, through its policy and staffing procedure, is simply telling indigent women, like Doe, that if they choose to carry their pregnancies to term, the city will provide physicians and medical facilities for full maternity care; but if they choose to exercise their constitutionally protected right to determine that they wish to terminate the pregnancy, the city will not provide physicians and facilities for the abortion procedure, even though it is probably safer than going through a full pregnancy and childbirth." 515 F. 2d 541, 544 (1975).

The Court of Appeals held that St. Louis could not in this way "interfer[e] in her decision of whether to bear a child or have an abortion simply because she is indigent and unable to afford private treatment," *ibid.*, because it was constitutionally impermissible that indigent women be " 'subjected to State coercion to bear children which they do not wish to bear [while] no other women similarly situated are so coerced,' " *id.*, at 545.

For the reasons set forth in my dissent in *Maher* v. *Roe*, I would affirm the Court of Appeals. Here the fundamental right of a woman freely to choose to terminate her pregnancy has been infringed by the city of St. Louis through a deliberate policy based on opposition to elective abortions on moral grounds by city officials. While it may still be possible for some indigent women to obtain abortions in clinics or private hospitals, it is clear that the city policy is a significant, and in some cases insurmountable, obstacle to indigent pregnant women who cannot pay for abortions in those private facilities. Nor is the closing of St. Louis' public hospitals an isolated instance with little practical significance. The importance of today's decision is greatly magnified by the fact that during 1975 and the first quarter of 1976 only about 18% of all public hospitals in the country provided abortion services, and in 10 States there were no public hospitals providing such services.[1]

A number of difficulties lie beneath the surface of the Court's holding. Public hospitals that do not permit the performance of elective abortions will frequently have physicians on their staffs who would willingly perform them. This may operate in some communities significantly to reduce the number of physicians who are both willing and able to perform abortions in a hospital setting. It is not a complete answer that many abortions may safely be performed in clinics, for some physicians will not be affiliated with those clinics, and some abortions may pose unacceptable risks if performed outside a hospital. Indeed, such an answer would be ironic, for if the result is to force some abortions to be performed in a clinic that properly should be performed in a hospital, the city policy will have operated to increase rather than reduce health risks associated with abortions; and in *Roe* v. *Wade,* 410 U. S. 113, 163 (1973), the Court permitted regulation by the State solely to *protect* maternal health.

The Court's holding will also pose difficulties in small communities where the public hospital is the only nearby health care facility. If such a public hospital is closed to abortions, any woman—rich or poor—will be seriously inconvenienced; and for some women—particularly poor women—the unavailability of abortions in the public hospital will be an insuperable obstacle. Indeed, a recent survey suggests that the decision in this case will be felt most strongly in rural areas, where the public hospital will in all likelihood be closed to elective abortions, and where there will not be sufficient demand to support a separate abortion clinic. . . .

1. Sullivan, Tietze, & Dryfoos, Legal Abortion in the United States, 1975–1976, 9 Family Planning Perspectives 116, 121, 128 (1977).

COLAUTTI, SECRETARY OF WELFARE OF PENNSYLVANIA, ET AL. *v.* FRANKLIN ET AL.

APPEAL FROM THE UNITED STATES DISTRICT COURT FOR THE EASTERN
DISTRICT OF PENNSYLVANIA

No. 77–891. Argued October 3, 1978—Decided January 9, 1979

BLACKMUN, J., delivered the opinion of the Court, in which BRENNAN, STEWART, MARSHALL, POWELL, and STEVENS, JJ., joined. WHITE, J., filed a dissenting opinion, in which BURGER, C. J., and REHNQUIST, J., joined.

MR. JUSTICE BLACKMUN delivered the opinion of the Court.

At issue here is the constitutionality of subsection (a) of § 5[1] of the Pennsylvania Abortion Control Act, 1974 Pa. Laws, Act No. 209, Pa. Stat. Ann., Tit. 35, § 6605 (a) (Purdon 1977). This statute subjects a physician who performs an abortion to potential criminal liability if he fails to utilize a statutorily prescribed technique when the fetus "is viable" or when there is "sufficient reason to believe that the fetus may be viable." . . .

1. Section 5 reads in pertinent part:

"(a) Every person who performs or induces an abortion shall prior thereto have made a determination based on his experience, judgment or professional competence that the fetus is not viable, and if the determination is that the fetus is viable or if there is sufficient reason to believe that the fetus may be viable, shall exercise that degree of professional skill, care and diligence to preserve the life and health of the fetus which such person would be required to exercise in order to preserve the life and health of any fetus intended to be born and not aborted and the abortion technique employed shall be that which would provide the best opportunity for the fetus to be aborted alive so long as a different technique would not be necessary in order to preserve the life or health of the mother.

.   .   .   .   .   .

"(d) Any person who fails to make the determination provided for in subsection (a) of this section, or who fails to exercise the degree of professional skill, care and diligence or to provide the abortion technique as provided for in subsection (a) of this section . . . shall be subject to such civil or criminal liability as would pertain to him had the fetus been a child who was intended to be born and not aborted."

III

The attack mounted by the plaintiffs-appellees upon § 5 (a) centers on both the viability-determination requirement and the stated standard of care. The former provision, requiring the physician to observe the care standard when he determines that the fetus is viable, or when "there is sufficient reason to believe that the fetus may be viable," is asserted to be unconstitutionally vague because it fails to inform the physician when his duty to the fetus arises, and because it does not make the physician's good-faith determination of viability conclusive. This provision is also said to be unconstitutionally overbroad, because it carves out a new time period prior to the stage of viability, and could have a restrictive effect on a couple who wants to abort a fetus determined by genetic testing to be defective.[8] The standard of care, and in particular the requirement that the physician employ the abortion technique "which would provide the best opportunity for the fetus to be aborted alive so long as a different technique would not be necessary in order to preserve the life or health of the mother," is said to be void for vagueness and to be unconstitutionally restrictive in failing to afford the physician sufficient professional discretion in determining which abortion technique is appropriate. . . .

IV

We agree with plaintiffs-appellees that the viability-determination requirement of § 5 (a) is ambiguous, and that its uncertainty is aggravated by the absence of a scienter requirement with respect to the finding of viability. Because we conclude that this portion of the statute is void for vagueness, we find it unnecessary to consider appellees' alternative arguments based on the alleged overbreadth of § 5 (a).

A

It is settled that, as a matter of due process, a criminal statute that "fails to give a person of ordinary intelligence fair notice that his contemplated conduct is forbidden by the statute," *United States* v. *Harriss,* 347 U. S. 612, 617 (1954), or is so indefinite that "it encourages arbitrary and erratic arrests and convictions," *Papachristou* v. *Jacksonville,* 405 U. S. 156, 162 (1972), is

---

8. The plaintiffs-appellees introduced evidence that modern medical technology makes it possible to detect whether a fetus is afflicted with such disorders as Tay-Sachs disease and Down's syndrome (mongolism). Such testing, however, often cannot be completed until after 18–20 weeks' gestation. App. 53a–56a (testimony of Hope Punnett, Ph. D.).

void for vagueness. See generally *Grayned* v. *City of Rockford,* 408 U. S. 104, 108–109 (1972). This appears to be especially true where the uncertainty induced by the statute threatens to inhibit the exercise of constitutionally protected rights. *Id.,* at 109; *Smith* v. *Goguen,* 415 U. S. 566, 573 (1974); *Keyishian* v. *Board of Regents,* 385 U. S. 589, 603–604 (1967).

Section 5 (a) requires every person who performs or induces an abortion to make a determination, "based on his experience, judgment or professional competence," that the fetus is not viable. If such person determines that the fetus is viable, or if "there is sufficient reason to believe that the fetus may be viable," then he must adhere to the prescribed standard of care. This requirement contains a double ambiguity. First, it is unclear whether the statute imports a purely subjective standard, or whether it imposes a mixed subjective and objective standard. Second, it is uncertain whether the phrase "may be viable" simply refers to viability, as that term has been defined in *Roe* and in *Planned Parenthood,* or whether it refers to an undefined penumbral or "gray" area prior to the stage of viability.

The statute requires the physician to conform to the prescribed standard of care if one of two conditions is satisfied: if he determines that the fetus "is viable," or "if there is sufficient reason to believe that the fetus may be viable." Apparently, the determination of whether the fetus "is viable" is to be based on the attending physician's "experience, judgment or professional competence," a subjective point of reference. But it is unclear whether the same phrase applies to the second triggering condition, that is, to "sufficient reason to believe that the fetus may be viable." In other words, it is ambiguous whether there must be "sufficient reason" from the perspective of the judgment, skill, and training of the attending physician, or "sufficient reason" from the perspective of a cross section of the medical community or a panel of experts. The latter, obviously, portends not an inconsequential hazard for the typical private practitioner who may not have the skills and technology that are readily available at a teaching hospital or large medical center.

The intended distinction between the phrases "is viable" and "may be viable" is even more elusive. Appellants argue that no difference is intended, and that the use of the "may be viable" words "simply incorporates the acknowledged medical fact that a fetus is 'viable' if it has that statistical 'chance' of survival recognized by the medical community." Brief for Appellants 28. The statute, however, does not support the contention that "may be viable" is synonymous with, or merely intended to explicate the meaning of, "viable." . . .

Since we must reject appellants' theory that "may be viable" means "viable," a second serious ambiguity appears in the statute. On the one hand, as appellees urge and as the District Court found, see 401 F. Supp., at 572, it may be that "may be viable" carves out a new time period during pregnancy when there is a remote possibility of fetal survival outside the womb, but the fetus has not yet attained the reasonable likelihood of survival that physicians associate with viability. On the other hand, although appellants do not argue this, it may be that "may be viable" refers to viability as physicians understand it, and "viable" refers to some undetermined stage later in pregnancy. We need not resolve this question. The crucial point is that "viable" and "may be viable" apparently refer to distinct conditions, and that one of these conditions differs in some indeterminate way from the definition of viability as set forth in *Roe* and in *Planned Parenthood.* . . .

B

The vagueness of the viability-determination requirement of § 5 (a) is compounded by the fact that the Act subjects the physician to potential criminal liability without regard to fault. Under § 5 (d), see n. 1, *supra,* a physician who fails to abide by the standard of care when there is sufficient reason to believe that the fetus "may be viable" is subject "to such civil or criminal liability as would pertain to him had the fetus been a child who was intended to be born and not aborted." To be sure, the Pennsylvania law of criminal homicide, made applicable to the physician by § 5 (d), conditions guilt upon a finding of scienter. See Pa. Stat. Ann., Tit. 18, §§ 2501–2504 (Purdon 1973 and Supp. 1978). The required mental state, however, is that of "intentionally, knowingly, recklessly or negligently caus[ing] the death of another human being." § 2501 (1973). Thus, the Pennsylvania law of criminal homicide requires scienter with respect to whether the physician's actions will result in the death of the fetus. But neither the Pennsylvania law of criminal homicide, nor the Abortion Control Act, requires that the physician be culpable in failing to find sufficient reason to believe that the fetus may be viable. . . .

The perils of strict criminal liability are particularly acute here because of the uncertainty of the viability determination itself. As the record in this case indicates, a physician determines whether or not a fetus is viable after considering a number of variables: the gestational age of the fetus, derived from the reported menstrual history of the woman; fetal weight, based on an inexact estimate of the size and condition of the uterus; the woman's general health and nutrition; the quality of the available medical facilities; and other factors.[14] Because of the number and the imprecision of these variables, the probability of any particular fetus' obtaining meaningful life outside the

14. See App. 5a–6a, 10a, 17a (testimony of Louis Gerstley III, M. D.); *id.,* at 77a–78a, 81a (testimony of Thomas W. Hilgers, M. D.); *id.,* at 93a–101a, 109a, 112a (testimony of William J. Keenan, M. D.).

womb can be determined only with difficulty. Moreover, the record indicates that even if agreement may be reached on the probability of survival, different physicians equate viability with different probabilities of survival, and some physicians refuse to equate viability with any numerical probability at all.[15] In the face of these uncertainties, it is not unlikely that experts will disagree over whether a particular fetus in the second trimester has advanced to the stage of viability. The prospect of such disagreement, in conjunction with a statute imposing strict civil and criminal liability for an erroneous determination of viability, could have a profound chilling effect on the willingness of physicians to perform abortions near the point of viability in the manner indicated by their best medical judgment.

Because we hold that the viability-determination provision of § 5 (a) is void on its face, we need not now decide whether, under a properly drafted statute, a finding of bad faith or some other type of scienter would be required before a physician could be held criminally responsible for an erroneous determination of viability. We reaffirm, however, that "the determination of whether a particular fetus is viable is, and must be, a matter for the judgment of the responsible attending physician." *Planned Parenthood of Central Missouri* v. *Danforth*, 428 U. S., at 64. State regulation that impinges upon this determination, if it is to be constitutional, must allow the attending physician "the room he needs to make his best medical judgment." *Doe* v. *Bolton*, 410 U. S., at 192. . . .

MR. JUSTICE WHITE, with whom THE CHIEF JUSTICE and MR. JUSTICE REHNQUIST join, dissenting.

Because the Court now withdraws from the States a substantial measure of the power to protect fetal life that was reserved to them in *Roe* v. *Wade*, 410 U. S. 113 (1973), and reaffirmed in *Planned Parenthood of Central Missouri* v. *Danforth*, 428 U. S. 52 (1976), I file this dissent.

I

In *Roe* v. *Wade*, the Court defined the term "viability" to signify the stage at which a fetus is "potentially able to live outside the mother's womb, albeit with artificial aid." This is the point at which the State's interest in protect-

---

15. See *id.*, at 8a (testimony of Dr. Gerstley) (viability means 5% chance of survival, "certainly at least two to three percent"); *id.*, at 104a (testimony of Dr. Keenan) (10% chance of survival would be viable); *id.*, at 144a (deposition of John Franklin, M. D.) (viability means "ten percent or better" probability of survival); *id.*, at 132a (testimony of Arturo Hervada, M. D.) (it is misleading to be obsessed with a particular percentage figure).

ing fetal life becomes sufficiently strong to permit it to "go so far as to proscribe abortion during that period, except when it is necessary to preserve the life or health of the mother." 410 U. S., at 163–164.

The Court obviously crafted its definition of viability with some care, and it chose to define that term not as that stage of development at which the fetus actually *is* able or actually *has* the ability to survive outside the mother's womb, with or without artificial aid, but as that point at which the fetus is *potentially* able to survive. In the ordinary usage of these words, being *able* and being *potentially able* do not mean the same thing. Potential ability is not actual ability. It is ability "[e]xisting in possibility, not in actuality." Webster's New International Dictionary (2d ed. 1958). The Court's definition of viability in *Roe* v. *Wade* reaches an earlier point in the development of the fetus than that stage at which a doctor could say with assurance that the fetus *would* survive outside the womb.

It was against this background that the Pennsylvania statute at issue here was adopted and the District Court's judgment was entered. Insofar as *Roe* v. *Wade* was concerned, Pennsylvania could have defined viability in the language of that case—"potentially able to live outside the mother's womb"—and could have forbidden all abortions after this stage of any pregnancy. The Pennsylvania Act, however, did not go so far. It forbade entirely only those abortions where the fetus had attained viability as defined in § 2 of the Act, that is, where the fetus had "the *capability* . . . to live outside the mother's womb albeit with artificial aid." Pa. Stat. Ann., Tit. 35, § 6602 (Purdon 1977) (emphasis added). But the State, understanding that it also had the power under *Roe* v. *Wade* to regulate where the fetus was only "potentially able" to exist outside the womb, also sought to regulate, but not forbid, abortions where there was sufficient reason to believe that the fetus "may be viable"; this language was reasonably believed by the State to be equivalent to what the Court meant in 1973 by the term "potentially able to live outside the mother's womb." Under § 5 (a), abortionists must not only determine whether the fetus is viable but also whether there is sufficient reason to believe that the fetus may be viable. If either condition exists, the method of abortion is regulated and a standard of care imposed. Under § 5 (d), breach of these regulations exposes the abortionist to the civil and criminal penalties that would be applicable if a live birth rather than an abortion had been intended. . . .

Affirmance of the District Court's judgment is untenable. The District Court originally thought § 5 (a) was vague because the term "viability" was itself vague. The Court scotched that notion in *Danforth*, and the District Court then sustained the Pennsylvania definition of viability. In doing so, it necessarily nullified the major reason for its prior invalidation of § 5 (a), which was that it incorporated the supposedly vague standard of § 2. But the District Court had also said that the "may be viable" standard was invalid as an impermissible effort to regulate a period of "potential" viability. This was the sole remaining articulated ground for invalidating § 5 (a). But this is the very ground that was urged and rejected in *Danforth*, where this Court sustained the Missouri provision defining viability as the stage at which the fetus "may" have the ability to survive outside the womb and reaffirmed the flexible concept of viability announced in *Roe*.

In affirming the District Court, the Court does not in so many words agree with the District Court but argues that it is too difficult to know whether the Pennsylvania Act simply intended, as the State urges, to go no further than *Roe* permitted in protecting a fetus that is potentially able to survive or whether it intended to carve out a protected period prior to viability as defined in *Roe*. The District Court, although otherwise seriously in error, had no such trouble with the Act. It understood the "may be viable" provision as an attempt to protect a period of potential life, precisely the kind of interest that *Roe* protected but which the District Court erroneously thought the State was not entitled to protect. . . . *Danforth*, as I have said, reaffirmed *Roe* in this respect. Only those with unalterable determination to invalidate the Pennsylvania Act can draw any measurable difference insofar as vagueness is concerned between "viability" defined as the ability to survive and "viability" defined as that stage at which the fetus may have the ability to survive. It seems to me that, in affirming, the Court is tacitly disowning the "may be" standard of the Missouri law as well as the "potential ability" component of viability as that concept was described in *Roe*. This is a further constitutionally unwarranted intrusion upon the police powers of the States.

II

Apparently uneasy with its work, the Court has searched for and seized upon two additional reasons to support affirmance, neither of which was relied upon by the District Court. The Court first notes that under § 5 (d), failure to make the determinations required by § 5 (a), or otherwise to comply with its provisions, subjects the abortionist to criminal prosecution under those laws that "would pertain to him had the fetus been a child who was intended to be born and not aborted." Although concededly the Pennsylvania law of criminal homicide conditions guilt upon a finding that the defendant intentionally, knowingly, recklessly, or negligently caused the death of another human being, the Court nevertheless goes on to declare that the abortionist could be successfully prosecuted for criminal homicide without any such fault or omission in determining whether or not the fetus is viable or may be viable. This alleged lack of a scienter requirement, the Court says, fortifies its holding that § 5 (a) is void for vagueness.

This seems to me an incredible construction of the Pennsylvania statutes.

The District Court suggested nothing of the sort, and appellees focus entirely on § 5 (a), ignoring the homicide statutes. The latter not only define the specified degrees of scienter that are required for the various homicides, but also provide that ignorance or mistake as to a matter of fact, for which there is a reasonable explanation, is a defense to a homicide charge if it negatives the mental state necessary for conviction. Pa. Stat. Ann., Tit. 18, § 304 (Purdon 1973). Given this background, I do not see how it can be seriously argued that a doctor who makes a good-faith mistake about whether a fetus is or is not viable could be successfully prosecuted for criminal homicide. This is the State's submission in this Court; the court below did not address the matter; and at the very least this is something the Court should not decide without hearing from the Pennsylvania courts. . . .

BELLOTTI, ATTORNEY GENERAL OF MASSACHUSETTS, ET AL. *v.* BAIRD ET AL.

APPEAL FROM THE UNITED STATES DISTRICT COURT FOR
THE DISTRICT OF MASSACHUSETTS

No. 78–329. Argued February 27, 1979—Decided July 2, 1979

[A Massachusetts statute requires parental consent before an abortion can be performed on an unmarried woman under the age of 18. If one or both parents refuse such consent, however, the abortion may be obtained by order of a judge of the superior court "for good cause shown." In appellees' class action challenging the constitutionality of the statute, a three-judge District Court held it unconstitutional. Subsequently, this Court vacated the District Court's judgment, *Bellotti v. Baird*, 428 U. S. 132, holding that the District Court should have abstained and certified to the Massachusetts Supreme Judicial Court appropriate questions concerning the meaning of the statute. On remand, the District Court certified several questions to the Supreme Judicial Court. Among the questions certified was whether the statute permits any minors—mature or immature—to obtain judicial consent to an abortion without any parental consultation whatsoever. The Supreme Judicial Court answered that, in general, it does not; that consent must be obtained for every nonemergency abortion unless no parent is available; and that an available parent must be given notice of any judicial proceedings brought by a minor to obtain consent for an abortion. Another question certified was whether, if the superior court finds that the minor is capable of making, and has, in fact, made and adhered to, an informed and reasonable decision to have an abortion, the court may refuse its consent on a finding that a parent's, or its own, contrary decision is a better one. The Supreme Judicial Court answered in the affirmative. Following the Supreme Judicial Court's judgment, the District Court again declared the statute unconstitutional and enjoined its enforcement, and the United States Supreme Court took it on appeal.]

POWELL, J., announced the judgment of the Court and delivered an opinion, in which BURGER, C. J., and STEWART and REHNQUIST, JJ., joined. REHNQUIST, J., filed a concurring opinion. STEVENS, J., filed an opinion concurring in the judgment, in which BRENNAN, MARSHALL, and BLACKMUN, JJ., joined. WHITE, J., filed a dissenting opinion.

121

MR. JUSTICE POWELL announced the judgment of the Court and delivered an opinion, in which THE CHIEF JUSTICE, MR. JUSTICE STEWART, and MR. JUSTICE REHNQUIST joined.

II

. . . A child, merely on account of his minority, is not beyond the protection of the Constitution. As the Court said in *In re Gault,* 387 U. S. 1, 13 (1967), "whatever may be their precise impact, neither the Fourteenth Amendment nor the Bill of Rights is for adults alone." . . . This observation, of course, is but the beginning of the analysis. The Court long has recognized that the status of minors under the law is unique in many respects. As Mr. Justice Frankfurter aptly put it: "Children have a very special place in life which law should reflect. Legal theories and their phrasing in other cases readily lead to fallacious reasoning if uncritically transferred to determination of a State's duty towards children." *May* v. *Anderson,* 345 U. S. 528, 536 (1953) (concurring opinion). The unique role in our society of the family, the institution by which "we inculcate and pass down many of our most cherished values, moral and cultural," *Moore* v. *East Cleveland,* 431 U. S. 494, 503–504 (1977) (plurality opinion), requires that constitutional principles be applied with sensitivity and flexibility to the special needs of parents and children. We have recognized three reasons justifying the conclusion that the constitutional rights of children cannot be equated with those of adults: the peculiar vulnerability of children; their inability to make critical decisions in an informed, mature manner; and the importance of the parental role in child rearing.

A

The Court's concern for the vulnerability of children is demonstrated in its decisions dealing with minors' claims to constitutional protection against deprivations of liberty or property interests by the State. With respect to many of these claims, we have concluded that the child's right is virtually coextensive with that of an adult. For example, the Court has held that the Fourteenth Amendment's guarantee against the deprivation of liberty without due process of law is applicable to children in juvenile delinquency proceedings. *In re Gault, supra.* In particular, minors involved in such proceedings are entitled to adequate notice, the assistance of counsel, and the opportunity to confront their accusers. They can be found guilty only upon proof beyond a reasonable doubt, and they may assert the privilege against compulsory self-incrimination. *In re Winship,* 397 U. S. 358 (1970); *In re Gault, supra.* See also *Ingraham* v. *Wright,* 430 U. S. 651, 674 (1977) (corporal punishment of schoolchildren implicates constitutionally protected liberty interest); cf. *Breed* v. *Jones*, 421 U. S. 519 (1975) (Double Jeopardy Clause prohibits prosecuting juvenile as an adult after an adjudicatory finding in juvenile court that he had violated a criminal statute). Similarly, in *Goss* v. *Lopez*, 419 U. S. 565 (1975), the Court held that children may not be deprived of certain property interests without due process.

These rulings have not been made on the uncritical assumption that the constitutional rights of children are indistinguishable from those of adults. Indeed, our acceptance of juvenile courts distinct from the adult criminal justice system assumes that juvenile offenders constitutionally may be treated differently from adults. In order to preserve this separate avenue for dealing with minors, the Court has said that hearings in juvenile delinquency cases need not necessarily "'conform with all of the requirements of a criminal trial or even of the usual administrative hearing.'" *In re Gault*, *supra*, at 30, quoting *Kent* v. *United States*, 383 U. S. 541, 562 (1966). Thus, juveniles are not constitutionally entitled to trial by jury in delinquency adjudications. *McKeiver* v. *Pennsylvania*, 403 U. S. 528 (1971). Viewed together, our cases show that although children generally are protected by the same constitutional guarantees against governmental deprivations as are adults, the State is entitled to adjust its legal system to account for children's vulnerability and their needs for "concern, . . . sympathy, and . . . paternal attention." *Id.*, at 550 (plurality opinion).

B

Second, the Court has held that the States validly may limit the freedom of children to choose for themselves in the making of important, affirmative choices with potentially serious consequences. These rulings have been grounded in the recognition that, during the formative years of childhood and adolescence, minors often lack the experience, perspective, and judgment to recognize and avoid choices that could be detrimental to them. . . .

Ginsberg v. *New York*, 390 U. S. 629 (1968), illustrates well the Court's concern over the inability of children to make mature choices, as the First Amendment rights involved are clear examples of constitutionally protected freedoms of choice. At issue was a criminal conviction for selling sexually oriented magazines to a minor under the age of 17 in violation of a New York state law. It was conceded that the conviction could not have stood under the First Amendment if based upon a sale of the same material to an adult. *Id.*, at 634. Notwithstanding the importance the Court always has attached to First Amendment rights, it concluded that "even where there is an invasion of protected freedoms 'the power of the state to control the conduct of children reaches beyond the scope of its authority over adults . . . ,'" *id.*, at 638, quoting *Prince* v. *Massachusetts*, 321 U. S. 158, 170 (1944). . . .

C

Third, the guiding role of parents in the upbringing of their children justifies limitations on the freedoms of minors. The State commonly protects its youth from adverse governmental action and from their own immaturity by requiring parental consent to or involvement in important decisions by minors.[16] But an additional and more important justification for state deference to parental control over children is that "[t]he child is not the mere creature of the State; those who nurture him and direct his destiny have the right, coupled with the high duty, to recognize and prepare him for additional obligations." *Pierce* v. *Society of Sisters*, 268 U. S. 510, 535 (1925). "The duty to prepare the child for 'additional obligations' . . . must be read to include the inculcation of moral standards, religious beliefs, and elements of good citizenship." *Wisconsin* v. *Yoder*, 406 U. S. 205, 233 (1972). This affirmative process of teaching, guiding, and inspiring by precept and example is essential to the growth of young people into mature, socially responsible citizens. . . .

III

With these principles in mind, we consider the specific constitutional questions presented by these appeals. In § 12S, Massachusetts has attempted to reconcile the constitutional right of a woman, in consultation with her physician, to choose to terminate her pregnancy as established by *Roe* v. *Wade*, 410 U. S. 113 (1973), and *Doe* v. *Bolton*, 410 U. S. 179 (1973), with the special interest of the State in encouraging an unmarried pregnant minor to seek the advice of her parents in making the important decision whether or not to bear a child. As noted above, § 12S was before us in *Bellotti I*, 428 U. S. 132 (1976), where we remanded the case for interpretation of its provisions by the Supreme Judicial Court of Massachusetts. We previously had held in *Planned Parenthood of Central Missouri* v. *Danforth*, 428 U. S. 52 (1976), that a State could not lawfully authorize an absolute parental veto over the decision of a minor to terminate her pregnancy. *Id.*, at 74. In *Bellotti I, supra*, we recognized that § 12S could be read as "fundamentally different from a statute that creates a 'parental veto,'" 428 U. S., at 145, thus "avoid[ing] or substantially modify[ing] the federal constitutional challenge to the statute." *Id.*, at 148. The question before us—in light of what we have said in the prior cases—is whether § 12S, as authoritatively inter-

16. See, *e. g.*, Mass. Gen. Laws Ann., ch. 207, §§ 7, 24, 25, 33, 33A (West 1958 and Supp. 1979) (parental consent required for marriage of person under 18); Mass. Gen. Laws Ann., ch. 119, § 55A (West Supp. 1979) (waiver of counsel by minor in juvenile delinquency proceedings must be made through parent or guardian).

preted by the Supreme Judicial Court, provides for parental notice and consent in a manner that does not unduly burden the right to seek an abortion. See *id.*, at 147. . . .

The pregnant minor's options are much different from those facing a minor in other situations, such as deciding whether to marry. A minor not permitted to marry before the age of majority is required simply to postpone her decision. She and her intended spouse may preserve the opportunity for later marriage should they continue to desire it. A pregnant adolescent, however, cannot preserve for long the possibility of aborting, which effectively expires in a matter of weeks from the onset of pregnancy.

Moreover, the potentially severe detriment facing a pregnant woman, see *Roe* v. *Wade*, 410 U. S., at 153, is not mitigated by her minority. Indeed, considering her probable education, employment skills, financial resources, and emotional maturity, unwanted motherhood may be exceptionally burdensome for a minor. In addition, the fact of having a child brings with it adult legal responsibility, for parenthood, like attainment of the age of majority, is one of the traditional criteria for the termination of the legal disabilities of minority. In sum, there are few situations in which denying a minor the right to make an important decision will have consequences so grave and indelible.

Yet, an abortion may not be the best choice for the minor. The circumstances in which this issue arises will vary widely. In a given case, alternatives to abortion, such as marriage to the father of the child, arranging for its adoption, or assuming the responsibilities of motherhood with the assured support of family, may be feasible and relevant to the minor's best interests. Nonetheless, the abortion decision is one that simply cannot be postponed, or it will be made by default with far-reaching consequences.

For these reasons, as we held in *Planned Parenthood of Central Missouri* v. *Danforth*, 428 U. S., at 74, "the State may not impose a blanket provision . . . requiring the consent of a parent or person *in loco parentis* as a condition for abortion of an unmarried minor during the first 12 weeks of her pregnancy." Although, as stated in Part II, *supra*, such deference to parents may be permissible with respect to other choices facing a minor, the unique nature and consequences of the abortion decision make it inappropriate "to give a third party an absolute, and possibly arbitrary, veto over the decision of the physician and his patient to terminate the patient's pregnancy, regardless of the reason for withholding the consent." 428 U. S., at 74. We therefore conclude that if the State decides to require a pregnant minor to obtain one or both parents' consent to an abortion, it also must provide an alternative procedure . . . whereby authorization for the abortion can be obtained.

A pregnant minor is entitled in such a proceeding to show either: (1) that she is mature enough and well enough informed to make her abortion decision, in consultation with her physician, independently of her parents' wishes; . . . or (2) that even if she is not able to make this decision independently, the desired abortion would be in her best interests. The proceeding in which this showing is made must assure that a resolution of the issue, and any appeals that may follow, will be completed with anonymity and sufficient expedition to provide an effective opportunity for an abortion to be obtained. In sum, the procedure must ensure that the provision requiring parental consent does not in fact amount to the "absolute, and possibly arbitrary, veto" that was found impermissible in *Danforth. Ibid.* . . .

Among the questions certified to the Supreme Judicial Court was whether § 12S permits any minors—mature or immature—to obtain judicial consent to an abortion without any parental consultation whatsoever. See n. 9, *supra.* The state court answered that, in general, it does not. "[T]he consent required by [§ 12S must] be obtained for every nonemergency abortion where the mother is less than eighteen years of age and unmarried." *Attorney General, supra,* at 750, 360 N. E. 2d, at 294. The text of § 12S itself states an exception to this rule, making consent unnecessary from any parent who has "died or has deserted his or her family."[26] The Supreme Judicial Court construed the statute as containing an additional exception: Consent need not be obtained "where no parent (or statutory substitute) is available." 371 Mass., at 750, 360 N. E. 2d, at 294. The court also ruled that an available parent must be given notice of any judicial proceedings brought by a minor to obtain consent for an abortion. . . . *Id.,* at 755–756, 360 N. E. 2d, at 297.

We think that, construed in this manner, § 12S would impose an undue burden upon the exercise by minors of the right to seek an abortion. As the District Court recognized, "there are parents who would obstruct, and perhaps altogether prevent, the minor's right to go to court." *Baird III,* 450 F. Supp., at 1001. There is no reason to believe that this would be so in the majority of cases where consent is withheld. But many parents hold strong views on the subject of abortion, and young pregnant minors, especially those living at home, are particularly vulnerable to their parents' efforts to obstruct both an abortion and their access to court. It would be unrealistic, therefore, to assume that the mere existence of a legal right to seek relief in superior court provides an effective avenue of relief for some of those who need it the most.

We conclude, therefore, that under state regulation such as that undertaken by Massachusetts, every minor must have the opportunity—if she so

26. The statute also provides that "[i]f both parents have died or have deserted their family, consent of the mother's guardian or other person having duties similar to a guardian, or any person who had assumed the care and custody of the mother is sufficient."

desires—to go directly to a court without first consulting or notifying her parents. If she satisfies the court that she is mature and well enough informed to make intelligently the abortion decision on her own, the court must authorize her to act without parental consultation or consent. If she fails to satisfy the court that she is competent to make this decision independently, she must be permitted to show that an abortion nevertheless would be in her best interests. If the court is persuaded that it is, the court must authorize the abortion. If, however, the court is not persuaded by the minor that she is mature or that the abortion would be in her best interests, it may decline to sanction the operation.

There is, however, an important state interest in encouraging a family rather than a judicial resolution of a minor's abortion decision. Also, as we have observed above, parents naturally take an interest in the welfare of their children—an interest that is particularly strong where a normal family relationship exists and where the child is living with one or both parents. These factors properly may be taken into account by a court called upon to determine whether an abortion in fact is in a minor's best interests. If, all things considered, the court determines that an abortion is in the minor's best interests, she is entitled to court authorization without any parental involvement. On the other hand, the court may deny the abortion request of an immature minor in the absence of parental consultation if it concludes that her best interests would be served thereby, or the court may in such a case defer decision until there is parental consultation in which the court may participate. But this is the full extent to which parental involvement may be required.[28] For the reasons stated above, the constitutional right to seek an abortion may not be unduly burdened by state-imposed conditions upon initial access to court.

(2)

Section 12S requires that both parents consent to a minor's abortion. The District Court found it to be "custom" to perform other medical and surgical procedures on minors with the consent of only one parent, and it concluded that "nothing about abortions . . . requires the minor's interest to be treated differently." *Baird I.* See *Baird III.*

We are not persuaded that, as a general rule, the requirement of obtaining both parents' consent unconstitutionally burdens a minor's right to seek an abortion. The abortion decision has implications far broader than those associated with most other kinds of medical treatment. At least when the par-

---

28. Of course, if the minor consults with her parents voluntarily and they withhold consent, she is free to seek judicial authorization for the abortion immediately.

ents are together and the pregnant minor is living at home, both the father and mother have an interest—one normally supportive—in helping to determine the course that is in the best interests of a daughter. Consent and involvement by parents in important decisions by minors long have been recognized as protective of their immaturity. In the case of the abortion decision, for reasons we have stated, the focus of the parents' inquiry should be the best interests of their daughter. As every pregnant minor is entitled in the first instance to go directly to the court for a judicial determination without prior parental notice, consultation, or consent, the general rule with respect to parental consent does not unduly burden the constitutional right. Moreover, where the pregnant minor goes to her parents and consent is denied, she still must have recourse to a prompt judicial determination of her maturity or best interests.

(3)

Another of the questions certified by the District Court to the Supreme Judicial Court was the following: "If the superior court finds that the minor is capable [of making], and has, in fact, made and adhered to, an informed and reasonable decision to have an abortion, may the court refuse its consent based on a finding that a parent's, or its own, contrary decision is a better one?" *Attorney General*, 371 Mass., at 747 n. 5 360 N. E. 2d, at 293 n. 5. To this the state court answered:

"[W]e do not view the judge's role as limited to a determination that the minor is capable of making, and has made, an informed and reasonable decision to have an abortion. Certainly the judge must make a determination of those circumstances, but, if the statutory role of the judge to determine the best interests of the minor is to be carried out, he must make a finding on the basis of all relevant views presented to him. We suspect that the judge will give great weight to the minor's determination, if informed and reasonable, but in circumstances where he determines that the best interests of the minor will not be served by an abortion, the judge's determination should prevail, assuming that his conclusion is supported by the evidence and adequate findings of fact." *Id.,* at 748, 360 N. E. 2d, at 293.

The Supreme Judicial Court's statement reflects the general rule that a State may require a minor to wait until the age of majority before being permitted to exercise legal rights independently. See n. 23, *supra.* But we are concerned here with the exercise of a constitutional right of unique character. See *supra*, at 642–643. As stated above, if the minor satisfies a court that she has attained sufficient maturity to make a fully informed decision, she then is entitled to make her abortion decision independently. We therefore agree with the District Court that § 12S cannot constitutionally permit judicial disregard of the abortion decision of a minor who has been determined to be mature and fully competent to assess the implications of the choice she has made. . . .

HARRIS, SECRETARY OF HEALTH AND HUMAN SERVICES v. McRAE ET AL.

APPEAL FROM THE UNITED STATES DISTRICT COURT FOR THE
EASTERN DISTRICT OF NEW YORK

No. 79–1268. Argued April 21, 1980—Decided June 30, 1980

STEWART, J., delivered the opinion of the Court, in which BURGER, C. J., and WHITE, POWELL, and REHNQUIST, JJ., joined. WHITE, J., filed a concurring opinion. BRENNAN, J., filed a dissenting opinion, in which MARSHALL and BLACKMUN, JJ., joined. MARSHALL, J., BLACKMUN, J., and STEVENS, J., filed dissenting opinions.

MR. JUSTICE STEWART delivered the opinion of the Court.

Since September 1976, Congress has prohibited—either by an amendment to the annual appropriations bill for the Department of Health, Education, and Welfare . . . or by a joint resolution—the use of any federal funds to reimburse the cost of abortions under the Medicaid program except under certain specified circumstances. This funding restriction is commonly known as the "Hyde Amendment," after its original congressional sponsor, Representative Hyde. The current version of the Hyde Amendment, applicable for fiscal year 1980, provides:

"[N]one of the funds provided by this joint resolution shall be used to perform abortions except where the life of the mother would be endangered if the fetus were carried to term; or except for such medical procedures necessary for the victims of rape or incest when such rape or incest has been reported promptly to a law enforcement agency or public health service." Pub. L. 96–123, § 109, 93 Stat. 926.

See also Pub. L. 96–86, § 118, 93 Stat. 662. This version of the Hyde Amendment is broader than that applicable for fiscal year 1977, which did not include the "rape or incest" exception, Pub. L. 94–439, § 209, 90 Stat. 1434, but narrower than that applicable for most of fiscal year 1978, . . . and all of fiscal year 1979, which had an additional exception for "instances where severe and long-lasting physical health damage to the mother would result if the pregnancy were carried to term when so determined by two physicians," Pub. L. 95–205, § 101, 91 Stat. 1460; Pub. L. 95–480, § 210, 92 Stat. 1586. . . .

On September 30, 1976, the day on which Congress enacted the version of the Hyde Amendment, these consolidated cases were fi'   e District Court for the Eastern District of New York. The plaintiffs   ta McRae, a New York Medicaid recipient then in the first trimester of a pregnancy that she wished to terminate; the New York City Health and Hospitals Corp., a public benefit corporation that operates 16 hospitals, 12 of which provide abortion services; and others—sought to enjoin the enforcement of the funding restriction on abortions. They alleged that the Hyde Amendment violated the First, Fourth, Fifth, and Ninth Amendments of the Constitution insofar as it limited the funding of abortions to those necessary to save the life of the mother, while permitting the funding of costs associated with childbirth. . . .

After a lengthy trial, which inquired into the medical reasons for abortions and the diverse religious views on the subject,[6] the District Court filed an opinion and entered a judgment invalidating all versions of the Hyde Amendment on constitutional grounds. . . . The District Court rejected the plaintiffs' statutory argument, concluding that even though Title XIX would otherwise have required a participating State to fund medically necessary abortions, the Hyde Amendment had substantively amended Title XIX to relieve a State of that funding obligation. Turning then to the constitutional issues, the District Court concluded that the Hyde Amendment, though valid under the Establishment Clause, violates the equal protection component of the Fifth Amendment's Due Process Clause and the Free Exercise Clause of the First Amendment. With regard to the Fifth Amendment, the District Court noted that when an abortion is "medically necessary to safeguard the pregnant woman's health, . . . the disentitlement to [M]edicaid assistance impinges directly on the woman's right to decide, in consultation with her physician and in reliance on his judgment, to terminate her pregnancy in order to preserve her health." . . . McRae v. Califano, 491 F. Supp. 630, 737. The court concluded that the Hyde Amendment violates the equal protection guarantee because, in its view, the decision of Congress to fund medically necessary services generally but only certain medically necessary abortions serves no legitimate governmental interest. As to the Free Exercise Clause of the First Amendment, the court held that insofar as a woman's decision to seek a medically necessary abortion may be a product of her religious beliefs under certain Protestant and Jewish tenets, the funding restrictions of the Hyde Amendment violate that constitutional guarantee as well. . . .

6. The trial, which was conducted between August 1977 and September 1978, produced a record containing more than 400 documentary and film exhibits and a transcript exceeding 5,000 pages.

We address first the appellees' argument that the Hyde Amendment, by restricting the availability of certain medically necessary abortions under Medicaid, impinges on the "liberty" protected by the Due Process Clause as recognized in *Roe* v. *Wade*, 410 U. S. 113, and its progeny. . . .

In *Maher* v. *Roe*, 432 U. S. 464, the Court was presented with the question whether the scope of personal constitutional freedom recognized in *Roe* v. *Wade* included an entitlement to Medicaid payments for abortions that are not medically necessary. At issue in *Maher* was a Connecticut welfare regulation under which Medicaid recipients received payments for medical services incident to childbirth, but not for medical services incident to nontherapeutic abortions. The District Court held that the regulation violated the Equal Protection Clause of the Fourteenth Amendment because the unequal subsidization of childbirth and abortion impinged on the "fundamental right to abortion" recognized in *Wade* and its progeny. . . .

The Hyde Amendment, like the Connecticut welfare regulation at issue in *Maher*, places no governmental obstacle in the path of a woman who chooses to terminate her pregnancy, but rather, by means of unequal subsidization of abortion and other medical services, encourages alternative activity deemed in the public interest. The present case does differ factually from *Maher* insofar as that case involved a failure to fund nontherapeutic abortions, whereas the Hyde Amendment withholds funding of certain medically necessary abortions. . . .

. . . [R]egardless of whether the freedom of a woman to choose to terminate her pregnancy for health reasons lies at the core or the periphery of the due process liberty recognized in *Wade*, it simply does not follow that a woman's freedom of choice carries with it a constitutional entitlement to the financial resources to avail herself of the full range of protected choices. The reason why was explained in *Maher*: although government may not place obstacles in the path of a woman's exercise of her freedom of choice, it need not remove those not of its own creation. Indigency falls in the latter category. The financial constraints that restrict an indigent woman's ability to enjoy the full range of constitutionally protected freedom of choice are the product not of governmental restrictions on access to abortions, but rather of her indigency. Although Congress has opted to subsidize medically necessary services generally, but not certain medically necessary abortions, the fact remains that the Hyde Amendment leaves an indigent woman with at least the same range of choice in deciding whether to obtain a medically necessary abortion as she would have had if Congress had chosen to subsidize no health care costs at all. We are thus not persuaded that the Hyde Amendment impinges on the constitutionally protected freedom of choice recognized in *Wade*. . . .

Although the liberty protected by the Due Process Clause affords protection against unwarranted government interference with freedom of choice in the context of certain personal decisions, it does not confer an entitlement to such funds as may be necessary to realize all the advantages of that freedom. To hold otherwise would mark a drastic change in our understanding of the Constitution. It cannot be that because government may not prohibit the use of contraceptives, *Griswold* v. *Connecticut*, 381 U. S. 479, or prevent parents from sending their child to a private school, *Pierce* v. *Society of Sisters*, 268 U. S. 510, government, therefore, has an affirmative constitutional obligation to ensure that all persons have the financial resources to obtain contraceptives or send their children to private schools. To translate the limitation on governmental power implicit in the Due Process Clause into an affirmative funding obligation would require Congress to subsidize the medically necessary abortion of an indigent woman even if Congress had not enacted a Medicaid program to subsidize other medically necessary services. . . .

The appellees also argue that the Hyde Amendment contravenes rights secured by the Religion Clauses of the First Amendment. It is the appellees' view that the Hyde Amendment violates the Establishment Clause because it incorporates into law the doctrines of the Roman Catholic Church concerning the sinfulness of abortion and the time at which life commences. Moreover, insofar as a woman's decision to seek a medically necessary abortion may be a product of her religious beliefs under certain Protestant and Jewish tenets, the appellees assert that the funding limitations of the Hyde Amendment impinge on the freedom of religion guaranteed by the Free Exercise Clause.

1

It is well settled that "a legislative enactment does not contravene the Establishment Clause if it has a secular legislative purpose, if its principal or primary effect neither advances nor inhibits religion, and if it does not foster an excessive governmental entanglement with religion." *Committee for Public Education* v. *Regan*, 444 U. S. 646, 653. Applying this standard, the District Court properly concluded that the Hyde Amendment does not run afoul of the Establishment Clause. Although neither a State nor the Federal Government can constitutionally "pass laws which aid one religion, aid all religions, or prefer one religion over another," *Everson* v. *Board of Education*, 330 U. S. 1, 15, it does not follow that a statute violates the Establishment Clause because it "happens to coincide or harmonize with the tenets of some or all religions." *McGowan* v. *Maryland*, 366 U. S. 420, 442. That the Judaeo-Christian religions oppose stealing does not mean that a State or the Federal Government may not, consistent with the Establishment Clause, enact laws prohibiting larceny. . . .

It remains to be determined whether the Hyde Amendment violates the equal protection component of the Fifth Amendment. This challenge is premised on the fact that, although federal reimbursement is available under Medicaid for medically necessary services generally, the Hyde Amendment does not permit federal reimbursement of all medically necessary abortions. The District Court held, and the appellees argue here, that this selective subsidization violates the constitutional guarantee of equal protection.

The guarantee of equal protection under the Fifth Amendment is not a source of substantive rights or liberties,[25] but rather a right to be free from invidious discrimination in statutory classifications and other governmental activity. It is well settled that where a statutory classification does not itself impinge on a right or liberty protected by the Constitution, the validity of classification must be sustained unless "the classification rests on grounds wholly irrelevant to the achievement of [any legitimate governmental] objective." *McGowan* v. *Maryland*, 366 U. S., at 425. This presumption of constitutional validity, however, disappears if a statutory classification is predicated on criteria that are, in a constitutional sense, "suspect," the principal example of which is a classification based on race, *e. g.*, *Brown* v. *Board of Education*, 347 U. S. 483.

1

For the reasons stated above, we have already concluded that the Hyde Amendment violates no constitutionally protected substantive rights. We now conclude as well that it is not predicated on a constitutionally suspect classification. . . .

Here, as in *Maher*, the principal impact of the Hyde Amendment falls on the indigent. But that fact does not itself render the funding restriction constitutionally invalid, for this Court has held repeatedly that poverty, standing alone, is not a suspect classification. See, *e. g.*, *James* v. *Valtierra*, 402 U. S. 137. That *Maher* involved the refusal to fund nontherapeutic abortions, whereas the present case involves the refusal to fund medically necessary abortions, has no bearing on the factors that render a classification "suspect" within the meaning of the constitutional guarantee of equal protection. . . .

25. An exception to this statement is to be found in *Reynolds* v. *Sims*, 377 U. S. 533, and its progeny. Although the Constitution of the United States does not confer the right to vote in state elections, see *Minor* v. *Happersett*, 21 Wall. 162, 178, *Reynolds* held that if a State adopts an electoral system, the Equal Protection Clause of the Fourteenth Amendment confers upon a qualified voter a substantive right to participate in the electoral process equally with other qualified voters. See, *e. g.*, *Dunn* v. *Blumstein*, 405 U. S. 330, 336.

MR. JUSTICE BRENNAN, with whom MR. JUSTICE MARSHALL and MR. JUSTICE BLACKMUN join, dissenting.

I agree entirely with my Brother STEVENS that the State's interest in protecting the potential life of the fetus cannot justify the exclusion of financially and medically needy women from the benefits to which they would otherwise be entitled solely because the treatment that a doctor has concluded is medically necessary involves an abortion. I write separately to express my continuing disagreement . . . with the Court's mischaracterization of the nature of the fundamental right recognized in *Roe* v. *Wade*, 410 U. S. 113 (1973), and its misconception of the manner in which that right is infringed by federal and state legislation withdrawing all funding for medically necessary abortions.

Roe v. *Wade* held that the constitutional right to personal privacy encompasses a woman's decision whether or not to terminate her pregnancy. *Roe* and its progeny . . . established that the pregnant woman has a right to be free from state interference with her choice to have an abortion—a right which, at least prior to the end of the first trimester, absolutely prohibits any governmental regulation of that highly personal decision. . . . The proposition for which these cases stand thus is not that the State is under an affirmative obligation to ensure access to abortions for all who may desire them; it is that the State must refrain from wielding its enormous power and influence in a manner that might burden the pregnant woman's freedom to choose whether to have an abortion. The Hyde Amendment's denial of public funds for medically necessary abortions plainly intrudes upon this constitutionally protected decision, for both by design and in effect it serves to coerce indigent pregnant women to bear children that they would otherwise elect not to have. . . .

When viewed in the context of the Medicaid program to which it is appended, it is obvious that the Hyde Amendment is nothing less than an attempt by Congress to circumvent the dictates of the Constitution and achieve indirectly what *Roe* v. *Wade* said it could not do directly. . . . Under Title XIX of the Social Security Act, the Federal Government reimburses participating States for virtually all medically necessary services it provides to the categorically needy. The sole limitation of any significance is the Hyde Amendment's prohibition against the use of any federal funds to pay for the costs of abortions (except where the life of the mother would be endangered if the fetus were carried to term). As my Brother STEVENS persuasively demonstrates, exclusion of medically necessary abortions from Medicaid coverage cannot be justified as a cost-saving device. Rather, the Hyde Amendment is a transparent attempt by the Legislative Branch to impose the political majority's judgment of the morally acceptable and socially desirable preference on a sensitive and intimate decision that the Constitution entrusts to the individual. Worse yet, the Hyde Amendment does not foist that majoritarian viewpoint with equal measure upon everyone in our Nation, rich and poor alike; rather, it imposes that viewpoint only upon that segment of our society which, because of its position of political powerlessness, is least able to defend its privacy rights from the encroachments of state-mandated morality. The instant legislation thus calls for more exacting judicial review than in most other cases. "When elected leaders cower before public pressure, this Court, more than ever, must not shirk its duty to enforce the Constitution for the benefit of the poor and powerless." *Beal* v. *Doe,* 432 U. S. 438, 462 (1977) (MARSHALL, J., dissenting). Though it may not be this Court's mission "to decide whether the balance of competing interests reflected in the Hyde Amendment is wise social policy," it most assuredly is our responsibility to vindicate the pregnant woman's constitutional right to decide whether to bear children free from governmental intrusion. . . .

A poor woman in the early stages of pregnancy confronts two alternatives: she may elect either to carry the fetus to term or to have an abortion. In the abstract, of course, this choice is hers alone, and the Court rightly observes that the Hyde Amendment "places no governmental obstacle in the path of a woman who chooses to terminate her pregnancy." But the reality of the situation is that the Hyde Amendment has effectively removed this choice from the indigent woman's hands. By funding all of the expenses associated with childbirth and none of the expenses incurred in terminating pregnancy, the Government literally makes an offer that the indigent woman cannot afford to refuse. It matters not that in this instance the Government has used the carrot rather than the stick. What is critical is the realization that as a practical matter, many poverty-stricken women will choose to carry their pregnancy to term simply because the Government provides funds for the associated medical services, even though these same women would have chosen to have an abortion if the Government had also paid for that option, or indeed if the Government had stayed out of the picture altogether and had defrayed the costs of neither procedure.

The fundamental flaw in the Court's due process analysis, then, is its failure to acknowledge that the discriminatory distribution of the benefits of governmental largesse can discourage the exercise of fundamental liberties just as effectively as can an outright denial of those rights through criminal and regulatory sanctions. Implicit in the Court's reasoning is the notion that as long as the Government is not obligated to provide its citizens with certain benefits or privileges, it may condition the grant of such benefits on the recipient's relinquishment of his constitutional rights.

MR. JUSTICE STEVENS, dissenting.

"The federal sovereign, like the States, must govern impartially. The concept of equal justice under law is served by the Fifth Amendment's guarantee of due process, as well as by the Equal Protection Clause of the Fourteenth Amendment." *Hampton* v. *Mow Sun Wong*, 426 U. S. 88, 100. When the sovereign provides a special benefit or a special protection for a class of persons, it must define the membership in the class by neutral criteria; it may not make special exceptions for reasons that are constitutionally insufficient. . . .

A fundamentally different question was decided in *Maher* v. *Roe*, 432 U. S. 464. Unlike these plaintiffs, the plaintiffs in *Maher* did not satisfy the neutral criterion of medical need; they sought a subsidy for nontherapeutic abortions—medical procedures which by definition they did not need. In rejecting that claim, the Court held that their constitutional right to choose that procedure did not impose a duty on the State to subsidize the exercise of that right. Nor did the fact that the State had undertaken to pay for the necessary medical care associated with childbirth require the State also to pay for abortions that were not necessary; for only necessary medical procedures satisfied the neutral statutory criteria. Nontherapeutic abortions were simply outside the ambit of the medical benefits program. Thus, in *Maher*, the plaintiffs' desire to exercise a constitutional right gave rise to neither special access nor special exclusion from the pool of benefits created by Title XIX.

These cases involve a special exclusion of women who, by definition, are confronted with a choice between two serious harms: serious health damage to themselves on the one hand and abortion on the other. The competing interests are the interest in maternal health and the interest in protecting potential human life. It is now part of our law that the pregnant woman's decision as to which of these conflicting interests shall prevail is entitled to constitutional protection.

If a woman has a constitutional right to place a higher value on avoiding either serious harm to her own health or perhaps an abnormal childbirth . . . than on protecting potential life, the exercise of that right cannot provide the basis for the denial of a benefit to which she would otherwise be entitled. The Court's sterile equal protection analysis evades this critical though simple point. The Court focuses exclusively on the "legitimate interest in protecting the potential life of the fetus." . . . It concludes that since the Hyde Amendments further that interest, the exclusion they create is rational and therefore constitutional. But it is misleading to speak of the Government's legitimate interest in the fetus without reference to the context in which that interest was held to be legitimate. For *Roe* v. *Wade* squarely held that the States may not protect that interest when a conflict with the interest in a pregnant woman's health exists. . . .

Nor can it be argued that the exclusion of this type of medically necessary treatment of the indigent can be justified on fiscal grounds. There are some especially costly forms of treatment that may reasonably be excluded from the program in order to preserve the assets in the pool and extend its benefits to the maximum number of needy persons. Fiscal considerations may compel certain difficult choices in order to improve the protection afforded to the entire benefited class. . . . But, ironically, the exclusion of medically necessary abortions harms the entire class as well as its specific victims. For the records in both *McRae* and *Zbaraz* demonstrate that the cost of an abortion is only a small fraction of the costs associated with childbirth. . . . Thus, the decision to tolerate harm to indigent persons who need an abortion in order to avoid "serious and long-lasting health damage" is one that is financed by draining money out of the pool that is used to fund all other necessary medical procedures. Unlike most invidious classifications, this discrimination harms not only its direct victims but also the remainder of the class of needy persons that the pool was designed to benefit. . . .

H. L. *v.* MATHESON, GOVERNOR OF UTAH, ET AL.

APPEAL FROM THE SUPREME COURT OF UTAH

No. 79–5903. Argued October 6, 1980—Decided March 23, 1981

BURGER, C. J., delivered the opinion of the Court, in which STEWART, WHITE, POWELL, and REHNQUIST, JJ., joined. POWELL, J., filed a concurring opinion, in which STEWART, J., joined. STEVENS, J., filed an opinion concurring in the judgment. MARSHALL, J., filed a dissenting opinion, in which BRENNAN and BLACKMUN, JJ., joined.

CHIEF JUSTICE BURGER delivered the opinion of the Court.

The question presented in this case is whether a state statute which requires a physician to "[n]otify, if possible," the parents of a dependent, unmarried minor girl prior to performing an abortion on the girl violates federal constitutional guarantees.

I

In the spring of 1978, appellant was an unmarried 15-year-old girl living with her parents in Utah and dependent on them for her support. She discovered she was pregnant. She consulted with a social worker and a physician. The physician advised appellant that an abortion would be in her best medical interest. However, because of Utah Code Ann. § 76–7–304 (1978), he refused to perform the abortion without first notifying appellant's parents.

Section 76–7–304, enacted in 1974, provides:

"To enable the physician to exercise his best medical judgment [in considering a possible abortion], he shall:

"(1) Consider all factors relevant to the well-being of the woman upon whom the abortion is to be performed including, but not limited to,

"(a) Her physical, emotional and psychological health and safety,

"(b) Her age,

"(c) Her familial situation.

"(2) *Notify, if possible, the parents or guardian of the woman upon whom the abortion is to be performed, if she is a minor* or the husband of the woman, if she is married." (Emphasis supplied.) . . .

Violation of this section is a misdemeanor punishable by imprisonment for not more than one year or a fine of not more than $1,000. . . .

Appellant believed "for [her] own reasons" that she should proceed with the abortion without notifying her parents. According to appellant, the social worker concurred in this decision.[3] While still in the first trimester of her pregnancy, appellant instituted this action in the Third Judicial District Court of Utah. . . . She sought a declaration that § 76–7–304 (2) is unconstitutional and an injunction prohibiting appellees, the Governor and the Attorney General of Utah, from enforcing the statute. Appellant sought to represent a class consisting of unmarried "minor women who are suffering unwanted pregnancies and desire to terminate the pregnancies but may not do so" because of their physicians' insistence on complying with § 76–7–304 (2). The trial judge declined to grant a temporary restraining order or a preliminary injunction.[5]

The trial judge held a hearing at which appellant was the only witness. Appellant affirmed the allegations of the complaint by giving monosyllabic answers to her attorney's leading questions.[6] However, when the State at-

3. Appellant's counsel stated in his jurisdictional statement and again in his brief that the physician concluded not only that an abortion would be in appellant's best interests, but also that parental notification would not be in appellant's best interests. However, at oral argument, counsel corrected this statement and conceded that there is no evidence to support this assertion. Tr. of Oral Arg. 8, 17.

5. The trial judge allowed appellant to proceed without appointment of a guardian *ad litem.* He noted that a guardian would be required to notify the parents.

6. The testimony was as follows:
"BY MR. DOLOWITZ [appellant's counsel]:
  "Q At the time that the Complaint in this matter was signed, you were pregnant?
  "A Yes.
  "Q You had consulted with a counselor about that pregnancy?
  "A Yeah.
  "Q You had determined after talking to the counselor that you felt you should get an abortion?
  "A Yes.
  "Q You felt that you did not want to notify your parents—
  "A Right.
  "Q —of that decision? You did not feel for your own reasons that you could discuss it with them?
  "A Right.
  "Q After discussing the matter with a counselor, you still believed that you should not discuss it with your parents?
  "A Right.
  "Q And they shouldn't be notified?
  "A Right.
  "Q After talking the matter over with a counselor, the counselor concurred in your decision that your parents should not be notified?
  "A Right.
  "Q You were advised that an abortion couldn't be performed without notifying them?
  "A Yes.

tempted to cross-examine appellant about her reasons for not wishing to notify her parents, appellant's counsel vigorously objected,[7] insisting that "the specifics of the reasons are really irrelevant to the Constitutional issue."[8] The only constitutionally permissible prerequisites for performance of an

---

"Q You then came to me to see about filing a suit?

"A Right.

"Q You and I discussed it as to whether or not you had a right to do what you wanted to do?

"A Yes.

"Q You decided that, after our discussion, you should still proceed with the action to try to obtain an abortion without notifying your parents?

"A Right.

"Q Now, at the time that you signed the Complaint and spoke with the counselor and spoke with me, you were in the first trimester of pregnancy, within your first twelve weeks of pregnancy?

"A Yes.

"Q You feel that, from talking to the counselor and thinking the situation over and discussing it with me, that you could make the decision on your own that you wished to abort the pregnancy?

"A Yes.

"Q You are living at home?

"A Yes.

"Q You still felt, even though you were living at home with your parents, that you couldn't discuss the matter with them?

"A Right."

Tr. 5–7.

7. "BY MR. McCARTHY [counsel for the State]:

"Q . . . Are you still living at home?

"A Yes.

"Q Are you dependent on your parents?

"A Yes.

"Q All your money comes from them?

"A Yes.

"Q How old are you now?

"A Fifteen.

"Q Aside from the issue of abortion, do you have any reason to feel that you can't talk to your parents about other problems?

"A Yes.

"Q What are those reasons?

"MR. DOLOWITZ: Now you are moving into the problem area that I indicated. . . . "

Id., at 8.

8. *Id.,* at 10. Appellant repeatedly pressed this point despite the trial court's statements that it could "conceive of a situation where a child probably wouldn't have to

abortion, he insisted, were the desire of the girl and the medical approval of a physician. . . . The trial judge sustained the objection, tentatively construing the statute to require appellant's physician to notify her parents "if he is able to physically contact them."

Thereafter, the trial judge entered findings of fact and conclusions of law. He concluded that appellant "is an appropriate representative to represent the class she purports to represent." . . . He construed the statute to require notice to appellant's parents "if it is physically possible." He concluded that § 76–7–304 (2) "do[es] not unconstitutionally restrict the right of privacy of a minor to obtain an abortion or to enter into a doctor-patient relationship." . . . Accordingly, he dismissed the complaint.

On appeal, the Supreme Court of Utah unanimously upheld the statute. . . .

The Utah Supreme Court held that notifying the parents of a minor seeking an abortion is "substantially and logically related" to the *Doe* factors set out in § 76–7–304 (1) because parents ordinarily possess information essential to a physician's exercise of his best medical judgment concerning the child. 604 P. 2d, at 909–910. The court also concluded that encouraging an unmarried pregnant minor to seek the advice of her parents in making the decision of whether to carry her child to term promotes a significant state interest in supporting the important role of parents in child-rearing. *Id.*, at 912. The court reasoned that since the statute allows no veto power over the minor's decision, it does not unduly intrude upon a minor's rights. . . .

Although we have held that a state may not constitutionally legislate a blanket, unreviewable power of parents to veto their daughter's abortion,[15] a statute setting out a "mere requirement of parental notice" does not violate the constitutional rights of an immature, dependent minor.[16] Four Justices in *Bellotti II* joined in stating:

"[Plaintiffs] suggest . . . that the mere requirement of parental notice [unduly burdens the right to seek an abortion]. As stated in Part II above, however, parental notice and consent are qualifications that typically may be imposed by the State on a minor's right to make important decisions. As immature minors often lack the ability to make fully informed choices that take account of both immediate and long-range consequences, a State

---

tell the parents" and that the statute "might be [u]nconstitutional as it relates to a particular fact situation but [c]onstitutional as it relates to another fact situation." *Id.*, at 10, 17. . . .

15. *Bellotti II*, 443 U. S., at 642–643, 653–656; *Danforth*, 428 U. S., at 74.

16. *Bellotti II*, *supra*, at 640, 649; *id.*, at 657 (dissenting opinion); *Danforth*, *supra*, at 90–91 (concurring opinion); see *Bellotti v. Baird*, 428 U. S. 132, 145, 147 (1976) (*Bellotti I*); cf. *Carey v. Population Services International*, 431 U. S. 678, 709–710 (1977).

reasonably may determine that parental consultation often is desirable and in the best interest of the minor. It may further determine, as a general proposition, that such consultation is particularly desirable with respect to the abortion decision—one that for some people raises profound moral and religious concerns. . . .

"'There can be little doubt that the State furthers a constitutionally permissible end by encouraging an unmarried pregnant minor to seek the help and advice of her parents in making the very important decision whether or not to bear a child. That is a grave decision, and a girl of tender years, under emotional stress, may be ill-equipped to make it without mature advice and emotional support. It seems unlikely that she will obtain adequate counsel and support from the attending physician at an abortion clinic, where abortions for pregnant minors frequently take place.'" *Id.*, at 640–641 (footnotes omitted), quoting *Danforth*, 428 U. S., at 91 (concurring opinion). . . .

The Utah statute gives neither parents nor judges a veto power over the minor's abortion decision.[17] As in *Bellotti I*, "we are concerned with a statute directed toward minors, as to whom there are unquestionably greater risks of inability to give an informed consent." 428 U. S., at 147. As applied to immature and dependent minors, the statute plainly serves the important considerations of family integrity[18] and protecting adolescents[19] which we identified in *Bellotti II*. In addition, as applied to that class, the statute serves a significant state interest by providing an opportunity for parents to supply essential medical and other information to a physician. The medical, emotional, and psychological consequences of an abortion are serious and can be lasting; this is particularly so when the patient is immature.[20] An adequate

17. The main premise of the dissent seems to be that a requirement of notice to the parents is the functional equivalent of a requirement of parental consent. In *Bellotti II*, however, we expressly declined to equate notice requirements with consent requirements. 443 U. S., at 640, 657.

18. *Bellotti II*. The short shrift given by the dissent to "parental authority and family integrity," *post*, at 447, runs contrary to a long line of constitutional cases in this Court. See cases cited *supra*, at 410.

19. *Bellotti II*, at 634–637.

20. Abortion is associated with an increased risk of complication in subsequent pregnancies. Maine, Does Abortion Affect Later Pregnancies?, 11 Family Planning Perspectives 98 (1979). The emotional and psychological effects of the pregnancy and abortion experience are markedly more severe in girls under 18 than in adults. Wallerstein, Kurtz, & Bar-Din, Psychosocial Sequelae of Therapeutic Abortion in Young Unmarried Women, 27 Arch. Gen. Psychiatry 828 (1972); see also Babikian & Goldman, A Study in Teen-Age Pregnancy, 128 Am. J. Psychiatry 755 (1971).

medical and psychological case history is important to the physician. Parents can provide medical and psychological data, refer the physician to other sources of medical history, such as family physicians, and authorize family physicians to give relevant data. . . .

As applied to the class properly before us, the statute plainly serves important state interests, is narrowly drawn to protect only those interests, and does not violate any guarantees of the Constitution. . . . The judgment of the Supreme Court of Utah is

Affirmed.

JUSTICE MARSHALL, with whom JUSTICE BRENNAN and JUSTICE BLACK-MUN join, dissenting.

In upholding the statute, the Utah Supreme Court concluded that the notification provision might encourage parental transmission of "additional information, which might prove invaluable to the physician in exercising his 'best medical judgment.'" . . . Yet neither the Utah courts nor the statute itself specifies the kind of information contemplated for this purpose, nor why it is available to the parents but not to the minor woman herself. Most parents lack the medical expertise necessary to supplement the physician's medical judgment, and at best could provide facts about the patient's medical history. It seems doubtful that a minor mature enough to become pregnant and to seek medical advice on her own initiative would be unable or unwilling to provide her physician with information crucial to the abortion decision. In addition, by law the physician already is obligated to obtain all information necessary to form his best medical judgment, . . . and nothing bars consultation with the parents should the physician find it necessary.

Even if mandatory parental notice serves a substantial state purpose in this regard, the Utah statute fails to implement it. Simply put, the statute on its face does not require or even encourage the transfer of information; it does not even call for a conversation between the physician and the parents. A letter from the physician to the parents would satisfy the statute, as would a brief telephone call made moments before the abortion. . . . Moreover, the statute is patently underinclusive if its aim is the transfer of information known to the parents but unavailable from the minor woman herself. The statute specifically excludes married minors from the parental notice requirement; only her husband need be told of the planned abortion, Utah Code Ann. § 76–7–304 (2) (1978), and Utah makes no claim that he possesses any information valuable to the physician's judgment but unavailable from the pregnant woman. Furthermore, no notice is required for other pregnancy-related care sought by the minor. See Utah Code Ann. § 78–14–5 (4) (f) (1977) (authorizing woman of any age to consent to pregnancy-related medical care). The minor woman may consent to surgical removal and analysis of amniotic fluid, caesarian delivery, and other medical care related to pregnancy. The physician's decisions concerning such procedures would be enhanced by parental information as much as would the abortion decision, yet only the abortion decision triggers the parental notice requirement. This result is especially anomalous given the comparatively lesser health risks associated with abortion as contrasted with other pregnancy-related medical care.[38] Thus, the statute not only fails to promote the transfer of information as is claimed, it does not apply to other closely related contexts in which such exchange of information would be no less important. The goal of promoting consultation between the physician and the parents of the pregnant minor cannot sustain a statute that is so ill-fitted to serve it. . . .

B

Appellees also claim the statute serves the legitimate purpose of improving the minor's decision by encouraging consultation between the minor woman and her parents. Appellees do not dispute that the State cannot legally or practically require such consultation. . . . Nor do appellees contest the fact that the decision is ultimately the minor's to make. . . . Nonetheless, the State seeks through the notice requirement to give parents the opportunity to contribute to the minor woman's abortion decision.

38. I am baffled by the majority's statement today that "[i]f the pregnant girl elects to carry her child to term, the *medical* decisions to be made entail few—perhaps none—of the potentially grave and emotional and psychological consequences of the decision to abort," *ante*, at 412–413. Choosing to participate in diagnostic tests involves risks to both mother and child, and also may burden the pregnant woman with knowledge that the child will be handicapped. See 3 National Institutes of Health, Prevention of Embryonic, Fetal, and Perinatal Disease 347–352 (R. Brent & M. Harris eds. 1976); Risks in the Practice of Modern Obstetrics 59–81, 369–370 (S. Aladjem ed. 1975). The decision to undergo surgery to save the child's life certainly carries as serious "emotional and psychological consequences" for the pregnant adolescent as does the decision to abort; in both instances, the minor confronts the task of calculating not only medical risks, but also all the issues involved in giving birth to a child. See *id.*, at 59–81. For an unwed adolescent, these issues include her future educational and job opportunities, as well as the more immediate problems of finding financial and emotional support for offspring dependent entirely on her. *Michael M.* v. *Sonoma County Superior Court, post*, at 470, and nn. 3 and 4 (REHNQUIST, J.) (plurality opinion). When surgery to save the child's life poses greater risks to the mother's life, the emotional and ethical dimensions of the medical care decision assume crisis proportion. Of course, for minors, the mere fact of pregnancy and the experience of childbirth can produce psychological upheaval.

Ideally, facilitation of supportive conversation would assist the pregnant minor during an undoubtedly difficult experience. Again, however, when measured against the rationality of the means employed, the Utah statute simply fails to advance this asserted goal. The statute imposes no requirement that the notice be sufficiently timely to permit any discussion between the pregnant minor and the parents. Moreover, appellant's claims require us to examine the statute's purpose in relation to the parents who the minor believes are likely to respond with hostility or opposition. In this light, the statute is plainly overbroad. Parental consultation hardly seems a legitimate state purpose where the minor's pregnancy resulted from incest, where a hostile or abusive parental response is assured, or where the minor's fears of such a response deter her from the abortion she desires. The absolute nature of the statutory requirement, with exception permitted only if the parents are physically unavailable, violates the requirement that regulations in this fundamentally personal area be carefully tailored to serve a significant state interest.[42] "The need to preserve the constitutional right and the unique nature of the abortion decision, especially when made by a minor, require a State to act with particular sensitivity when it legislates to foster parental involvement in this matter." *Bellotti II*, 443 U. S., at 642 (POWELL, J.). Because Utah's absolute notice requirement demonstrates no such sensitivity, I cannot approve its interference with the minor's private consultation with the physician during the first trimester of her pregnancy.

C

Finally, appellees assert a state interest in protecting parental authority and family integrity. . . . This Court, of course, has recognized that the "primary role of the parents in the upbringing of their children is now established beyond debate as an enduring American tradition." *Wisconsin* v. *Yoder*, 406 U. S. 205, 232 (1972). See *Prince* v. *Massachusetts*, 321 U. S. 158 (1944); *Meyer* v. *Nebraska*, 262 U. S. 390 (1923). Indeed, "those who nurture [the child] and direct his destiny have the right, coupled with the high duty, to recognize and prepare him for additional obligations." *Pierce* v. *Society of Sisters*, 268 U. S., at 535. Similarly, our decisions "have respected the private realm of family life which the state cannot enter." *Prince* v. *Massachusetts, supra*, at 166. See also *Moore* v. *East Cleveland*, 431 U. S., at 505.

42. State-sponsored counseling services, in contrast, could promote family dialogue and also improve the minor's decision-making process. Appellant H. L., for example, consulted with a counselor who supported her decision. The role of counselors can be significant in facilitating the pregnant woman's adjustment to decisions related to her pregnancy. See Smith, A Follow-Up Study of Women Who Request Abortion, 43 Am. J. Orthopsychiatry 574, 583–585 (1973).

The critical thrust of these decisions has been to protect the privacy of individual families from unwarranted state intrusion.[44] Ironically, appellees invoke these decisions in seeking to justify state interference in the normal functioning of the family. Through its notice requirement, the State in fact enters the private realm of the family rather than leaving unaltered the pattern of interactions chosen by the family. Whatever its motive, state intervention is hardly likely to resurrect parental authority that the parents themselves are unable to preserve.[45] . . .

44. *Wynn* v. *Carey,* 582 F. 2d, at 1385–1386; Note, The Minor's Right of Privacy: Limitations on State Action after *Danforth* and *Carey,* 77 Colum. L. Rev. 1216, 1224 (1977).

45. "The fact that the minor became pregnant and sought an abortion contrary to the parents' wishes indicates that whatever control the parent once had over the minor has diminished, if not evaporated entirely. And we believe that enforcing a single, albeit important, parental decision—at a time when the minor is near to majority status—by an instrument as blunt as a state statute is extremely unlikely to restore parental control." *Poe* v. *Gerstein,* 517 F. 2d 787, 793–794 (CA5 1975), summarily aff'd, 428 U. S. 901 (1976).

CITY OF AKRON v. AKRON CENTER FOR REPRODUCTIVE HEALTH, INC., ET AL.

CERTIORARI TO THE UNITED STATES COURT OF APPEALS
FOR THE SIXTH CIRCUIT

No. 81–746. Argued November 30, 1982—Decided June 15, 1983

POWELL, J., delivered the opinion of the Court, in which BURGER, C. J., and BRENNAN, MARSHALL, BLACKMUN, and STEVENS, JJ., joined. O'CONNOR, J., filed a dissenting opinion, in which WHITE and REHNQUIST, JJ., joined.

JUSTICE POWELL delivered the opinion of the Court.

In this litigation we must decide the constitutionality of several provisions of an ordinance enacted by the city of Akron, Ohio, to regulate the performance of abortions. Today we also review abortion regulations enacted by the State of Missouri, see *Planned Parenthood Assn. of Kansas City, Mo., Inc.* v. *Ashcroft*, and by the State of Virginia, see *Simopoulos* v. *Virginia.*

These cases come to us a decade after we held in *Roe* v. *Wade*, 410 U. S. 113 (1973), that the right of privacy, grounded in the concept of personal liberty guaranteed by the Constitution, encompasses a woman's right to decide whether to terminate her pregnancy. Legislative responses to the Court's decision have required us on several occasions, and again today, to define the limits of a State's authority to regulate the performance of abortions. And arguments continue to be made, in these cases as well, that we erred in interpreting the Constitution. Nonetheless, the doctrine of *stare decisis,* while perhaps never entirely persuasive on a constitutional question, is a doctrine that demands respect in a society governed by the rule of law.[1] We respect it today, and reaffirm *Roe* v. *Wade.*

---

1. There are especially compelling reasons for adhering to *stare decisis* in applying the principles of *Roe* v. *Wade*. That case was considered with special care. It was first argued during the 1971 Term, and reargued—with extensive briefing—the following Term. The decision was joined by THE CHIEF JUSTICE and six other Justices. Since *Roe* was decided in January 1973, the Court repeatedly and consistently has accepted and applied the basic principle that a woman has a fundamental right to make the highly personal choice whether or not to terminate her pregnancy. . . .

I

In February 1978 the City Council of Akron enacted Ordinance No. 160–1978, entitled "Regulation of Abortions." . . . The ordinance sets forth 17 provisions that regulate the performance of abortions, see Akron Codified Ordinances, ch. 1870, 5 of which are at issue in this case:

(i) Section 1870.03 requires that all abortions performed after the first trimester of pregnancy be performed in a hospital. . . .

(ii) Section 1870.05 sets forth requirements for notification of and consent by parents before abortions may be performed on unmarried minors. . . .

(iii) Section 1870.06 requires that the attending physician make certain specified statements to the patient "to insure that the consent for an abortion is truly informed consent." . . .

(iv) Section 1870.07 requires a 24-hour waiting period between the time the woman signs a consent form and the time the abortion is performed. . . .

(v) Section 1870.16 requires that fetal remains be "disposed of in a humane and sanitary manner." . . .

A violation of any section of the ordinance is punishable as a criminal misdemeanor. § 1870.18. If any provision is invalidated, it is to be severed from the remainder of the ordinance. . . . The ordinance became effective on May 1, 1978. . . .

In *Roe* v. *Wade*, the Court held that the "right of privacy, . . . founded in the Fourteenth Amendment's concept of personal liberty and restrictions upon state action, . . . is broad enough to encompass a woman's decision whether or not to terminate her pregnancy." 410 U. S., at 153. Although the Constitution does not specifically identify this right, the history of this Court's constitutional adjudication leaves no doubt that "the full scope of the liberty guaranteed by the Due Process Clause cannot be found in or limited by the precise terms of the specific guarantees elsewhere provided in the Constitution." *Poe* v. *Ullman*, 367 U. S. 497, 543 (1961) (Harlan, J., dissenting from dismissal of appeal). Central among these protected liberties is an individual's "freedom of personal choice in matters of marriage and family life." *Roe*, 410 U. S., at 169 (Stewart, J., concurring). . . .

At the same time, the Court in *Roe* acknowledged that the woman's fundamental right "is not unqualified and must be considered against important state interests in abortion." *Roe*, 410 U. S., at 154. But restrictive state regulation of the right to choose abortion, as with other fundamental rights subject to searching judicial examination, must be supported by a compelling state interest. *Id.*, at 155. We have recognized two such interests that may justify state regulation of abortions. . . .

First, a State has an "important and legitimate interest in protecting the potentiality of human life." *Id.,* at 162. Although this interest exists "throughout the course of the woman's pregnancy," *Beal* v. *Doe,* 432 U. S. 438, 446 (1977), it becomes compelling only at viability, the point at which the fetus "has the capability of meaningful life outside the mother's womb," *Roe, supra,* at 163. See *Planned Parenthood of Central Missouri* v. *Danforth,* 428 U. S. 52, 63–65 (1976). At viability this interest in protecting the potential life of the unborn child is so important that the State may proscribe abortions altogether, "except when it is necessary to preserve the life or health of the mother." *Roe,* 410 U. S., at 164.

Second, because a State has a legitimate concern with the health of women who undergo abortions, "a State may properly assert important interests in safeguarding health [and] in maintaining medical standards." We held in *Roe,* however, that this health interest does not become compelling until "approximately the end of the first trimester" of pregnancy. . . . Until that time, a pregnant woman must be permitted, in consultation with her physician, to decide to have an abortion and to effectuate that decision "free of interference by the State." . . .

This does not mean that a State never may enact a regulation touching on the woman's abortion right during the first weeks of pregnancy. Certain regulations that have no significant impact on the woman's exercise of her right may be permissible where justified by important state health objectives. In *Danforth, supra,* we unanimously upheld two Missouri statutory provisions, applicable to the first trimester, requiring the woman to provide her informed written consent to the abortion and the physician to keep certain records, even though comparable requirements were not imposed on most other medical procedures. See 428 U. S., at 65–67, 79–81. The decisive factor was that the State met its burden of demonstrating that these regulations furthered important health-related state concerns. . . . But even these minor regulations on the abortion procedure during the first trimester may not interfere with physician-patient consultation or with the woman's choice between abortion and childbirth.

From approximately the end of the first trimester of pregnancy, the State "may regulate the abortion procedure to the extent that the regulation reasonably relates to the preservation and protection of maternal health." . . . *Roe,* 410 U. S., at 163. The State's discretion to regulate on this basis does not, however, permit it to adopt abortion regulations that depart from accepted medical practice. We have rejected a State's attempt to ban a particular second-trimester abortion procedure, where the ban would have increased the costs and limited the availability of abortions without promoting important health benefits. See *Danforth,* 428 U. S., at 77–78. If a State requires licensing or undertakes to regulate the performance of abortions during this period, the health standards adopted must be "legitimately related

to the objective the State seeks to accomplish." *Doe*, 410 U. S., at 195. . . .
There can be no doubt that § 1870.03's second-trimester hospitalization
requirement places a significant obstacle in the path of women seeking an
abortion. A primary burden created by the requirement is additional cost to
the woman. The Court of Appeals noted that there was testimony that a
second-trimester abortion costs more than twice as much in a hospital as in a
clinic. See 651 F. 2d, at 1209 (in-hospital abortion costs $850–$900, whereas
a dilatation-and-evacuation (D&E) abortion performed in a clinic costs
$350–$400). . . . Moreover, the court indicated that second-trimester abortions were rarely performed in Akron hospitals. *Ibid.* (only nine second-
trimester abortions performed in Akron hospitals in the year before
trial). . . . Thus, a second-trimester hospitalization requirement may force
women to travel to find available facilities, resulting in both financial expense and additional health risk. . . .

Akron does not contend that § 1870.03 imposes only an insignificant burden on women's access to abortion, but rather defends it as a reasonable
health regulation. This position had strong support at the time of *Roe* v.
Wade, as hospitalization for second-trimester abortions was recommended
by the American Public Health Association (APHA), see *Roe*, 410 U. S., at
143–146, and the American College of Obstetricians and Gynecologists
(ACOG), see Standards for Obstetric-Gynecologic Services 65 (4th ed.
1974). Since then, however, the safety of second-trimester abortions has increased dramatically.[22] The principal reason is that the D&E procedure is
now widely and successfully used for second-trimester abortions.[23] The
Court of Appeals found that there was "an abundance of evidence that D&E
is the safest method of performing post-first trimester abortions today." 651
F. 2d, at 1209. The availability of the D&E procedure during the interval
between approximately 12 and 16 weeks of pregnancy, a period during
which other second-trimester abortion techniques generally cannot be
used,[24] has meant that women desiring an early second-trimester abortion no

---

22. The death-to-case ratio for all second-trimester abortions in this country fell
from 14.4 deaths per 100,000 abortions in 1972 to 7.6 per 100,000 in 1977. See Tyler,
Cates, Schulz, Selik, & Smith, Second-Trimester Induced Abortion in the United
States, published in Second-Trimester Abortion 17–20.

23. At the time *Roe* was decided, the D&E procedure was used only to perform first-
trimester abortions.

24. Instillation procedures, the primary means of performing a second-trimester
abortion before the development of D&E, generally cannot be performed until approximately the 16th week of pregnancy because until that time the amniotic sac
is too small. See Grimes & Cates, Dilatation and Evacuation, published in Second-
Trimester Abortion 121.

longer are forced to incur the health risks of waiting until at least the 16th week of pregnancy.

For our purposes, an even more significant factor is that experience indicates that D&E may be performed safely on an outpatient basis in appropriate nonhospital facilities. The evidence is strong enough to have convinced the APHA to abandon its prior recommendation of hospitalization for all second-trimester abortions. . . .

These developments, and the professional commentary supporting them, constitute impressive evidence that—at least during the early weeks of the second trimester—D&E abortions may be performed as safely in an outpatient clinic as in a full-service hospital. . . . We conclude, therefore, that "present medical knowledge," *Roe, supra,* at 163, convincingly undercuts Akron's justification for requiring that *all* second-trimester abortions be performed in a hospital. . . .

We turn next to § 1870.05(B), the provision prohibiting a physician from performing an abortion on a minor pregnant woman under the age of 15 unless he obtains "the informed written consent of one of her parents or her legal guardian" or unless the minor obtains "an order from a court having jurisdiction over her that the abortion be performed or induced." The District Court invalidated this provision because "[i]t does not establish a procedure by which a minor can avoid a parental veto of her abortion decision by demonstrating that her decision is, in fact, informed. Rather, it requires, in all cases, both the minor's informed consent and either parental consent or a court order." 479 F. Supp., at 1201. The Court of Appeals affirmed on the same basis. . . .

The relevant legal standards are not in dispute. The Court has held that "the State may not impose a blanket provision . . . requiring the consent of a parent or person *in loco parentis* as a condition for abortion of an unmarried minor." *Danforth, supra,* at 74. In *Bellotti* v. *Baird,* 443 U. S. 622 (1979) *(Bellotti II)*, a majority of the Court indicated that a State's interest in protecting immature minors will sustain a requirement of a consent substitute, either parental or judicial. See *id.,* at 640–642 (plurality opinion for four Justices); *id.,* at 656–657 (WHITE, J., dissenting) (expressing approval of absolute parental or judicial consent requirement). . . . The *Bellotti II* plurality cautioned, however, that the State must provide an alternative procedure whereby a pregnant minor may demonstrate that she is sufficiently mature to make the abortion decision herself or that, despite her immaturity, an abortion would be in her best interests. 443 U. S., at 643–644. Under these decisions, it is clear that Akron may not make a blanket determination that *all* minors under the age of 15 are too immature to make this decision or that an abortion never may be in the minor's best interests without parental approval.

Akron's ordinance does not create expressly the alternative procedure required by *Bellotti II*. But Akron contends that the Ohio Juvenile Court will qualify as a "court having jurisdiction" within the meaning of § 1870.05(B), and that "it is not to be assumed that during the course of the juvenile proceedings the Court will not construe the ordinance in a manner consistent with the constitutional requirement of a determination of the minor's ability to make an informed consent." Brief for Petitioner in No. 81–746, p. 28. Akron concludes that the courts below should not have invalidated § 1870.05(B) on its face. The city relies on *Bellotti* v. *Baird*, 428 U. S. 132 (1976) *(Bellotti I)*, in which the Court did not decide whether a State's parental consent provisions were unconstitutional as applied to mature minors, holding instead that "abstention is appropriate where an unconstrued state statute is susceptible of a construction by the state judiciary 'which might avoid in whole or in part the necessity for federal constitutional adjudication, or at least materially change the nature of the problem.'" *Id.*, at 146–147 (quoting *Harrison* v. *NAACP*, 360 U. S. 167, 177 (1959)). See also *H. L.* v. *Matheson*, 450 U. S. 398 (1981) (refusing to decide whether parental notice statute would be constitutional as applied to mature minors). . . .

We do not think that the abstention principle should have been applied here. It is reasonable to assume, as we did in *Bellotti I* and *Matheson*, that a state court presented with a state statute specifically governing abortion consent procedures for pregnant minors will attempt to construe the statute consistently with constitutional requirements. This suit, however, concerns a municipal ordinance that creates no procedures for making the necessary determinations. Akron seeks to invoke the Ohio statute governing juvenile proceedings, but that statute neither mentions minors' abortions nor suggests that the Ohio Juvenile Court has authority to inquire into a minor's maturity or emancipation. . . . In these circumstances, we do not think that the Akron ordinance, as applied in Ohio juvenile proceedings, is reasonably susceptible of being construed to create an "opportunity for case-by-case evaluations of the maturity of pregnant minors." *Bellotti II* (plurality opinion). We therefore affirm the Court of Appeals' judgment that § 1870.05(B) is unconstitutional.

V

The Akron ordinance provides that no abortion shall be performed except "with the informed written consent of the pregnant woman, . . . given freely and without coercion." § 1870.06(A). Furthermore, "in order to insure that the consent for an abortion is truly informed consent," the woman must be "orally informed by her attending physician" of the status of her pregnancy, the development of her fetus, the date of possible viability, the physical and emotional complications that may result from an abortion, and the availability of agencies to provide her with assistance and information with respect to birth control, adoption, and childbirth. § 1870.06(B). In addition, the attending physician must inform her "of the particular risks associated with her own pregnancy and the abortion technique to be employed . . . [and] other information which in his own medical judgment is relevant to her decision as to whether to have an abortion or carry her pregnancy to term." § 1870.06(C). . . .

The validity of an informed consent requirement . . . rests on the State's interest in protecting the health of the pregnant woman. The decision to have an abortion has "implications far broader than those associated with most other kinds of medical treatment," *Bellotti II*, 443 U. S., at 649 (plurality opinion), and thus the State legitimately may seek to ensure that it has been made "in the light of all attendant circumstances—psychological and emotional as well as physical—that might be relevant to the well-being of the patient." *Colautti* v. *Franklin*, 439 U. S., at 394. . . . This does not mean, however, that a State has unreviewable authority to decide what information a woman must be given before she chooses to have an abortion. It remains primarily the responsibility of the physician to ensure that appropriate information is conveyed to his patient, depending on her particular circumstances. *Danforth*'s recognition of the State's interest in ensuring that this information be given will not justify abortion regulations designed to influence the woman's informed choice between abortion or childbirth. . . .

B

Viewing the city's regulations in this light, we believe that § 1870.06(B) attempts to extend the State's interest in ensuring "informed consent" beyond permissible limits. First, it is fair to say that much of the information required is designed not to inform the woman's consent but rather to persuade her to withhold it altogether. Subsection (3) requires the physician to inform his patient that "the unborn child is a human life from the moment of conception," a requirement inconsistent with the Court's holding in *Roe* v. *Wade* that a State may not adopt one theory of when life begins to justify its regulation of abortions. See 410 U. S., at 159–162. Moreover, much of the detailed description of "the anatomical and physiological characteristics of the particular unborn child" required by subsection (3) would involve at best speculation by the physician. . . . And subsection (5), that begins with the dubious statement that "abortion is a major surgical procedure" . . . and proceeds to describe numerous possible physical and psychological complications of abortion, . . . is a "parade of horribles" intended to suggest that abortion is a particularly dangerous procedure.

An additional, and equally decisive, objection to § 1870.06(B) is its intrusion upon the discretion of the pregnant woman's physician. This provision specifies a litany of information that the physician must recite to each woman regardless of whether in his judgment the information is relevant to her personal decision. For example, even if the physician believes that some of the risks outlined in subsection (5) are nonexistent for a particular patient, he remains obligated to describe them to her. In *Danforth* the Court warned against placing the physician in just such an "undesired and uncomfortable straitjacket." 428 U. S., at 67, n. 8. Consistent with its interest in ensuring informed consent, a State may require that a physician make certain that his patient understands the physical and emotional implications of having an abortion. But Akron has gone far beyond merely describing the general subject matter relevant to informed consent. By insisting upon recitation of a lengthy and inflexible list of information, Akron unreasonably has placed "obstacles in the path of the doctor upon whom [the woman is] entitled to rely for advice in connection with her decision." *Whalen* v. *Roe*, 429 U. S., at 604, n. 33. . . .

C

Section 1870.06(C) presents a different question. Under this provision, the "attending physician" must inform the woman

"of the particular risks associated with her own pregnancy and the abortion technique to be employed including providing her with at least a general description of the medical instructions to be followed subsequent to the abortion in order to insure her safe recovery, and shall in addition provide her with such other information which in his own medical judgment is relevant to her decision as to whether to have an abortion or carry her pregnancy to term."

The information required clearly is related to maternal health and to the State's legitimate purpose in requiring informed consent. Nonetheless, the Court of Appeals determined that it interfered with the physician's medical judgment "in exactly the same way as section 1870.06(B). It requires the doctor to make certain disclosures in all cases, regardless of his own professional judgment as to the desirability of doing so." 651 F. 2d, at 1207. This was a misapplication of *Danforth.* There we construed "informed consent" to mean "the giving of information to the patient as to just what would be done and as to its consequences." 428 U. S., at 67, n. 8. We see no significant difference in Akron's requirement that the woman be told of the particular risks of her pregnancy and the abortion technique to be used, and be given general instructions on proper postabortion care. Moreover, in contrast to subsection (B), § 1870.06(C) merely describes in general terms the information to be disclosed. It properly leaves the precise nature and amount of this disclosure to the physician's discretion and "medical judgment."

The Court of Appeals also held, however, that § 1870.06(C) was invalid because it required that the disclosure be made by the "attending physician." The court found that "the practice of all three plaintiff clinics has been for the counseling to be conducted by persons other than the doctor who performs the abortion," 651 F. 2d, at 1207, and determined that Akron had not justified requiring the physician personally to describe the health risks. Akron challenges this holding as contrary to our cases that emphasize the importance of the physician-patient relationship. In Akron's view, as in the view of the dissenting judge below, the "attending physician" requirement "does no more than seek to ensure that there is in fact a true physician-patient relationship even for the woman who goes to an abortion clinic." *Id.,* at 1217 (Kennedy, J., concurring in part and dissenting in part). . . .

We are not convinced, however, that there is as vital a state need for insisting that the physician performing the abortion, or for that matter any physician, personally counsel the patient in the absence of a request. The State's interest is in ensuring that the woman's consent is informed and unpressured; the critical factor is whether she obtains the necessary information and counseling from a qualified person, not the identity of the person from whom she obtains it. . . . Akron and intervenors strongly urge that the nonphysician counselors at the plaintiff abortion clinics are not trained or qualified to perform this important function. The courts below made no such findings, however, and on the record before us we cannot say that the woman's consent to the abortion will not be informed if a physician delegates the counseling task to another qualified individual. . . .

The Akron ordinance prohibits a physician from performing an abortion until 24 hours after the pregnant woman signs a consent form. § 1870.07.[42] The District Court upheld this provision on the ground that it furthered Akron's interest in ensuring "that a woman's abortion decision is made after careful consideration of all the facts applicable to her particular situation." 479 F. Supp., at 1204. The Court of Appeals reversed, finding that the inflexible waiting period had "no medical basis," and that careful consideration of the abortion decision by the woman "is beyond the state's power to require." 651 F. 2d, at 1208. We affirm the Court of Appeals' judgment. . . .

---

42. This provision does not apply if the physician certifies in writing that "there is an emergency need for an abortion to be performed or induced such that continuation of the pregnancy poses an immediate threat and grave risk to the life or physical health of the pregnant woman." § 1870.12.

We find that Akron has failed to demonstrate that any legitimate state interest is furthered by an arbitrary and inflexible waiting period. There is no evidence suggesting that the abortion procedure will be performed more safely. Nor are we convinced that the State's legitimate concern that the woman's decision be informed is reasonably served by requiring a 24-hour delay as a matter of course. The decision whether to proceed with an abortion is one as to which it is important to "affor[d] the physician adequate discretion in the exercise of his medical judgment." *Colautti* v. *Franklin*, 439 U. S., at 387. In accordance with the ethical standards of the profession, a physician will advise the patient to defer the abortion when he thinks this will be beneficial to her. . . . But if a woman, after appropriate counseling, is prepared to give her written informed consent and proceed with the abortion, a State may not demand that she delay the effectuation of that decision.

VII

Section § 1870.16 of the Akron ordinance requires physicians performing abortions to "insure that the remains of the unborn child are disposed of in a humane and sanitary manner." The Court of Appeals found that the word "humane" was impermissibly vague as a definition of conduct subject to criminal prosecution. The court invalidated the entire provision, declining to sever the word "humane" in order to uphold the requirement that disposal be "sanitary." See 651 F. 2d, at 1211. We affirm this judgment.

Akron contends that the purpose of § 1870.16 is simply "'to preclude the mindless dumping of aborted fetuses onto garbage piles.'" *Planned Parenthood Assn.* v. *Fitzpatrick*, 401 F. Supp. 554, 573 (ED Pa. 1975) (three-judge court) (quoting State's characterization of legislative purpose), summarily aff'd *sub nom. Franklin* v. *Fitzpatrick*, 428 U. S. 901 (1976). . . . It is far from clear, however, that this provision has such a limited intent. The phrase "humane and sanitary" does, as the Court of Appeals noted, suggest a possible intent to "mandate some sort of 'decent burial' of an embryo at the earliest stages of formation." 651 F. 2d, at 1211. This level of uncertainty is fatal where criminal liability is imposed. See *Colautti* v. *Franklin, supra*, at 396. Because § 1870.16 fails to give a physician "fair notice that his contemplated conduct is forbidden," *United States* v. *Harriss*, 347 U. S. 612, 617 (1954), we agree that it violates the Due Process Clause. . . .

JUSTICE O'CONNOR, with whom JUSTICE WHITE and JUSTICE REHNQUIST join, dissenting.

In *Roe* v. *Wade*, 410 U. S. 113 (1973), the Court held that the "right of privacy . . . founded in the Fourteenth Amendment's concept of personal liberty and restrictions upon state action . . . is broad enough to encompass a woman's decision whether or not to terminate her pregnancy." *Id.,* at 153. The parties in these cases have not asked the Court to re-examine the validity of that holding and the court below did not address it. Accordingly, the Court does not re-examine its previous holding. Nonetheless, it is apparent from the Court's opinion that neither sound constitutional theory nor our need to decide cases based on the application of neutral principles can accommodate an analytical framework that varies according to the "stages" of pregnancy, where those stages, and their concomitant standards of review, differ according to the level of medical technology available when a particular challenge to state regulation occurs. The Court's analysis of the Akron regulations is inconsistent both with the methods of analysis employed in previous cases dealing with abortion, and with the Court's approach to fundamental rights in other areas.

Our recent cases indicate that a regulation imposed on "a lawful abortion 'is not unconstitutional unless it unduly burdens the right to seek an abortion.'" *Maher* v. *Roe,* 432 U. S. 464, 473 (1977) (quoting *Bellotti* v. *Baird,* 428 U. S. 132, 147 (1977) *(Bellotti I)).* See also *Harris* v. *McRae,* 448 U. S. 297, 314 (1980). In my view, this "unduly burdensome" standard should be applied to the challenged regulations throughout the entire pregnancy without reference to the particular "stage" of pregnancy involved. If the particular regulation does not "unduly burde[n]" the fundamental right, *Maher, supra,* at 473, then our evaluation of that regulation is limited to our determination that the regulation rationally relates to a legitimate state purpose. Irrespective of what we may believe is wise or prudent policy in this difficult area, "the Constitution does not constitute us as 'Platonic Guardians' nor does it vest in this Court the authority to strike down laws because they do not meet our standards of desirable social policy, 'wisdom,' or 'common sense.'" *Plyler* v. *Doe,* 457 U. S. 202, 242 (1982) (BURGER, C. J., dissenting).

I

The trimester or "three-stage" approach adopted by the Court in *Roe,* . . . and, in a modified form, employed by the Court to analyze the regulations in these cases, cannot be supported as a legitimate or useful framework for accommodating the woman's right and the State's interests. The decision of the Court today graphically illustrates why the trimester approach is a completely unworkable method of accommodating the conflicting personal rights and compelling state interests that are involved in the abortion context.

As the Court indicates today, the State's compelling interest in maternal health changes as medical technology changes, and any health regulation must not "depart from accepted medical practice." . . . In applying this standard, the Court holds that "the safety of second-trimester abortions has increased dramatically" since 1973, when *Roe* was decided. . . . Although a regulation such as one requiring that all second-trimester abortions be performed in hospitals "had strong support" in 1973 "as a reasonable health regulation," *ante*, at 435, this regulation can no longer stand because, according to the Court's diligent research into medical and scientific literature, the dilation and evacuation (D&E) procedure, used in 1973 only for first-trimester abortions, "is now widely and successfully used for second-trimester abortions." . . . Further, the medical literature relied on by the Court indicates that the D&E procedure may be performed in an appropriate nonhospital setting for "at least . . . the early weeks of the second trimester. . . . " *Ante*, at 437. The Court then chooses the period of 16 weeks of gestation as that point at which D&E procedures may be performed safely in a nonhospital setting, and thereby invalidates the Akron hospitalization regulation.

It is not difficult to see that despite the Court's purported adherence to the trimester approach adopted in *Roe*, the lines drawn in that decision have now been "blurred" because of what the Court accepts as technological advancement in the safety of abortion procedure. The State may no longer rely on a "bright line" that separates permissible from impermissible regulation, and it is no longer free to consider the second trimester as a unit and weigh the risks posed by all abortion procedures throughout that trimester. . . . Rather, the State must continuously and conscientiously study contemporary medical and scientific literature in order to determine whether the effect of a particular regulation is to "depart from accepted medical practice" insofar as particular procedures and particular periods within the trimester are concerned. Assuming that legislative bodies are able to engage in this exacting task . . . it is difficult to believe that our Constitution *requires* that they do it as a prelude to protecting the health of their citizens. It is even more difficult to believe that this Court, without the resources available to those bodies entrusted with making legislative choices, believes itself competent to make these inquiries and to revise these standards every time the American College of Obstetricians and Gynecologists (ACOG) or similar group revises its views about what is and what is not appropriate medical procedure in this area. Indeed, the ACOG Standards on which the Court relies were changed in 1982 after trial in the present cases. Before ACOG changed its Standards in 1982, it recommended that all mid-trimester abortions be performed in a hospital. See 651 F. 2d 1198, 1209 (CA6 1981). As today's decision indicates, medical technology is changing, and this change will necessitate our continued functioning as the Nation's "*ex officio* medical board with powers to approve or disapprove medical and operative practices and standards throughout the United States." *Planned Parenthood of Central Missouri* v. *Danforth*, 428 U. S. 52, 99 (1976) (WHITE, J., concurring in part and dissenting in part).

Just as improvements in medical technology inevitably will move *forward* the point at which the State may regulate for reasons of maternal health, different technological improvements will move *backward* the point of viability at which the State may proscribe abortions except when necessary to preserve the life and health of the mother.

In 1973, viability before 28 weeks was considered unusual. The 14th edition of L. Hellman & J. Pritchard, Williams Obstetrics (1971), on which the Court relied in *Roe* for its understanding of viability, stated, at 493, that "[a]ttainment of a [fetal] weight of 1,000 g [or a fetal age of approximately 28 weeks' gestation] is . . . widely used as the criterion of viability." However, recent studies have demonstrated increasingly earlier fetal viability.[5] It is certainly reasonable to believe that fetal viability in the first trimester of pregnancy may be possible in the not too distant future. Indeed, the Court has explicitly acknowledged that *Roe* left the point of viability "flexible for anticipated advancements in medical skill." *Colautti* v. *Franklin*, 439 U. S. 379, 387 (1979). "[W]e recognized in *Roe* that viability was a matter of medical judgment, skill, and technical ability, and we preserved the flexibility of the term." *Danforth, supra*, at 64.

The *Roe* framework, then, is clearly on a collision course with itself. As the medical risks of various abortion procedures decrease, the point at which

5. One study shows that infants born alive with a gestational age of less than 25 weeks and weight between 500 and 1,249 grams have a 20% chance of survival. See Phillip, Little, Polivy, & Lucey, Neonatal Mortality Risk for the Eighties: The Importance of Birth Weight/Gestational Age Groups, 68 Pediatrics 122 (1981). Another recent comparative study shows that preterm infants with a weight of 1,000 grams or less born in one hospital had a 42% rate of survival. Kopelman, The Smallest Preterm Infants: Reasons for Optimism and New Dilemmas, 132 Am. J. Diseases of Children 461 (1978). An infant weighing 484 grams and having a gestational age of 22 weeks at birth is now thriving in a Los Angeles hospital, and the attending physician has stated that the infant has a "95% chance of survival." Washington Post, Mar. 31, 1983, p. A2, col. 2. The aborted fetus in *Simopoulos* v. *Virginia, post*, p. 506, weighed 495 grams and had a gestational age of approximately 22 weeks.

Recent developments promise even greater success in overcoming the various respiratory and immunological neonatal complications that stand in the way of increased fetal viability. See, *e. g.*, Beddis, Collins, Levy, Godfrey, & Silverman, New Technique for Servo-Control of Arterial Oxygen Tension in Preterm Infants, 54 Archives of Disease in Childhood 278 (1979). "There is absolutely no question that in the current era there has been a sustained and progressive improvement in the outlook for survival of small premature infants." Stern, Intensive Care of the Pre-Term Infant, 26 Danish Med. Bull. 144 (1979).

the State may regulate for reasons of maternal health is moved further forward to actual childbirth. As medical science becomes better able to provide for the separate existence of the fetus, the point of viability is moved further back toward conception. Moreover, it is clear that the trimester approach violates the fundamental aspiration of judicial decisionmaking through the application of neutral principles "sufficiently absolute to give them roots throughout the community and continuity over significant periods of time. . . . " A. Cox, The Role of the Supreme Court in American Government 114 (1976). The *Roe* framework is inherently tied to the state of medical technology that exists whenever particular litigation ensues. Although legislatures are better suited to make the necessary factual judgments in this area, the Court's framework forces legislatures, as a matter of constitutional law, to speculate about what constitutes "accepted medical practice" at any given time. Without the necessary expertise or ability, courts must then pretend to act as science review boards and examine those legislative judgments.

The Court adheres to the *Roe* framework because the doctrine of *stare decisis* "demands respect in a society governed by the rule of law." Although respect for *stare decisis* cannot be challenged, "this Court's considered practice [is] not to apply *stare decisis* as rigidly in constitutional as in nonconstitutional cases." *Glidden Co.* v. *Zdanok,* 370 U. S. 530, 543 (1962). Although we must be mindful of the "desirability of continuity of decision in constitutional questions . . . when convinced of former error, this Court has never felt constrained to follow precedent. In constitutional questions, where correction depends upon amendment and not upon legislative action this Court throughout its history has freely exercised its power to reexamine the basis of its constitutional decisions." *Smith* v. *Allwright,* 321 U. S. 649, 665 (1944) (footnote omitted).

Even assuming that there is a fundamental right to terminate pregnancy in some situations, there is no justification in law or logic for the trimester framework adopted in *Roe* and employed by the Court today on the basis of *stare decisis.* For the reasons stated above, that framework is clearly an unworkable means of balancing the fundamental right and the compelling state interests that are indisputably implicated. . . .

The fallacy inherent in the *Roe* framework is apparent: just because the State has a compelling interest in ensuring maternal safety once an abortion may be more dangerous than childbirth, it simply does not follow that the State has *no* interest before that point that justifies state regulation to ensure that first-trimester abortions are performed as safely as possible. . . .

The state interest in potential human life is likewise extant throughout pregnancy. In *Roe,* the Court held that although the State had an important and legitimate interest in protecting potential life, that interest could not become compelling until the point at which the fetus was viable. The difficulty with this analysis is clear: *potential* life is no less potential in the first weeks of pregnancy than it is at viability or afterward. At any stage in pregnancy, there is the *potential* for human life. Although the Court refused to "resolve the difficult question of when life begins," *id.*, at 159, the Court chose the point of viability—when the fetus is *capable* of life independent of its mother—to permit the complete proscription of abortion. The choice of viability as the point at which the state interest in *potential* life becomes compelling is no less arbitrary than choosing any point before viability or any point afterward. Accordingly, I believe that the State's interest in protecting potential human life exists throughout the pregnancy.

III

Although the State possesses compelling interests in the protection of potential human life and in maternal health throughout pregnancy, not every regulation that the State imposes must be measured against the State's compelling interests and examined with strict scrutiny. This Court has acknowledged that "the right in *Roe* v. *Wade* can be understood only by considering both the woman's interest and the nature of the State's interference with it. *Roe* did not declare an unqualified 'constitutional right to an abortion.' . . . Rather, the right protects the woman from unduly burdensome interference with her freedom to decide whether to terminate her pregnancy." *Maher*, 432 U. S., at 473–474. The Court and its individual Justices have repeatedly utilized the "unduly burdensome" standard in abortion cases.[8]

---

8. See *Bellotti* v. *Baird*, 428 U. S. 132, 147 (1976) *(Bellotti I)* (State may not "impose undue burdens upon a minor capable of giving an informed consent." In *Bellotti I*, the Court left open the question whether a judicial hearing would unduly burden the *Roe* right of an adult woman. See 428 U. S., at 147); *Bellotti* v. *Baird*, 443 U. S. 622, 640 (1979) *(Bellotti II)* (opinion of POWELL, J.) (State may not "unduly burden the right to seek an abortion"); *Harris* v. *McRae*, 448 U. S. 297, 314 (1980) ("The doctrine of *Roe* v. *Wade*, the Court held in *Maher*, 'protects the woman from unduly burdensome interference with her freedom to decide whether to terminate her pregnancy,' [432 U. S.], at 473–474, such as the severe criminal sanctions at issue in *Roe* v. *Wade, supra*, or the absolute requirement of spousal consent for an abortion challenged in *Planned Parenthood of Central Missouri* v. *Danforth*, 428 U. S. 52"); *Beal* v. *Doe*, 432 U. S. 438, 446 (1977) (The state interest in protecting potential human life "does not, at least until approximately the third trimester, become sufficiently compelling to justify unduly burdensome state interference . . . "); *Carey* v. *Population Services International*, 431 U. S. 678, 705 (1977) (POWELL, J., concurring in part and concurring in judgment) ("In my view, [*Roe* and *Griswold* v. *Connecticut*, 381 U. S. 479 (1965),] make clear that the [compelling state interest] standard has been invoked only when the state regulation entirely frustrates or heavily burdens the exercise of constitutional rights in this area. See *Bellotti* v. *Baird*, 428 U. S. 132, 147 (1976)"). Even though the Court did not explicitly use the "unduly burdensome" standard in

The requirement that state interference "infringe[s] substantially" or "heavily burden[s]" a right before heightened scrutiny is applied is not novel in our fundamental-rights jurisprudence, or restricted to the abortion context. In *San Antonio Independent School District* v. *Rodriguez*, 411 U. S. 1, 37–38 (1973), we observed that we apply "strict judicial scrutiny" only when legislation may be said to have "'deprived,' 'infringed,' or 'interfered' with the free exercise of some such fundamental personal right or liberty." If the impact of the regulation does not rise to the level appropriate for our strict scrutiny, then our inquiry is limited to whether the state law bears "some rational relationship to legitimate state purposes." *Id.*, at 40. Even in the First Amendment context, we have required in some circumstances that state laws "infringe substantially" on protected conduct, *Gibson* v. *Florida Legislative Investigation Committee*, 372 U. S. 539, 545 (1963), or that there be "a significant encroachment upon personal liberty," *Bates* v. *City of Little Rock*, 361 U. S. 516, 524 (1960). . . .

The "unduly burdensome" standard is particularly appropriate in the abortion context because of the *nature* and *scope* of the right that is involved. The privacy right involved in the abortion context "cannot be said to be absolute." *Roe*, 410 U. S., at 154. "*Roe* did not declare an unqualified 'constitutional right to an abortion.'" *Maher*, 432 U. S., at 473. Rather, the *Roe* right is intended to protect against state action "drastically limiting the availability and safety of the desired service," *id.*, at 472, against the imposition of an "absolute obstacle" on the abortion decision, *Danforth*, 428 U. S., at 70–71, n. 11, or against "official interference" and "coercive restraint" imposed on the abortion decision, *Harris*, 448 U. S., at 328 (WHITE, J., concurring). That a state regulation may "inhibit" abortions to some degree does not require that we find that the regulation is invalid. See *H. L.* v. *Matheson*, 450 U. S. 398, 413 (1981).

The abortion cases demonstrate that an "undue burden" has been found for the most part in situations involving absolute obstacles or severe limitations on the abortion decision. In *Roe*, the Court invalidated a Texas statute that criminalized *all* abortions except those necessary to save the life of the mother. In *Danforth*, the Court invalidated a state prohibition of abortion by saline amniocentesis because the ban had "the effect of inhibiting . . . the vast majority of abortions after the first 12 weeks." 428 U. S., at 79. The Court today acknowledges that the regulation in *Danforth* effectively represented "a *complete* prohibition on abortions in certain circumstances" (emphasis added). In *Danforth*, the Court also invalidated state regulations

---

evaluating the informed-consent requirement in *Planned Parenthood of Central Missouri* v. *Danforth, supra*, the informed-consent requirement for first-trimester abortions in *Danforth* was upheld because it did not "unduly burde[n] the right to seek an abortion." *Bellotti I, supra*, at 147.

requiring parental or spousal consent as a prerequisite to a first-trimester abortion because the consent requirements effectively and impermissibly delegated a "veto power" to parents and spouses during the first trimester of pregnancy. In both *Bellotti I*, 428 U. S. 132 (1977), and *Bellotti* v. *Baird*, 443 U. S. 622 (1979) *(Bellotti II)*, the Court was concerned with effective parental veto over the abortion decision. . . .

Section 1870.03 of the Akron ordinance requires that second-trimester abortions be performed in hospitals. . . .

The hospitalization requirement does not impose an undue burden, and it is not necessary to apply an exacting standard of review. Further, the regulation has a "rational relation" to a valid state objective of ensuring the health and welfare of its citizens. See *Williamson* v. *Lee Optical Co.*, 348 U. S. 483, 491 (1955). . . .

Section 1870.05(B)(2) of the Akron ordinance provides that no physician shall perform an abortion on a minor under 15 years of age unless the minor gives written consent, and the physician first obtains the informed written consent of a parent or guardian, or unless the minor first obtains "an order from a court having jurisdiction over her that the abortion be performed or induced." . . .

Assuming, *arguendo*, that the Court is correct in holding that a parental notification requirement would be unconstitutional as applied to mature minors,[12] I see no reason to assume that the Akron ordinance and the State Juvenile Court statute compel state judges to notify the parents of a mature minor if such notification was contrary to the minor's best interests. Further, there is no reason to believe that the state courts would construe the consent requirement to impose any type of parental or judicial veto on the abortion decisions of mature minors. In light of the Court's complete lack of knowledge about how the Akron ordinance will operate, and how the Akron ordinance and the State Juvenile Court statute interact, our "'scrupulous regard for the rightful independence of state governments'" counsels against "unnecessary interference by the federal courts with proper and val-

12. In my view, no decision of this Court has yet held that parental notification in the case of mature minors is unconstitutional. Although the plurality opinion of JUSTICE POWELL in *Bellotti II* suggested that the state statute in that case was unconstitutional because, *inter alia*, it failed to provide *all* minors with an opportunity "to go directly to a court without first consulting or notifying her parents," 443 U. S., at 647, the Court in *H. L.* v. *Matheson* held that *unemancipated and immature* minors had "no constitutional right to notify a court in lieu of notifying their parents." 450 U. S., at 412, n. 22. Furthermore, the Court in *H. L.* v. *Matheson* expressly did *not* decide that a parental notification requirement would be unconstitutional if the State otherwise permitted *mature* minors to make abortion decisions free of parental or judicial "veto." See *id.*, at 406–407.

idly administered state concerns, a course so essential to the balanced working of our federal system." *Harrison* v. *NAACP* (quoting *Matthews* v. *Rodgers*, 284 U. S. 521, 525 (1932)).

The Court invalidates the informed-consent provisions of § 1870.06(B) and § 1870.06(C) of the Akron ordinance. . . . Although it finds that subsections (1), (2), (6), and (7) of § 1870.06(B) are "certainly . . . not objectionable," it refuses to sever those provisions from subsections (3), (4), and (5) because the city requires that the "acceptable" information be provided by the attending physician when "much, if not all of it, could be given by a qualified person assisting the physician," *ibid*. Despite the fact that the Court finds that § 1870.06(C) "properly leaves the precise nature and amount of . . . disclosure to the physician's discretion and 'medical judgment,'" the Court also finds § 1870.06(C) unconstitutional because it requires that the disclosure be made by the attending physician, rather than by other "qualified persons" who work at abortion clinics. . . .

The validity of subsections (3), (4), and (5) is not before the Court because it appears that the city of Akron conceded their unconstitutionality before the court below. See Brief for City of Akron in No. 79–3757 (CA6), p. 35; Reply Brief for City of Akron in No. 79–3757 (CA6), pp. 5–9. In my view, the remaining subsections of § 1870.06(B) are separable from the subsections conceded to be unconstitutional. Section 1870.19 contains a separability clause which creates a "'presumption of divisibility'" and places "the burden . . . on the litigant who would escape its operation." *Carter* v. *Carter Coal Co.*, 298 U. S. 238, 335 (1936) (opinion of Cardozo, J.). Akron Center has failed to show that severance of subsections (3), (4), and (5) would "create a program quite different from the one the legislature actually adopted." *Sloan* v. *Lemon*, 413 U. S. 825, 834 (1973).

The remainder of § 1870.06(B), and § 1870.06 (C), impose no undue burden or drastic limitation on the abortion decision. The city of Akron is merely attempting to ensure that the decision to abort is made in light of that knowledge that the city deems relevant to informed choice. As such, these regulations do not impermissibly affect any privacy right under the Fourteenth Amendment.

Section 1870.07 of the Akron ordinance requires a 24-hour waiting period between the signing of a consent form and the actual performance of the abortion, except in cases of emergency. . . .

The waiting period does not apply in cases of medical emergency. Therefore, should the physician determine that the waiting period would increase risks significantly, he or she need not require the woman to wait. The Court's concern in this respect is simply misplaced. Although the waiting period may impose an additional cost on the abortion decision, this increased cost does not unduly burden the availability of abortions or impose an absolute obstacle to access to abortions. Further, the State is not required to "fine-tune" its abortion statutes so as to minimize the costs of abortions. *H. L.* v. *Matheson*, 450 U. S., at 413.

Assuming, *arguendo*, that any additional costs are such as to impose an undue burden on the abortion decision, the State's compelling interests in maternal physical and mental health and protection of fetal life clearly justify the waiting period. As we acknowledged in *Danforth*, 428 U. S., at 67, the decision to abort is "a stressful one," and the waiting period reasonably relates to the State's interest in ensuring that a woman does not make this serious decision in undue haste. The decision also has grave consequences for the fetus, whose life the State has a compelling interest to protect and preserve. "[N]o other [medical] procedure involves the purposeful termination of a potential life." *Harris*, 448 U. S., at 325. The waiting period is surely a small cost to impose to ensure that the woman's decision is well considered in light of its certain and irreparable consequences on fetal life, and the possible effects on her own. . . .

Finally, § 1870.16 of the Akron ordinance requires that "[a]ny physician who shall perform or induce an abortion upon a pregnant woman shall insure that the remains of the unborn child are disposed of in a humane and sanitary manner." The Court finds this provision void for vagueness. I disagree.

In *Planned Parenthood Assn.* v. *Fitzpatrick*, 401 F. Supp. 554 (ED Pa. 1975) (three-judge court), summarily aff'd *sub nom. Franklin* v. *Fitzpatrick*, 428 U. S. 901 (1976), the District Court upheld a "humane disposal" provision against a vagueness attack in light of the State's representation that the intent of the Act "'is to preclude the mindless dumping of aborted fetuses onto garbage piles.'" 401 F. Supp., at 573. The District Court held that different concerns would be implicated if the statute were, at some point, determined to require "expensive burial." *Ibid.* In the present cases, the city of Akron has informed this Court that the intent of the "humane" portion of its statute, as distinguished from the "sanitary" portion, is merely to ensure that fetuses will not be "'dump[ed] . . . on garbage piles.'" Brief for Petitioner in No. 81–746, p. 48. In light of the fact that the city of Akron indicates no intent to require that physicians provide "decent burials" for fetuses, and that "humane" is no more vague than the term "sanitary," the vagueness of which Akron Center does not question, I cannot conclude that the statute is void for vagueness. . . .

PLANNED PARENTHOOD ASSOCIATION OF KANSAS CITY, MISSOURI, INC., ET AL. *v.* ASHCROFT, ATTORNEY GENERAL OF MISSOURI, ET AL.

CERTIORARI TO THE UNITED STATES COURT OF
APPEALS FOR THE EIGHTH CIRCUIT

No. 81–1255. Argued November 30, 1982—Decided June 15, 1983

POWELL, J., announced the judgment of the Court in Part VI and delivered the opinion of the Court with respect to Parts I and II, in which BURGER, C. J., and BRENNAN, MARSHALL, BLACKMUN, and STEVENS, JJ., joined, and an opinion with respect to Parts III, IV, and V, in which BURGER, C. J., joined. BLACKMUN, J., filed an opinion concurring in part and dissenting in part, in which BRENNAN, MARSHALL, and STEVENS, JJ., joined. O'CONNOR, J., filed an opinion concurring in the judgment in part and dissenting in part, in which WHITE and REHNQUIST, JJ., joined.

JUSTICE POWELL announced the judgment of the Court in Part VI and delivered the opinion of the Court with respect to Parts I and II and an opinion with respect to Parts III, IV, and V, in which THE CHIEF JUSTICE joins.

. . . The statutory provision at issue in this case requires the attendance of a second physician at the abortion of a viable fetus. § 188.030.3. This section requires that the second physician "take all reasonable steps in keeping with good medical practice . . . to preserve the life and health of the viable unborn child; provided that it does not pose an increased risk to the life or health of the woman." See n. 3, *supra.* It also provides that the second physician "shall take control of and provide immediate medical care for a child born as a result of the abortion."

The lower courts invalidated § 188.030.3. . . . The plaintiffs, respondents here on this issue, urge affirmance on the grounds that the second-physician requirement distorts the traditional doctor-patient relationship, and is both impractical and costly. They note that Missouri does not require two physicians in attendance for any other medical or surgical procedure, including childbirth or delivery of a premature infant.

The first physician's primary concern will be the life and health of the woman. Many third-trimester abortions in Missouri will be emergency operations, . . . as the State permits these late abortions only when they are necessary to preserve the life or the health of the woman. It is not unreasonable for the State to assume that during the operation the first physician's attention and skills will be directed to preserving the woman's health, and not to protecting the actual life of those fetuses who survive the abortion procedure. Viable fetuses will be in immediate and grave danger because of their premature birth. A second physician, in situations where Missouri permits third-trimester abortions, may be of assistance to the woman's physician in preserving the health and life of the child.

By giving immediate medical attention to a fetus that is delivered alive, the second physician will assure that the State's interests are protected more fully than the first physician alone would be able to do. And given the compelling interest that the State has in preserving life, we cannot say that the Missouri requirement of a second physician in those unusual circumstances where Missouri permits a third-trimester abortion is unconstitutional. Preserving the life of a viable fetus that is aborted may not often be possible, . . . but the State legitimately may choose to provide safeguards for the comparatively few instances of live birth that occur. We believe the second-physician requirement reasonably furthers the State's compelling interest in protecting the lives of viable fetuses, and we reverse the judgment of the Court of Appeals holding that § 188.030.3 is unconstitutional. . . .

SIMOPOULOS v. VIRGINIA

APPEAL FROM THE SUPREME COURT OF VIRGINIA

No. 81–185. Argued November 30, 1982—Decided June 15, 1983

POWELL, J., delivered the opinion of the Court, in which BURGER, C. J., and BRENNAN, MARSHALL, and BLACKMUN, JJ., joined, and in Parts I and II of which WHITE, REHNQUIST, and O'CONNOR, JJ., joined. O'CONNOR, J., filed an opinion concurring in part and concurring in the judgment, in which WHITE and REHNQUIST, JJ., joined. STEVENS, J., filed a dissenting opinion.

JUSTICE POWELL delivered the opinion of the Court.

. . . In furtherance of its compelling interest in maternal health, Virginia has enacted a hospitalization requirement for abortions performed during the second trimester. As a general proposition, physicians' offices are not regulated under Virginia law. . . . Virginia law does not, however, permit a physician licensed in the practice of medicine and surgery to perform an abortion during the second trimester of pregnancy unless "such procedure is performed in a hospital licensed by the State Department of Health." . . .

It is readily apparent that Virginia's second-trimester hospitalization requirement differs from those at issue in *City of Akron, ante,* at 431–432, and *Planned Parenthood Assn. of Kansas City, Mo., Inc.* v. *Ashcroft.* In those cases, we recognized the medical fact that, "at least during the early weeks of the second trimester[,] D&E abortions may be performed as safely in an outpatient clinic as in a full-service hospital." *City of Akron.* The requirements at issue, however, mandated that "all second-trimester abortions must be performed in general, acute-care facilities." *Ashcroft, ante,* at 481. In contrast, the Virginia statutes and regulations do not require that second-trimester abortions be performed exclusively in full-service hospitals. Under Virginia's hospitalization requirement, outpatient surgical hospitals may qualify for licensing as "hospitals" in which second-trimester abortions lawfully may be performed. Thus, our decisions in *City of Akron* and *Ashcroft* are not controlling here.

In view of its interest in protecting the health of its citizens, the State necessarily has considerable discretion in determining standards for the licensing of medical facilities. Although its discretion does not permit it to adopt abortion regulations that depart from accepted medical practice, it does have a legitimate interest in regulating second-trimester abortions and setting forth the standards for facilities in which such abortions are performed.

On their face, the Virginia regulations appear to be generally compatible with accepted medical standards governing outpatient second-trimester abortions. The American Public Health Association (APHA) (Resolution No. 7907), although recognizing "that greater use of the Dilatation and Evacuation procedure makes it possible to perform the vast majority of second trimester abortions during or prior to the 16th week after the last menstrual period," still "[u]rges endorsement of the provision of second trimester abortion in free-standing qualified clinics that meet the state standards required for certification." APHA, The Right to Second Trimester Abortion 1, 2 (1979). The medical profession has not thought that a State's standards need be relaxed merely because the facility performs abortions: "Ambulatory care facilities providing abortion services should meet the same standards of care as those recommended for other surgical procedures performed in the physician's office and outpatient clinic or the free-standing and hospital-based ambulatory setting." American College of Obstetricians and Gynecologists (ACOG), Standards for Obstetric-Gynecologic Services 54 (5th ed. 1982). . . . ("Free-standing or hospital-based ambulatory surgical facilities should be licensed to conform to requirements of state or federal legislation"). Indeed, the medical profession's standards for outpatient surgical facilities are stringent: "Such facilities should maintain the same surgical, anesthetic, and personnel standards as recommended for hospitals." . . .

Given the plain language of the Virginia regulations and the history of their adoption, we see no reason to doubt that an adequately equipped clinic could, upon proper application, obtain an outpatient hospital license permitting the performance of second-trimester abortions. We conclude that Virginia's requirement that second-trimester abortions be performed in licensed clinics is not an unreasonable means of furthering the State's compelling interest in "protecting the woman's own health and safety." *Roe,* 410 U. S., at 150. . . .

THORNBURGH, GOVERNOR OF PENNSYLVANIA, ET AL. v. AMERICAN COLLEGE OF OBSTETRICIANS AND GYNECOLOGISTS ET AL.

APPEAL FROM THE UNITED STATES COURT OF APPEALS
FOR THE THIRD CIRCUIT

No. 84–495. Argued November 5, 1985—Decided June 11, 1986

BLACKMUN, J., delivered the opinion of the Court, in which BRENNAN, MARSHALL, POWELL, and STEVENS, JJ., joined. STEVENS, J., filed a concurring opinion. BURGER, C. J., filed a dissenting opinion. WHITE, J., filed a dissenting opinion, in which REHNQUIST, J., joined. O'CONNOR, J., filed a dissenting opinion, in which REHNQUIST, J., joined.

JUSTICE BLACKMUN delivered the opinion of the Court.

IV

. . . This case, as it comes to us, concerns the constitutionality of six provisions of the Pennsylvania Act that the Court of Appeals struck down as facially invalid: § 3205 ("informed consent"); § 3208 ("printed information"); §§ 3214(a) and (h) (reporting requirements); § 3211(a) (determination of viability); § 3210(b) (degree of care required in postviability abortions); and § 3210(c) (second-physician requirement). We have no reason to address the validity of the other sections of the Act challenged in the District Court. . . .

We turn to the challenged statutes:

1. Section 3205 ("informed consent") and § 3208 ("printed information"). Section 3205(a) requires that the woman give her "voluntary and informed consent" to an abortion. Failure to observe the provisions of § 3205 subjects the physician to suspension or revocation of his license, and subjects any other person obligated to provide information relating to informed consent to criminal penalties. § 3205(c). A requirement that the woman give what is truly a voluntary and informed consent, as a general proposition, is, of course, proper and is surely not unconstitutional. See *Planned Parenthood of Central Missouri* v. *Danforth,* 428 U. S. 52, 67 (1976). But the State may not require the delivery of information designed "to influence the woman's informed choice between abortion or childbirth." *Akron,* 462 U. S., at 443–444.

171

Appellants refer to the Akron ordinance, Brief for Appellants 67, as did this Court in *Akron* itself, 462 U. S., at 445, as "a litany of information" and as "'a parade of horribles'" of dubious validity plainly designed to influence the woman's choice. They would distinguish the Akron situation, however, from the Pennsylvania one. Appellants assert that statutes "describing the general subject matter relevant to informed consent," *ibid.*, and stating "in general terms the information to be disclosed," *id.*, at 447, are permissible, and they further assert that the Pennsylvania statutes do no more than that.

We do not agree. We conclude that, like Akron's ordinance, §§ 3205 and 3208 fail the *Akron* measurement. The two sections prescribe in detail the method for securing "informed consent." Seven explicit kinds of information must be delivered to the woman at least 24 hours before her consent is given, and five of these must be presented by the woman's physician. The five are: (a) the name of the physician who will perform the abortion, (b) the "fact that there may be detrimental physical and psychological effects which are not accurately foreseeable," (c) the "particular medical risks associated with the particular abortion procedure to be employed," (d) the probable gestational age, and (e) the "medical risks associated with carrying her child to term." The remaining two categories are (f) the "fact that medical assistance benefits may be available for prenatal care, childbirth and neonatal care," and (g) the "fact that the father is liable to assist" in the child's support, "even in instances where the father has offered to pay for the abortion." §§ 3205(a)(1) and (2). The woman also must be informed that materials printed and supplied by the Commonwealth that describe the fetus and that list agencies offering alternatives to abortion are available for her review. If she chooses to review the materials but is unable to read, the materials "shall be read to her," and any answer she seeks must be "provided her in her own language." § 3205(a)(2)(iii). She must certify in writing, prior to the abortion, that all this has been done. § 3205(a)(3). The printed materials "shall include the following statement":

> "'There are many public and private agencies willing and able to help you to carry your child to term, and to assist you and your child after your child is born, whether you choose to keep your child or place her or him for adoption. The Commonwealth of Pennsylvania strongly urges you to contact them before making a final decision about abortion. The law requires that your physician or his agent give you the opportunity to call agencies like these before you undergo an abortion.'" § 3208(a)(1).

The materials must describe the "probable anatomical and physiological characteristics of the unborn child at two-week gestational increments from fertilization to full term, including any relevant information on the possibility of the unborn child's survival." § 3208(a)(2). . . .

The requirements of §§ 3205(a)(2)(i) and (ii) that the woman be advised that medical assistance benefits may be available, and that the father is responsible for financial assistance in the support of the child similarly are poorly disguised elements of discouragement for the abortion decision. Much of this would be nonmedical information beyond the physician's area of expertise and, for many patients, would be irrelevant and inappropriate. For a patient with a life-threatening pregnancy, the "information" in its very rendition may be cruel as well as destructive of the physician–patient relationship. As any experienced social worker or other counselor knows, theoretical financial responsibility often does not equate with fulfillment. And a victim of rape should not have to hear gratuitous advice that an unidentified perpetrator is liable for support if she continues the pregnancy to term. Under the guise of informed consent, the Act requires the dissemination of information that is not relevant to such consent, and, thus, it advances no legitimate state interest.

The requirements of §§ 3205(a)(1)(ii) and (iii) that the woman be informed by the physician of "detrimental physical and psychological effects" and of all "particular medical risks" compound the problem of medical attendance, increase the patient's anxiety, and intrude upon the physician's exercise of proper professional judgment. This type of compelled information is the antithesis of informed consent. That the Commonwealth does not, and surely would not, compel similar disclosure of every possible peril of necessary surgery or of simple vaccination, reveals the anti-abortion character of the statute and its real purpose. Pennsylvania, like Akron, "has gone far beyond merely describing the general subject matter relevant to informed consent." *Akron*, 162 U. S., at 445. In addition, the Commonwealth would require the physician to recite its litany "regardless of whether in his judgment the information is relevant to [the patient's] personal decision." *Ibid.* These statutory defects cannot be saved by any facts that might be forthcoming at a subsequent hearing. Section 3205's informational requirements therefore are facially unconstitutional. . . .

WHITE, J., dissenting.

II

As it has evolved in the decisions of this Court, the freedom recognized by the Court in *Roe* v. *Wade* and its progeny is essentially a negative one, based not on the notion that abortion is a good in itself, but only on the view that the legitimate goals that may be served by state coercion of private choices regarding abortion are, at least under some circumstances, outweighed by the damage to individual autonomy and privacy that such coercion entails. In other words, the evil of abortion does not justify the evil of forbidding it. Cf. *Stanley* v. *Georgia*, 394 U. S. 557 (1969). But precisely because *Roe* v. *Wade* is not premised on the notion that abortion is itself desirable (either as a matter of constitutional entitlement or of social policy), the decision does not command the States to fund or encourage abortion, or even to approve of it. Rather, we have recognized that the States may legitimately adopt a policy of encouraging normal childbirth rather than abortion so long as the measures through which that policy is implemented do not amount to direct compulsion of the woman's choice regarding abortion. *Harris* v. *McRae*, 448 U. S. 297 (1980); *Maher* v. *Roe*, 432 U. S. 464 (1977); *Beal* v. *Doe*, 432 U. S. 438 (1977). The provisions before the Court today quite obviously represent the State's effort to implement such a policy.

The majority's opinion evinces no deference toward the State's legitimate policy. Rather, the majority makes it clear from the outset that it simply disapproves of any attempt by Pennsylvania to legislate in this area. The history of the state legislature's decade-long effort to pass a constitutional abortion statute is recounted as if it were evidence of some sinister conspiracy. In fact, of course, the legislature's past failure to predict the evolution of the right first recognized in *Roe* v. *Wade* is understandable and is in itself no ground for condemnation. Moreover, the legislature's willingness to pursue permissible policies through means that go to the limits allowed by existing precedents is no sign of *mens rea*. The majority, however, seems to find it necessary to respond by changing the rules to invalidate what before would have seemed permissible. The result is a decision that finds no justification in the Court's previous holdings, departs from sound principles of constitutional and statutory interpretation, and unduly limits the State's power to implement the legitimate (and in some circumstances compelling) policy of encouraging normal childbirth in preference to abortion. . . .

One searches the majority's opinion in vain for a convincing reason why the apparently laudable policy of promoting informed consent becomes unconstitutional when the subject is abortion. The majority purports to find support in *Akron* v. *Akron Center for Reproductive Health, Inc.*, 462 U. S. 416 (1983). But *Akron* is not controlling. The informed-consent provisions struck down in that case, as characterized by the majority, required the physician to advance tendentious statements concerning the unanswerable question of when human life begins, to offer merely speculative descriptions of the anatomical features of the fetus carried by the woman seeking the abortion, and to recite a "parade of horribles" suggesting that abortion is "a particularly dangerous procedure." I have no quarrel with the general proposition, for which I read *Akron* to stand, that a campaign of state-promulgated disinformation cannot be justified in the name of "informed consent" or "freedom of choice." But the Pennsylvania statute before us cannot be accused of sharing the flaws of the ordinance at issue in *Akron*. As the majority concedes, the statute does not, on its face, require that the patient be given any information that is false or unverifiable. Moreover, it is unquestionable that all of the information required would be relevant in many cases to a woman's decision whether or not to obtain an abortion.

Why, then, is the statute unconstitutional? The majority's argument, while primarily rhetorical, appears to offer three answers. First, the information that must be provided will in some cases be irrelevant to the woman's decision. This is true. Its pertinence to the question of the statute's constitutionality, however, is beyond me. Legislators are ordinarily entitled to proceed on the basis of rational generalizations about the subject matter of legislation, and the existence of particular cases in which a feature of a statute performs no function (or is even counterproductive) ordinarily does not render the statute unconstitutional or even constitutionally suspect. Only where the statute is subject to heightened scrutiny by virtue of its impingement on some fundamental right or its employment of a suspect classification does the imprecision of the "fit" between the statute's ends and means become potentially damning. Here, there is nothing to trigger such scrutiny, for the statute does not directly infringe the allegedly fundamental right at issue—the woman's right to choose an abortion. Indeed, I fail to see how providing a woman with accurate information—whether relevant or irrelevant—could ever be deemed to impair *any* constitutionally protected interest (even if, as the majority hypothesizes, the information may upset her). Thus, the majority's observation that the statute may require the provision of irrelevant information in some cases is itself an irrelevancy.

Second, the majority appears to reason that the informed-consent provisions are invalid because the information they require may increase the woman's "anxiety" about the procedure and even "influence" her in her choice. Again, both observations are undoubtedly true; but they by no means cast the constitutionality of the provisions into question. It is in the very nature of informed-consent provisions that they may produce some anxiety in the patient and influence her in her choice. This is in fact their reason for existence, and—provided that the information required is accurate and nonmisleading—it is an entirely salutary reason. If information may reasonably affect the patient's choice, the patient should have that information; and, as one authority has observed, "the greater the likelihood that particular information will influence [the patient's] decision, the more essential the information arguably becomes for securing her informed consent." Appleton, Doctors, Patients and the Constitution, 63 Wash. U. L. Q. 183, 211 (1985). That the result of the provision of information may be that some women will forgo abortions by no means suggests that providing the information is unconstitutional, for the ostensible objective of *Roe* v. *Wade* is not maximizing the number of abortions, but maximizing choice. Moreover, our decisions in *Maher*, *Beal*, and *Harris* v. *McRae* all indicate that the

State may encourage women to make their choice in favor of childbirth rather than abortion, and the provision of accurate information regarding abortion and its alternatives is a reasonable and fair means of achieving that objective.

Third, the majority concludes that the informed-consent provisions are invalid because they "intrud[e] upon the discretion of the pregnant woman's physician," violate "the privacy of the informed-consent dialogue between the woman and her physician," *ibid.*, and "officially structur[e]" that dialogue, *ante*, at 763. The provisions thus constitute "state medicine" that "infringes upon [the physician's] professional responsibilities." *Ibid.* This is nonsensical. I can concede that the Constitution extends its protection to certain zones of personal autonomy and privacy, see *Griswold* v. *Connecticut*, 381 U. S., at 502 (WHITE, J., concurring in judgment), and I can understand, if not share, the notion that that protection may extend to a woman's decision regarding abortion. But I cannot concede the possibility that the Constitution provides more than minimal protection for the manner in which a physician practices his or her profession or for the "dialogues" in which he or she chooses to participate in the course of treating patients. I had thought it clear that regulation of the practice of medicine, like regulation of other professions and of economic affairs generally, was a matter peculiarly within the competence of legislatures, and that such regulation was subject to review only for rationality. See, *e. g., Williamson* v. *Lee Optical of Oklahoma, Inc.*, 348 U. S. 483 (1955). . . .

WEBSTER, ATTORNEY GENERAL OF MISSOURI, ET AL. *v.* REPRODUCTIVE HEALTH SERVICES ET AL.

APPEAL FROM THE UNITED STATES COURT OF APPEALS FOR THE EIGHTH CIRCUIT

No. 88–605. Argued April 26, 1989—Decided July 3, 1989

REHNQUIST, C. J., announced the judgment of the Court and delivered the opinion for a unanimous Court with respect to Part II–C, the opinion of the Court with respect to Parts I, II–A, and II–B, in which WHITE, O'CONNOR, SCALIA, and KENNEDY, JJ., joined, and an opinion with respect to Parts II–D and III, in which WHITE and KENNEDY, JJ., joined. O'CONNOR, J., and SCALIA, J., filed opinions concurring in part and concurring in the judgment. BLACKMUN, J., filed an opinion concurring in part and dissenting in part, in which BRENNAN and MARSHALL, JJ., joined. STEVENS, J., filed an opinion concurring in part and dissenting in part.

CHIEF JUSTICE REHNQUIST announced the judgment of the Court and delivered the opinion of the Court with respect to Parts I, II–A, II–B, and II–C, and an opinion with respect to Parts II–D and III, in which JUSTICE WHITE and JUSTICE KENNEDY join.

Decision of this case requires us to address four sections of the Missouri Act: (a) the preamble; (b) the prohibition on the use of public facilities or employees to perform abortions; (c) the prohibition on public funding of abortion counseling; and (d) the requirement that physicians conduct viability tests prior to performing abortions. We address these *seriatim.*

A

The Act's preamble, as noted, sets forth "findings" by the Missouri legislature that "[t]he life of each human being begins at conception," and that "[u]nborn children have protectable interests in life, health, and well-being." Mo. Rev. Stat. §§ 1.205.1(1), (2) (1986). The Act then mandates that state laws be interpreted to provide unborn children with "all the rights, privileges, and immunities available to other persons, citizens, and residents of this state," subject to the Constitution and this Court's precedents. § 1.205.2. . . . In invalidating the preamble, the Court of Appeals relied on

177

this Court's dictum that "'a State may not adopt one theory of when life begins to justify its regulation of abortions.'" 851 F. 2d, at 1075–1076, quoting *Akron* v. *Akron Center for Reproductive Health, Inc.,* 462 U. S. 416, 444 (1983), in turn citing *Roe* v. *Wade,* 410 U. S., at 159–162. It rejected Missouri's claim that the preamble was "abortion-neutral," and "merely determine[d] when life begins in a nonabortion context, a traditional state prerogative." 851 F. 2d, at 1076. The court thought that "[t]he only plausible inference" from the fact that "every remaining section of the bill save one regulates the performance of abortions" was that "the state intended its abortion regulations to be understood against the backdrop of its theory of life." . . .

The State contends that the preamble itself is precatory and imposes no substantive restrictions on abortions, and that appellees therefore do not have standing to challenge it. Brief for Appellants 21–24. Appellees, on the other hand, insist that the preamble is an operative part of the Act intended to guide the interpretation of other provisions of the Act. Brief for Appellees 19–23. They maintain, for example, that the preamble's definition of life may prevent physicians in public hospitals from dispensing certain forms of contraceptives, such as the intrauterine device.

In our view, the Court of Appeals misconceived the meaning of the *Akron* dictum, which was only that a State could not "justify" an abortion regulation otherwise invalid under *Roe* v. *Wade* on the ground that it embodied the State's view about when life begins. Certainly the preamble does not by its terms regulate abortion or any other aspect of appellees' medical practice. The Court has emphasized that *Roe* v. *Wade* "implies no limitation on the authority of a State to make a value judgment favoring childbirth over abortion." *Maher* v. *Roe,* 432 U. S., at 474. The preamble can be read simply to express that sort of value judgment. . . .

Section 188.210 provides that "[i]t shall be unlawful for any public employee within the scope of his employment to perform or assist an abortion, not necessary to save the life of the mother," while § 188.215 makes it "unlawful for any public facility to be used for the purpose of performing or assisting an abortion not necessary to save the life of the mother." . . . The Court of Appeals held that these provisions contravened this Court's abortion decisions. 851 F. 2d, at 1082–1083. We take the contrary view. . . .

. . . Relying on *Maher,* the Court in *Poelker* v. *Doe,* 432 U. S. 519, 521 (1977), held that the city of St. Louis committed "no constitutional violation . . . in electing, as a policy choice, to provide publicly financed hospital services for childbirth without providing corresponding services for nontherapeutic abortions."

More recently, in *Harris* v. *McRae,* 448 U. S. 297 (1980), the Court up-

held "the most restrictive version of the Hyde Amendment," which withheld from States federal funds under the Medicaid program to reimburse
the costs of abortions, "'except where the life of the mother would be endangered if the fetus were carried to term.'" *Ibid.* (quoting Pub. L. 94–439,
§ 209, 90 Stat. 1434). As in *Maher* and *Poelker,* the Court required only a
showing that Congress' authorization of "reimbursement for medically necessary services generally, but not for certain medically necessary abortions"
was rationally related to the legitimate governmental goal of encouraging
childbirth. 448 U. S., at 325.

The Court of Appeals distinguished these cases on the ground that "[t]o
prevent access to a public facility does more than demonstrate a political
choice in favor of childbirth; it clearly narrows and in some cases forecloses
the availability of abortion to women." 851 F. 2d, at 1081. The court reasoned that the ban on the use of public facilities "could prevent a woman's
chosen doctor from performing an abortion because of his unprivileged status at other hospitals or because a private hospital adopted a similar anti-
abortion stance." *Ibid.* It also thought that "[s]uch a rule could increase the
cost of obtaining an abortion and delay the timing of it as well." *Ibid.*

We think that this analysis is much like that which we rejected in *Maher,*
Poelker, and *McRae.* As in those cases, the State's decision here to use public
facilities and staff to encourage childbirth over abortion "places no governmental obstacle in the path of a woman who chooses to terminate her pregnancy." *McRae,* 448 U. S., at 315. Just as Congress' refusal to fund abortions
in *McRae* left "an indigent woman with at least the same range of choice in
deciding whether to obtain a medically necessary abortion as she would have
had if Congress had chosen to subsidize no health care costs at all," *id.,* at
317, Missouri's refusal to allow public employees to perform abortions in
public hospitals leaves a pregnant woman with the same choices as if the
State had chosen not to operate any public hospitals at all. The challenged
provisions only restrict a woman's ability to obtain an abortion to the extent
that she chooses to use a physician affiliated with a public hospital. This cir-
cumstance is more easily remedied, and thus considerably less burdensome,
than indigency, which "may make it difficult—and in some cases, perhaps,
impossible—for some women to have abortions" without public funding.
Maher, 432 U. S., at 474. Having held that the State's refusal to fund abortions does not violate *Roe* v. *Wade,* it strains logic to reach a contrary result
for the use of public facilities and employees. If the State may "make a value
judgment favoring childbirth over abortion and . . . implement that judgment by the allocation of public funds," *Maher, supra,* at 474, surely it may
do so through the allocation of other public resources, such as hospitals and
medical staff. . . .

D

Section 188.029 of the Missouri Act provides:

"Before a physician performs an abortion on a woman he has reason to believe is carrying an unborn child of twenty or more weeks gestational age, the physician shall first determine if the unborn child is viable by using and exercising that degree of care, skill, and proficiency commonly exercised by the ordinarily skillful, careful, and prudent physician engaged in similar practice under the same or similar conditions. In making this determination of viability, the physician shall perform or cause to be performed such medical examinations and tests as are necessary to make a finding of the gestational age, weight, and lung maturity of the unborn child and shall enter such findings and determination of viability in the medical record of the mother." . . .

The viability-testing provision of the Missouri Act is concerned with promoting the State's interest in potential human life rather than in maternal health. Section 188.029 creates what is essentially a presumption of viability at 20 weeks, which the physician must rebut with tests indicating that the fetus is not viable prior to performing an abortion. It also directs the physician's determination as to viability by specifying consideration, if feasible, of gestational age, fetal weight, and lung capacity. The District Court found that "the medical evidence is uncontradicted that a 20-week fetus is *not* viable," and that "23¹/₂ to 24 weeks gestation is the earliest point in pregnancy where a reasonable possibility of viability exists." 662 F. Supp., at 420. But it also found that there may be a 4-week error in estimating gestational age, *id.*, at 421, which supports testing at 20 weeks.

In *Roe* v. *Wade*, the Court recognized that the State has "important and legitimate" interests in protecting maternal health and in the potentiality of human life. 410 U. S., at 162. During the second trimester, the State "may, if it chooses, regulate the abortion procedure in ways that are reasonably related to maternal health." *Id.*, at 164. After viability, when the State's interest in potential human life was held to become compelling, the State "may, if it chooses, regulate, and even proscribe, abortion except where it is necessary, in appropriate medical judgment, for the preservation of the life or health of the mother." *Id.*, at 165. . . .

In *Colautti* v. *Franklin*, 439 U. S. 379 (1979), upon which appellees rely, the Court held that a Pennsylvania statute regulating the standard of care to be used by a physician performing an abortion of a possibly viable fetus was void for vagueness. *Id.*, at 390–401. But in the course of reaching that conclusion, the Court reaffirmed its earlier statement in *Planned Parenthood of*

Central Mo. v. *Danforth,* 428 U. S. 52, 64 (1976), that "'the determination of whether a particular fetus is viable is, and must be, a matter for the judgment of the responsible attending physician.'" 439 U. S., at 396. JUSTICE BLACKMUN, *post,* at 545, n. 6, ignores the statement in *Colautti* that "neither the legislature nor the courts may proclaim one of the elements entering into the ascertainment of viability—be it weeks of gestation or fetal weight or any other single factor—as the determinant of when the State has a compelling interest in the life or health of the fetus." 439 U. S., at 388–389. To the extent that § 188.029 regulates the method for determining viability, it undoubtedly does superimpose state regulation on the medical determination whether a particular fetus is viable. The Court of Appeals and the District Court thought it unconstitutional for this reason. 851 F. 2d, at 1074–1075; 662 F. Supp., at 423. To the extent that the viability tests increase the cost of what are in fact second-trimester abortions, their validity may also be questioned under *Akron,* 462 U. S., at 434–435, where the Court held that a requirement that second-trimester abortions must be performed in hospitals was invalid because it substantially increased the expense of those procedures.

We think that the doubt cast upon the Missouri statute by these cases is not so much a flaw in the statute as it is a reflection of the fact that the rigid trimester analysis of the course of a pregnancy enunciated in *Roe* has resulted in subsequent cases like *Colautti* and *Akron* making constitutional law in this area a virtual Procrustean bed. Statutes specifying elements of informed consent to be provided abortion patients, for example, were invalidated if they were thought to "structur[e] . . . the dialogue between the woman and her physician." *Thornburgh* v. *American College of Obstetricians and Gynecologists,* 476 U. S. 747, 763 (1986). As the dissenters in *Thornburgh* pointed out, such a statute would have been sustained under any traditional standard of judicial review, *id.,* at 802 (WHITE, J., dissenting), or for any other surgical procedure except abortion. *Id.,* at 783 (Burger, C. J., dissenting). . . .

In the first place, the rigid *Roe* framework is hardly consistent with the notion of a Constitution cast in general terms, as ours is, and usually speaking in general principles, as ours does. The key elements of the *Roe* framework—trimesters and viability—are not found in the text of the Constitution or in any place else one would expect to find a constitutional principle. Since the bounds of the inquiry are essentially indeterminate, the result has been a web of legal rules that have become increasingly intricate, resembling a code of regulations rather than a body of constitutional doctrine. . . . JUSTICE WHITE has put it, the trimester framework has left this Cou serve as the country's "*ex officio* medical board with powers to app disapprove medical and operative practices and standards throug

United States." *Planned Parenthood of Central Mo.* v. *Danforth*, 428 U. S., at 99 (opinion concurring in part and dissenting in part).

In the second place, we do not see why the State's interest in protecting potential human life should come into existence only at the point of viability, and that there should therefore be a rigid line allowing state regulation after viability but prohibiting it before viability. The dissenters in *Thornburgh*, writing in the context of the *Roe* trimester analysis, would have recognized this fact by positing against the "fundamental right" recognized in *Roe* the State's "compelling interest" in protecting potential human life throughout pregnancy. "[T]he State's interest, if compelling after viability, is equally compelling before viability." *Thornburgh*, 476 U. S., at 795 (WHITE, J., dissenting); see *id.*, at 828 (O'CONNOR, J., dissenting) ("State has compelling interests in ensuring maternal health and in protecting potential human life, and these interests exist 'throughout pregnancy'") (citation omitted).

The tests that § 188.029 requires the physician to perform are designed to determine viability. The State here has chosen viability as the point at which its interest in potential human life must be safeguarded. See Mo. Rev. Stat. § 188.030 (1986) ("No abortion of a viable unborn child shall be performed unless necessary to preserve the life or health of the woman"). It is true that the tests in question increase the expense of abortion, and regulate the discretion of the physician in determining the viability of the fetus. Since the tests will undoubtedly show in many cases that the fetus is not viable, the tests will have been performed for what were in fact second-trimester abortions. But we are satisfied that the requirement of these tests permissibly furthers the State's interest in protecting potential human life, and we therefore believe § 188.029 to be constitutional.

JUSTICE BLACKMUN takes us to task for our failure to join in a "great issues" debate as to whether the Constitution includes an "unenumerated" general right to privacy as recognized in cases such as *Griswold* v. *Connecticut*, 381 U. S. 479 (1965), and *Roe*. But *Griswold* v. *Connecticut*, unlike *Roe*, did not purport to adopt a whole framework, complete with detailed rules and distinctions, to govern the cases in which the asserted liberty interest would apply. As such, it was far different from the opinion, if not the holding, of *Roe* v. *Wade*, which sought to establish a constitutional framework for judging state regulation of abortion during the entire term of pregnancy. That framework sought to deal with areas of medical practice traditionally subject to state regulation, and it sought to balance once and for all by reference only to the calendar the claims of the State to protect the fetus as a ▸ of human life against the claims of a woman to decide for herself ▸ er or not to abort a fetus she was carrying. The experience of the

Court in applying *Roe* v. *Wade* in later cases, see *supra*, at 518, n. 15, suggests to us that there is wisdom in not unnecessarily attempting to elaborate the abstract differences between a "fundamental right" to abortion, as the Court described it in *Akron*, 462 U. S. at 420, n. 1, a "limited fundamental constitutional right," which JUSTICE BLACKMUN today treats *Roe* as having established, *post*, at 555, or a liberty interest protected by the Due Process Clause, which we believe it to be. The Missouri testing requirement here is reasonably designed to ensure that abortions are not performed where the fetus is viable—an end which all concede is legitimate—and that is sufficient to sustain its constitutionality.

JUSTICE BLACKMUN also accuses us, *inter alia*, of cowardice and illegitimacy in dealing with "the most politically divisive domestic legal issue of our time." There is no doubt that our holding today will allow some governmental regulation of abortion that would have been prohibited under the language of cases such as *Colautti* v. *Franklin*, 439 U. S. 379 (1979), and *Akron* v. *Akron Center for Reproductive Health, Inc.*, *supra*. But the goal of constitutional adjudication is surely not to remove inexorably "politically divisive" issues from the ambit of the legislative process, whereby the people through their elected representatives deal with matters of concern to them. The goal of constitutional adjudication is to hold true the balance between that which the Constitution puts beyond the reach of the democratic process and that which it does not. We think we have done that today. JUSTICE BLACKMUN's suggestion that legislative bodies, in a Nation where more than half of our population is women, will treat our decision today as an invitation to enact abortion regulation reminiscent of the dark ages not only misreads our views but does scant justice to those who serve in such bodies and the people who elect them.

III

Both appellants and the United States as *Amicus Curiae* have urged that we overrule our decision in *Roe* v. *Wade*. Brief for Appellants 12–18; Brief for United States as *Amicus Curiae* 8–24. The facts of the present case, however, differ from those at issue in *Roe*. Here, Missouri has determined that viability is the point at which its interest in potential human life must be safeguarded. In *Roe*, on the other hand, the Texas statute criminalized the performance of *all* abortions, except when the mother's life was at stake. 410 U. S., at 117–118. This case therefore affords us no occasion to revisit the holding of *Roe*, which was that the Texas statute unconstitutionally infringed the right to an abortion derived from the Due Process Clause, *id.*, at 164, and we leave it undisturbed. To the extent indicated in our opinion, we would modify and narrow *Roe* and succeeding cases. . . .

JUSTICE SCALIA, concurring in part and concurring in the judgment.

I join Parts I, II–A, II–B, and II–C of the opinion of the Court. As to Part II–D, I share JUSTICE BLACKMUN's view that it effectively would over-rule *Roe* v. *Wade*, 410 U. S. 113 (1973). I think that should be done, but would do it more explicitly. Since today we contrive to avoid doing it, and indeed to avoid almost any decision of national import, I need not set forth my reasons, some of which have been well recited in dissents of my colleagues in other cases.

The outcome of today's case will doubtless be heralded as a triumph of judicial statesmanship. It is not that, unless it is statesmanlike needlessly to prolong this Court's self-awarded sovereignty over a field where it has little proper business since the answers to most of the cruel questions posed are political and not juridical—a sovereignty which therefore quite properly, but to the great damage of the Court, makes it the object of the sort of organized public pressure that political institutions in a democracy ought to receive.

JUSTICE O'CONNOR's assertion, that a "'fundamental rule of judicial re-straint'" requires us to avoid reconsidering *Roe,* cannot be taken seriously. By finessing *Roe* we do not, as she suggests, adhere to the strict and vener-able rule that we should avoid "'decid[ing] questions of a constitutional na-ture.'" We have not disposed of this case on some statutory or procedural ground, but have decided, and could not avoid deciding, whether the Mis-souri statute meets the requirements of the United States Constitution. The only choice available is whether, in deciding that constitutional question, we should use *Roe* v. *Wade* as the benchmark, or something else. What is in-volved, therefore, is not the rule of avoiding constitutional issues where pos-sible, but the quite separate principle that we will not "'formulate a rule of constitutional law broader than is required by the precise facts to which it is to be applied.'" The latter is a sound general principle, but one often de-parted from when good reason exists. Just this Term, for example, in an opinion authored by JUSTICE O'CONNOR, despite the fact that we had al-ready held a racially based set-aside unconstitutional because unsupported by evidence of identified discrimination, which was all that was needed to decide the case, we went on to outline the criteria for properly tailoring race-based remedies in cases where such evidence is present. *Richmond* v. *J. A. Croson Co.,* 488 U. S. 469, 506–508 (1989). Also this Term, in an opinion joined by JUSTICE O'CONNOR, we announced the constitutional rule that deprivation of the right to confer with counsel during trial violates the Sixth Amendment even if no prejudice can be shown, despite our finding that there had been no such deprivation on the facts before us—which was all that was needed to decide that case. *Perry* v. *Leeke,* 488 U. S. 272, 278–280

(1989); see *id.*, at 285 (KENNEDY, J., concurring in part). I have not identified with certainty the first instance of our deciding a case on broader constitutional grounds than absolutely necessary, but it is assuredly no later than *Marbury* v. *Madison,* 1 Cranch 137 (1803), where we held that mandamus could constitutionally issue against the Secretary of State, although that was unnecessary given our holding that the law authorizing issuance of the mandamus by this Court was unconstitutional. . . .

The real question, then, is whether there are valid reasons to go beyond the most stingy possible holding today. It seems to me there are not only valid but compelling ones. Ordinarily, speaking no more broadly than is absolutely required avoids throwing settled law into confusion; doing so today preserves a chaos that is evident to anyone who can read and count. Alone sufficient to justify a broad holding is the fact that our retaining control, through *Roe,* of what I believe to be, and many of our citizens recognize to be, a political issue, continuously distorts the public perception of the role of this Court. We can now look forward to at least another Term with carts full of mail from the public, and streets full of demonstrators, urging us— their unelected and life-tenured judges who have been awarded those extraordinary, undemocratic characteristics precisely in order that we might follow the law despite the popular will—to follow the popular will. Indeed, I expect we can look forward to even more of that than before, given our indecisive decision today. And if these reasons for taking the unexceptional course of reaching a broader holding are not enough, then consider the nature of the constitutional question we avoid: In most cases, we do no harm by not speaking more broadly than the decision requires. Anyone affected by the conduct that the avoided holding would have prohibited will be able to challenge it himself and have his day in court to make the argument. Not so with respect to the harm that many States believed, pre-*Roe,* and many may continue to believe, is caused by largely unrestricted abortion. That will continue to occur if the States have the constitutional power to prohibit it, and would do so, but we skillfully avoid telling them so. Perhaps those abortions cannot constitutionally be proscribed. That is surely an arguable question, the question that reconsideration of *Roe* v. *Wade* entails. But what is not at all arguable, it seems to me, is that we should decide now and not insist that we be run into a corner before we grudgingly yield up our judgment. The only sound reason for the latter course is to prevent a change in the law—but to think that desirable begs the question to be decided. . . .

JUSTICE BLACKMUN, with whom JUSTICE BRENNAN and JUSTICE MARSHALL join, concurring in part and dissenting in part.

Today, *Roe* v. *Wade,* 410 U. S. 113 (1973), and the fundamental constitutional right of women to decide whether to terminate a pregnancy, survive but are not secure. Although the Court extricates itself from this case without making a single, even incremental, change in the law of abortion, the plurality and JUSTICE SCALIA would overrule *Roe* (the first silently, the other explicitly) and would return to the States virtually unfettered authority to control the quintessentially intimate, personal, and life-directing decision whether to carry a fetus to term. Although today, no less than yesterday, the Constitution and the decisions of this Court prohibit a State from enacting laws that inhibit women from the meaningful exercise of that right, a plurality of this Court implicitly invites every state legislature to enact more and more restrictive abortion regulations in order to provoke more and more test cases, in the hope that sometime down the line the Court will return the law of procreative freedom to the severe limitations that generally prevailed in this country before January 22, 1973. Never in my memory has a plurality announced a judgment of this Court that so foments disregard for the law and for our standing decisions.

Nor in my memory has a plurality gone about its business in such a deceptive fashion. At every level of its review, from its effort to read the real meaning out of the Missouri statute, to its intended evisceration of precedents and its deafening silence about the constitutional protections that it would jettison, the plurality obscures the portent of its analysis. With feigned restraint, the plurality announces that its analysis leaves *Roe* "undisturbed," albeit "modif[ied] and narrow[ed]." But this disclaimer is totally meaningless. The plurality opinion is filled with winks, and nods, and knowing glances to those who would do away with *Roe* explicitly, but turns a stone face to anyone in search of what the plurality conceives as the scope of a woman's right under the Due Process Clause to terminate a pregnancy free from the coercive and brooding influence of the State. The simple truth is that *Roe* would not survive the plurality's analysis, and that the plurality provides no substitute for *Roe*'s protective umbrella.

I fear for the future. I fear for the liberty and equality of the millions of women who have lived and come of age in the 16 years since *Roe* was decided. I fear for the integrity of, and public esteem for, this Court. . . .

. . . In the plurality's view, the viability-testing provision imposes a burden on second-trimester abortions as a way of furthering the State's interest in protecting the potential life of the fetus. Since under the *Roe* framework, the State may not fully regulate abortion in the interest of potential life (as opposed to maternal health) until the third trimester, the plurality finds it necessary, in order to save the Missouri testing provision, to throw out *Roe*'s trimester framework. In flat contradiction to *Roe*, 410 U. S., at 163, the plurality concludes that the State's interest in potential life is compelling before viability, and upholds the testing provision because it "permissibly furthers" that state interest. . . .

Had the plurality read the statute as written, it would have had no cause to reconsider the *Roe* framework. As properly construed, the viability-testing provision does not pass constitutional muster under even a rational-basis standard, the least restrictive level of review applied by this Court. See *Williamson* v. *Lee Optical Co.,* 348 U. S. 483 (1955). By mandating tests to determine fetal weight and lung maturity for every fetus thought to be more than 20 weeks gestational age, the statute requires physicians to undertake procedures, such as amniocentesis, that, in the situation presented, have no medical justification, impose significant additional health risks on both the pregnant woman and the fetus, and bear no rational relation to the State's interest in protecting fetal life. . . . As written, § 188.029 is an arbitrary imposition of discomfort, risk, and expense, furthering no discernible interest except to make the procurement of an abortion as arduous and difficult as possible. Thus, were it not for the plurality's tortured effort to avoid the plain import of § 188.029, it could have struck down the testing provision as patently irrational irrespective of the *Roe* framework. . . .

The plurality eschews this straightforward resolution, in the hope of precipitating a constitutional crisis. Far from avoiding constitutional difficulty, the plurality attempts to engineer a dramatic retrenchment in our jurisprudence by exaggerating the conflict between its untenable construction of § 188.029 and the *Roe* trimester framework.

No one contests that under the *Roe* framework the State, in order to promote its interest in potential human life, may regulate and even proscribe nontherapeutic abortions once the fetus becomes viable. *Roe,* 410 U. S., at 164–165. If, as the plurality appears to hold, the testing provision simply requires a physician to use appropriate and medically sound tests to determine whether the fetus is actually viable when the estimated gestational age is greater than 20 weeks (and therefore within what the District Court found to be the margin of error for viability . . .), then I see little or no conflict with *Roe.* . . . Nothing in *Roe,* or any of its progeny, holds that a State may not effectuate its compelling interest in the potential life of a viable fetus by seeking to ensure that no viable fetus is mistakenly aborted because of the inherent lack of precision in estimates of gestational age. A requirement that a physician make a finding of viability, one way or the other, for every fetus that falls within the range of possible viability does no more than preserve the State's recognized authority. Although, as the plurality correctly points out, such a testing requirement would have the effect of imposing additional costs on second-trimester abortions where the tests indicated that the fetus was not viable, these costs would be merely incidental to, and a necessary accommodation of, the State's unquestioned right to prohibit nontherapeutic abortions after the point of viability. In short, the testing provision, as construed by the plurality, is consistent with the *Roe* framework and could be upheld effortlessly under current doctrine. . . .

How ironic it is, then, and disingenuous, that the plurality scolds the

Court of Appeals for adopting a construction of the statute that fails to avoid constitutional difficulties. . . . By distorting the statute, the plurality manages to avoid invalidating the testing provision on what should have been noncontroversial constitutional grounds; having done so, however, the plurality rushes headlong into a much deeper constitutional thicket, brushing past an obvious basis for upholding § 188.029 in search of a pretext for scuttling the trimester framework. Evidently, from the plurality's perspective, the real problem with the Court of Appeals' construction of § 188.029 is not that it raised a constitutional difficulty, but that it raised the wrong constitutional difficulty—one not implicating *Roe*. The plurality has remedied that, traditional canons of construction and judicial forbearance notwithstanding.

B

Having set up the conflict between § 188.029 and the *Roe* trimester framework, the plurality summarily discards *Roe*'s analytic core as "'unsound in principle and unworkable in practice.'" . . . quoting *Garcia* v. *San Antonio Metropolitan Transit Authority*, 469 U. S. 528, 546 (1985). This is so, the plurality claims, because the key elements of the framework do not appear in the text of the Constitution, because the framework more closely resembles a regulatory code than a body of constitutional doctrine, and because under the framework the State's interest in potential human life is considered compelling only after viability, when, in fact, that interest is equally compelling throughout pregnancy. . . . The plurality does not bother to explain these alleged flaws in *Roe*. Bald assertion masquerades as reasoning. The object, quite clearly, is not to persuade, but to prevail.

1

The plurality opinion is far more remarkable for the arguments that it does not advance than for those that it does. The plurality does not even mention, much less join, the true jurisprudential debate underlying this case: whether the Constitution includes an "unenumerated" general right to privacy as recognized in many of our decisions, most notably *Griswold* v. *Connecticut*, 381 U. S. 479 (1965), and *Roe*, and, more specifically, whether, and to what extent, such a right to privacy extends to matters of childbearing and family life, including abortion. See, *e. g.*, *Eisenstadt* v. *Baird*, 405 U. S. 438 (1972) (contraception); *Loving* v. *Virginia*, 388 U. S. 1 (1967) (marriage); *Skinner* v. *Oklahoma ex rel. Williamson*, 316 U. S. 535 (1942) (procreation); *Pierce* v. *Society of Sisters*, 268 U. S. 510 (1925) (childrearing). . . . These are questions of unsurpassed significance in this Court's interpretation of the Constitution, and mark the battleground upon which this case was fought, by the parties, by the Solicitor General as *amicus* on behalf of petitioners, and by an unprecedented number of *amici*. On these grounds, abandoned by the plurality, the Court should decide this case.

But rather than arguing that the text of the Constitution makes no mention of the right to privacy, the plurality complains that the critical elements of the *Roe* framework—trimesters and viability—do not appear in the Constitution and are, therefore, somehow inconsistent with a Constitution cast in general terms. Were this a true concern, we would have to abandon most of our constitutional jurisprudence. As the plurality well knows, or should know, the "critical elements" of countless constitutional doctrines nowhere appear in the Constitution's text. The Constitution makes no mention, for example, of the First Amendment's "actual malice" standard for proving certain libels, see *New York Times Co.* v. *Sullivan*, 376 U. S. 254 (1964), or of the standard for determining when speech is obscene. See *Miller* v. *California*, 413 U. S. 15 (1973). Similarly, the Constitution makes no mention of the rational-basis test, or the specific verbal formulations of intermediate and strict scrutiny by which this Court evaluates claims under the Equal Protection Clause. The reason is simple. Like the *Roe* framework, these tests or standards are not, and do not purport to be, rights protected by the Constitution. Rather, they are judge-made methods for evaluating and measuring the strength and scope of constitutional rights or for balancing the constitutional rights of individuals against the competing interests of government. . . .

2

The plurality next alleges that the result of the trimester framework has "been a web of legal rules that have become increasingly intricate, resembling a code of regulations rather than a body of constitutional doctrine." Again, if this were a true and genuine concern, we would have to abandon vast areas of our constitutional jurisprudence. The plurality complains that under the trimester framework the Court has distinguished between a city ordinance requiring that second-trimester abortions be performed in clinics and a state law requiring that these abortions be performed in hospitals, or between laws requiring that certain information be furnished to a woman by a physician or his assistant and those requiring that such information be furnished by the physician exclusively. *Ante*, at 518, n. 15, citing *Simopoulos* v. *Virginia*, 462 U. S. 506 (1983), and *Akron* v. *Akron Center for Reproductive Health, Inc.*, 462 U. S. 416 (1983). Are these distinctions any finer, or more "regulatory," than the distinctions we have often drawn in our First Amendment jurisprudence, where, for example, we have held that a "release time" program permitting public-school students to leave school grounds during school hours to receive religious instruction does not violate the Establishment Clause, even though a release-time program permitting religious instruction on school grounds does violate the Clause? Compare *Zorach* v. *Clauson*, 343 U. S. 306 (1952), with *Illinois ex rel. McCollum* v. *Board of Education of School Dist. No. 71, Champaign County*, 333 U. S. 203 (1948). Our Fourth Amendment jurisprudence recognizes factual distinctions no less intricate. Just this Term, for example, we held that while an aerial observation from a helicopter hovering at 400 feet does not violate any reasonable expectation of privacy, such an expectation of privacy would be violated by a helicopter observation from an unusually low altitude. *Florida* v. *Riley*, 488 U. S. 445, 451 (1989) (O'CONNOR, J., concurring in judgment). Similarly, in a Sixth Amendment case, the Court held that although an overnight ban on attorney-client communication violated the constitutionally guaranteed right to counsel, *Geders* v. *United States*, 425 U. S. 80 (1976), that right was not violated when a trial judge separated a defendant from his lawyer during a 15-minute recess after the defendant's direct testimony. *Perry* v. *Leeke*, 488 U. S. 272 (1989).

That numerous constitutional doctrines result in narrow differentiations between similar circumstances does not mean that this Court has abandoned adjudication in favor of regulation. Rather, these careful distinctions reflect the process of constitutional adjudication itself, which is often highly fact specific, requiring such determinations as whether state laws are "unduly burdensome" or "reasonable" or bear a "rational" or "necessary" relation to asserted state interests. In a recent due process case, THE CHIEF JUSTICE wrote for the Court: "[M]any branches of the law abound in nice distinctions that may be troublesome but have been thought nonetheless necessary: 'I do not think we need trouble ourselves with the thought that my view depends upon differences of degree. The whole law does so as soon as it is civilized.'" *Daniels* v. *Williams*, 474 U. S. 327, 334 (1986), quoting *LeRoy Fibre Co.* v. *Chicago, M. & St. P. R. Co.*, 232 U. S. 340, 354 (1914) (Holmes, J., partially concurring).

These "differences of degree" fully account for our holdings in *Simopoulos, supra*, and *Akron, supra*. Those decisions rest on this Court's reasoned and accurate judgment that hospitalization and doctor-counseling requirements unduly burdened the right of women to terminate a pregnancy and were not rationally related to the State's asserted interest in the health of pregnant women, while Virginia's *substantially less restrictive* regulations were not unduly burdensome and did rationally serve the State's interest. . . . That the Court exercised its best judgment in evaluating these markedly different statutory schemes no more established the Court as an " 'ex officio* medical board,' " quoting *Planned Parenthood of Central Mo.* v.

Danforth, 428 U. S. 52, 99 (1976) (opinion of WHITE, J., concurring in part and dissenting in part), than our decisions involving religion in the public schools establish the Court as a national school board, or our decisions concerning prison regulations establish the Court as a bureau of prisons. See *Thornburgh* v. *Abbott,* 490 U. S. 401 (1989) (adopting different standard of First Amendment review for incoming as opposed to outgoing prison mail). If, in delicate and complicated areas of constitutional law, our legal judgments "have become increasingly intricate," it is not, as the plurality contends, because we have overstepped our judicial role. Quite the opposite: the rules are intricate because we have remained conscientious in our duty to do justice carefully, especially when fundamental rights rise or fall with our decisions.

3

Finally, the plurality asserts that the trimester framework cannot stand because the State's interest in potential life is compelling throughout pregnancy, not merely after viability. The opinion contains not one word of rationale for its view of the State's interest. This "it-is-so-because-we-say-so" jurisprudence constitutes nothing other than an attempted exercise of brute force; reason, much less persuasion, has no place.

In answering the plurality's claim that the State's interest in the fetus is uniform and compelling throughout pregnancy, I cannot improve upon what JUSTICE STEVENS has written:

"I should think it obvious that the State's interest in the protection of an embryo—even if that interest is defined as 'protecting those who will be citizens' . . . —increases progressively and dramatically as the organism's capacity to feel pain, to experience pleasure, to survive, and to react to its surroundings increases day by day. The development of a fetus—and pregnancy itself—are not static conditions, and the assertion that the government's interest is static simply ignores this reality. . . . [U]nless the religious view that a fetus is a 'person' is adopted . . . there is a fundamental and well-recognized difference between a fetus and a human being; indeed, if there is not such a difference, the permissibility of terminating the life of a fetus could scarcely be left to the will of the state legislatures. And if distinctions may be drawn between a fetus and a human being in terms of the state interest in their protection—even though the fetus represents one of 'those who will be citizens'—it seems to me quite odd to argue that distinctions may not also be drawn between the state interest in protecting the freshly fertilized egg and the state interest in protecting the 9-month-gestated, fully sentient fetus on the eve of birth. Recognition of this distinction is supported not only by logic, but also by history and by our shared experiences." *Thornburgh,* 476 U. S., at 778–779 (footnote omitted).

See also *Roe,* 410 U. S., at 129–147.

For my own part, I remain convinced, as six other Members of this Court 16 years ago were convinced, that the *Roe* framework, and the viability standard in particular, fairly, sensibly, and effectively functions to safeguard the constitutional liberties of pregnant women while recognizing and accommodating the State's interest in potential human life. The viability line reflects the biological facts and truths of fetal development; it marks that threshold moment prior to which a fetus cannot survive separate from the woman and cannot reasonably and objectively be regarded as a subject of rights or interests distinct from, or paramount to, those of the pregnant woman. At the same time, the viability standard takes account of the undeniable fact that as the fetus evolves into its postnatal form, and as it loses its dependence on the uterine environment, the State's interest in the fetus' potential human life, and in fostering a regard for human life in general, becomes compelling. As a practical matter, because viability follows "quickening"—the point at which a woman feels movement in her womb—and because viability occurs no earlier than 23 weeks gestational age, it establishes an easily applicable standard for regulating abortion while providing a pregnant woman ample time to exercise her fundamental right with her responsible physician to terminate her pregnancy. . . . Although I have stated previously for a majority of this Court that "[c]onstitutional rights do not always have easily ascertainable boundaries," to seek and establish those boundaries remains the special responsibility of this Court. *Thornburgh,* 476 U. S., at 771. In *Roe,* we discharged that responsibility as logic and science compelled. The plurality today advances not one reasonable argument as to why our judgment in that case was wrong and should be abandoned. . . .

The plurality pretends that *Roe* survives, explaining that the facts of this case differ from those in *Roe:* here, Missouri has chosen to assert its interest in potential life only at the point of viability, whereas, in *Roe,* Texas had asserted that interest from the point of conception, criminalizing all abortions, except where the life of the mother was at stake. This, of course, is a distinction without a difference. The plurality repudiates every principle for which *Roe* stands; in good conscience, it cannot possibly believe that *Roe* lies "undisturbed" merely because this case does not call upon the Court to reconsider the Texas statute, or one like it. If the Constitution permits a State to enact any statute that reasonably furthers its interest in potential life, and if that interest arises as of conception, why would the Texas statute fail to pass muster? One suspects that the plurality agrees. It is impossible to read the plurality opinion and especially its final paragraph, without recognizing its implicit invitation to every State to enact more and more restrictive abortion laws, and to assert their interest in potential life as of the moment of conception. All these laws will satisfy the plurality's nonscrutiny, until sometime, a new regime of old dissenters and new appointees will declare what the plurality intends: that *Roe* is no longer good law. . . .

Thus, "not with a bang, but a whimper," the plurality discards a landmark case of the last generation, and casts into darkness the hopes and visions of every woman in this country who had come to believe that the Constitution guaranteed her right to exercise some control over her unique ability to bear children. The plurality does so either oblivious or insensitive to the fact that millions of women, and their families, have ordered their lives around the right to reproductive choice, and that this right has become vital to the full participation of women in the economic and political walks of American life. The plurality would clear the way once again for government to force upon women the physical labor and specific and direct medical and psychological harms that may accompany carrying a fetus to term. The plurality would clear the way again for the State to conscript a woman's body and to force upon her a "distressful life and future." *Roe*, 410 U. S., at 153. The result, as we know from experience, see Cates & Rochat, Illegal Abortions in the United States: 1972–1974, 8 Family Planning Perspectives 86, 92 (1976), would be that every year hundreds of thousands of women, in desperation, would defy the law, and place their health and safety in the unclean and unsympathetic hands of back-alley abortionists, or they would attempt to perform abortions upon themselves, with disastrous results. Every year, many women, especially poor and minority women, would die or suffer debilitating physical trauma, all in the name of enforced morality or religious dictates or lack of compassion, as it may be.

Of the aspirations and settled understandings of American women, of the inevitable and brutal consequences of what it is doing, the tough-approach plurality utters not a word. This silence is callous. It is also profoundly destructive of this Court as an institution. To overturn a constitutional decision is a rare and grave undertaking. To overturn a constitutional decision that secured a fundamental personal liberty to millions of persons would be unprecedented in our 200 years of constitutional history. Although the doctrine of *stare decisis* applies with somewhat diminished force in constitutional cases generally, even in ordinary constitutional cases "any departure from . . . *stare decisis* demands special justification." *Arizona* v. *Rumsey*, 467 U. S. 203, 212 (1984). See also *Vasquez* v. *Hillery*, 474 U. S. 254, 266 (1986) ("[T]he careful observer will discern that any detours from the straight path of *stare decisis* in our past have occurred for articulable reasons, and only when the Court has felt obliged 'to bring its opinions into agreement with experience and with facts newly ascertained,'" quoting *Burnet* v. *Coronado Oil & Gas Co.*, 285 U. S. 393, 412 (1932) (Brandeis, J., dissenting)). This requirement of justification applies with unique force where, as here, the Court's abrogation of precedent would destroy people's firm belief, based on past decisions of this Court, that they possess an unabridgeable right to undertake certain conduct. . . .

OHIO v. AKRON CENTER FOR REPRODUCTIVE HEALTH ET AL.

APPEAL FROM THE UNITED STATES COURT OF APPEALS FOR
THE SIXTH CIRCUIT

No. 88–805. Argued November 29, 1989—Decided June 25, 1990

KENNEDY, J., announced the judgment of the Court, and delivered the opinion of the Court with respect to Parts I, II, III, and IV, in which REHNQUIST, C. J., and WHITE, STEVENS, O'CONNOR, and SCALIA, JJ., joined, and an opinion with respect to Part V, in which REHNQUIST, C. J., and WHITE and SCALIA, JJ., joined. SCALIA, J., filed a concurring opinion. STEVENS, J., filed an opinion concurring in part and concurring in the judgment. BLACKMUN, J., filed a dissenting opinion, in which BRENNAN and MARSHALL, JJ., joined.

JUSTICE KENNEDY announced the judgment of the Court and delivered the opinion of the Court with respect to Parts I, II, III, and IV[†], and an opinion with respect to Part V, in which THE CHIEF JUSTICE, JUSTICE WHITE, and JUSTICE SCALIA join.

The Court of Appeals held invalid an Ohio statute that, with certain exceptions, prohibits any person from performing an abortion on an unmarried, unemancipated, minor woman absent notice to one of the woman's parents or a court order of approval. We reverse, for we determine that the statute accords with our precedents on parental notice and consent in the abortion context and does not violate the Fourteenth Amendment.

. . . We have decided five cases addressing the constitutionality of parental notice or parental consent statutes in the abortion context. See *Planned Parenthood of Central Mo. v. Danforth*, 428 U. S. 52 (1976); *Bellotti v. Baird*, 443 U. S. 622 (1979); *H. L. v. Matheson*, 450 U. S. 398 (1981); *Planned Parenthood Assn. of Kansas City, Mo., Inc. v. Ashcroft*, 462 U. S. 476 (1983); *Akron v. Akron Center for Reproductive Health, Inc.*, 462 U. S. 416 (1983). We do not need to determine whether a statute that does not accord with these cases would violate the Constitution, for we conclude that H. B. 319 is consistent with them.

[†] JUSTICE STEVENS and JUSTICE O'CONNOR join only Parts I, II, III, and IV of the opinion.

A

This dispute turns, to a large extent, on the adequacy of H. B. 319's judicial bypass procedure. In analyzing this aspect of the dispute, we note that, although our cases have required bypass procedures for parental consent statutes, we have not decided whether parental notice statutes must contain such procedures. See *Matheson,* and n. 25 (upholding a notice statute without a bypass procedure as applied to immature, dependent minors). We leave the question open, because, whether or not the Fourteenth Amendment requires notice statutes to contain bypass procedures, H. B. 319's bypass procedure meets the requirements identified for parental consent statutes in *Danforth, Bellotti, Ashcroft,* and *Akron. Danforth* established that, in order to prevent another person from having an absolute veto power over a minor's decision to have an abortion, a State must provide some sort of bypass procedure if it elects to require parental consent. See 428 U. S., at 74. As we hold today in *Hodgson* v. *Minnesota,* it is a corollary to the greater intrusiveness of consent statutes that a bypass procedure that will suffice for a consent statute will suffice also for a notice statute. See also *Matheson* (notice statutes are not equivalent to consent statutes because they do not give anyone a veto power over a minor's abortion decision).

The principal opinion in *Bellotti* stated four criteria that a bypass procedure in a consent statute must satisfy. Appellees contend that the bypass procedure does not satisfy these criteria. We disagree. First, the *Bellotti* principal opinion indicated that the procedure must allow the minor to show that she possesses the maturity and information to make her abortion decision, in consultation with her physician, without regard to her parents' wishes. See 443 U. S., at 643 (opinion of Powell, J.). The Court reaffirmed this requirement in *Akron* by holding that a State cannot presume the immaturity of girls under the age of 15. 462 U. S., at 440. In the case now before us, we have no difficulty concluding that H. B. 319 allows a minor to show maturity in conformity with the principal opinion in *Bellotti.* The statute permits the minor to show that she "is sufficiently mature and well enough informed to decide intelligently whether to have an abortion." Ohio. Rev. Code Ann. § 2151.85(C)(1) (Supp. 1988).

Second, the *Bellotti* principal opinion indicated that the procedure must allow the minor to show that, even if she cannot make the abortion decision by herself, "the desired abortion would be in her best interests." 443 U. S., at 644. We believe that H. B. 319 satisfies the *Bellotti* language as quoted. The statute requires the juvenile court to authorize the minor's consent where the court determines that the abortion is in the minor's best interest and in cases where the minor has shown a pattern of physical, sexual, or emotional abuse. See § 2151.85(C)(2).

Third, the *Bellotti* principal opinion indicated that the procedure must insure the minor's anonymity. See 443 U. S., at 644. H. B. 319 satisfies this standard. Section 2151.85 (D) provides that "[t]he [juvenile] court shall not notify the parents, guardian, or custodian of the complainant that she is pregnant or that she wants to have an abortion." Section 2151.85(F) further states:

"Each hearing under this section shall be conducted in a manner that will preserve the anonymity of the complainant. The complaint and all other papers and records that pertain to an action commenced under this section shall be kept confidential and are not public records."

Section 2505.073(B), in a similar fashion, requires the court of appeals to preserve the minor's anonymity and confidentiality of all papers on appeal. The State, in addition, makes it a criminal offense for an employee to disclose documents not designated as public records. See §§ 102.03(B), 102.99(B).

Appellees argue that the complaint forms prescribed by the Ohio Supreme Court will require the minor to disclose her identity. Unless the minor has counsel, she must sign a complaint form to initiate the bypass procedure and, even if she has counsel, she must supply the name of one of her parents at four different places. See App. 6–14 (pleading forms). Appellees would prefer protections similar to those included in the statutes that we reviewed in *Bellotti* and *Ashcroft*. The statute in *Bellotti* protected anonymity by permitting use of a pseudonym, see *Planned Parenthood League of Massachusetts v. Bellotti*, 641 F. 2d 1006, 1025 (CA1 1981), and the statute in *Ashcroft* allowed the minor to sign the petition with her initials, see 462 U. S., at 491, n. 16. Appellees also maintain that the Ohio laws requiring court employees not to disclose public documents are irrelevant because the right to anonymity is broader than the right not to have officials reveal one's identity to the public at large.

Confidentiality differs from anonymity, but we do not believe that the distinction has constitutional significance in the present context. The distinction has not played a part in our previous decisions, and, even if the *Bellotti* principal opinion is taken as setting the standard, we do not find complete anonymity critical. H. B. 319, like the statutes in *Bellotti* and *Ashcroft*, takes reasonable steps to prevent the public from learning of the minor's identity. We refuse to base a decision on the facial validity of a statute on the mere possibility of unauthorized, illegal disclosure by state employees. H. B. 319, like many sophisticated judicial procedures, requires participants to provide identifying information for administrative purposes, not for public disclosure.

Fourth, the *Bellotti* principal opinion indicated that courts must conduct a bypass procedure with expedition to allow the minor an effective opportunity to obtain the abortion. See 443 U. S., at 644. H. B. 319, as noted above, requires the trial court to make its decision within five "business day[s]" after the minor files her complaint, § 2151.85(B)(1); requires the court of appeals to docket an appeal within four "days" after the minor files a notice of appeal, § 2505.073(A); and requires the court of appeals to render a decision within five "days" after docketing the appeal, *ibid.*

The District Court and the Court of Appeals assumed that all of the references to days in §§ 2151.85(B)(1) and 2505.073(A) meant business days as opposed to calendar days. Cf. Ohio Rule App. Proc. 14(A) (excluding nonbusiness days from computations of less than seven days). They calculated, as a result, that the procedure could take up to 22 calendar days because the minor could file at a time during the year in which the 14 business days needed for the bypass procedure would encompass 3 Saturdays, 3 Sundays, and 2 legal holidays. Appellees maintain, on the basis of an affidavit included in the record, that a 3-week delay could increase by a substantial measure both the costs and the medical risks of an abortion. See App. 18. They conclude, as did those courts, that H. B. 319 does not satisfy the *Bellotti* principal opinion's expedition requirement.

As a preliminary matter, the 22-day calculation conflicts with two well-known rules of construction discussed in our abortion cases and elsewhere. "Where fairly possible, courts should construe a statute to avoid a danger of unconstitutionality." . . . (opinion of Powell, J.). Although we recognize that the other federal courts "'are better schooled in and more able to interpret the laws of their respective States'" than are we, *Frisby* v. *Schultz,* 487 U. S. 474, 482 (1988), the Court of Appeals' decision strikes us as dubious. Interpreting the term "days" in § 2505.073(A) to mean business days instead of calendar days seems inappropriate and unnecessary because of the express and contrasting use of "business day[s]" in § 2151.85(B)(1). In addition, because appellees are making a facial challenge to a statute, they must show that "no set of circumstances exists under which the Act would be valid." *Webster* v. *Reproductive Health Services,* 492 U. S. 490, 524 (1989) (O'CONNOR, J., concurring). The Court of Appeals should not have invalidated the Ohio statute on a facial challenge based upon a worst-case analysis that may never occur. Cf. Ohio Rev. Code § 2505.073(A) (Supp. 1988) (allowing the court of appeals, upon the minor's motion, to shorten or extend the time periods). Moreover, under our precedents, the mere possibility that the procedure may require up to 22 days in a rare case is plainly insufficient to invalidate the statute on its face. *Ashcroft,* for example, upheld a Missouri statute that contained a bypass procedure that could require 17 calendar days plus a sufficient time for deliberation and decisionmaking at both the trial and appellate levels. See 462 U. S., at 477, n. 4, 491, n. 16.

B

Appellees ask us, in effect, to extend the criteria used by some members of the Court in *Bellotti* and the cases following it by imposing three additional requirements on bypass procedures. First, they challenge the constructive authorization provisions in H. B. 319, which enable a minor to obtain an abortion without notifying one of her parents if either the juvenile court or the court of appeals fails to act within the prescribed time limits. See Ohio Rev. Code Ann. §§ 2151.85(B)(1), 2505.073(A), and § 2919.12(B)(1)(a)(iv) (1987 and Supp. 1988). They speculate that the absence of an affirmative order when a court fails to process the minor's complaint will deter the physician from acting.

We discern no constitutional defect in the statute. Absent a demonstrated pattern of abuse or defiance, a State may expect that its judges will follow mandated procedural requirements. There is no showing that the time limitations imposed by H. B. 319 will be ignored. With an abundance of caution, and concern for the minor's interests, Ohio added the constructive authorization provisions in H. B. 319 to ensure expedition of the bypass procedures even if these time limits are not met. The State represents that a physician can obtain certified documentation from the juvenile or appellate court that constructive authorization has occurred. Brief for Appellant 36. We did not require a similar safety net in the bypass procedures in n. 4, and find no defect in the procedures that Ohio has provided.

Second, appellees ask us to rule that a bypass procedure cannot require a minor to prove maturity or best interests by a standard of clear and convincing evidence. They maintain that, when a State seeks to deprive an individual of liberty interests, it must take upon itself the risk of error. See *Santosky* v. *Kramer*, 455 U. S. 745, 755 (1982). House Bill 319 violates this standard, in their opinion, not only by placing the burden of proof upon the minor, but also by imposing a heightened standard of proof.

This contention lacks merit. A State does not have to bear the burden of proof on the issues of maturity or best interests. The principal opinion in *Bellotti* indicates that a State may require the minor to prove these facts in a bypass procedure. See 443 U. S., at 643 (opinion of Powell, J.). A State, moreover, may require a heightened standard of proof when, as here, the bypass procedure contemplates an *ex parte* proceeding at which no one opposes the minor's testimony. We find the clear and convincing standard used in H. B. 319 acceptable. The Ohio Supreme Court has stated:

"Clear and convincing evidence is that measure or degree of proof which will produce in the mind of the trier of facts a firm belief or conviction as to the allegations sought to be established. It is intermediate, being more than a mere preponderance, but not to the extent of such certainty as is required beyond a reasonable doubt as in criminal cases. It does not mean clear and unequivocal." *Cross* v. *Ledford,* 161 Ohio St. 469, 477, 120 N. E. 2d 118, 123 (1954) (emphasis deleted).

Our precedents do not require the State to set a lower standard. Given that the minor is assisted in the courtroom by an attorney as well as a guardian ad litem, this aspect of H. B. 319 is not infirm under the Constitution.

Third, appellees contend that the pleading requirements in H. B. 319 create a trap for the unwary. The minor, under the statutory scheme and the requirements prescribed by the Ohio Supreme Court, must choose among three pleading forms. See Ohio Rev. Code § 2151.85(C) (Supp. 1988); App. 6–14. The first alleges only maturity and the second alleges only best interests. She may not attempt to prove both maturity and best interests unless she chooses the third form, which alleges both of these facts. Appellees contend that the complications imposed by this scheme deny a minor the opportunity, required by the principal opinion in *Bellotti,* to prove either maturity or best interests or both. See 443 U. S., at 643–644.

Even on the assumption that the pleading scheme could produce some initial confusion because few minors would have counsel when pleading, the simple and straightforward procedure does not deprive the minor of an opportunity to prove her case. It seems unlikely that the Ohio courts will treat a minor's choice of complaint form without due care and understanding for her unrepresented status. In addition, we note that the minor does not make a binding election by the initial choice of pleading form. The minor, under H. B. 319, receives appointed counsel after filing the complaint and may move for leave to amend the pleadings. See 2151.85(B) (2); Ohio Rule Juvenile Proc. 22(B); see also *Hambleton* v. *R. G. Barry Corp.,* 12 Ohio St. 3d 179, 183–184, 465 N. E. 2d 1298, 1302 (1984) (finding a liberal amendment policy in the state civil rules). Regardless of whether Ohio could have written a simpler statute, H. B. 319 survives a facial challenge. . . .

HODGSON ET AL. v. MINNESOTA ET AL.

CERTIORARI TO THE UNITED STATES COURT OF APPEALS
FOR THE EIGHTH CIRCUIT

No. 88–1125. Argued November 29, 1989—Decided June 25, 1990

STEVENS, J., announced the judgment of the Court and delivered the opinion of the Court with respect to Parts I, II, IV, and VII, in which BRENNAN, MARSHALL, BLACKMUN, and O'CONNOR, JJ., joined, an opinion with respect to Part III, in which BRENNAN, J., joined, an opinion with respect to Parts V and VI, in which O'CONNOR, J., joined, and a dissenting opinion with respect to Part VIII. O'CONNOR, J., filed an opinion concurring in part and concurring in the judgment. MARSHALL, J., filed an opinion concurring in part, concurring in the judgment in part, and dissenting in part, in which BRENNAN and BLACKMUN, JJ., joined. SCALIA, J., filed an opinion concurring in the judgment in part and dissenting in part. KENNEDY, J., filed an opinion concurring in the judgment in part and dissenting in part, in which REHNQUIST, C. J., and WHITE and SCALIA, JJ., joined.

JUSTICE STEVENS announced the judgment of the Court and delivered the opinion of the Court with respect to Parts I, II, IV, and VII, an opinion with respect to Part III in which JUSTICE BRENNAN joins, an opinion with respect to Parts V and VI in which JUSTICE O'CONNOR joins, and a dissenting opinion with respect to Part VIII.

A Minnesota statute, Minn. Stat. §§ 144.343(2)–(7) (1988), provides, with certain exceptions, that no abortion shall be performed on a woman under 18 years of age until at least 48 hours after both of her parents have been notified. In subdivisions 2–4 of the statute the notice is mandatory unless (1) the attending physician certifies that an immediate abortion is necessary to prevent the woman's death and there is insufficient time to provide the required notice; (2) both of her parents have consented in writing; or (3) the woman declares that she is a victim of parental abuse or neglect, in which event notice of her declaration must be given to the proper authorities. The United States Court of Appeals for the Eighth Circuit, sitting en banc, unanimously held this provision unconstitutional. In No. 88–1309, we granted the State's petition to review that holding. Subdivision 6 of the same statute provides that if a court enjoins the enforcement of subdivision 2, the same notice requirement shall be effective unless the pregnant woman obtains a court order permitting the abortion to proceed. By a vote of 7 to 3, the Court of Appeals upheld the constitutionality of subdivision 6. In No. 88–1125, we granted the plaintiffs' petition to review that holding.

For reasons that follow, we now conclude that the requirement of notice to both of the pregnant minor's parents is not reasonably related to legitimate state interests and that subdivision 2 is unconstitutional. A different majority of the Court, for reasons stated in separate opinions, concludes that subdivision 6 is constitutional. Accordingly, the judgment of the Court of Appeals in its entirety is affirmed.

I

The parental notice statute was enacted in 1981 as an amendment to the Minors' Consent to Health Services Act. The earlier statute, which remains in effect as subdivision 1 of § 144.343 and as § 144.346, had modified the common-law requirement of parental consent for any medical procedure performed on minors. It authorized "[a]ny minor" to give effective consent without any parental involvement for the treatment of "pregnancy and conditions associated therewith, venereal disease, alcohol and other drug abuse." . . . The statute, unlike others of its age, . . . applied to abortion services.

The 1981 amendment qualified the authority of an "unemancipated minor" . . . to give effective consent to an abortion by requiring that either her physician or an agent notify "the parent" personally or by certified mail at least 48 hours before the procedure is performed. . . . The term "parent" is defined in subdivision 3 to mean "both parents of the pregnant woman if they are both living." No exception is made for a divorced parent, a noncustodial parent, or a biological parent who never married or lived with the pregnant woman's mother. . . . The statute does provide, however, that if only one parent is living, or "if the second one cannot be located through reasonably diligent effort," notice to one parent is sufficient. . . .

Subdivision 6 authorizes a judicial bypass of the two-parent notice requirement if subdivision 2 is ever "temporarily or permanently" enjoined by judicial order. If the pregnant minor can convince "any judge of a court of competent jurisdiction" that she is "mature and capable of giving informed consent to the proposed abortion," or that an abortion without notice to both parents would be in her best interest, the court can authorize the physician to proceed without notice. The statute provides that the bypass procedure shall be confidential, that it shall be expedited, that the minor has a right to court-appointed counsel, and that she shall be afforded free access to the court "24 hours a day, seven days a week." An order denying an abortion can be appealed on an expedited basis, but an order authorizing an abortion without notification is not subject to appeal. . . .

Three separate but related interests—the interest in the welfare of the pregnant minor, the interest of the parents, and the interest of the family unit—are relevant to our consideration of the constitutionality of the 48-hour waiting period and the two-parent notification requirement.

The State has a strong and legitimate interest in the welfare of its young citizens, whose immaturity, inexperience, and lack of judgment may sometimes impair their ability to exercise their rights wisely. See *Bellotti II*, 443 U. S., at 634–639 (opinion of Powell, J.); *Prince* v. *Massachusetts*, 321 U. S. 158, 166–167 (1944).[31] That interest, which justifies state-imposed requirements that a minor obtain his or her parent's consent before undergoing an operation, marrying, or entering military service, see *Parham* v. *J. R.*, 442 U. S. 584, 603–604 (1979); *Planned Parenthood of Central Mo.* v. *Danforth*, 428 U. S., at 95 (WHITE, J., concurring in part and dissenting in part); *id.*, at 102–103 (STEVENS, J., concurring in part and dissenting in part), extends also to the minor's decision to terminate her pregnancy. Although the Court has held that parents may not exercise "an absolute, and possibly arbitrary, veto" over that decision, *Danforth*, 428 U. S., at 74, it has never challenged a State's reasonable judgment that the decision should be made after notification to and consultation with a parent. See *Ohio* v. *Akron Center for Reproductive Health, post*, at 510–511; *Akron* v. *Akron Center for Reproductive Health, Inc.*, 462 U. S. 416, 428, n. 10, 439 (1983); *H. L.* v. *Matheson*, 450 U. S., at 409–410; *Bellotti II*, 443 U. S., at 640–641 (opinion of Powell, J.); *Danforth*, 428 U. S., at 75. As Justice Stewart, joined by Justice Powell, pointed out in his concurrence in *Danforth:*

"There can be little doubt that the State furthers a constitutionally permissible end by encouraging an unmarried pregnant minor to seek the help and advice of her parents in making the very important decision whether or not to bear a child." *Id.*, at 91.

Parents have an interest in controlling the education and upbringing of their children but that interest is "a counterpart of the responsibilities they have assumed." *Lehr* v. *Robertson*, 463 U. S. 248, 257 (1983); see also *Parham*, 442 U. S., at 602 (citing 1 W. Blackstone, Commentaries *447; 2 J. Kent, Commentaries on American Law *190); *Pierce* v. *Society of Sisters*, 268 U. S. 510, 535 (1925). The fact of biological parentage generally offers a

---

31. "Properly understood . . . the tradition of parental authority is not inconsistent with our tradition of individual liberty; rather, the former is one of the basic presuppositions of the latter. Legal restrictions on minors, especially those supportive of the parental role, may be important to the child's chances for the full growth and maturity that make eventual participation in a free society meaningful and rewarding." *Bellotti II*, 443 U. S., at 638–639 (opinion of Powell, J.). . . .

person only "an opportunity . . . to develop a relationship with his off-spring." *Lehr*, 463 U. S., at 262; see also *Caban* v. *Mohammed*, 441 U. S. 380, 397 (1979) (Stewart, J., dissenting). But the demonstration of commitment to the child through the assumption of personal, financial, or custodial responsibility may give the natural parent a stake in the relationship with the child rising to the level of a liberty interest. See *Stanley* v. *Illinois*, 405 U. S. 645, 651 (1972); *Lehr*, 463 U. S., at 261; *Michael H.* v. *Gerald D.*, 491 U. S. 110, 157–160 (1989) (WHITE, J., dissenting); cf. *Caban*, 441 U. S., at 393, n. 14. But see *Michael H.*, 491 U. S., at 123–127 (plurality opinion).

While the State has a legitimate interest in the creation and dissolution of the marriage contract, see *Sosna* v. *Iowa*, 419 U. S. 393, 404 (1975); *Maynard* v. *Hill*, 125 U. S. 190, 205 (1888), the family has a privacy interest in the upbringing and education of children and the intimacies of the marital relationship which is protected by the Constitution against undue state interference. See *Wisconsin* v. *Yoder*, 406 U. S. 205, 233–234 (1972); *Griswold* v. *Connecticut*, 381 U. S., at 495–496 (Goldberg, J., concurring); *Poe* v. *Ullman*, 367 U. S. 497, 551–552 (1961) (Harlan, J., dissenting); *Gilbert* v. *Minnesota*, 254 U. S. 325, 335–336 (1920) (Brandeis, J., dissenting); see also *Michael H.*, 491 U. S., at 132 (O'CONNOR, J., concurring in part); *Roberts* v. *United States Jaycees*, 468 U. S. 609, 618–620 (1984); *Cleveland Bd. of Education* v. *LaFleur*, 414 U. S., at 639–640. The family may assign one parent to guide the children's education and the other to look after their health.[32] "The statist notion that governmental power should supersede parental authority in *all* cases because *some* parents abuse and neglect children is repugnant to American tradition." *Parham*, 442 U. S., at 603. We have long held that there exists a "private realm of family life which the state cannot enter." *Prince* v. *Massachusetts*, 321 U. S., at 166. Thus, when the government intrudes on choices concerning the arrangement of the household, this Court has carefully examined the "governmental interests advanced and the extent to which they are served by the challenged regulation." *Moore* v. *East Cleveland*, 431 U. S. 494, 499 (1977) (plurality opinion); *id.*, at 507, 510–511 (BRENNAN, J., concurring); see also *Meyer* v. *Nebraska*, 262 U. S. 390, 399–400 (1923). . . .

We think it is clear that a requirement that a minor wait 48 hours after notifying a single parent of her intention to get an abortion would reasonably further the legitimate state interest in ensuring that the minor's decision is knowing and intelligent. We have held that when a parent or another person has assumed "primary responsibility" for a minor's well-being, the State may properly enact "laws designed to aid discharge of that respon-

---

32. Under common-law principles, one parent has authority to act as agent for the other in matters of their child's upbringing and education. See E. Spencer, Law of Domestic Relations 432 (1911); T. Reeve, Law of Baron and Femme 295 (1816).

sibility." *Ginsberg* v. *New York*, 390 U. S. 629, 639 (1968). To the extent that subdivision 2 of the Minnesota statute requires notification of only one parent, it does just that. The brief waiting period provides the parent the opportunity to consult with his or her spouse and a family physician, and it permits the parent to inquire into the competency of the doctor performing the abortion, discuss the religious or moral implications of the abortion decision, and provide the daughter needed guidance and counsel in evaluating the impact of the decision on her future. See *Zbaraz* v. *Hartigan*, 763 F. 2d 1532, 1552 (CA7 1985) (Coffey, J., dissenting), aff'd by an equally divided Court, 484 U. S. 171 (1987).

The 48-hour delay imposes only a minimal burden on the right of the minor to decide whether or not to terminate her pregnancy. Although the District Court found that scheduling factors, weather, and the minor's school and work commitments may combine, in many cases, to create a delay of a week or longer between the initiation of notification and the abortion, 648 F. Supp., at 765, there is no evidence that the 48-hour period itself is unreasonable or longer than appropriate for adequate consultation between parent and child. The statute does not impose any period of delay once a court, acting *in loco parentis,* or the parents express their agreement that the minor is mature or that the procedure would be in her best interest. . . .

It is equally clear that the requirement that *both* parents be notified, whether or not both wish to be notified or have assumed responsibility for the upbringing of the child, does not reasonably further any legitimate state interest. The usual justification for a parental consent or notification provision is that it supports the authority of a parent who is presumed to act in the minor's best interest and thereby assures that the minor's decision to terminate her pregnancy is knowing, intelligent, and deliberate. To the extent that such an interest is legitimate, it would be fully served by a requirement that the minor notify one parent who can then seek the counsel of his or her mate or any other party, when such advice and support is deemed necessary to help the child make a difficult decision. In the ideal family setting, of course, notice to either parent would normally constitute notice to both. A statute requiring two-parent notification would not further any state interest in those instances. In many families, however, the parent notified by the child would not notify the other parent. In those cases the State has no legitimate interest in questioning one parent's judgment that notice to the other parent would not assist the minor or in presuming that the parent who has assumed parental duties is incompetent to make decisions regarding the health and welfare of the child.

Not only does two-parent notification fail to serve any state interest with respect to functioning families, it disserves the state interest in protecting and assisting the minor with respect to dysfunctional families. The record reveals that in the thousands of dysfunctional families affected by this statute, the two-parent notice requirement proved positively harmful to the minor and her family. The testimony at trial established that this requirement, ostensibly designed for the benefit of the minor, resulted in major trauma to the child, and often to a parent as well. In some cases, the parents were divorced and the second parent did not have custody or otherwise participate in the child's upbringing. App. 244–245; *id.*, at 466; *id.*, at 115. In these circumstances, the privacy of the parent and child was violated, even when they suffered no other physical or psychological harm. In other instances, however, the second parent had either deserted or abused the child, *id.*, at 462, 464, had died under tragic circumstances, *id.*, at 120–121, or was not notified because of the considered judgment that notification would inflict unnecessary stress on a parent who was ill. *Id.*, at 204, 465. . . . In these circumstances, the statute was not merely ineffectual in achieving the State's goals but actually counterproductive. The focus on notifying the second parent distracted both the parent and minor from the minor's imminent abortion decision. . . .

The Court holds that the constitutional objection to the two-parent notice requirement is removed by the judicial bypass option provided in subdivision 6 of the Minnesota statute. I respectfully dissent from that holding.

A majority of the Court has previously held that a statute requiring one parent's consent to a minor's abortion will be upheld if the State provides an "'alternative procedure whereby a pregnant minor may demonstrate that she is sufficiently mature to make the abortion decision herself or that, despite her immaturity, an abortion would be in her best interests.'" *Planned Parenthood Assn. of Kansas City, Mo., Inc.* v. *Ashcroft*, 462 U. S. 476, 491 (1983) (opinion of Powell, J.); *id.*, at 505 (opinion of O'CONNOR, J.). Indeed, in *Bellotti II*, four Members of the Court expressed the same opinion about a statute requiring the consent of both parents. See 443 U. S., at 643–644 (opinion of Powell, J.). Neither of those precedents should control our decision today.

In *Bellotti II*, eight Members of the Court joined the judgment holding the Massachusetts statute unconstitutional. Thus, the Court did not *hold* that the judicial bypass set forth in that statute was valid; it held just the opposite. Moreover, the discussion of the minimum requirements for a valid judicial bypass in Justice Powell's opinion was joined by only three other Members of the Court. Indeed, neither the arguments of the parties, nor any of the opinions in the case, considered the significant difference between a statute requiring the involvement of *both* parents in the abortion decision and a statute that merely requires the involvement of one. Thus, the doctrine of *stare decisis* does not require that the standards articulated in Justice Powell's opinion be applied to a statute that mandates the involvement of both parents.

Unlike *Bellotti II*, the judgment in *Ashcroft* sustained the constitutionality of the statute containing a judicial bypass as an alternative to the requirement of *one* parent's consent to a minor's abortion. The distinctions between notice and consent and between notification of both parents rather than just one arguably constitute a sufficient response to an argument resting on *stare decisis*. Further analysis is necessary, however, because, at least on the surface, the consent requirement would appear to be more onerous than a requirement of mere notice. . . .

A judicial bypass that is designed to handle exceptions from a reasonable general rule, and thereby preserve the constitutionality of that rule, is quite different from a requirement that a minor—or a minor and one of her parents—must apply to a court for permission to avoid the application of a rule that is not reasonably related to legitimate state goals. A requirement that a minor acting with the consent of *both* parents apply to a court for permission to effectuate her decision clearly would constitute an unjustified official interference with the privacy of the minor and her family. The requirement that the bypass procedure must be invoked when the minor and one parent agree that the other parent should not be notified represents an equally unjustified governmental intrusion into the family's decisional process. When the parents are living together and have joint custody over the child, the State has no legitimate interest in the communication between father and mother about the child. "[W]here the parents are divorced, the minor and/or custodial parent, and not a court, is in the best position to determine whether notifying the non-custodial parent would be in the child's best interests." App. to Pet. for Cert. in No. 88–1125, p. 69a. As the Court of Appeals panel originally concluded, the "minor and custodial parent, . . . by virtue of their major interest and superior position, should alone have the opportunity to decide to whom, if anyone, notice of the minor's abortion decision should be given." *Ibid.* (citation omitted). I agree with that conclusion. . . .

PLANNED PARENTHOOD OF SOUTHEASTERN PENNSYLVANIA ET AL. v. ROBERT P. CASEY, ET AL.

Nos. 91–744, 91–902. Argued April 22, 1992.—Decided June 29, 1992.

O'CONNOR, KENNEDY, and SOUTER, JJ., announced the judgment of the Court and delivered the opinion of the Court with respect to Parts I, II, III, V–A, V–C, and VI, in which BLACKMUN and STEVENS, JJ., joined, an opinion with respect to Part V–E, in which STEVENS, J., joined, and an opinion with respect to Parts IV, V–B, and V–D. STEVENS, J., filed an opinion concurring in part and dissenting in part. BLACKMUN, J., filed an opinion concurring in part, concurring in the judgment in part, and dissenting in part. REHNQUIST, C. J., filed an opinion concurring in the judgment in part and dissenting in part, in which WHITE, SCALIA, and THOMAS, JJ., joined. SCALIA, J., filed an opinion concurring in the judgment in part and dissenting in part, in which REHNQUIST, C. J., and WHITE and THOMAS, JJ., joined.

JUSTICE O'CONNOR, JUSTICE KENNEDY, and JUSTICE SOUTER announced the judgment of the Court and delivered the opinion of the Court with respect to Parts I, II, III, V–A, V–C, and VI, an opinion with respect to Part V–E, in which JUSTICE STEVENS joins, and an opinion with respect to Parts IV, V–B, and V–D.

I

Liberty finds no refuge in a jurisprudence of doubt. Yet 19 years after our holding that the Constitution protects a woman's right to terminate her pregnancy in its early stages, *Roe* v. *Wade,* 410 U. S. 113, 93 S.Ct. 705, 35 L. Ed. 2d 147 (1973), that definition of liberty is still questioned. Joining the respondents as *amicus curiae,* the United States, as it has done in five other cases in the last decade, again asks us to overrule *Roe.* See Brief for Respondents 104–117; Brief for United States as *Amicus Curiae* 8.

At issue in these cases are five provisions of the Pennsylvania Abortion Control Act of 1982 as amended in 1988 and 1989. 18 Pa. Cons. Stat. §§ 3203–3220 (1990). Relevant portions of the Act are set forth in the appendix. The Act requires that a woman seeking an abortion give her informed consent prior to the abortion procedure, and specifies that she be provided with certain information at least 24 hours before the abortion is performed. § 3205. For a minor to obtain an abortion, the Act requires the informed consent of one of her parents, but provides for a judicial bypass option if the minor does not wish to or cannot obtain a parent's consent. § 3206. Another provision of the Act requires that, unless certain exceptions apply, a married woman seeking an abortion must sign a statement indicating that she has notified her husband of her intended abortion. § 3209. The Act exempts compliance with these three requirements in the event of a "medical emergency," which is defined in § 3203 of the Act. See §§ 3203, 3205(a), 3206(a), 3209(c). In addition to the above provisions regulating the performance of abortions, the Act imposes certain reporting requirements on facilities that provide abortion services. §§ 3207(b), 3214(a), 3214(f).

Before any of these provisions took effect, the petitioners, who are five abortion clinics and one physician representing himself as well as a class of physicians who provide abortion services, brought this suit seeking declaratory and injunctive relief. Each provision was challenged as unconstitutional on its face. The District Court entered a preliminary injunction against the enforcement of the regulations, and, after a 3-day bench trial, held all the provisions at issue here unconstitutional, entering a permanent injunction against Pennsylvania's enforcement of them. 744 F. Supp. 1323 (ED Pa. 1990). The Court of Appeals for the Third Circuit affirmed in part and reversed in part, upholding all of the regulations except for the husband notification requirement. 947 F. 2d 682 (1991). We granted certiorari. 502 U. S. 112 S.Ct. 631, 632, 117 L. Ed. 2d 104 (1992).

The Court of Appeals found it necessary to follow an elaborate course of reasoning even to identify the first premise to use to determine whether the statute enacted by Pennsylvania meets constitutional standards. See 947 F. 2d, at 687–698. And at oral argument in this Court, the attorney for the parties challenging the statute took the position that none of the enactments can be upheld without overruling *Roe* v. *Wade*. Tr. of Oral Arg. 5–6. We disagree with that analysis; but we acknowledge that our decisions after *Roe* cast doubt upon the meaning and reach of its holding. Further, THE CHIEF JUSTICE admits that he would overrule the central holding of *Roe* and adopt the rational relationship test as the sole criterion of constitutionality. State and federal courts as well as legislatures throughout the Union must have guidance as they seek to address this subject in conformance with the Constitution. Given these premises, we find it imperative to review once more the principles that define the rights of the woman and the legitimate authority of the State respecting the termination of pregnancies by abortion procedures.

After considering the fundamental constitutional questions resolved by *Roe*, principles of institutional integrity, and the rule of *stare decisis*, we are led to conclude this: the essential holding of *Roe* v. *Wade* should be retained and once again reaffirmed.

It must be stated at the outset and with clarity that *Roe*'s essential holding, the holding we reaffirm, has three parts. First is a recognition of the right of the woman to choose to have an abortion before viability and to obtain it without undue interference from the State. Before viability, the State's interests are not strong enough to support a prohibition of abortion or the imposition of a substantial obstacle to the woman's effective right to elect the procedure. Second is a confirmation of the State's power to restrict abortions after fetal viability, if the law contains exceptions for pregnancies with endanger a woman's life or health. And third is the principle that the State has legitimate interests from the outset of the pregnancy in protecting the health of the woman and the life of the fetus that may become a child. These principles do not contradict one another; and we adhere to each.

II

Constitutional protection of the woman's decision to terminate her pregnancy derives from the Due Process Clause of the Fourteenth Amendment. It declares that no State shall "deprive any person of life, liberty, or property, without due process of law." The controlling word in the case before us is "liberty." Although a literal reading of the Clause might suggest that it governs only the procedures by which a State may deprive persons of liberty, for at least 105 years, at least since *Mugler* v. *Kansas,* 123 U. S. 623, 660–661, 8 S.Ct. 273, 291, 31 L. Ed. 205 (1887), the Clause has been understood to contain a substantive component as well, one "barring certain government actions regardless of the fairness of the procedures used to implement them." *Daniels* v. *Williams,* 474 U. S. 327, 331, 106 S.Ct. 662, 665, 88 L. Ed. 2d 662 (1986). As Justice Brandeis (joined by Justice Holmes) observed, "[d]espite arguments to the contrary which had seemed to me persuasive, it is settled that the due process clause of the Fourteenth Amendment applies to matters of substantive law as well as to matters of procedure. Thus all fundamental rights comprised within the term liberty are protected by the Federal Constitution from invasion by the States." *Whitney* v. *California,* 274 U. S. 357, 373, 47 S.Ct. 641, 647, 71 L. Ed. 1095 (1927) (Brandeis, J., concurring). "[T]he guaranties of due process, though having their roots in Magna Carta's '*per legem terrae*' and considered as procedural safeguards 'against executive usurpation and tyranny,' have in this country 'become bulwarks also against arbitrary legislation.'" *Poe* v. *Ullman,* 367 U. S. 497, 541, 81 S.Ct. 1752, 1776, 6 L. Ed. 2d 989 (1961) (Harlan, J., dissenting from dismissal on jurisdictional grounds) (quoting *Hurtado* v. *California,* 110 U. S. 516, 532, 4 S.Ct. 111, 119, 28 L. Ed. 232 (1884)).

The most familiar of the substantive liberties protected by the Fourteenth Amendment are those recognized by the Bill of Rights. We have held that the Due Process Clause of the Fourteenth Amendment incorporates most of the Bill of Rights against the States. See, *e. g., Duncan* v. *Louisiana,* 391 U. S. 145, 147–148, 88 S.Ct. 1444, 1446, 20 L. Ed. 2d 491 (1968). It is tempting, as a means of curbing the discretion of federal judges, to suppose that liberty encompasses no more than those rights already guaranteed to the individual against federal interference by the express provisions of the first eight amendments to the Constitution. See *Adamson* v. *California,* 332 U. S. 46, 68–92, 67 S.Ct. 1672, 1683–1697, 91 L. Ed. 1903 (1947) (Black, J., dissenting). But of course this Court has never accepted that view.

It is also tempting, for the same reason, to suppose that the Due Process Clause protects only those practices, defined at the most specific level, that were protected against government interference by other rules of law when the Fourteenth Amendment was ratified. See *Michael H.* v. *Gerald D.,* 491 U. S. 110, 127–128, n. 6, 109 S.Ct. 2333, 2344, n. 6, 105 L. Ed. 2d 91 (1989) (opinion of SCALIA, J.). But such a view would be inconsistent with our law. It is a promise of the Constitution that there is a realm of personal liberty which the government may not enter. We have vindicated this principle before. Marriage is mentioned nowhere in the Bill of Rights and interracial marriage was illegal in most States in the 19th century, but the Court was no doubt correct in finding it to be an aspect of liberty protected against state interference by the substantive component of the Due Process Clause in *Loving* v. *Virginia,* 388 U. S. 1, 12, 87 S.Ct. 1817, 1824, 18 L. Ed. 2d 1010 (1967) (relying, in an opinion for eight Justices, on the Due Process Clause). Similar examples may be found in *Turner* v. *Safley,* 482 U. S. 78, 94–99, 107 S.Ct. 2254, 2265–2267, 96 L. Ed. 2d 64 (1987); in *Carey* v. *Population Services International,* 431 U. S. 678, 684–686, 97 S.Ct. 2010, 2015–2017, 52 L. Ed. 2d 675 (1977); in *Griswold* v. *Connecticut,* 381 U. S. 479, 481–482, 85 S.Ct. 1678, 1680–1681, 14 L. Ed. 2d 510 (1965), as well as in the separate opinions of a majority of the Members of the Court in that case, *id.,* at 486–488, 85 S.Ct., at 1682–1683 (Goldberg, J., joined by Warren, C. J., and Brennan, J., concurring) (expressly relying on due process), *id.,* at 500–502, 85 S.Ct., at 1690–1691 (Harlan, J., concurring in judgment) (same), *id.,* at 502–507, 85 S.Ct., at 1691–1694 (WHITE, J., concurring in judgment) (same); in *Pierce* v. *Society of Sisters,* 268 U. S. 510, 534–535, 45 S.Ct. 571, 573, 69 L. Ed. 1070 (1925); and in *Meyer* v. *Nebraska,* 262 U. S. 390, 399–403, 43 S.Ct. 625, 627, 67 L. Ed. 1042 (1923).

Neither the Bill of Rights nor the specific practices of States at the time of the adoption of the Fourteenth Amendment marks the outer limits of the substantive sphere of liberty which the Fourteenth Amendment protects. See U. S. Const., Amend. 9. As the second Justice Harlan recognized:

"[T]he full scope of the liberty guaranteed by the Due Process Clause cannot be found in or limited by the precise terms of the specific guarantees elsewhere provided in the Constitution. This 'liberty' is not a series of isolated points pricked out in terms of the taking of property; the freedom of speech, press, and religion; the right to keep and bear arms; the freedom from unreasonable searches and seizures; and so on. It is a rational continuum which, broadly speaking, includes a freedom from all substantial arbitrary impositions and purposeless restraints, . . . and which also recognizes, what a reasonable and sensitive judgment must, that certain interests require particularly careful scrutiny of the state needs asserted to justify their abridgment." *Poe* v. *Ullman, supra,* 367 U. S., at 543, 81 S.Ct., at 1777 (Harlan, J., dissenting from dismissal on jurisdictional grounds).

Justice Harlan wrote these words in addressing an issue the full Court did not reach in *Poe* v. *Ullman,* but the Court adopted his position four Terms later in *Griswold* v. *Connecticut, supra.* In *Griswold,* we held that the Constitution does not permit a State to forbid a married couple to use contraceptives. That same freedom was later guaranteed, under the Equal Protection Clause, for unmarried couples. See *Eisenstadt* v. *Baird,* 405 U. S. 438, 92 S.Ct. 1029, 31 L. Ed. 2d 349 (1972). Constitutional protection was extended to the sale and distribution of contraceptives in *Carey* v. *Population Services International, supra.* It is settled now, as it was when the Court heard arguments in *Roe* v. *Wade,* that the Constitution places limits on a State's right to interfere with a person's most basic decisions about family and parenthood, see *Carey* v. *Population Services International, supra; Moore* v. *East Cleveland,* 431 U. S. 494, 97 S.Ct. 1932, 52 L. Ed. 2d 531 (1977); *Eisenstadt* v. *Baird, supra; Loving* v. *Virginia, supra; Griswold* v. *Connecticut, supra; Skinner* v. *Oklahoma ex rel. Williamson,* 316 U. S. 535, 62 S.Ct. 1110, 86 L. Ed. 1655 (1942); *Pierce* v. *Society of Sisters, supra; Meyer* v. *Nebraska, supra,* as well as bodily integrity. See, *e. g., Washington* v. *Harper,* 494 U. S. 210, 221–222, 110 S.Ct. 1028, 1036–1037, 108 L. Ed. 2d 178 (1990); *Winston* v. *Lee,* 470 U. S. 753, 105 S.Ct. 1611, 84 L. Ed. 2d 662 (1985); *Rochin* v. *California,* 342 U. S. 165, 72 S.Ct. 205, 96 L. Ed. 183 (1952).

The inescapable fact is that adjudication of substantive due process claims may call upon the Court in interpreting the Constitution to exercise that same capacity which by tradition courts always have exercised: reasoned judgment. Its boundaries are not susceptible of expression as a simple rule. That does not mean we are free to invalidate state policy choices with which we disagree; yet neither does it permit us to shrink from the duties of our office. As Justice Harlan observed:

"Due process has not been reduced to any formula; its content cannot be determined by reference to any code. The best that can be said is that through the course of this Court's decisions it has represented the balance which our Nation, built upon postulates of respect for the liberty of the individual, has struck between that liberty and the demands of organized society. If the supplying of content to this Constitutional concept has of necessity been a rational process, it certainly has not been one where judges have felt free to roam where unguided speculation might take them. The balance of which I speak is the balance struck by this country, having regard to what history teaches are the traditions from which it developed as well as the traditions from which it broke. That tradition is a living thing. A decision of this Court which radically departs from it could not long survive, while a decision which builds on what has survived is likely to be sound. No formula could serve as a substitute, in this area, for judgment and restraint." *Poe* v. *Ullman*, 367 U. S., at 542, 81 S.Ct., at 1776 (Harlan, J., dissenting from dismissal on jurisdictional grounds).

See also *Rochin* v. *California, supra,* 342 U. S., at 171–172, 72 S.Ct., at 209 (Frankfurter, J., writing for the Court) ("To believe that this judicial exercise of judgment could be avoided by freezing 'due process of law' at some fixed stage of time or thought is to suggest that the most important aspect of constitutional adjudication is a function for inanimate machines and not for judges").

Men and women of good conscience can disagree, and we suppose some always shall disagree, about the profound moral and spiritual implications of terminating a pregnancy, even in its earliest stage. Some of us as individuals find abortion offensive to our most basic principles of morality, but that cannot control our decision. Our obligation is to define the liberty of all, not to mandate our own moral code. The underlying constitutional issue is whether the State can resolve these philosophic questions in such a definitive way that a woman lacks all choice in the matter, except perhaps in those rare circumstances in which the pregnancy is itself a danger to her own life or health, or is the result of rape or incest.

It is conventional constitutional doctrine that where reasonable people disagree the government can adopt one position or the other. See, *e. g., Ferguson* v. *Skrupa*, 372 U. S. 726, 83 S.Ct. 1028, 10 L. Ed. 2d 93 (1963); *Williamson* v. *Lee Optical of Oklahoma, Inc.*, 348 U. S. 483, 75 S.Ct. 461, 99 L. Ed. 563 (1955). That theorem, however, assumes a state of affairs in which the choice does not intrude upon a protected liberty. Thus, while some people might disagree about whether or not the flag should be saluted, or disagree about the proposition that it may not be defiled, we have ruled that a State may not compel or enforce one view or the other. See *West Virginia State Bd. of Education* v. *Barnette*, 319 U. S. 624, 63 S.Ct. 1178, 87 L. Ed. 1628 (1943); *Texas* v. *Johnson*, 491 U. S. 397, 109 S.Ct. 2533, 105 L. Ed. 2d 342 (1989).

Our law affords constitutional protection to personal decisions relating to marriage, procreation, contraception, family relationships, child rearing, and education. *Carey* v. *Population Services International,* 431 U. S., at 685, 97 S.Ct., at 2016. Our cases recognize "the right of the *individual,* married or single, to be free from unwarranted governmental intrusion into matters so fundamentally affecting a person as the decision whether to bear or beget a child." *Eisenstadt* v. *Baird, supra,* 405 U. S., at 453, 92 S.Ct., at 1038 (emphasis in original). Our precedents "have respected the private realm of family life which the state cannot enter." *Prince* v. *Massachusetts,* 321 U. S. 158, 166, 64 S.Ct. 438, 442, 88 L. Ed. 645 (1944). These matters, involving the most intimate and personal choices a person may make in a lifetime, choices central to personal dignity and autonomy, are central to the liberty protected by the Fourteenth Amendment. At the heart of liberty is the right to define one's own concept of existence, of meaning, of the universe, and of the mystery of human life. Beliefs about these matters could not define the attributes of personhood were they formed under compulsion of the State.

These considerations begin our analysis of the woman's interest in terminating her pregnancy but cannot end it, for this reason: though the abortion decision may originate within the zone of conscience and belief, it is more than a philosophic exercise. Abortion is a unique act. It is an act fraught with consequences for others: for the woman who must live with the implications of her decision; for the persons who perform and assist in the procedure; for the spouse, family, and society which must confront the knowledge that these procedures exist, procedures some deem nothing short of an act of violence against innocent human life; and, depending on one's beliefs, for the life or potential life that is aborted. Though abortion is conduct, it does not follow that the State is entitled to proscribe it in all instances. That is because the liberty of the woman is at stake in a sense unique to the human condition and so unique to the law. The mother who carries a child to full term is subject to anxieties, to physical constraints, to pain that only she must bear. That these sacrifices have from the beginning of the human race been endured by woman with a pride that ennobles her in the eyes of others and gives to the infant a bond of love cannot alone be grounds for the State to insist she make the sacrifice. Her suffering is too intimate and personal for the State to insist, without more, upon its own vision of the woman's role, however dominant that vision has been in the course of our history and our culture. The destiny of the woman must be shaped to a large extent on her own conception of her spiritual imperatives and her place in society.

It should be recognized, moreover, that in some critical respects the abortion decision is of the same character as the decision to use contraception, to which *Griswold* v. *Connecticut, Eisenstadt* v. *Baird,* and *Carey* v. *Population Services International,* afford constitutional protection. We have no doubt as to the correctness of those decisions. They support the reasoning in *Roe* relating to the woman's liberty because they involve personal decisions concerning not only the meaning of procreation but also human responsibility and respect for it. As with abortion, reasonable people will have differences of opinion about these matters. One view is based on such reverence for the wonder of creation that any pregnancy ought to be welcomed and carried to full term no matter how difficult it will be to provide for the child and ensure its well-being. Another is that the inability to provide for the nurture and care of that infant is a cruelty to the child and an anguish to the parent. These are intimate views with infinite variations, and their deep, personal character underlay our decisions in *Griswold, Eisenstadt,* and *Carey.* The same concerns are present when the woman confronts the reality that, perhaps despite her attempts to avoid it, she has become pregnant.

It was this dimension of personal liberty that *Roe* sought to protect, and its holding invoked the reasoning and the tradition of the precedents we have discussed, granting protection to substantive liberties of the person. *Roe* was, of course, an extension of those cases and, as the decision itself indicated, the separate States could act in some degree to further their own legitimate interests in protecting pre-natal life. The extent to which the legislatures of the States might act to outweigh the interests of the woman in choosing to terminate her pregnancy was a subject of debate both in *Roe* itself and in decisions following it.

While we appreciate the weight of the arguments made on behalf of the State in the case before us, arguments which in their ultimate formulation conclude that *Roe* should be overruled, the reservations any of us may have in reaffirming the central holding of *Roe* are outweighed by the explication of individual liberty we have given combined with the force of *stare decisis.* We turn now to that doctrine.

III

A

The obligation to follow precedent begins with necessity, and a contrary necessity marks its outer limit. With Cardozo, we recognize that no judicial system could do society's work if it eyed each issue afresh in every case that raised it. See B. Cardozo, The Nature of the Judicial Process 149 (1921). Indeed, the very concept of the rule of law underlying our own Constitution requires such continuity over time that a respect for precedent is, by definition, indispensable. See Powell, Stare Decisis and Judicial Restraint, 1991 Journal of Supreme Court History 13, 16. At the other extreme, a different necessity would make itself felt if a prior judicial ruling should come to be seen so clearly as error that its enforcement was for that very reason doomed.

Even when the decision to overrule a prior case is not, as in the rare, latter instance, virtually foreordained, it is common wisdom that the rule of *stare decisis* is not an "inexorable command," and certainly it is not such in every constitutional case, see *Burnet* v. *Coronado Oil Gas Co.*, 285 U. S. 393, 405–411, 52 S.Ct. 443, 446–449, 76 L. Ed. 815 (1932) (Brandeis, J., dissenting). See also *Payne* v. *Tennessee*, 501 U. S. 111 S.Ct. 2597, 115 L. Ed. 2d 720 (1991) (SOUTER, J., joined by KENNEDY, J., concurring); *Arizona* v. *Rumsey*, 467 U. S. 203, 212, 104 S.Ct. 2305, 2310, 81 L. Ed. 2d 164 (1984). Rather, when this Court reexamines a prior holding, its judgment is customarily informed by a series of prudential and pragmatic considerations designed to test the consistency of overruling a prior decision with the ideal of the rule of law, and to gauge the respective costs of reaffirming and overruling a prior case. Thus, for example, we may ask whether the rule has proved to be intolerable simply in defying practical workability, *Swift & Co.* v. *Wickham*, 382 U. S. 111, 116, 86 S.Ct. 258, 261, 15 L. Ed. 2d 194 (1965); whether the rule is subject to a kind of reliance that would lend a special hardship to the consequences of overruling and add inequity to the cost of repudiation, *e. g.*, *United States* v. *Title Ins. & Trust Co.*, 265 U. S. 472, 486, 44 S.Ct. 621, 623, 68 L. Ed. 1110 (1924); whether related principles of law have so far developed as to have left the old rule no more than a remnant of abandoned doctrine, see *Patterson* v. *McLean Credit Union*, 491 U.S. 164, 173–174, 109 S.Ct. 2363, 2371, 105 L. Ed. 2d 132 (1989); or whether facts have so changed or come to be seen so differently, as to have robbed the old rule of significant application or justification, *e. g.*, *Burnet, supra*, 285 U. S., at 412, 52 S.Ct., at 449 (Brandeis, J., dissenting).

So in this case we may inquire whether *Roe*'s central rule has been found unworkable; whether the rule's limitation on state power could be removed without serious inequity to those who have relied upon it or significant damage to the stability of the society governed by the rule in question; whether the law's growth in the intervening years has left *Roe*'s central rule a doctrinal anachronism discounted by society; and whether *Roe*'s premises of fact have so far changed in the ensuing two decades as to render its central holding somehow irrelevant or unjustifiable in dealing with the issue it addressed.

1

Although *Roe* has engendered opposition, it has in no sense proven "unworkable," see *Garcia* v. *San Antonio Metropolitan Transit Authority*, 469 U. S. 528, 546, 105 S.Ct. 1005, 1015, 83 L. Ed. 2d 1016 (1985), representing as it does a simple limitation beyond which a state law is unenforceable. While *Roe* has, of course, required judicial assessment of state laws affecting the exercise of the choice guaranteed against government infringement, and although the need for such review will remain as a consequence of today's decision, the required determinations fall within judicial competence.

2

The inquiry into reliance counts the cost of a rule's repudiation as it would fall on those who have relied reasonably on the rule's continued application. Since the classic case for weighing reliance heavily in favor of following the earlier rule occurs in the commercial context, see *Payne* v. *Tennessee*, where advance planning of great precision is most obviously a necessity, it is no cause for surprise that some would find no reliance worthy of consideration in support of *Roe.* . . .

To eliminate the issue of reliance that easily, however, one would need to limit cognizable reliance to specific instances of sexual activity. But to do this would be simply to refuse to face the fact that for two decades of economic and social developments, people have organized intimate relationships and made choices that define their views of themselves and their places in society, in reliance on the availability of abortion in the event that contraception should fail. The ability of women to participate equally in the economic and social life of the Nation has been facilitated by their ability to control their reproductive lives. See, *e. g.,* R. Petchesky, Abortion and Woman's Choice 109, 133, n. 7 (rev. ed. 1990). The Constitution serves human values, and while the effect of reliance on *Roe* cannot be exactly measured, neither can the certain cost of overruling *Roe* for people who have ordered their thinking and living around that case be dismissed.

3

No evolution of legal principle has left *Roe*'s doctrinal footings weaker than they were in 1973. No development of constitutional law since the case was decided has implicitly or explicitly left *Roe* behind as a mere survivor of obsolete constitutional thinking.

It will be recognized, of course, that *Roe* stands at an intersection of two lines of decisions, but in whichever doctrinal category one reads the case, the result for present purposes will be the same. The *Roe* Court itself placed its holding in the succession of cases most prominently exemplified by *Griswold* v. *Connecticut,* 381 U. S. 479, 85 S.Ct. 1678, 14 L. Ed. 2d 510 (1965), see *Roe,* 410 U. S., at 152–153, 93 S.Ct., at 726. When it is so seen, *Roe* is clearly in no jeopardy, since subsequent constitutional developments have neither disturbed, nor do they threaten to diminish, the scope of recognized protection accorded to the liberty relating to intimate relationships, the family, and decisions about whether or not to beget or bear a child. See, *e. g., Carey* v. *Population Services International,* 431 U. S. 678, 97 S.Ct. 2010, 52 L. Ed. 2d 675 (1977); *Moore* v. *East Cleveland,* 431 U. S. 494, 97 S.Ct. 1932, 52 L. Ed. 2d 531 (1977). . . .

From what we have said so far it follows that it is a constitutional liberty of the woman to have some freedom to terminate her pregnancy. We conclude that the basic decision in *Roe* was based on a constitutional analysis which we cannot now repudiate. The woman's liberty is not so unlimited, however, that from the outset the State cannot show its concern for the life of the unborn, and at a later point in fetal development the State's interest in life has sufficient force so that the right of the woman to terminate the pregnancy can be restricted.

That brings us, of course, to the point where much criticism has been directed at *Roe,* a criticism that always inheres when the Court draws a specific rule from what in the Constitution is but a general standard. We conclude, however, that the urgent claims of the woman to retain the ultimate control over her destiny and her body, claims implicit in the meaning of liberty, require us to perform that function. Liberty must not be extinguished for want of a line that is clear. And it falls to us to give some real substance to the woman's liberty to determine whether to carry her pregnancy to full term.

We conclude the line should be drawn at viability, so that before that time the woman has a right to choose to terminate her pregnancy. We adhere to this principle for two reasons. First, as we have said, is the doctrine of *stare decisis.* Any judicial act of line-drawing may seem somewhat arbitrary, but *Roe* was a reasoned statement, elaborated with great care. We have twice reaffirmed it in the face of great opposition. See *Thornburgh* v. *American College of Obstetricians & Gynecologists,* 476 U. S., at 759, 106 S.Ct., at 2178; *Akron I,* 462 U. S., at 419–420, 103 S.Ct., at 2487–2488. Although we must overrule those parts of *Thornburgh* and *Akron I* which, in our view, are inconsistent with *Roe*'s statement that the State has a legitimate interest in promoting the life or potential life of the unborn, the central premise of those cases represents an unbroken commitment by this Court to the essential holding of *Roe.* It is that premise which we reaffirm today.

The second reason is that the concept of viability, as we noted in *Roe,* is the time at which there is a realistic possibility of maintaining and nourishing a life outside the womb, so that the independent existence of the second life can in reason and all fairness be the object of state protection that now overrides the rights of the woman. See *Roe* v. *Wade,* 410 U. S., at 163, 93 S.Ct., at 731. Consistent with other constitutional norms, legislatures may draw lines which appear arbitrary without the necessity of offering a justification. But courts may not. We must justify the lines we draw. And there is no line other than viability which is more workable. To be sure, as we have said, there may be some medical developments that affect the precise point of viability, but this is an imprecision within tolerable limits given that the medical community and all those who must apply its discoveries will continue to explore the matter. The viability line also has, as a practical matter, an element of fairness. In some broad sense it might be said that a woman who fails to act before viability has consented to the State's intervention on behalf of the developing child.

The woman's right to terminate her pregnancy before viability is the most central principle of *Roe* v. *Wade*. It is a rule of law and a component of liberty we cannot renounce.

On the other side of the equation is the interest of the State in the protection of potential life. The *Roe* Court recognized the State's "important and legitimate interest in protecting the potentiality of human life." *Roe*. The weight to be given this state interest, not the strength of the woman's interest, was the difficult question faced in *Roe*. We do not need to say whether each of us, had we been Members of the Court when the valuation of the State interest came before it as an original matter, would have concluded, as the *Roe* Court did, that its weight is insufficient to justify a ban on abortions prior to viability even when it is subject to certain exceptions. The matter is not before us in the first instance, and coming as it does after nearly 20 years of litigation in *Roe*'s wake we are satisfied that the immediate question is not the soundness of *Roe*'s resolution of the issue, but the precedential force that must be accorded to its holding. And we have concluded that the essential holding of *Roe* should be reaffirmed.

Yet it must be remembered that *Roe* v. *Wade* speaks with clarity in establishing not only the woman's liberty but also the State's "important and legitimate interest in potential life." *Roe, supra,* at 163, 93 S.Ct., at 731. That portion of the decision in *Roe* has been given too little acknowledgement and implementation by the Court in its subsequent cases. Those cases decided that any regulation touching upon the abortion decision must survive strict scrutiny, to be sustained only if drawn in narrow terms to further a compelling state interest. See *e. g., Akron I,* 462 U. S., at 427. Not all of the cases decided under that formulation can be reconciled with the holding in *Roe* itself that the State has legitimate interests in the health of the woman and in protecting the potential life within her. In resolving this tension, we choose to rely upon *Roe*, as against the later cases.

Roe established a trimester framework to govern abortion regulations. Under this elaborate but rigid construct, almost no regulation at all is permitted during the first trimester of pregnancy; regulations designed to protect the woman's health, but not to further the State's interest in potential life, are permitted during the second trimester; and during the third trimester, when the fetus is viable, prohibitions are permitted provided the life or health of the mother is not at stake. *Roe* v. *Wade*, 410 U. S., at 163–166, 93 S.Ct., at 731–733. Most of our cases since *Roe* have involved the application of rules derived from the trimester framework. See, *e. g., Thornburgh* v. *American College of Obstetricians and Gynecologists, supra; Akron I, supra.*

The trimester framework no doubt was erected to ensure that the woman's right to choose not become so subordinate to the State's interest in promoting fetal life that her choice exists in theory but not in fact. We do not agree, however, that the trimester approach is necessary to accomplish this objective. A framework of this rigidity was unnecessary and in its later interpretation sometimes contradicted the State's permissible exercise of its powers.

Though the woman has a right to choose to terminate or continue her pregnancy before viability, it does not at all follow that the State is prohibited from taking steps to ensure that this choice is thoughtful and informed. Even in the earliest stages of pregnancy, the State may enact rules and regulations designed to encourage her to know that there are philosophic and social arguments of great weight that can be brought to bear in favor of continuing the pregnancy to full term and that there are procedures and institutions to allow adoption of unwanted children as well as a certain degree of state assistance if the mother chooses to raise the child herself. "'[T]he Constitution does not forbid a State or city, pursuant to democratic processes, from expressing a preference for normal childbirth.'" *Webster* v. *Reproductive Health Services,* 492 U. S., at 511, 109 S.Ct., at 3053 (opinion of the Court) (quoting *Poelker* v. *Doe,* 432 U. S. 519, 521, 97 S.Ct. 2391, 2392, 53 L. Ed. 2d 528 (1977)). It follows that States are free to enact laws to provide a reasonable framework for a woman to make a decision that has such profound and lasting meaning. This, too, we find consistent with *Roe*'s central premises, and indeed the inevitable consequence of our holding that the State has an interest in protecting the life of the unborn.

We reject the trimester framework, which we do not consider to be part of the essential holding of *Roe*. See *Webster* v. *Reproductive Health Services, supra,* 492 U. S., at 518, 109 S.Ct., at 3056 (opinion of REHNQUIST, C.J.); *id.,* at 529, 109 S.Ct., at 3062 (O'CONNOR, J., concurring in part and concurring in judgment) (describing the trimester framework as "problematic"). Measures aimed at ensuring that a woman's choice contemplates the consequences for the fetus do not necessarily interfere with the right recognized in *Roe*, although those measures have been found to be inconsistent with the rigid trimester framework announced in that case. A logical reading of the central holding in *Roe* itself, and a necessary reconciliation of the liberty of the woman and the interest of the State in promoting prenatal life, require, in our view, that we abandon the trimester framework as a rigid prohibition on all previability regulation aimed at the protection of fetal life. The trimester framework suffers from these basic flaws: in its formulation it misconceives the nature of the pregnant woman's interest; and in practice it undervalues the State's interest in potential life, as recognized in *Roe*. . . .

The very notion that the State has a substantial interest in potential life leads to the conclusion that not all regulations must be deemed unwarranted. Not all burdens on the right to decide whether to terminate a pregnancy will be undue. In our view, the undue burden standard is the appropriate means of reconciling the State's interest with the woman's constitutionally protected liberty.

The concept of an undue burden has been utilized by the Court as well as individual members of the Court, including two of us, in ways that could be considered inconsistent. See *e. g., Hodgson* v. *Minnesota*, 497 U. S., at 417 (O'CONNOR, J., concurring in part and concurring in judgment); *Akron II*, 497 U. S., at 502 (opinion of KENNEDY, J.); *Thornburgh* v. *American College of Obstetricians and Gynecologists*, 476 U. S., at 828–829, 106 S.Ct., at 2214 (O'CONNOR, J., dissenting); *Akron I, supra*, 462 U. S., at 461–466, 103 S.Ct., at 2509–2511 (O'CONNOR, J., dissenting); *Harris* v. *McRae, supra*, 448 U. S., at 314, 100 S.Ct., at 2686; *Maher* v. *Roe, supra*, 432 U. S., at 473, 97 S.Ct., at 2382; *Beal* v. *Doe*, 432 U. S. 438, 446, 97 S.Ct. 2366, 2371, 53 L. Ed. 2d 464 (1977); *Bellotti I, supra*, 428 U. S., at 147, 96 S.Ct., at 2866. Because we set forth a standard of general application to which we intend to adhere, it is important to clarify what is meant by an undue burden.

A finding of an undue burden is a shorthand for the conclusion that a state regulation has the purpose or effect of placing a substantial obstacle in the path of a woman seeking an abortion of a nonviable fetus. A statute with this purpose is invalid because the means chosen by the State to further the interest in potential life must be calculated to inform the woman's free choice, not hinder it. And a statute which, while furthering the interest in potential life or some other valid state interest, has the effect of placing a substantial obstacle in the path of a woman's choice cannot be considered a permissible means of serving its legitimate ends. To the extent that the opinions of the Court or of individual Justices use the undue burden standard in a manner that is inconsistent with this analysis, we set out what in our view should be the controlling standard. . . . (attempting to "define the doctrine of abuse of the writ with more precision" after acknowledging tension among earlier cases). In our considered judgment, an undue burden is an unconstitutional burden. See *Akron II, supra*, 497 U. S., at 502 (opinion of KENNEDY, J.). Understood another way, we answer the question, left open in previous opinions discussing the undue burden formulation, whether a law designed to further the State's interest in fetal life which imposes an undue burden on the woman's decision before fetal viability could be constitutional. See, *e. g.*, *Akron I*, 462 U. S., at 462–463 (O'CONNOR, J., dissenting). The answer is no.

Some guiding principles should emerge. What is at stake is the woman's right to make the ultimate decision, not a right to be insulated from all others in doing so. Regulations which do no more than create a structural mechanism by which the State, or the parent or guardian of a minor, may express profound respect for the life of the unborn are permitted, if they are not a substantial obstacle to the woman's exercise of the right to choose. See *infra* (addressing Pennsylvania's parental consent requirement). Unless it has that effect on her right of choice, a state measure designed to persuade her to choose childbirth over abortion will be upheld if reasonably related to that goal. Regulations designed to foster the health of a woman seeking an abortion are valid if they do not constitute an undue burden.

Even when jurists reason from shared premises, some disagreement is inevitable. Compare *Hodgson*, 497 U. S., at 417 (opinion of KENNEDY, J.) with *id.*, 110 S.Ct. (O'CONNOR, J., concurring in part and concurring in judgment in part). That is to be expected in the application of any legal standard which must accommodate life's complexity. We do not expect it to be otherwise with respect to the undue burden standard. We give this summary:

(a) To protect the central right recognized by *Roe* v. *Wade* while at the same time accommodating the State's profound interest in potential life, we will employ the undue burden analysis as explained in this opinion. An undue burden exists, and therefore a provision of law is invalid, if its purpose or effect is to place a substantial obstacle in the path of a woman seeking an abortion before the fetus attains viability.

(b) We reject the rigid trimester framework of *Roe* v. *Wade*. To promote the State's profound interest in potential life, throughout pregnancy the State may take measures to ensure that the woman's choice is informed, and measures designed to advance this interest will not be invalidated as long as their purpose is to persuade the woman to choose childbirth over abortion. These measures must not be an undue burden on the right.

(c) As with any medical procedure, the State may enact regulations to further the health or safety of a woman seeking an abortion. Unnecessary health regulations that have the purpose or effect of presenting a substantial obstacle to a woman seeking an abortion impose an undue burden on the right.

(d) Our adoption of the undue burden analysis does not disturb the central holding of *Roe* v. *Wade*, and we reaffirm that holding. Regardless of whether exceptions are made for particular circumstances, a State may not prohibit any woman from making the ultimate decision to terminate her pregnancy before viability.

(e) We also reaffirm *Roe*'s holding that "subsequent to viability, the State in promoting its interest in the potentiality of human life may, if it chooses, regulate, and even proscribe, abortion except where it is necessary, in appropriate medical judgment, for the preservation of the life or health of the mother." *Roe* v. *Wade*, 410 U. S., at 164–165, 93 S.Ct., at 732.

These principles control our assessment of the Pennsylvania statute, and we now turn to the issue of the validity of its challenged provisions.

V

The Court of Appeals applied what it believed to be the undue burden standard and upheld each of the provisions except for the husband notification requirement. We agree generally with this conclusion, but refine the undue burden analysis in accordance with the principles articulated above. We now consider the separate statutory sections at issue.

A

Because it is central to the operation of various other requirements, we begin with the statute's definition of medical emergency. Under the statute, a medical emergency is

"[t]hat condition which, on the basis of the physician's good faith clinical judgment, so complicates the medical condition of a pregnant woman as to necessitate the immediate abortion of her pregnancy to avert her death or for which a delay will create serious risk of substantial and irreversible impairment of a major bodily function." 18 Pa. Cons. Stat. (1990). § 3203. . . .

The District Court found that there were three serious conditions which would not be covered by the statute: preeclampsia, inevitable abortion, and premature ruptured membrane. 744 F.Supp., at 1378. Yet, as the Court of Appeals observed, 947 F. 2d, at 700–701, it is undisputed that under some circumstances each of these conditions could lead to an illness with substantial and irreversible consequences. While the definition could be interpreted in an unconstitutional manner, the Court of Appeals construed the phrase "serious risk" to include those circumstances. *Id.*, at 701. It stated: "we read the medical emergency exception as intended by the Pennsylvania legislature to assure that compliance with its abortion regulations would not in any way pose a significant threat to the life or health of a woman." *Ibid.* As we said in *Brockett* v. *Spokane Arcades, Inc.*, 472 U. S. 491, 499–500, 105 S.Ct. 2794, 2799–2800, 86 L. Ed. 2d 394 (1985): "Normally, . . . we defer to the construction of a state statute given it by the lower federal courts." Indeed, we have said that we will defer to lower court interpretations of state law unless they amount to "plain" error. *Palmer* v. *Hoffman*, 318 U. S. 109, 118, 63 S.Ct. 477, 482, 87 L. Ed. 645 (1943). This "'reflect[s] our belief that district courts and courts of appeals are better schooled in and more able to interpret the laws of their respective States.'" *Frisby* v. *Schultz*, 487 U. S. 474, 482, 108 S.Ct. 2495, 2501, 101 L. Ed. 2d 420 (1988) (citation omitted). We adhere to that course today, and conclude that, as construed by the Court of Appeals, the medical emergency definition imposes no undue burden on a woman's abortion right.

B

We next consider the informed consent requirement. 18 Pa. Cons. Stat. Ann. § 3205. Except in a medical emergency, the statute requires that at least 24 hours before performing an abortion a physician inform the woman of the nature of the procedure, the health risks of the abortion and of childbirth, and the "probable gestational age of the unborn child." The physician or a qualified nonphysician must inform the woman of the availability of printed materials published by the State describing the fetus and providing information about medical assistance for childbirth, information about child support from the father, and a list of agencies which provide adoption and other services as alternatives to abortion. An abortion may not be performed unless the woman certifies in writing that she has been informed of the availability of these printed materials and has been provided them if she chooses to view them.

Our prior decisions establish that as with any medical procedure, the State may require a woman to give her written informed consent to an abortion. See *Planned Parenthood of Central Mo.* v. *Danforth*, 428 U. S., at 67, 96 S.Ct., at 2840. In this respect, the statute is unexceptional. Petitioners challenge the statute's definition of informed consent because it includes the provision of specific information by the doctor and the mandatory 24-hour waiting period. The conclusions reached by a majority of the Justices in the separate opinions filed today and the undue burden standard adopted in this opinion require us to overrule in part some of the Court's past decisions, decisions driven by the trimester framework's prohibition of all previability regulations designed to further the State's interest in fetal life. . . .

To the extent *Akron I* and *Thornburgh* find a constitutional violation when the government requires, as it does here, the giving of truthful, nonmisleading information about the nature of the procedure, the attendant health risks and those of childbirth, and the "probable gestational age" of the fetus, those cases go too far, are inconsistent with *Roe*'s acknowledgment of an important interest in potential life, and are overruled. This is clear even on the very terms of *Akron I* and *Thornburgh*. Those decisions, along with *Danforth*, recognize a substantial government interest justifying a requirement that a woman be apprised of the health risks of abortion and childbirth. *E. g., Danforth, supra*, 428 U. S., at 66–67, 96 S.Ct., at 2840. It cannot be questioned that psychological well-being is a facet of health. Nor can it be doubted that most women considering an abortion would deem the impact on the fetus relevant, if not dispositive, to the decision. In attempting to ensure that a woman apprehend the full consequences of her decision, the State furthers the legitimate purpose of reducing the risk that a woman may elect an abortion, only to discover later, with devastating psychological consequences, that her decision was not fully informed. If the information the State requires to be made available to the woman is truthful and not misleading, the requirement may be permissible.

We also see no reason why the State may not require doctors to inform a woman seeking an abortion of the availability of materials relating to the consequences to the fetus, even when those consequences have no direct relation to her health. An example illustrates the point. We would think it constitutional for the State to require that in order for there to be informed consent to a kidney transplant operation the recipient must be supplied with information about risks to the donor as well as risks to himself or herself. A requirement that the physician make available information similar to that mandated by the statute here was described in *Thornburgh* as "an outright attempt to wedge the Commonwealth's message discouraging abortion into the privacy of the informed-consent dialogue between the woman and her physician." 476 U. S., at 762, 106 S.Ct., at 2179. We conclude, however, that informed choice need not be defined in such narrow terms that all considerations of the effect on the fetus are made irrelevant. As we have made clear, we depart from the holdings of *Akron I* and *Thornburgh* to the extent that we permit a State to further its legitimate goal of protecting the life of the unborn by enacting legislation aimed at ensuring a decision that is mature and informed, even when in so doing the State expresses a preference for childbirth over abortion. In short, requiring that the woman be informed of the availability of information relating to fetal development and the assistance available should she decide to carry the pregnancy to full term is a reasonable measure to insure an informed choice, one which might cause the woman to choose childbirth over abortion. This requirement cannot be considered a substantial obstacle to obtaining an abortion, and, it follows, there is no undue burden. . . .

Our analysis of Pennsylvania's 24-hour waiting period between the provision of the information deemed necessary to informed consent and the performance of an abortion under the undue burden standard requires us to reconsider the premise behind the decision in *Akron I* invalidating a parallel requirement. In *Akron I* we said: "Nor are we convinced that the State's legitimate concern that the woman's decision be informed is reasonably served by requiring a 24-hour delay as a matter of course." 462 U. S., at 450, 103 S.Ct., at 2503. We consider that conclusion to be wrong. The idea that important decisions will be more informed and deliberate if they follow some period of reflection does not strike us as unreasonable, particularly where the statute directs that important information become part of the background of the decision. The statute, as construed by the Court of Appeals, permits avoidance of the waiting period in the event of a medical emergency and the record evidence shows that in the vast majority of cases, a 24-hour delay does not create any appreciable health risk. In theory, at least, the waiting period is a reasonable measure to implement the State's interest in protecting the life of the unborn, a measure that does not amount to an undue burden.

Whether the mandatory 24-hour waiting period is nonetheless invalid because in practice it is a substantial obstacle to a woman's choice to terminate her pregnancy is a closer question. The findings of fact by the District Court indicate that because of the distances many women must travel to reach an abortion provider, the practical effect will often be a delay of much more than a day because the waiting period requires that a woman seeking an abortion make at least two visits to the doctor. The District Court also found that in many instances this will increase the exposure of women seeking abortions to "the harassment and hostility of anti-abortion protestors demonstrating outside a clinic." 744 F. Supp., at 1351. As a result, the District Court found that for those women who have the fewest financial resources, those who must travel long distances, and those who have difficulty explaining their whereabouts to husbands, employers, or others, the 24-hour waiting period will be "particularly burdensome." *Id.,* at 1352.

These findings are troubling in some respects, but they do not demonstrate that the waiting period constitutes an undue burden. We do not doubt that, as the District Court held, the waiting period has the effect of "increasing the cost and risk of delay of abortions," *id.,* at 1378, but the District Court did not conclude that the increased costs and potential delays amount to substantial obstacles. Rather, applying the trimester framework's strict prohibition of all regulation designed to promote the State's interest in potential life before viability, see *id.,* at 1374, the District Court concluded that the waiting period does not further the state "interest in maternal health" and "infringes the physician's discretion to exercise sound medical judgment." *Id.,* at 1378. Yet, as we have stated, under the undue burden standard a State is permitted to enact persuasive measures which favor childbirth over abortion, even if those measures do not further a health interest. And while the waiting period does limit a physician's discretion, that is not, standing alone, a reason to invalidate it. In light of the construction given the statute's definition of medical emergency by the Court of Appeals, and the District Court's findings, we cannot say that the waiting period imposes a real health risk.

We also disagree with the District Court's conclusion that the "particularly burdensome" effects of the waiting period on some women require its invalidation. A particular burden is not of necessity a substantial obstacle. Whether a burden falls on a particular group is a distinct inquiry from whether it is a substantial obstacle even as to the women in that group. And the District Court did not conclude that the waiting period is such an obstacle even for the women who are most burdened by it. Hence, on the record before us, and in the context of this facial challenge, we are not convinced that the 24-hour waiting period constitutes an undue burden. . . .

C

Section 3209 of Pennsylvania's abortion law provides, except in cases of medical emergency, that no physician shall perform an abortion on a married woman without receiving a signed statement from the woman that she has notified her spouse that she is about to undergo an abortion. The woman has the option of providing an alternative signed statement certifying that her husband is not the man who impregnated her; that her husband could not be located; that the pregnancy is the result of spousal sexual assault which she has reported; or that the woman believes that notifying her husband will cause him or someone else to inflict bodily injury upon her. A physician who performs an abortion on a married woman without receiving the appropriate signed statement will have his or her license revoked, and is liable to the husband for damages.

The District Court heard the testimony of numerous expert witnesses, and made detailed findings of fact regarding the effect of this statute. These included:

"273. The vast majority of women consult their husbands prior to deciding to terminate their pregnancy. . . .

.   .   .   .   .

"279. The 'bodily injury' exception could not be invoked by a married woman whose husband, if notified, would, in her reasonable belief, threaten to (a) publicize her intent to have an abortion to family, friends or acquaintances; (b) retaliate against her in future child custody or divorce proceedings; (c) inflict psychological intimidation or emotional harm upon her, her children or other persons; (d) inflict bodily harm on other persons such as children, family members or other loved ones; or (e) use his control over finances to deprive of necessary monies for herself or her children. . . .

.   .   .   .   .

"281. Studies reveal that family violence occurs in two million families in the United States. This figure, however, is a conservative one that substantially understates (because battering is usually not reported until it reaches life-threatening proportions) the actual number of families affected by domestic violence. In fact, researchers estimate that one of every two women will be battered at some time in their life. . . .

"282. A wife may not elect to notify her husband of her intention to have an abortion for a variety of reasons, including the husband's illness, concern about her own health, the imminent failure of the marriage, or the husband's absolute opposition to the abortion. . . .

"283. The required filing of the spousal consent form would require plaintiff-clinics to change their counseling procedures and force women to reveal their most intimate decision-making on pain of criminal sanctions. The confidentiality of these revelations could not be guaranteed, since the woman's records are not immune from subpoena. . . .

"284. Women of all class levels, educational backgrounds, and racial, ethnic and religious groups are battered. . . .

"285. Wife-battering or abuse can take on many physical and psychological forms. The nature and scope of the battering can cover a broad range of actions and be gruesome and torturous. . . .

"286. Married women, victims of battering, have been killed in Pennsylvania and throughout the United States. . . .

"287. Battering can often involve a substantial amount of sexual abuse, including marital rape and sexual mutilation. . . .

"288. In a domestic abuse situation, it is common for the battering husband to also abuse the children in an attempt to coerce the wife. . . .

"289. Mere notification of pregnancy is frequently a flashpoint for battering and violence within the family. The number of battering incidents is high during the pregnancy and often the worst abuse can be associated with pregnancy. . . . The battering husband may deny parentage and use the pregnancy as an excuse for abuse. . . .

"290. Secrecy typically shrouds abusive families. Family members are instructed not to tell anyone, especially police or doctors, about the abuse and violence. Battering husbands often threaten their wives or her children with further abuse if she tells an outsider of the violence and tells her that nobody will believe her. A battered woman, therefore, is highly unlikely to disclose the violence against her for fear of retaliation by the abuser. . . .

"291. Even when confronted directly by medical personnel or other helping professionals, battered women often will not admit to the battering because they have not admitted to themselves that they are battered. . . .

.   .   .   .   .

"294. A woman in a shelter or a safe house unknown to her husband is not 'reasonably likely' to have bodily harm inflicted upon her by her batterer, however her attempt to notify her husband pursuant to section 3209 could accidentally disclose her whereabouts to her husband. Her fear of future ramifications would be realistic under the circumstances.

"295. Marital rape is rarely discussed with others or reported to law enforcement authorities, and of those reported only few are prosecuted. . . .

"296. It is common for battered women to have sexual intercourse with their husbands to avoid being battered. While this type of coercive sexual activity would be spousal sexual assault as defined by the Act, many women may not consider it to be so and others would fear disbelief. . . .

"297. The marital rape exception to section 3209 cannot be claimed by women who are victims of coercive sexual behavior other than penetration. The 90-day reporting requirement of the spousal sexual assault statute, 18 Pa. Con. Stat. Ann. § 3218(c), further narrows the class of sexually abused wives who can claim the exception, since many of these women may be psychologically unable to discuss or report the rape for several years after the incident. . . .

"298. Because of the nature of the battering relationship, battered women are unlikely to avail themselves of the exceptions to section 3209 of the Act, regardless of whether the section applies to them." 744 F. Supp., at 1360–1362.

These findings are supported by studies of domestic violence. The American Medical Association (AMA) has published a summary of the recent research in this field, which indicates that in an average 12-month period in this country, approximately two million women are the victims of severe assaults by their male partners. In a 1985 survey, women reported that nearly one of every eight husbands had assaulted their wives during the past year. The AMA views these figures as "marked underestimates," because the nature of these incidents discourages women from reporting them, and because surveys typically exclude the very poor, those who do not speak

English well, and women who are homeless or in institutions or hospitals when the survey is conducted. According to the AMA, "[r]esearchers on family violence agree that the true incidence of partner violence is probably *double* the above estimates; or four million severely assaulted women per year. Studies suggest that from one-fifth to one-third of all women will be physically assaulted by a partner or ex-partner during their lifetime." AMA Council on Scientific Affairs, Violence Against Women 7 (1991) (emphasis in original). Thus on an average day in the United States, nearly 11,000 women are severely assaulted by their male partners. Many of these incidents involve sexual assault. *Id.*, at 3–4; Shields & Hanneke, Battered Wives' Reactions to Marital Rape, in The Dark Side of Families: Current Family Violence Research 131, 144 (D. Finkelhor, R. Gelles, G. Hataling, & M. Straus eds. 1983). In families where wife-beating takes place, moreover, child abuse is often present as well. Violence Against Women, at 12.

Other studies fill in the rest of this troubling picture. Physical violence is only the most visible form of abuse. Psychological abuse, particularly forced social and economic isolation of women, is also common. L. Walker, The Battered Woman Syndrome 27–28 (1984). Many victims of domestic violence remain with their abusers, perhaps because they perceive no superior alternative. Herbert, Silver, & Ellard, Coping with an Abusive Relationship: I. How and Why do Women Stay?, 53 J. Marriage & the Family 311 (1991). Many abused women who find temporary refuge in shelters return to their husbands, in large part because they have no other source of income. Aguirre, Why Do They Return? Abused Wives in Shelters, 30 J.Nat.Assn. of Social Workers 350, 352 (1985). Returning to one's abuser can be dangerous. Recent Federal Bureau of Investigation statistics disclose that 8.8% of all homicide victims in the United States are killed by their spouse. Mercy & Saltzman, Fatal Violence Among Spouses in the United States, 1976–85, 79 Am.J.Public Health 595 (1989). Thirty percent of female homicide victims are killed by their male partners. Domestic Violence: Terrorism in the Home, Hearing before the Subcommittee on Children, Family, Drugs and Alcoholism of the Senate Committee on Labor and Human Resources, 101st Cong., 2d Sess., 3 (1990).

The limited research that has been conducted with respect to notifying one's husband about an abortion, although involving samples too small to be representative, also supports the District Court's findings of fact. The vast majority of women notify their male partners of their decision to obtain an abortion. In many cases in which married women do not notify their husbands, the pregnancy is the result of an extramarital affair. Where the husband is the father, the primary reason women do not notify their husbands is that the husband and wife are experiencing marital difficulties, often accompanied by incidents of violence. Ryan & Plutzer, When Married Women

Have Abortions: Spousal Notification and Marital Interaction, 51 J. Marriage & the Family 41, 44 (1989).
This information and the District Court's findings reinforce what common sense would suggest. In well-functioning marriages, spouses discuss important intimate decisions such as whether to bear a child. But there are millions of women in this country who are the victims of regular physical and psychological abuse at the hands of their husbands. Should these women become pregnant, they may have very good reasons for not wishing to inform their husbands of their decision to obtain an abortion. Many may have justifiable fears of physical abuse, but may be no less fearful of the consequences of reporting prior abuse to the Commonwealth of Pennsylvania. Many may have a reasonable fear that notifying their husbands will provoke further instances of child abuse; these women are not exempt from § 3209's notification requirement. Many may fear devastating forms of psychological abuse from their husbands, including verbal harassment, threats of future violence, the destruction of possessions, physical confinement to the home, the withdrawal of financial support, or the disclosure of the abortion to family and friends. These methods of psychological abuse may act as even more of a deterrent to notification than the possibility of physical violence, but women who are the victims of the abuse are not exempt from § 3209's notification requirement. And many women who are pregnant as a result of sexual assaults by their husbands will be unable to avail themselves of the exception for spousal sexual assault, § 3209(b)(3), because the exception requires that the woman have notified law enforcement authorities within 90 days of the assault, and her husband will be notified of her report once an investigation begins. § 3128(c). If anything in this field is certain, it is that victims of spousal sexual assault are extremely reluctant to report the abuse to the government; hence, a great many spousal rape victims will not be exempt from the notification requirement imposed by § 3209.

The spousal notification requirement is thus likely to prevent a significant number of women from obtaining an abortion. It does not merely make abortions a little more difficult or expensive to obtain; for many women, it will impose a substantial obstacle. We must not blind ourselves to the fact that the significant number of women who fear for their safety and the safety of their children are likely to be deterred from procuring an abortion as surely as if the Commonwealth had outlawed abortion in all cases. . . .

We recognize that a husband has a "deep and proper concern and interest . . . in his wife's pregnancy and in the growth and development of the fetus she is carrying." With regard to the children he has fathered and raised, the Court has recognized his "cognizable and substantial" interest in their custody. *Stanley* v. *Illinois*, 405 U. S. 645, 651–652, 92 S.Ct. 1208, 1213, 31 L. Ed. 2d 551 (1972); see also *Quilloin* v. *Walcott*, 434 U. S. 246,

98 S.Ct. 549, 54 L. Ed. 2d 511 (1978); *Caban* v. *Mohammed*, 441 U. S. 380, 99 S.Ct. 1760, 60 L. Ed. 2d 297 (1979); *Lehr* v. *Robertson*, 463 U. S. 248, 103 S.Ct. 2985, 77 L. Ed. 2d 614 (1983). If this case concerned a State's ability to require the mother to notify the father before taking some action with respect to a living child raised by both, therefore, it would be reasonable to conclude as a general matter that the father's interest in the welfare of the child and the mother's interest are equal.

Before birth, however, the issue takes on a very different cast. It is an inescapable biological fact that state regulation with respect to the child a woman is carrying will have a far greater impact on the mother's liberty than on the father's. The effect of state regulation on a woman's protected liberty is doubly deserving of scrutiny in such a case, as the State has touched not only upon the private sphere of the family but upon the very bodily integrity of the pregnant woman. Cf. *Cruzan* v. *Director, Missouri Dept. of Health*, 497 U. S. The Court has held that "when the wife and the husband disagree on this decision, the view of only one of the two marriage partners can prevail. Inasmuch as it is the woman who physically bears the child and who is the more directly and immediately affected by the pregnancy, as between the two, the balance weighs in her favor." This conclusion rests upon the basic nature of marriage and the nature of our Constitution: "[T]he marital couple is not an independent entity with a mind and heart of its own, but an association of two individuals each with a separate intellectual and emotional makeup. If the right of privacy means anything, it is the right of the *individual*, married or single, to be free from unwarranted governmental intrusion into matters so fundamentally affecting a person as the decision whether to bear or beget a child." *Eisenstadt* v. *Baird*, 405 U. S., at 453, 92 S.Ct., at 1038 (emphasis in original). The Constitution protects individuals, men and women alike, from unjustified state interference, even when that interference is enacted into law for the benefit of their spouses.

There was a time, not so long ago, when a different understanding of the family and of the Constitution prevailed. In *Bradwell* v. *Illinois*, 16 Wall. 130, 21 L. Ed. 442 (1873), three Members of this Court reaffirmed the common-law principle that "a woman had no legal existence separate from her husband, who was regarded as her head and representative in the social state; and, notwithstanding some recent modifications of this civil status, many of the special rules of law flowing from and dependent upon this cardinal principle still exist in full force in most States." *Id.*, at 141 (Bradley J., joined by Swayne and Field, JJ., concurring in judgment). Only one generation has passed since this Court observed that "woman is still regarded as the center of home and family life," with attendant "special responsibilities" that precluded full and independent legal status under the Constitution. *Hoyt* v. *Florida*, 368 U. S. 57, 62, 82 S.Ct. 159, 162, 7 L. Ed. 2d 118

(1961). These views, of course, are no longer consistent with our understanding of the family, the individual, or the Constitution.

In keeping with our rejection of the common-law understanding of a woman's role within the family, the Court held in *Danforth* that the Constitution does not permit a State to require a married woman to obtain her husband's consent before undergoing an abortion. 428 U. S., at 69, 96 S.Ct., at 2841. The principles that guided the Court in *Danforth* should be our guides today. For the great many women who are victims of abuse inflicted by their husbands, or whose children are the victims of such abuse, a spousal notice requirement enables the husband to wield an effective veto over his wife's decision. Whether the prospect of notification itself deters such women from seeking abortions, or whether the husband, through physical force or psychological pressure or economic coercion, prevents his wife from obtaining an abortion until it is too late, the notice requirement will often be tantamount to the veto found unconstitutional in *Danforth*. . . .

D

We next consider the parental consent provision. Except in a medical emergency, an unemancipated young woman under 18 may not obtain an abortion unless she and one of her parents (or guardian) provides informed consent as defined above. If neither a parent nor a guardian provides consent, a court may authorize the performance of an abortion upon a determination that the young woman is mature and capable of giving informed consent and has in fact given her informed consent, or that an abortion would be in her best interests.

We have been over most of this ground before. Our cases establish, and we reaffirm today, that a State may require a minor seeking an abortion to obtain the consent of a parent or guardian, provided that there is an adequate judicial bypass procedure. See, *e. g., Akron II,* 497 U. S., at 502, *Hodgson,* 497 U. S., at 417, *Akron I, supra,* 462 U. S., at 440, 103 S.Ct., at 2497; *Bellotti II, supra* 443 U. S., at 643–644 (plurality opinion). Under these precedents, in our view, the one-parent consent requirement and judicial bypass procedure are constitutional.

The only argument made by petitioners respecting this provision and to which our prior decisions do not speak is the contention that the parental consent requirement is invalid because it requires informed parental consent. For the most part, petitioners' argument is a reprise of their argument with respect to the informed consent requirement in general, and we reject it for the reasons given above. Indeed, some of the provisions regarding informed consent have particular force with respect to minors: the waiting period, for example, may provide the parent or parents of a pregnant young woman the opportunity to consult with her in private, and to discuss the consequences of her decision in the context of the values and moral or religious principles of their family. See *Hodgson, supra,* 497 U. S., at 417.

E

Under the recordkeeping and reporting requirements of the statute, every facility which performs abortions is required to file a report stating its name and address as well as the name and address of any related entity, such as a controlling or subsidiary organization. In the case of state-funded institutions, the information becomes public.

For each abortion performed, a report must be filed identifying: the physician (and the second physician where required); the facility; the referring physician or agency; the woman's age; the number of prior pregnancies and prior abortions she has had; gestational age; the type of abortion procedure; the date of the abortion; whether there were any pre-existing medical conditions which would complicate pregnancy; medical complications with the abortion; where applicable, the basis for the determination that the abortion was medically necessary; the weight of the aborted fetus; and whether the woman was married, and if so, whether notice was provided or the basis for the failure to give notice. Every abortion facility must also file quarterly reports showing the number of abortions performed broken down by trimester. See 18 Pa. Cons. Stat. §§ 3207, 3214 (1990). In all events, the identity of each woman who has had an abortion remains confidential.

In *Danforth,* 428 U. S., at 80, we held that recordkeeping and reporting provisions "that are reasonably directed to the preservation of maternal health and that properly respect a patient's confidentiality and privacy are permissible." We think that under this standard, all the provisions at issue here except that relating to spousal notice are constitutional. Although they do not relate to the State's interest in informing the woman's choice, they do relate to health. The collection of information with respect to actual patients is a vital element of medical research, and so it cannot be said that the requirements serve no purpose other than to make abortions more difficult. Nor do we find that the requirements impose a substantial obstacle to a woman's choice. At most they might increase the cost of some abortions by a slight amount. While at some point increased cost could become a substantial obstacle, there is no such showing on the record before us. . . .

JUSTICE BLACKMUN, concurring in part, concurring in the judgment in part, and dissenting in part.

Three years ago, in *Webster* v. *Reproductive Health Serv.,* 492 U. S. 490, 109 S.Ct. 3040, 106 L. Ed. 2d 410 (1989), four Members of this Court appeared poised to "cas[t] into darkness the hopes and visions of every woman in this country" who had come to believe that the Constitution guaranteed her the right to reproductive choice. *Id.*, at 557, 109 S.Ct., at 3077 (BLACK-MUN, J., dissenting). See *id.*, at 499, 109 S.Ct., at 3046 (opinion of REHNQUIST, C.J.); *id.*, at 532, 109 S.Ct., at 3064 (opinion of SCALIA, J.). All that remained between the promise of *Roe* and the darkness of the plurality was a single, flickering flame. Decisions since *Webster* gave little reason to hope that this flame would cast much light. See, *e. g., Ohio* v. *Akron Center for Reproductive Health,* 497 U. S. 502, 524 (1990) (opinion of BLACKMUN, J.). But now, just when so many expected the darkness to fall, the flame has grown bright.

I do not underestimate the significance of today's joint opinion. Yet I remain steadfast in my belief that the right to reproductive choice is entitled to the full protection afforded by this Court before *Webster*. And I fear for the darkness as four Justices anxiously await the single vote necessary to extinguish the light.

I

Make no mistake, the joint opinion of Justices O'CONNOR, KENNEDY, and SOUTER is an act of personal courage and constitutional principle. In contrast to previous decisions in which Justices O'CONNOR and KENNEDY postponed reconsideration of *Roe* v. *Wade,* 410 U. S. 113, 93 S.Ct. 705, 35 L. Ed. 2d 147 (1973), the authors of the joint opinion today join JUSTICE STEVENS and me in concluding that "the essential holding of *Roe* should be retained and once again reaffirmed." In brief, five Members of this Court today recognize that "the Constitution protects a woman's right to terminate her pregnancy in its early stages."

A fervent view of individual liberty and the force of *stare decisis* have led the Court to this conclusion. Today a majority reaffirms that the Due Process Clause of the Fourteenth Amendment establishes "a realm of personal liberty which the government may not enter,"—a realm whose outer limits cannot be determined by interpretations of the Constitution that focus only on the specific practices of States at the time the Fourteenth Amendment was adopted. Included within this realm of liberty is "'the right of the *individual,* married or single, to be free from unwarranted governmental intrusion into matters so fundamentally affecting a person as the decision whether to bear or beget a child.'" *Eisenstadt* v. *Baird,* 405 U. S. 438, 453, 92 S.Ct. 1029, 1038, 31 L. Ed. 2d 349 (1972) (emphasis in original). "These matters, involving the most intimate and personal choices a person may make in a lifetime, choices central to personal dignity and autonomy, are *central* to the liberty protected by the Fourteenth Amendment." (Emphasis added.) Finally, the Court today recognizes that in the case of abortion, "the liberty of the woman is at stake in a sense unique to the human condition and so unique to the law. The mother who carries a child to full term is subject to anxieties, to physical constraints, to pain that only she must bear." The Court's reaffirmation of *Roe*'s central holding is also based on the force of *stare decisis*. "[N]o erosion of principle going to liberty or personal autonomy has left *Roe*'s central holding a doctrinal remnant; *Roe* portends no developments at odds with other precedent for the analysis of personal liberty; and no changes of fact have rendered viability more or less appropriate as the point at which the balance of interests tips." Indeed, the Court acknowledges that *Roe*'s limitation on state power could not be removed "without serious inequity to those who have relied upon it or significant damage to the stability of the society governed by the rule in question." In the 19 years since *Roe* was decided, that case has shaped more than reproductive planning—"an entire generation has come of age free to assume *Roe*'s concept of liberty in defining the capacity of women to act in society and to make reproductive decisions." The Court understands that, having "call[ed] the contending sides . . . to end their national division by accepting a common mandate rooted in the Constitution," a decision to overrule *Roe* "would seriously weaken the Court's capacity to exercise the judicial power and to function as the Supreme Court of a Nation dedicated to the rule of law." What has happened today should serve as a model for future Justices and a warning to all who have tried to turn this Court into yet another political branch.

In striking down the Pennsylvania statute's spousal notification requirement, the Court has established a framework for evaluating abortion regulations that responds to the social context of women facing issues of reproductive choice. . . . In determining the burden imposed by the challenged regulation, the Court inquires whether the regulation's "*purpose or effect* is to place a substantial obstacle in the path of a woman seeking an abortion before the fetus attains viability." (emphasis added). The Court reaffirms: "The proper focus of constitutional inquiry is the group for whom the law is a restriction, not the group for whom the law is irrelevant." Looking at this group, the Court inquires, based on expert testimony, empirical studies, and common sense, whether "in a large fraction of the cases in which [the restriction] is relevant, it will operate as a substantial obstacle to a woman's choice to undergo an abortion." "A statute with this purpose is invalid because the means chosen by the State to further the interest in potential life must be calculated to inform the woman's free choice, not hinder it." And is applying its test, the Court remains sensitive to the unique role of women in the decision-making process. Whatever may have been the practice when the Fourteenth Amendment was adopted, the Court observes, "[w]omen do not lose their constitutionally protected liberty when they marry. The Constitution protects all individuals, male or female, married or unmarried, from the abuse of governmental power, even when that power is employed for the supposed benefit of a member of the individual's family." . . .

Lastly, while I believe that the joint opinion errs in failing to invalidate the other regulations, I am pleased that the joint opinion has not ruled out the possibility that these regulations may be shown to impose an unconstitutional burden. The joint opinion makes clear that its specific holdings are based on the insufficiency of the record before it. I am confident that in the future evidence will be produced to show that "in a large fraction of the cases in which [these regulations are] relevant, [they] will operate as a substantial obstacle to a woman's choice to undergo an abortion."

II

Today, no less than yesterday, the Constitution and decisions of this Court require that a State's abortion restrictions be subjected to the strictest of judicial scrutiny. Our precedents and the joint opinion's principles require us to subject all non–*de minimis* abortion regulations to strict scrutiny. Under this standard, the Pennsylvania statute's provisions requiring content-based counseling, a 24-hour delay, informed parental consent, and reporting of abortion-related information must be invalidated.

A

The Court today reaffirms the long recognized rights of privacy and bodily integrity. As early as 1891, the Court held, "[n]o right is held more sacred, or is more carefully guarded by the commonlaw, than the right of every individual to the possession and control of his own person, free from all restraint or interference of others. . . . " *Union Pacific R. Co.* v. *Botsford,* 141 U. S. 250, 251, 11 S.Ct. 1000, 1001, 35 L. Ed. 734 (1891). Throughout this century, this Court also has held that the fundamental right of privacy protects citizens against governmental intrusion in such intimate family matters as procreation, childrearing, marriage, and contraceptive choice. See *ante,* at 2804–2805. These cases embody the principle that personal decisions that profoundly affect bodily integrity, identity, and destiny should be largely beyond the reach of government. *Eisenstadt,* 405 U. S., at 453, 92 S.Ct., at 1038. In *Roe* v. *Wade,* this Court correctly applied these principles to a woman's right to choose abortion.

State restrictions on abortion violate a woman's right of privacy in two ways. First, compelled continuation of a pregnancy infringes upon a woman's right to bodily integrity by imposing substantial physical intrusions and significant risks of physical harm. During pregnancy, women experience dramatic physical changes and a wide range of health consequences. Labor and delivery pose additional health risks and physical demands. In short, restrictive abortion laws force women to endure physical invasions far more substantial than those this Court has held to violate the constitutional principle of bodily integrity in other contexts. See, *e. g., Winston* v. *Lee*, 470 U. S. 753, 105 S.Ct. 1611, 84 L. Ed. 2d 662 (1985) (invalidating surgical removal of bullet from murder suspect); *Rochin* v. *California*, 342 U. S. 165, 72 S.Ct. 205, 96 L. Ed. 183 (1952) (invalidating stomach-pumping). . . .

Further, when the State restricts a woman's right to terminate her pregnancy, it deprives a woman of the right to make her own decision about reproduction and family planning—critical life choices that this Court long has deemed central to the right to privacy. The decision to terminate or continue a pregnancy has no less an impact on a woman's life than decisions about contraception or marriage. 410 U. S., at 153, 93 S.Ct., at 727. Because motherhood has a dramatic impact on a woman's educational prospects, employment opportunities, and self-determination, restrictive abortion laws deprive her of basic control over her life. For these reasons, "the decision whether or not to beget or bear a child" lies at "the very heart of this cluster of constitutionally protected choices." *Carey* v. *Population Services, Int'l*, 431 U. S. 678, 97 S.Ct. 2010, 52 L. Ed. 2d 675 (1977).

A State's restrictions on a woman's right to terminate her pregnancy also implicate constitutional guarantees of gender equality. State restrictions on abortion compel women to continue pregnancies they otherwise might terminate. By restricting the right to terminate pregnancies, the State conscripts women's bodies into its service, forcing women to continue their pregnancies, suffer the pains of childbirth, and in most instances, provide years of maternal care. The State does not compensate women for their services; instead, it assumes that they owe this duty as a matter of course. This assumption—that women can simply be forced to accept the "natural" status and incidents of motherhood—appears to rest upon a conception of women's role that has triggered the protection of the Equal Protection Clause. See, *e. g., Mississippi Univ. for Women* v. *Hogan*, 458 U. S. 718, 724–726, 102 S.Ct. 3331, 3336–3337, 73 L. Ed. 2d 1090 (1982); *Craig* v. *Boren*, 429 U. S. 190, 198–199, 97 S.Ct. 451, 457–458, 50 L. Ed. 2d 397 (1976). . . . The joint opinion recognizes that these assumptions about women's place in society "are no longer consistent with our understanding of the family, the individual, or the Constitution."

B

The Court has held that limitations on the right of privacy are permissible only if they survive "strict" constitutional scrutiny—that is, only if the governmental entity imposing the restriction can demonstrate that the limitation is both necessary and narrowly tailored to serve a compelling governmental interest. *Griswold* v. *Connecticut*, 381 U. S. 479, 485, 85 S.Ct. 1678, 1682, 14 L. Ed. 2d 510 (1965). We have applied this principle specifically in the context of abortion regulations. *Roe* v. *Wade*, 410 U. S., at 155, 93 S.Ct., at 728. . . .

Roe implemented these principles through a framework that was designed "to insure that the woman's right to choose not become so subordinate to the State's interest in promoting fetal life that her choice exists in theory but not in fact." *Roe* identified two relevant State interests: "an interest in preserving and protecting the health of the pregnant woman" and an interest in "protecting the potentiality of human life." 410 U. S., at 162, 93 S.Ct., at 731. With respect to the State's interest in the health of the mother, "the 'compelling' point . . . is at approximately the end of the first trimester," because it is at that point that the mortality rate in abortion approaches that in childbirth. *Roe*, 410 U. S., at 163, 93 S.Ct., at 731. With respect to the State's interest in potential life, "the 'compelling' point is at viability," because it is at that point that the fetus "presumably has the capability of meaningful life outside the mother's womb." *Ibid.* In order to fulfill the requirement of narrow tailoring, "the State is obligated to make a reasonable effort to limit the effect of its regulations to the period in the trimester during which its health interest will be furthered." *Akron*, 462 U. S., at 434, 103 S.Ct., at 2495.

In my view, application of this analytical framework is no less warranted than when it was approved by seven Members of this Court in *Roe*. Strict scrutiny of state limitations on reproductive choice still offers the most secure protection of the woman's right to make her own reproductive decisions, free from state coercion. No majority of this Court has ever agreed upon an alternative approach. The factual premises of the trimester framework have not been undermined, see *Webster*, 492 U. S., at 553, 109 S.Ct., at 3075 (BLACKMUN, J., dissenting), and the *Roe* framework is far more administrable, and far less manipulable, than the "undue burden" standard adopted by the joint opinion. . . .

CHIEF JUSTICE REHNQUIST, with whom JUSTICE WHITE, JUSTICE SCALIA, and JUSTICE THOMAS join, concurring in the judgment in part and dissenting in part.

The joint opinion, following its newly-minted variation on *stare decisis*, retains the outer shell of *Roe* v. *Wade*, 410 U. S. 113, 93 S.Ct. 705, 35 L. Ed. 2d 147 (1973), but beats a wholesale retreat from the substance of that case. We believe that *Roe* was wrongly decided, and that it can and should be overruled consistently with our traditional approach to *stare decisis* in constitutional cases. We would adopt the approach of the plurality in *Webster* v. *Reproductive Health Services,* 492 U. S. 490, 109 S.Ct. 3040, 106 L. Ed. 2d 410 (1989), and uphold the challenged provisions of the Pennsylvania statute in their entirety.

I

In ruling on this case below, the Court of Appeals for the Third Circuit first observed that "this appeal does not directly implicate *Roe;* this case involves the regulation of abortions rather than their outright prohibition." 947 F. 2d 682, 687 (1991). Accordingly, the court directed its attention to the question of the standard of review for abortion regulations. In attempting to settle on the correct standard, however, the court confronted the confused state of this Court's abortion jurisprudence. After considering the several opinions in *Webster* v. *Reproductive Health Services, supra,* and *Hodgson* v. *Minnesota,* 497 U. S. 417, 110 S.Ct. 2926, 111 L. Ed. 2d 344 (1990), the Court of Appeals concluded that JUSTICE O'CONNOR's "undue burden" test was controlling, as that was the narrowest ground on which we had upheld recent abortion regulations. 947 F. 2d, at 693–697 ("'When a fragmented court decides a case and no single rationale explaining the result enjoys the assent of five Justices, the holding of the Court may be viewed as that position taken by those Members who concurred in the judgments on the narrowest grounds'" (quoting *Marks* v. *United States,* 430 U. S. 188, 193, 97 S.Ct. 990, 993, 51 L. Ed. 2d 260 (1977) (internal quotation marks omitted)). Applying this standard, the Court of Appeals upheld all of the challenged regulations except the one requiring a woman to notify her spouse of an intended abortion.

In arguing that this Court should invalidate each of the provisions at issue, petitioners insist that we reaffirm our decision in *Roe* v. *Wade, supra,* in which we held unconstitutional a Texas statute making it a crime to procure an abortion except to save the life of the mother. . . . We agree with the Court of Appeals that our decision in *Roe* is not directly implicated by the Pennsylvania statute, which does not prohibit, but simply regulates, abortion. But, as the Court of Appeals found, the state of our post-*Roe* decisional law dealing with the regulation of abortion is confusing and uncertain, indicating that a reexamination of that line of cases is in order. Unfortunately for those who must apply this Court's decisions, the reexamination undertaken today leaves the Court no less divided than beforehand. Although they reject the trimester framework that formed the underpinning of *Roe,* Justices O'CONNOR, KENNEDY, and SOUTER adopt a revised undue burden standard to analyze the challenged regulations. We conclude, however, that such an outcome is an unjustified constitutional compromise, one which leaves the Court in a position to closely scrutinize all types of abortion regulations despite the fact that it lacks the power to do so under the Constitution. . . .

We have held that a liberty interest protected under the Due Process Clause of the Fourteenth Amendment will be deemed fundamental if it is "implicit in the concept of ordered liberty." *Palko* v. *Connecticut*, 302 U. S. 319, 325, 58 S.Ct. 149, 152, 82 L. Ed. 288 (1937). Three years earlier, in *Snyder* v. *Massachusetts*, 291 U. S. 97, 54 S.Ct. 330, 78 L. Ed. 674 (1934), we referred to a "principle of justice so rooted in the traditions and conscience of our people as to be ranked as fundamental." *Id.*, at 105, 54 S.Ct., at 332; see also *Michael H.* v. *Gerald D.*, 491 U. S. 110, 122, 109 S.Ct. 2333, 2341, 105 L. Ed. 2d 91 (1989) (plurality opinion) (citing the language from *Snyder*). These expressions are admittedly not precise, but our decisions implementing this notion of "fundamental" rights do not afford any more elaborate basis on which to base such a classification.

In construing the phrase "liberty" incorporated in the Due Process Clause of the Fourteenth Amendment, we have recognized that its meaning extends beyond freedom from physical restraint. In *Pierce* v. *Society of Sisters*, 268 U. S. 510, 45 S.Ct. 571, 69 L. Ed. 1070 (1925), we held that it included a parent's right to send a child to private school; in *Meyer* v. *Nebraska*, 262 U. S. 390, 43 S.Ct. 625, 67 L. Ed. 1042 (1923), we held that it included a right to teach a foreign language in a parochial school. Building on these cases, we have held that the term "liberty" includes a right to marry, *Loving* v. *Virginia*, 388 U. S. 1, 87 S.Ct. 1817, 18 L. Ed. 2d 1010 (1967); a right to procreate, *Skinner* v. *Oklahoma ex rel. Williamson*, 316 U. S. 535, 62 S.Ct. 1110, 86 L. Ed. 1655 (1942); and a right to use contraceptives, *Griswold* v. *Connecticut*, 381 U. S. 479, 85 S.Ct. 1678, 14 L. Ed. 2d 510 (1965); *Eisenstadt* v. *Baird*, 405 U. S. 438, 92 S.Ct. 1029, 31 L. Ed. 2d 349 (1972). But a reading of these opinions makes clear that they do not endorse any all-encompassing "right to privacy."

In *Roe* v. *Wade*, the Court recognized a "guarantee of personal privacy" which "is broad enough to encompass a woman's decision whether or not to terminate her pregnancy." 410 U. S., at 152–153, 93 S.Ct., at 727. We are now of the view that, in terming this right fundamental, the Court in *Roe* read the earlier opinions upon which it based its decision much too broadly. Unlike marriage, procreation and contraception, abortion "involves the purposeful termination of potential life." *Harris* v. *McRae*, 448 U. S. 297, 325, 100 S.Ct. 2671, 2692, 65 L. Ed. 2d 784 (1980). The abortion decision must therefore "be recognized as *sui generis*, different in kind from the others that the Court has protected under the rubric of personal or family privacy and autonomy." *Thornburgh* v. *American College of Obstetricians and Gynecologists, supra*, 476 U S., at 792, 106 S.Ct., at 2195 (WHITE, J., dissenting). One cannot ignore the fact that a woman is not isolated in her pregnancy, and that the decision to abort necessarily involves the destruction of a fetus. See *Michael H.* v. *Gerald D., supra,* 491 U. S., at 124, n. 4, 109 S.Ct., at 2342, n. 4 (To look "at the act which is assertedly the subject of a liberty interest in isolation from its effect upon other people [is] like inquiring whether there is a liberty interest in firing a gun where the case at hand happens to involve its discharge into another person's body").

Nor do the historical traditions of the American people support the view that the right to terminate one's pregnancy is "fundamental." The common law which we inherited from England made abortion after "quickening" an offense. At the time of the adoption of the Fourteenth Amendment, statutory prohibitions or restrictions on abortion were commonplace; in 1868, at least 28 of the then-37 States and 8 Territories had statutes banning or limiting abortion. J. Mohr, Abortion in America 200 (1978). By the turn of the century virtually every State had a law prohibiting or restricting abortion on its books. By the middle of the present century, a liberalization trend had set in. But 21 of the restrictive abortion laws in effect in 1868 were still in effect in 1973 when *Roe* was decided, and an overwhelming majority of the States prohibited abortion unless necessary to preserve the life or health of the mother. *Roe* v. *Wade,* 410 U. S., at 139–140, 93 S.Ct., at 720; *id.,* at 176–177, n. 2, 93 S.Ct., at 738–739, n. 2 (REHNQUIST, J., dissenting). On this record, it can scarcely be said that any deeply rooted tradition of relatively unrestricted abortion in our history supported the classification of the right to abortion as "fundamental" under the Due Process Clause of the Fourteenth Amendment. . . .

The joint opinion of Justices O'CONNOR, KENNEDY, and SOUTER cannot bring itself to say that *Roe* was correct as an original matter, but the authors are of the view that "the immediate question is not the soundness of *Roe*'s resolution of the issue, but the precedential force that must be accorded to its holding." Instead of claiming that *Roe* was correct as a matter of original constitutional interpretation, the opinion therefore contains an elaborate discussion of *stare decisis.* This discussion of the principle of *stare decisis* appears to be almost entirely dicta, because the joint opinion does not apply that principle in dealing with *Roe. Roe* decided that a woman had a fundamental right to an abortion. The joint opinion rejects that view. *Roe* decided that abortion regulations were to be subjected to "strict scrutiny" and could be justified only in the light of "compelling state interests." The joint opinion rejects that view. See *Roe* v. *Wade, supra,* 410 U. S., at 162–164, 93 S.Ct., at 731–732. *Roe* analyzed abortion regulation under a rigid trimester framework, a framework which has guided this Court's decisionmaking for 19 years. The joint opinion rejects that framework.

Stare decisis is defined in Black's Law Dictionary as meaning "to abide by, or adhere to, decided cases." Black's Law Dictionary 1406 (6th ed. 1990).

Whatever the "central holding" of Roe that is left after the joint opinion finishes dissecting it is surely not the result of that principle. While purporting to adhere to precedent, the joint opinion instead revises it. Roe continues to exist, but only in the way a storefront on a western movie set exists: a mere facade to give the illusion of reality. Decisions following Roe, such as Akron v. Akron Center for Reproductive Health, Inc., 462 U. S. 416, 103 S.Ct. 2481, 76 L. Ed. 2d 687 (1983), and Thornburgh v. American College of Obstetricians and Gynecologists, 476 U. S. 747, 106 S.Ct. 2169, 90 L. Ed. 2d 779 (1986), are frankly overruled in part under the "undue burden" standard expounded in the joint opinion.

In our view, authentic principles of stare decisis do not require that any portion of the reasoning in Roe be kept intact. "Stare decisis is not . . . a universal, inexorable command," especially in cases involving the interpretation of the Federal Constitution. Burnet v. Coronado Oil & Gas Co., 285 U. S. 393, 405, 52 S.Ct. 443, 446, 76 L. Ed. 815 (1932) (Brandeis, J., dissenting). Erroneous decisions in such constitutional cases are uniquely durable, because correction through legislative action, save for constitutional amendment, is impossible. It is therefore our duty to reconsider constitutional interpretations that "depar[t] from a proper understanding" of the Constitution. Garcia v. San Antonio Metropolitan Transit Authority, 469 U. S., at 557, 105 S.Ct., at 1020; see United States v. Scott, 437 U. S. 82, 101, 98 S.Ct. 2187, 2199, 57 L. Ed. 2d 65 (1978) ("'[I]n cases involving the Federal Constitution, . . . [t]he Court bows to the lessons of experience and the force of better reasoning, recognizing that the process of trial and error, so fruitful in the physical sciences, is appropriate also in the judicial function.'" (quoting Burnet v. Coronado Oil & Gas Co., supra, 285 U. S., at 406–408, 52 S.Ct., at 447–448 (Brandeis, J., dissenting))); Smith v. Allwright, 321 U. S. 649, 665, 64 S.Ct. 757, 765, 88 L. Ed. 987 (1944). Our constitutional watch does not cease merely because we have spoken before on an issue; when it becomes clear that a prior constitutional interpretation is unsound we are obliged to reexamine the question. See, e. g., West Virginia State Bd. of Education v. Barnette, 319 U. S. 624, 642, 63 S.Ct. 1178, 1187, 87 L. Ed. 1628 (1943); Erie R. Co. v. Tompkins, 304 U. S. 64, 74–78, 58 S.Ct. 817, 820–822, 82 L. Ed. 1188 (1938).

The joint opinion discusses several stare decisis factors which, it asserts, point toward retaining a portion of Roe. Two of these factors are that the main "factual underpinning" of Roe has remained the same, and that its doctrinal foundation is no weaker now than it was in 1973. Of course, what might be called the basic facts which gave rise to Roe have remained the same—women become pregnant, there is a point somewhere, depending on medical technology, where a fetus becomes viable, and women give birth to children. But this is only to say that the same facts which gave rise to Roe will continue to give rise to similar cases. It is not a reason, in and of itself, why those cases must be decided in the same incorrect manner as was the first case to deal with the question. And surely there is no requirement, in considering whether to depart from *stare decisis* in a constitutional case, that a decision be more wrong now than it was at the time it was rendered. If that were true, the most outlandish constitutional decision could survive forever, based simply on the fact that it was no more outlandish later than it was when originally rendered.

Nor does the joint opinion faithfully follow this alleged requirement. The opinion frankly concludes that *Roe* and its progeny were wrong in failing to recognize that the State's interests in maternal health and in the protection of unborn human life exist throughout pregnancy. But there is no indication that these components of *Roe* are any more incorrect at this juncture than they were at its inception.

The joint opinion also points to the reliance interests involved in this context in its effort to explain why precedent must be followed for precedent's sake. Certainly it is true that where reliance is truly at issue, as in the case of judicial decisions that have formed the basis for private decisions, "[c]onsiderations in favor of *stare decisis* are at their acme." *Payne* v. *Tennessee,* 501 U. S., 111 S.Ct., at 2610. But, as the joint opinion apparently agrees, *ante,* at 2809, any traditional notion of reliance is not applicable here. The Court today cuts back on the protection afforded by *Roe,* and no one claims that this action defeats any reliance interest in the disavowed trimester framework. Similarly, reliance interests would not be diminished were the Court to go further and acknowledge the full error of *Roe,* as "reproductive planning could take virtually immediate account of" this action.

The joint opinion thus turns to what can only be described as an unconventional—and unconvincing—notion of reliance, a view based on the surmise that the availability of abortion since *Roe* has led to "two decades of economic and social developments" that would be undercut if the error of *Roe* were recognized. *Ibid.* The joint opinion's assertion of this fact is undeveloped and totally conclusory. In fact, one can not be sure to what economic and social developments the opinion is referring. Surely it is dubious to suggest that women have reached their "places in society" in reliance upon *Roe,* rather than as a result of their determination to obtain higher education and compete with men in the job market, and of society's increasing recognition of their ability to fill positions that were previously thought to be reserved only for men. *Ibid.* . . .

Taking the joint opinion on its own terms, we doubt that its distinction between *Roe,* on the one hand, and *Plessy* and *Lochner,* on the other, withstands analysis. The joint opinion acknowledges that the Court improved its stature by overruling *Plessy* in *Brown* on a deeply divisive issue. And our decision in *West Coast Hotel,* which overruled *Adkins* v. *Children's Hospital, su-*

pra, and *Lochner,* was rendered at a time when Congress was considering President Franklin Roosevelt's proposal to "reorganize" this Court and enable him to name six additional Justices in the event that any member of the Court over the age of 70 did not elect to retire. It is difficult to imagine a situation in which the Court would face more intense opposition to a prior ruling than it did at that time, and, under the general principle proclaimed in the joint opinion, the Court seemingly should have responded to this opposition by stubbornly refusing to reexamine the *Lochner* rationale, lest it lose legitimacy by appearing to "overrule under fire."

The joint opinion agrees that the Court's stature would have been seriously damaged if in *Brown* and *West Coast Hotel* it had dug in its heels and refused to apply normal principles of *stare decisis* to the earlier decisions. But the opinion contends that the Court was entitled to overrule *Plessy* and *Lochner* in those cases, despite the existence of opposition to the original decisions, only because both the Nation and the Court had learned new lessons in the interim. This is at best a feebly supported, *post hoc* rationalization for those decisions.

For example, the opinion asserts that the Court could justifiably overrule its decision in *Lochner* only because the Depression had convinced "most people" that constitutional protection of contractual freedom contributed to an economy that failed to protect the welfare of all. Surely the joint opinion does not mean to suggest that people saw this Court's failure to uphold minimum wage statutes as the cause of the Great Depression! In any event, the *Lochner* Court did not base its rule upon the policy judgment that an unregulated market was fundamental to a stable economy; it simply believed, erroneously, that "liberty" under the Due Process Clause protected the "right to make a contract." *Lochner* v. *New York,* 198 U. S., at 53, 25 S.Ct., at 541. Nor is it the case that the people of this Nation only discovered the dangers of extreme laissez faire economics because of the Depression. State laws regulating maximum hours and minimum wages were in existence well before that time. A Utah statute of that sort enacted in 1896 was involved in our decision in *Holden* v. *Hardy,* 169 U. S. 366, 18 S.Ct. 383, 42 L. Ed. 780 (1898), and other states followed suit shortly afterwards. See, *e. g., Muller* v. *Oregon,* 208 U. S. 412, 28 S.Ct. 324, 52 L. Ed. 551 (1908); *Bunting* v. *Oregon,* 243 U. S. 426, 37 S.Ct. 435, 61 L.Ed. 830 (1917). These statutes were indeed enacted because of a belief on the part of their sponsors that "freedom of contract" did not protect the welfare of workers, demonstrating that that belief manifested itself more than a generation before the Great Depression. Whether "most people" had come to share it in the hard times of the 1930's is, insofar as anything the joint opinion advances, entirely speculative. The crucial failing at that time was not that workers were not paid a fair wage, but that there was no work available at *any* wage.

When the Court finally recognized its error in *West Coast Hotel,* it did not engage in the *post hoc* rationalization that the joint opinion attributes to it today; it did not state that *Lochner* had been based on an economic view that had fallen into disfavor, and that it therefore should be overruled. Chief Justice Hughes in his opinion for the Court simply recognized what Justice Holmes had previously recognized in his *Lochner* dissent, that "[t]he Constitution does not speak of freedom of contract." *West Coast Hotel Co.* v. *Parrish,* 300 U. S., at 391, 57 S.Ct., at 581; *Lochner* v. *New York, supra,* 198 U. S., at 75, 25 S.Ct., at 546 (Holmes, J., dissenting) ("[A] Constitution is not intended to embody a particular economic theory, whether of paternalism and the organic relation of the citizen to the State or of *laissez faire*"). Although the Court did acknowledge in the last paragraph of its opinion the state of affairs during the then-current Depression, the theme of the opinion is that the Court had been mistaken as a matter of constitutional law when it embraced "freedom of contract" 32 years previously. . . .

Section 3209 of the Act contains the spousal notification provision. It requires that, before a physician may perform an abortion on a married woman, the woman must sign a statement indicating that she has notified her husband of her planned abortion. A woman is not required to notify her husband if (1) her husband is not the father, (2) her husband, after diligent effort, cannot be located, (3) the pregnancy is the result of a spousal sexual assault that has been reported to the authorities, or (4) the woman has reason to believe that notifying her husband is likely to result in the infliction of bodily injury upon her by him or by another individual. In addition, a woman is exempted from the notification requirement in the case of a medical emergency. 18 Pa. Cons. Stat. § 3209 (1990).

We first emphasize that Pennsylvania has not imposed a spousal *consent* requirement of the type the Court struck down in *Planned Parenthood of Central Mo.* v. *Danforth,* 428 U. S., at 67–72, 96 S.Ct., at 2840–2842. Missouri's spousal consent provision was invalidated in that case because of the Court's view that it unconstitutionally granted to the husband "a veto power exercisable for any reason whatsoever or for no reason at all." *Id.,* at 71, 96 S.Ct., at 2842. But this case involves a much less intrusive requirement of spousal *notification,* not consent. Such a law requiring only notice to the husband "does not give any third party the legal right to make the [woman's] decision for her, or to prevent her from obtaining an abortion should she choose to have one performed." *Hodgson* v. *Minnesota, supra,* 497 U. S., at 496 (KENNEDY, J., concurring in judgment in part and dissenting in part); see *H. L.* v. *Matheson,* 450 U. S., at 411, n. 17, 101 S.Ct., at 1172, n. 17. *Danforth* thus does not control our analysis. Petitioners contend that it should, however; they argue that the real effect of such a notice requirement is to give the power to husbands to veto a woman's abortion choice. The District Court indeed found that the notification provision created a risk that some woman who would otherwise have an abortion will be prevented from having one. 947 F. 2d, at 712. For example, petitioners argue, many notified husbands will prevent abortions through physical force, psychological coercion, and other types of threats. But Pennsylvania has incorporated exceptions in the notice provision in an attempt to deal with these problems. For instance, a woman need not notify her husband if the pregnancy is result of a reported sexual assault, or if she has reason to believe that she would suffer bodily injury as a result of the notification. 18 Pa. Cons. Stat. § 3209(b) (1990). Furthermore, because this is a facial challenge to the Act, it is insufficient for petitioners to show that the notification provision "might operate unconstitutionally under some conceivable set of circumstances." *United States* v. *Salerno*, 481 U. S. 739, 745, 107 S.Ct. 2095, 2100, 95 L. Ed. 2d 697 (1987). Thus, it is not enough for petitioners to show that, in some "worst-case" circumstances, the notice provision will operate as a grant of veto power to husbands. *Ohio* v. *Akron Center for Reproductive Health*, 497 U. S., at 514, 110 S.Ct. Because they are making a facial challenge to the provision, they must "show that no set of circumstances exists under which the [provision] would be valid." *Ibid.* (internal quotation marks omitted). This they have failed to do. . . .

The question before us is therefore whether the spousal notification requirement rationally furthers any legitimate state interests. We conclude that it does. First, a husband's interests in procreation within marriage and in the potential life of his unborn child are certainly substantial ones. See *Planned Parenthood of Central Mo.* v. *Danforth*, 428 U. S., at 69, 96 S.Ct., at 2841 ("We are not unaware of the deep and proper concern and interest that a devoted and protective husband has in his wife's pregnancy and in the growth and development of the fetus she is carrying"); *id.*, at 93, 96 S.Ct., at 2852 (WHITE, J., concurring in part and dissenting in part); *Skinner* v. *Oklahoma ex rel. Williamson*, 316 U. S., at 541, 62 S.Ct., at 1113. The State itself has legitimate interests both in protecting these interests of the father and in protecting the potential life of the fetus, and the spousal notification requirement is reasonably related to advancing those state interests. By providing that a husband will usually know of his spouse's intent to have an abortion, the provision makes it more likely that the husband will participate in deciding the fate of his unborn child, a possibility that might otherwise have been denied him. This participation might in some cases result in a decision to proceed with the pregnancy. As Judge Alito observed in his dissent below, "[t]he Pennsylvania legislature could have rationally believed that some married women are initially inclined to obtain an abortion without their husbands' knowledge because of perceived problems—such as economic constraints, future plans, or the husbands' previously expressed opposition—that may be obviated by discussion prior to the abortion." 947 F. 2d, at 726 (Alito, J., concurring in part and dissenting in part).

The State also has a legitimate interest in promoting "the integrity of the marital relationship." 18 Pa. Cons. Stat. § 3209(a) (1990). This Court has previously recognized "the importance of the marital relationship in our society." *Planned Parenthood of Central Mo.* v. *Danforth, supra,* 428 U.S., at 69, 96 S.Ct., at 2841. In our view, the spousal notice requirement is a rational attempt by the State to improve truthful communication between spouses and encourage collaborative decisionmaking, and thereby fosters marital integrity. See *Labine* v. *Vincent,* 401 U. S. 532, 538, 91 S.Ct. 1017, 1020, 28 L. Ed. 2d 288 (1971) ("[T]he power to make rules to establish, protect, and strengthen family life" is committed to the state legislatures). Petitioners argue that the notification requirement does not further any such interest; they assert that the majority of wives already notify their husbands of their abortion decisions, and the remainder have excellent reasons for keeping their decisions a secret. In the first case, they argue, the law is unnecessary, and in the second case it will only serve to foster marital discord and threats of harm. Thus, petitioners see the law as a totally irrational means of furthering whatever legitimate interest the State might have. But, in our view, it is unrealistic to assume that every husband-wife relationship is either (1) so perfect that this type of truthful and important communication will take place as a matter of course, or (2) so imperfect that, upon notice, the husband will react selfishly, violently, or contrary to the best interests of his wife. See *Planned Parenthood of Central Mo.* v. *Danforth, supra,* 428 U. S., at 103–104, 96 S.Ct., at 2857 (STEVENS, J., concurring in part and dissenting in part) (making a similar point in the context of a parental consent statute). The spousal notice provision will admittedly be unnecessary in some circumstances, and possibly harmful in others, but "the existence of particular cases in which a feature of a statute performs no function (or is even counterproductive) ordinarily does not render the statute unconstitutional or even constitutionally suspect." *Thornburgh* v. *American College of Obstetricians and Gynecologists,* 476 U. S., at 800, 106 S.Ct., at 2199 (WHITE, J., dissenting). The Pennsylvania Legislature was in a position to weigh the likely benefits of the provision against its likely adverse effects, and presumably concluded, on balance, that the provision would be beneficial. Whether this was a wise decision or not, we cannot say that it was irrational. We therefore conclude that the spousal notice provision comports with the Constitution. See *Harris* v. *McRae,* 448 U. S., at 325–326, 100 S.Ct., at 2692–2693 ("It is not the mission of this Court or any other to decide whether the balance of competing interests . . . is wise social policy"). . . .

JUSTICE SCALIA, with whom THE CHIEF JUSTICE, JUSTICE WHITE, and JUSTICE THOMAS join, concurring in the judgment in part and dissenting in part.

. . . I will not swell the United States Reports with repetition of what I have said before; and applying the rational basis test, I would uphold the Pennsylvania statute in its entirety. I must, however, respond to a few of the more outrageous arguments in today's opinion, which it is beyond human nature to leave unanswered. I shall discuss each of them under a quotation from the Court's opinion to which they pertain.

"The inescapable fact is that adjudication of substantive due process claims may call upon the Court in interpreting the Constitution to exercise that same capacity which by tradition courts always have exercised: reasoned judgment." . . .

The authors of the joint opinion, of course, do not squarely contend that *Roe* v. *Wade* was a *correct* application of "reasoned judgment"; merely that it must be followed, because of *stare decisis*. But in their exhaustive discussion of all the factors that go into the determination of when *stare decisis* should be observed and when disregarded, they never mention "how wrong was the decision on its face?" Surely, if "[t]he Court's power lies . . . in its legitimacy, a product of substance and perception," the "substance" part of the equation demands that plain error be acknowledged and eliminated. *Roe* was plainly wrong—even on the Court's methodology of "reasoned judgment," and even more so (of course) if the proper criteria of text and tradition are applied.

The emptiness of the "reasoned judgment" that produced *Roe* is displayed in plain view by the fact that, after more than 19 years of effort by some of the brightest (and most determined) legal minds in the country, after more than 10 cases upholding abortion rights in this Court, and after dozens upon dozens of *amicus* briefs submitted in this and other cases, the best the Court can do to explain how it is that the word "liberty" *must* be thought to include the right to destroy human fetuses is to rattle off a collection of adjectives that simply decorate a value judgment and conceal a political choice. The right to abort, we are told, inheres in "liberty" because it is among "a person's most basic decisions"; it involves a "most intimate and personal choic[e]"; it is "central to personal dignity and autonomy," *ibid.;* it "originate[s] within the zone of conscience and belief," *ibid.;* it is "too intimate and personal" for state interference; it reflects "intimate views" of a "deep, personal character"; it involves "intimate relationships, and notions of "personal autonomy and bodily integrity"; and it concerns a particularly "'important decisio[n]'" (citation omitted). . . . But it is obvious to anyone applying "reasoned judgment" that the same adjectives can be applied to many forms of conduct that this Court (including one of the Justices in today's majority, see *Bowers* v. *Hardwick*, 478 U. S. 186, 106 S.Ct. 2841, 92 L. Ed. 2d 140 (1986)) has held are *not* entitled to constitutional protection—because, like abortion, they are forms of conduct that have long been criminalized in American society. Those adjectives might be applied, for example, to homosexual sodomy, polygamy, adult incest, and suicide, all of which are equally "intimate" and "deep[ly] personal" decisions involving "personal autonomy and bodily integrity," and all of which can constitutionally be proscribed because it is our unquestionable constitutional tradition that they are proscribable. It is not reasoned judgment that supports the Court's decision; only personal predilection. . . .

"Liberty finds no refuge in a jurisprudence of doubt."

One might have feared to encounter this august and sonorous phrase in an opinion defending the real *Roe* v. *Wade*, rather than the revised version fabricated today by the authors of the joint opinion. The shortcomings of *Roe* did not include lack of clarity: Virtually all regulation of abortion before the third trimester was invalid. But to come across this phrase in the joint opinion—which calls upon federal district judges to apply an "undue burden" standard as doubtful in application as it is unprincipled in origin—is really more than one should have to bear.

The joint opinion frankly concedes that the amorphous concept of "undue burden" has been inconsistently applied by the Members of this Court in the few brief years since that "test" was first explicitly propounded by JUSTICE O'CONNOR in her dissent in *Akron I, supra*. . . . Because the three Justices now wish to "set forth a standard of general application," the joint opinion announces that "it is important to clarify what is meant by an undue burden," *ibid.* I certainly agree with that, but I do not agree that the joint opinion succeeds in the announced endeavor. To the contrary, its efforts at clarification make clear only that the standard is inherently manipulable and will prove hopelessly unworkable in practice.

The joint opinion explains that a state regulation imposes an "undue burden" if it "has the purpose or effect of placing a substantial obstacle in the path of a woman seeking an abortion of a nonviable fetus." An obstacle is "substantial," we are told, if it is "calculated[,] [not] to inform the woman's free choice, [but to] hinder it." . . . This latter statement cannot possibly mean what it says. *Any* regulation of abortion that is intended to advance what the joint opinion concedes is the State's "substantial" interest in protecting unborn life will be "calculated [to] hinder" a decision to have an abortion. It thus seems more accurate to say that the joint opinion would uphold abortion regulations only if they do not *unduly* hinder the woman's decision. That, of course, brings us right back to square one: Defining an "undue burden" as an "undue hindrance" (or a "substantial obstacle") hardly "clarifies" the test. Consciously or not, the joint opinion's verbal shell game will conceal raw judicial policy choices concerning what is "appropriate" abortion legislation. . . .

The rootless nature of the "undue burden" standard, a phrase plucked out of context from our earlier abortion decisions, is further reflected in the fact that the joint opinion finds it necessary expressly to repudiate the more narrow formulations used in JUSTICE O'CONNOR's earlier opinions. Those opinions stated that a statute imposes an "undue burden" if it imposes "*absolute* obstacles or *severe* limitations on the abortion decision," *Akron I*, 462 U. S., at 464, 103 S.Ct., at 2510 (O'CONNOR, J., dissenting) (emphasis added); see also *Thornburgh* v. *American College of Obstetricians and Gynecologists*, 476 U. S. 747, 828, 106 S.Ct. 2169, 2214, 90 L. Ed. 2d 779 (1986) (O'CONNOR, J., dissenting). Those strong adjectives are conspicuously missing from the joint opinion, whose authors have for some unexplained reason now determined that a burden is "undue" if it merely imposes a "substantial" obstacle to abortion decisions. JUSTICE O'CONNOR has also abandoned (again without explanation) the view she expressed in *Planned Parenthood Assn. of Kansas City, Mo., Inc.* v. *Ashcroft*, 462 U. S. 476, 103 S.Ct. 2517, 76 L. Ed. 2d 733 (1983) (dissenting opinion), that a medical regulation which imposes an "undue burden" could nevertheless be upheld if it "reasonably relate[s] to the preservation and protection of maternal health," *id.*, at 505, 103 S.Ct., at 2532 (citation and internal quotation marks omitted). In today's version, even health measures will be upheld only "*if they do not constitute an undue burden*" (emphasis added). Gone too is Justice O'CONNOR's statement that "the State possesses *compelling* interests in the protection of potential human life . . . throughout pregnancy," *Akron I, supra*, 462 U. S., at 461, 103 S.Ct., at 2509 (emphasis added); see also *Ashcroft, supra*, 462 U. S., at 505, 103 S.Ct., at 2532 (O'CONNOR, J., concurring in judgment in part and dissenting in part); *Thornburgh, supra*, 476 U. S., at 828, 106 S.Ct., at 2214 (O'CONNOR, J., dissenting); instead, the State's interest in unborn human life is stealthily downgraded to a merely "substantial" or "profound" interest. (That had to be done, of course, since designating the interest as "compelling" throughout pregnancy would have been, shall we say, a "substantial obstacle" to the joint opinion's determined effort to reaffirm what it views as the "central holding" of *Roe*. See *Akron I*, 462 U. S., at 420, n. 1, 103 S.Ct., at 2487, n. 1.) And "viability" is no longer the "arbitrary" dividing line previously decried by JUSTICE O'CONNOR in *Akron I, id.*, at 461, 103 S.Ct., at 2509; the Court now announces that "the attainment of viability may continue to serve as the critical fact." . . . It is difficult to maintain the illusion that we are interpreting a Constitution rather than inventing one, when we amend its provisions so breezily.

Because the portion of the joint opinion adopting and describing the undue-burden test provides no more useful guidance than the empty phrases discussed above, one must turn to pages . . . applying that standard to the present facts for further guidance. In evaluating Pennsylvania's abortion law, the joint opinion relies extensively on the factual findings of the District Court, and repeatedly qualifies its conclusions by noting that they are contingent upon the record developed in this case. Thus, the joint opinion would uphold the 24-hour waiting period contained in the Pennsylvania statute's informed consent provision, 18 Pa. Cons. Stat. § 3205 (1990), because "the record evidence shows that in the vast majority of cases, a 24-hour delay does not create any appreciable health risk." The three Justices therefore conclude that "on the record before us, . . . we are not convinced that the 24-hour waiting period constitutes an undue burden." The requirement that a doctor provide the information pertinent to informed consent would also be upheld because "there is no evidence on this record that [this requirement] would amount in practical terms to a substantial obstacle to a woman seeking an abortion." . . . Similarly, the joint opinion would uphold the reporting requirements of the Act, §§ 3207, 3214, because "there is no . . . showing on the record before us" that these requirements constitute a "substantial obstacle" to abortion decisions. But at the same time the opinion pointedly observes that these reporting requirements may increase the costs of abortions and that "at some point [that fact] could become a substantial obstacle," *ibid.* Most significantly, the joint opinion's conclusion that the spousal notice requirement of the Act, see § 3209, imposes an "undue burden" is based in large measure on the District Court's "detailed findings of fact," which the joint opinion sets out at great length.

I do not, of course, have any objection to the notion that, in applying legal principles, one should rely only upon the facts that are contained in the record or that are properly subject to judicial notice. . . . But what is remarkable about the joint opinion's fact-intensive analysis is that it does not result in any measurable clarification of the "undue burden" standard. Rather, the approach of the joint opinion is, for the most part, simply to highlight certain facts in the record that apparently strike the three Justices as particularly significant in establishing (or refuting) the existence of an undue burden; after describing these facts, the opinion then simply announces that the provision either does or does not impose a "substantial obstacle" or an "undue burden." . . . We do not know whether the same conclusions could have been reached on a different record, or in what respects the record would have had to differ before an opposite conclusion would have been appropriate. The inherently standardless nature of this inquiry invites the district judge to give effect to his personal preferences about abortion. By finding and relying upon the right facts, he can invalidate, it would seem, almost any abortion restriction that strikes him as "undue"—subject, of course, to the possibility of being reversed by a Circuit Court or Supreme Court that is as unconstrained in reviewing his decision as he was in making it.

To the extent I can discern *any* meaningful content in the "undue burden" standard as applied in the joint opinion, it appears to be that a State may not regulate abortion in such a way as to reduce significantly its incidence. The joint opinion repeatedly emphasizes that an important factor in the "undue burden" analysis is whether the regulation "prevents[s] a significant number of women from obtaining an abortion," *ante,* at 2829; whether a "significant number of women . . . are likely to be deterred from procuring an abortion," *ibid.;* and whether the regulation often "deters" women from seeking abortions, *ante,* at 2830–2831. We are not told, however, what forms of "deterrence" are impermissible or what degree of success in deterrence is too much to be tolerated. If, for example, a State required a woman to read a pamphlet describing, with illustrations, the facts of fetal development before she could obtain an abortion, the effect of such legislation might be to "deter" a "significant number of women" from procuring abortions, thereby seemingly allowing a district judge to invalidate it as an undue burden. Thus, despite flowery rhetoric about the State's "substantial" and "profound" interest in "potential human life," and criticism of *Roe* for undervaluing that interest, the joint opinion permits the State to pursue that interest only so long as it is not too successful. As JUSTICE BLACKMUN recognizes (with evident hope), . . . the "undue burden" standard may ultimately require the invalidation of each provision upheld today if it can be shown, on a better record, that the State is too effectively "express|ing| a preference for childbirth over abortion." . . . Reason finds no refuge in this jurisprudence of confusion.

"While we appreciate the weight of the arguments . . . that *Roe* should be overruled, the reservations any of us may have in reaffirming the central holding of *Roe* are outweighed by the explication of individual liberty we have given combined with the force of *stare decisis.*"

The Court's reliance upon *stare decisis* can best be described as contrived. It insists upon the necessity of adhering not to all of *Roe,* but only to what it calls the "central holding." It seems to me that *stare decisis* ought to be applied even to the doctrine of *stare decisis,* and I confess never to have heard of this new, keep-what-you-want-and-throw-away-the-rest version. I wonder whether, as applied to *Marbury* v. *Madison,* 1 Cranch 137, 2 L. Ed. 60 (1803), for example, the new version of *stare decisis* would be satisfied if we allowed courts to review the constitutionality of only those statutes that (like the one in *Marbury*) pertain to the jurisdiction of the courts.

I am certainly not in a good position to dispute that the Court *has saved* the "central holding" of *Roe,* since to do that effectively I would have to know what the Court has saved, which in turn would require me to understand (as I do not) what the "undue burden" test means. I must confess, however, that I have always thought, and I think a lot of other people have always thought, that the arbitrary trimester framework, which the Court today discards, was quite as central to *Roe* as the arbitrary viability test, which the Court today retains. It seems particularly ungrateful to carve the trimester framework out of the core of *Roe*, since its very rigidity (in sharp contrast to the utter indeterminability of the "undue burden" test) is probably the only reason the Court is able to say, in urging *stare decisis*, that *Roe* "has in no sense proven 'unworkable.'" . . . I suppose the Court is entitled to call a "central holding" whatever it wants to call a "central holding"—which is, come to think of it, perhaps one of the difficulties with this modified version of *stare decisis*. I thought I might note, however, that the following portions of *Roe* have not been saved:

- Under *Roe*, requiring that a woman seeking an abortion be provided truthful information about abortion before giving informed written consent is unconstitutional, if the information is designed to influence her choice, *Thornburgh*, 476 U. S., at 759–765, 106 S.Ct., at 2178–2181; *Akron I*, 462 U. S., 442–445, 103 S.Ct., at 2499–2500. Under the joint opinion's "undue burden" regime (as applied today, at least) such a requirement is constitutional.

- Under *Roe*, requiring that information be provided by a doctor, rather than by nonphysician counselors, is unconstitutional, *Akron I, supra*, at 446–449, 103 S.Ct., at 2501–2502. Under the "undue burden" regime (as applied today, at least) it is not.

- Under *Roe*, requiring a 24-hour waiting period between the time the woman gives her informed consent and the time of the abortion is unconstitutional, *Akron I, supra*, at 449–451, 103 S.Ct., at 2502–2503. Under the "undue burden" regime (as applied today, at least) it is not.

- Under *Roe*, requiring detailed reports that include demographic data about each woman who seeks an abortion and various information about each abortion is unconstitutional, *Thornburgh, supra*, 476 U. S., at 765––768, 106 S.Ct., at 2181–2183. Under the "undue burden" regime (as applied today, at least) it generally is not.

"Where, in the performance of its judicial duties, the Court decides a case in such a way as to resolve the sort of intensely divisive controversy reflected in Roe . . . , its decision has a dimension that the resolution of the normal case does not carry. It is the dimension present whenever the Court's interpretation of the Constitution calls the contending sides of a national controversy to end their national division by accepting a common mandate rooted in the Constitution."

The Court's description of the place of *Roe* in the social history of the United States is unrecognizable. Not only did *Roe* not, as the Court suggests, *resolve* the deeply divisive issue of abortion; it did more than anything else to nourish it, by elevating it to the national level where it is infinitely more difficult to resolve. National politics were not plagued by abortion protests, national abortion lobbying, or abortion marches on Congress, before *Roe* v. *Wade* was decided. Profound disagreement existed among our citizens over the issue—as it does over other issues, such as the death penalty—but that disagreement was being worked out at the state level. As with many other issues, the division of sentiment within each State was not as closely balanced as it was among the population of the Nation as a whole, meaning not only that more people would be satisfied with the results of state-by-state resolution, but also that those results would be more stable. Pre-*Roe*, moreover, political compromise was possible. . . .

"[T]o overrule under fire . . . would subvert the Court's legitimacy . . . .

"To all those who will be . . . tested by following, the Court implicitly undertakes to remain steadfast. . . . The promise of constancy, once given, binds its maker for as long as the power to stand by the decision survives and . . . the commitment [is not] obsolete. . . .

"[The American people's] belief in themselves as . . . a people [who aspire to live according to the rule of law] is not readily separable from their understanding of the Court invested with the authority to decide their constitutional cases and speak before all others for their constitutional ideals. If the Court's legitimacy should be undermined, then, so would the country be in its very ability to see itself through its constitutional ideals."

The Imperial Judiciary lives. It is instructive to compare this Nietzschean vision of us unelected, life-tenured judges—leading a Volk who will be "tested by following," and whose very "belief in themselves" is mystically bound up in their "understanding" of a Court that "speak[s] before all others for their constitutional ideals"—with the somewhat more modest role envisioned for these lawyers by the Founders.

"The judiciary . . . has . . . no direction either of the strength or of the wealth of the society, and can take no active resolution whatever. It may truly be said to have neither FORCE nor WILL but merely judgment. . . ." The Federalist No. 78, pp. 393–394 (G. Wills ed. 1982).

Or, again, to compare this ecstasy of a Supreme Court in which there is, especially on controversial matters, no shadow of change or hint of alteration ("There is a limit to the amount of error that can plausibly be imputed to prior courts," . . .) with the more democratic views of a more humble man:

"[T]he candid citizen must confess that if the policy of the Government upon vital questions affecting the whole people is to be irrevocably fixed by decisions of the Supreme Court, . . . the people will have ceased to be their own rulers, having to that extent practically resigned their Government into the hands of that eminent tribunal." A. Lincoln, First Inaugural Address (Mar. 4, 1861), reprinted in Inaugural Addresses of the Presidents of the United States, S. Doc. No. 101–10, p. 139 (1989).

It is particularly difficult, in the circumstances of the present decision, to sit still for the Court's lengthy lecture upon the virtues of "constancy," of "remain[ing] steadfast," of adhering to "principle." Among the five Justices who purportedly adhere to *Roe*, at most three agree upon the *principle* that constitutes adherence (the joint opinion's "undue burden" standard)—and that principle is inconsistent with *Roe*, see 410 U. S., at 154–156, 93 S.Ct., at 727–728. . . . To make matters worse, two of the three, in order thus to remain steadfast, had to abandon previously stated positions. It is beyond me how the Court expects these accommodations to be accepted "as grounded truly in principle, not as compromises with social and political pressures having, as such, no bearing on the principled choices that the Court is obliged to make." The only principle the Court "adheres" to, it seems to me, is the principle that the Court must be seen as standing by *Roe*. That is not a principle of law (which is what I thought the Court was talking about), but a principle of *Real-politik*—and a wrong one at that.

I cannot agree with, indeed I am appalled by, the Court's suggestion that the decision whether to stand by an erroneous constitutional decision must be strongly influenced—*against* overruling, no less—by the substantial and continuing public opposition the decision has generated. The Court's judgment that any other course would "subvert the Court's legitimacy" must be another consequence of reading the error-filled history book that described the deeply divided country brought together by *Roe*. In my history-book, the Court was covered with dishonor and deprived of legitimacy by *Dred Scott* v. *Sandford*, 19 How. 393, 15 L. Ed. 691 (1857), an erroneous (and widely opposed) opinion that it did not abandon, rather than by *West Coast Hotel Co.* v. *Parrish*, 300 U. S. 379, 57 S.Ct. 578, 81 L. Ed. 703 (1937), which produced the famous "switch in time" from the Court's erroneous (and widely opposed) constitutional opposition to the social measures of the New

Deal. (Both *Dred Scott* and one line of the cases resisting the New Deal rested upon the concept of "substantive due process" that the Court praises and employs today. Indeed, *Dred Scott* was "very possibly the first application of substantive due process in the Supreme Court, the original precedent for *Lochner* v. *New York* and *Roe* v. *Wade*." D. Currie, The Constitution in the Supreme Court 271 (1985) (footnotes omitted).)

But whether it would "subvert the Court's legitimacy" or not, the notion that we would decide a case differently from the way we otherwise would have in order to show that we can stand firm against public disapproval is frightening. It is a bad enough idea, even in the head of someone like me, who believes that the text of the Constitution, and our traditions, say what they say and there is no fiddling with them. But when it is in the mind of a Court that believes the Constitution has an evolving meaning; that the Ninth Amendment's reference to "othe[r]" rights is not a disclaimer, but a charter for action, *ibid.;* and that the function of this Court is to "speak before all others for [the people's] constitutional ideals" unrestrained by meaningful text or tradition—then the notion that the Court must adhere to a decision for as long as the decision faces "great opposition" and the Court is "under fire" acquires a character of almost czarist arrogance. We are offended by these marchers who descend upon us, every year on the anniversary of *Roe*, to protest our saying that the Constitution requires what our society has never thought the Constitution requires. These people who refuse to be "tested by following" must be taught a lesson. We have no Cossacks, but at least we can stubbornly refuse to abandon an erroneous opinion that we might otherwise change—to show how little they intimidate us.

Of course, as THE CHIEF JUSTICE points out, we have been subjected to what the Court calls "political pressure" by *both* sides of this issue. Maybe today's decision *not* to overrule *Roe* will be seen as buckling to pressure from *that* direction. Instead of engaging in the hopeless task of predicting public perception—a job not for lawyers but for political campaign managers—the Justices should do what is *legally* right by asking two questions: (1) Was *Roe* correctly decided? (2) Has *Roe* succeeded in producing a settled body of law? If the answer to both questions is no, *Roe* should undoubtedly be overruled.

In truth, I am as distressed as the Court is—and expressed my distress several years ago, see *Webster*, 492 U. S., at 535, 109 S.Ct., at 3065—about the "political pressure" directed to the Court: the marches, the mail, the protests aimed at inducing us to change our opinions. How upsetting it is, that so many of our citizens (good people, not lawless ones, on both sides of this abortion issue, and on various sides of other issues as well) think that we Justices should properly take into account their views, as though we were engaged not in ascertaining an objective law but in determining some kind of social consensus. The Court would profit, I think, from giving less attention to the *fact* of this distressing phenomenon, and more attention to the *cause* of it. That cause permeates today's opinion: a new mode of constitutional adjudication that relies not upon text and traditional practice to determine the law, but upon what the Court calls "reasoned judgment," *ante,* at 2806, which turns out to be nothing but philosophical predilection and moral intuition. All manner of "liberties," the Court tells us, inhere in the Constitution and are enforceable by this Court—not just those mentioned in the text or established in the traditions of our society. Why even the Ninth Amendment—which says only that "[t]he enumeration in the Constitution of certain rights shall not be construed to deny or disparage others retained by the people"—is, despite our contrary understanding for almost 200 years, a literally boundless source of additional, unnamed, unhinted—at "rights," definable and enforceable by us, through "reasoned judgment."

What makes all this relevant to the bothersome application of "political pressure" against the Court are the twin facts that the American people love democracy and the American people are not fools. As long as this Court thought (and the people thought) that we Justices were doing essentially lawyers' work up here—reading text and discerning our society's traditional understanding of that text—the public pretty much left us alone. Texts and traditions are facts to study, not convictions to demonstrate about. But if in reality our process of constitutional adjudication consists primarily of making *value judgments;* if we can ignore a long and clear tradition clarifying an ambiguous text, as we did, for example, five days ago in declaring unconstitutional invocations and benedictions at public-high-school graduation ceremonies, *Lee* v. *Weisman,* 505 U. S., S.Ct., L. Ed. 2d (1992); if, as I say, our pronouncement of constitutional law rests primarily on value judgments, then a free and intelligent people's attitude towards us can be expected to be (*ought* to be) quite different. The people know that their value judgments are quite as good as those taught in any law school—maybe better. If, indeed, the "liberties" protected by the Constitution are, as the Court says, undefined and unbounded, then the people *should* demonstrate, to protest that we do not implement *their* values instead of *ours.* Not only that, but confirmation hearings for new Justices *should* deteriorate into question-and-answer sessions in which Senators go through a list of their constituents' most favored and most disfavored alleged constitutional rights, and seek the nominee's commitment to support or oppose them. Value judgments, after all, should be voted on, not dictated; and if our Constitution has somehow accidently committed them to the Supreme Court, at least we can have a sort of plebiscite each time a new nominee to that body is put forward. JUSTICE BLACKMUN not only regards this prospect with equanimity, he solicits it.

*   *   *

There is a poignant aspect to today's opinion. Its length, and what might be called its epic tone, suggest that its authors believe they are bringing to an end a troublesome era in the history of our Nation and of our Court. "It is the dimension" of authority, they say, to "cal[l] the contending sides of national controversy to end their national division by accepting a common mandate rooted in the Constitution."

There comes vividly to mind a portrait by Emanuel Leutze that hangs in the Harvard Law School: Roger Brooke Taney, painted in 1859, the 82d year of his life, the 24th of his Chief Justiceship, the second after his opinion in *Dred Scott*. He is all in black, sitting in a shadowed red armchair, left hand resting upon a pad of paper in his lap, right hand hanging limply, almost lifelessly, beside the inner arm of the chair. He sits facing the viewer, and staring straight out. There seems to be on his face, and in his deep-set eyes, an expression of profound sadness and disillusionment. Perhaps he always looked that way, even when dwelling upon the happiest of thoughts. But those of us who know how the lustre of his great Chief Justiceship came to be eclipsed by *Dred Scott* cannot help believing that he had that case—its already apparent consequences for the Court, and its soon-to-be-played-out consequences for the Nation—burning on his mind. I expect that two years earlier he, too, had thought himself "call[ing] the contending sides of national controversy to end their national division by accepting a common mandate rooted in the Constitution."

It is no more realistic for us in this case, than it was for him in that, to think that an issue of the sort they both involved—an issue involving life and death, freedom and subjugation—can be "speedily and finally settled" by the Supreme Court, as President James Buchanan in his inaugural address said the issue of slavery in the territories would be. See Inaugural Addresses of the Presidents of the United States, S. Doc. No. 101–10, p. 126 (1989). Quite to the contrary, by foreclosing all democratic outlet for the deep passions this issue arouses, by banishing the issue from the political forum that gives all participants, even the losers, the satisfaction of a fair hearing and an honest fight, by continuing the imposition of a rigid national rule instead of allowing for regional differences, the Court merely prolongs and intensifies the anguish.

We should get out of this area, where we have no right to be, and where we do neither ourselves nor the country any good by remaining.

INDEX